W9-BCF-324

Martha

Martha

The Life of Martha Mitchell

by Winzola McLendon

 Random House New York

 Published in the United States by Random House, Inc., New York, and simultaneously in Canada by Random House of Canada Limited, Toronto.

Library of Congress Cataloging in Publication Data
McLendon, Winzola.
Martha : the life of Martha Mitchell.
Includes index.
1. Mitchell, Martha, 1918–1974 2. Wives—United States—Biography. 3. Mitchell, John Newton, 1913–
4. Lawyers—United States—Biography. I. Title.
HQ1413.M57M3 301.41'2'0924 [B] 77-90289
ISBN 0-394-41124-2

Manufactured in the United States of America
9 8 7 6 5 4 3 2
First Edition

To Bennie

Author's Note

THE MAIN SUBSTANCE OF THIS BOOK AND THE REASON FOR ITS being comes from a long association with Martha Mitchell, in which I was accepted by her in the dual role of intimate friend and working member of the press. Martha relied most strongly on my presence in the difficult period after her husband left her in September 1973.

As a reporter, I wrote about Martha for several publications; in writing this biography I have shamelessly cribbed from these articles and have drawn heavily on my notes and tapes made during the preparation of them. My gratitude, therefore, to: the Chicago *Tribune,* Features and News, Inc., *Ladies' Home Journal, Look, McCall's,* New Era Features, the New York *Times,* (Long Island) *Newsday,* the Washington *Star,* and the *Washingtonian.*

Since Martha's death, I have conducted more than 150 interviews, in person and by telephone. Particularly helpful to me were Martha's son Clyde Jay Jennings and her cousin ("by marriage") S. Ray West, Jr., who gave generously of their time and information. My thanks go also to Mr. and Mrs. S. Ray West, Sr., and to Martha's distant cousin J. A. Franklin of Chester, South Carolina, who supplied material about her maternal ancestors.

I also referred to newspaper and magazine articles, wire-service stories, radio and television transcripts, and books written by others in order to refresh my memory and corroborate the accuracy of historical events as well as to reinforce my own insights. My thanks to: *Esquire, Girl Talk, Ladies' Home Journal, Life, Look, McCall's, New Times, New York, Newsweek, Parade, People, Potomac, Time,* and the *Washingtonian*;

Also, the Alabama *Journal,* Arkansas *Gazette,* Associated Press, Birmingham (Alabama) *News,* Chicago *Daily News,* Chicago *Sun-Times,* Chicago *Tribune, Commercial Appeal* (Memphis), Connecticut *Sunday Herald, Daily Siftings Herald* (Arkansas), Features and News, Inc., Greenwood (Mississippi) *Commonwealth,* Houston *Post,* Knight Newspaper Syndicate, Inc., Knight News Service, Los Angeles *Examiner,* Los Angeles *Times,* London *Daily Mail,* London *Times,* Manchester (New Hampshire) *Union Leader,* Mansfield (Ohio) *News Journal,* Memphis *Press-Scimitar,* Nashville *Banner,* New Era Features, New York *Daily News,* New York *Post,* New York *Times,* (Long Island) *Newsday,* Palm Springs (California) *Daily Enterprise,* Philadelphia *Bulletin,* Philadelphia *Daily News,* Philadelphia *Inquirer,* Pine Bluff (Arkansas) *Commercial,* Pine Bluff *Graphic,* St. Petersburg (Florida) *Times,* United Press International, *Wall Street Journal,* Washington *Daily News,* Washington *Post,* Washington *Star,* Women's News Service, *Women's Wear Daily,* "Washington Merry-Go-Round" (Jack Anderson);

American Broadcasting Company, AM-Detroit, British Broadcasting Corporation, Columbia Broadcasting System, David Frost Interviews, *Empathy* (WWDC-Washington), *The Merv Griffin Show, The Mike Douglas Show,* Mike Wallace—*CBS 60 Minutes,* National Broadcasting Company, *Panorama*—Metromedia Washington; *The Pat Collins Show, Today, Tomorrow,* and WCVB-TV Boston.

And I am grateful to the authors of: *All The President's Men,* by Carl Bernstein and Bob Woodward; *An American Melodrama: The Presidential Campaign of 1968,* by Lewis Chester, Godfrey Hodgson and Bruce Page; *An American Life: One Man's Road to Watergate,* by Jeb Stuart Magruder; *At That Point In Time,* by Fred Thompson; *Before the Fall: An Inside View of the Pre-Watergate White House,* by William Safire; *Blind Ambition: The White House Years,* by John Dean; *The End of a Presidency,* by the staff of the New York *Times*; *The Ends of Power,* by H. R. Haldeman with Joseph DiMona; *The Final Days,* by Bob Woodward and Carl Bernstein; *No Final Victories: A Life in Politics from John F. Kennedy to Watergate,* by Lawrence F. O'Brien; *The Great Coverup: Nixon and the Scandal of Watergate,* by Barry Sussman; "Impeachment of Richard M. Nixon, President of the United States: The Final Report of the Judiciary, House of Representatives," Peter W. Rodino, Jr., Chairman, introduction by R. W. Apple, Jr., of the New York *Times*; *Land of Cypress and Pine: More Southeast Arkansas History,* by James W. Leslie; *The Last Nixon Watch,* by John Osborne; *Laughing All the Way,* by Barbara Howar; *The Making of the President 1972,* by Theodore H. White; *Marathon: The Pursuit of the Presidency 1972–1976,* by Jules Witcover; *Nixon Agonistes: The Crisis of the Self-Made Man,* by Garry Wills; *The Nixon Watch,* by John Osborne; *The Palace Guard,* by Dan Rather and Gary Paul Gates; *Perfectly Clear: Nixon from Whittier to Watergate,* by Frank Mankiewicz; *A Piece of Tape: The Watergate Story: Fact and Fiction,* by James W. McCord, Jr.; *The Right and The Power: The Prosecution of Watergate,* by Leon Jaworski; *The Senate Watergate Report,*, with an introduction by Daniel Schorr, (2 Vols., Dell); *U.S. v. Richard M. Nixon: The Final Crisis,* by Frank Mankiewicz; *The Watergate Hearings, Break-in and Cover-up: Proceedings of the Senate Select Committee on Presidential Campaign Activities,* as edited by the staff of the New York *Times,* with a narrative by R.W. Apple, Jr.; *Watergate: The Full Inside Story,* by the London *Sunday Times* team, Lewis Chester, Cal McCrystal, Stephen Aris and William Shawcross; *Wheeling and Dealing: Confessions of a Capitol Hill Power Broker,* by Bobby Baker with Larry L. King; *The White House Transcripts: Submission of Recorded Presidential Conversations to the Committee on the Judiciary of the House of Representatives by President Richard Nixon,* with an introduction by R.W. Apple, Jr., of the New York *Times*; and *The Women of Watergate,* by Madeleine Edmondson and Alden Duer Cohen.

I am grateful, too, to my friends in the media who so generously shared information and understanding. Most of them are named within the pages of this book. But there are more to whom I owe my thanks: Vince Colondra of *The Mike Douglas Show*; Colleen Dishon of the Chicago *Tribune*; David English, editor of the London *Daily Mail*; Richard Kaplan, editor of *Sunday Woman Magazine*; Tom Parsons, news editor of the Pine Bluff *Commercial,* and Kay Young of the same paper; Chester Pearce, KADL-TV-Radio, Pine Bluff; Ellen Wadley and Frances Foley of CBS News; Les Whitten, Washington author and columnist; and Jean Sprain Wilson, NBC.

There are others who gave time, support and encouragement during the research and writing of this book. I am grateful to all of them, both those named in the text and those who are not. I owe a special thanks to Joyce-Anne Pottorff, the periodicals assistant at the Public Library of Pine Bluff and Jefferson County, who was so helpful in my research of the early Martha, as well Joe Boswell, the florist who decorated the church for Martha's first wedding; and her former Pine Bluff schoolmates or college friends: Estelle Triplett Bettwy, John Erickson, Nancy Peterson Hill, Mrs. Walker Jones (the former Katie Shepherd) and Mrs. T. Waller Lewis.

I also am grateful to the people who knew Martha well during her marriage to Clyde Jennings, and others who were close to her when John Mitchell was a Wall Street bond lawyer. I was able to round out the story of Martha's Washington years from information supplied by former Cabinet wives, White House and Justice Department aides, members of the CREEP staff, and others whose lives touched briefly on Martha's. Therefore, my thanks to: Mrs. William N. (Buffie) Cafritz, Judge G. Harrold Carswell, the FBI agents who do not wish to be identified, former counsel to President Nixon John Dean, Mrs. Clement Haynsworth, Barbara Howar, Navy Captain Kenneth Hughes, who was aide to the new Attorney General during the 1969 Inaugural week; my friend of many years Charlotte Levine; Florence Lowe, Ritta Noto, Bill Weidner, former resident manager of the Essex House, and Hollywood record and film producer Michael Viner.

Also extremely helpful were the people who shared with me information about Martha's final years, among them Lee Flarity of Flair, Inc.; New York interior decorator Richard Ridge; Roosevelt Zanders of Zanders Limousine Service and Martha's lawyers and doctors, whose names appear in the text.

There are other doctors, too, who helped me understand Martha's medical problems. Many of them are from the National Naval Medical Center: Captain Michael Bohan, former Assistant Chief of Medicine; Captain William L. Brannon, chairman of the Department of Neurology; Commander John T. O'Brian, Department of Endocrinology; Lieutenant Commander Robert Bradley Slease, Department of Hemotology-Oncology Branch. Then there were Dr. Robert Martin, National Institutes of Health; Navy Captain William Milton Narva, Bureau of Medicine and Surgery; and Dr. George Kolodner, psychiatrist and director of the Kolmac Clinic, which runs a comprehensive program on alcohol abuse. My thanks, too, to Martha's nurses at the New York Hospital for Special Surgery and at her apartment during her final days; and Evelyn Hyman, acting director of the Counseling Employment Agency, which supplied the nurses although Martha was unable to pay their salaries.

I particularly want to thank Rosely Himmelstein, a superb copy editor at Random House, who in the process of working on this manuscript became my friend.

The support and encouragement and independent research of my sister Elaine (Mrs. Donald) Conley, and my sister-in-law Vivian McLendon Kelley also are most gratefully acknowledged.

Above all, I am indebted to three people:

- My friend of fifteen years and editor of this manuscript, Robert Loomis, who with kindness and concern and intelligent editing guided this book to completion. His greatest achievement, though, was keeping our friendship intact while winning most of our arguments.
- My daughter, Martha Elizabeth (M'Liz) Beardsley, herself a professional journalist, who kept order amid chaos during the preparation of this life history. In addition to researching, filing, typing and indexing, she read the manuscript in its many stages, offering encouragement and constructive criticism.
- My husband, John Benjamin (Bennie) McLendon, who understood that this was something I had to do; without his support and affection this book would never have been finished.

Martha Mitchell "captivated Middle America, cheered the Right, infuriated the Left, flipped the pompous, and thoroly [sic] *disproved the theory that the meek shall inherit the earth."*

—London *Times*

Martha

Chapter One

MARTHA MITCHELL DIDN'T WANT TO GO TO CALIFORNIA THE weekend of June 17, 1972. Not that she had a premonition about the Watergate break-in or the terrifying role she'd play in the first clumsy attempts to cover it up. She didn't want to go because Pat Nixon would be there. At this point the relationship between the two women—never good at best—had deteriorated to the point where they avoided each other's company as much as possible. Martha didn't even want to hear the name "Pat Nixon" and referred to the First Lady only as *her* or *she.* There is no record of what Pat Nixon called Martha.

The purpose of the California trip, as given to the press, was for John Mitchell, by then director of the Committee for the Re-Election of the President (an organization quickly dubbed CREEP, which had been set up to run Richard Nixon's 1972 campaign), to attend various meetings and fund-raisers in connection with the campaign. One meeting, scheduled for June 17 with top California backers of Hubert Humphrey, was canceled at the last minute when Humphrey surprised his supporters by deciding to stay in the race for the Democratic presidential nomination.

Actually, the reason for the weekend junket was to lure big names from show business into the Nixon camp. As Martha liked to tell it, the

Administration just couldn't stand the fact that its image was not glamorous. Thinking that entertainment's top stars would change its look, the Administration did everything, including giving special tax breaks, to coax these people over to its side. Still, the stars didn't flock to Nixon the way they did to Democrats in general and to any Kennedy in particular. In fact, they not only didn't flock, some didn't even act civil to a Nixonite when they met one. Martha still was smarting over the way TV-star Lily Tomlin refused to speak to her, off camera, when Martha did a cameo appearance on *Laugh-In*.

Some of the CREEP staff thought the best way to get celebrity participation was to have Henry Kissinger, then the President's assistant for national security and the Administration's in-house glamour symbol, go to California for a "Celebrities for Nixon" soirée. Henry agreed to go, along with John and Martha Mitchell, to a party to be given by the late Taft Schreiber, president of the Music Corporation of America, at his house in Beverly Hills.

Invitations, listing Martha, John and Henry as honor guests, were sent out to a select list; CREEP officials were ecstatic at the great response. But at the last minute Henry Kissinger had to bow out to go to China. The rumor was that Taft Schreiber wanted to cancel the party but changed his mind when the White House produced Pat Nixon as a substitute. Schreiber was placated. Martha refused to go.

Tremendous pressure was put on her by various people connected with CREEP until she finally gave in.

On the afternoon of Friday, June 16, John and a reluctant Martha left Washington for Los Angeles in a Gulfstream II jet. With them for the six-and-a-half-hour flight were the Mitchells' eleven-year-old daughter, Martha Elizabeth, Jr. (called "Marty" by most people and "Junior" by her father); the Robert Mardians—he was a former Justice Department assistant attorney general who came to CREEP with John Mitchell; Jeb Stuart Magruder, the number-two man at CREEP and a former White House aide; Mitchell's secretary, Lea Jablonsky, who had been Martha's first secretary at CREEP; and two executive vice-presidents of Gulf Oil and their wives.

Others from CREEP joined the party at the Beverly Hills Hotel, among them John Mitchell's aide at the Committee, Fred LaRue and Mrs. LaRue, security guard Steve King, scheduling officer Herbert (Bart) Porter and his wife, and Jeb Magruder's wife, Gail.

The Mitchell party had a whole wing of the hotel, with John and Martha sharing a two-bedroom suite with Marty and Lea Jablonsky. The rest of the people were in rooms to the side and across the hall. It was late in the day by the time they got to the hotel; everyone retired early.

The following morning, Saturday, Martha was awakened around six-thirty, California time, by the sound of a ringing telephone. She answered from her side of the bed and remembered that an operator said the White House was calling and either Bob Haldeman or John Ehrlichman wanted to speak to John Mitchell.

Martha never was sure which one called since she always thought of the two top presidential aides as the Katzenjammer Kids and often confused their names. Since she wanted to go back to sleep, Martha asked John if he would take the call in the sitting room. He did and never came back to bed.

John Mitchell later said he first heard about the Watergate break-in on Saturday morning while accompanying California Governor Ronald Reagan to a series of political meetings in Los Angeles. Martha remained adamant about the time of the White House call and insisted that was when John first learned that five men were captured during a break-in and burglary at the Democratic National Committee headquarters at the Watergate.

Martha slept until about eleven o'clock, had breakfast in her room and left for a beauty parlor appointment. When she came back to the suite she noticed various members of their party dashing about "like mad people," in and out of the Mitchells' sitting room, in and out of their own rooms. She didn't know what was going on, nor did she ask. Martha had other things on her mind. She was going to the Merritt T. Smith studio to pose for her formal campaign pictures to be sent to the hundreds of people who'd requested autographed photographs. (Three years later, the pictures were stacked in a small room off the kitchen of her New York apartment; none had been sent out by CREEP.)

Still in the yellow evening dress she'd worn for the last picture, Martha returned to the suite to find the LaRues, the Mardians and John drinking and looking dejected. She recalled that one of them was bent over with his head in his hands. Martha thought, "My God, what is going on?" No one answered when she asked what was wrong and reminded them that they'd all come out there to have a good time. Someone poured another drink, others got up and started milling around in the hall between the rooms. Martha went to her bedroom to redo her makeup and comb her hair in preparation for the Taft Schreiber party.

Everyone left soon after to get to the party ahead of Mrs. Nixon. When the Mitchell car pulled up in front of the hilltop mansion, John stepped out first. As Martha started to follow, the zipper of her dress broke, all the way down her back. Without saying anything to John, she and Lea, who was riding with them, drove back to the hotel so Martha could change.

By the time Martha and Lea started back up the hill to the Schreibers' there was a traffic jam on the narrow, winding road, causing Martha to be late joining the receiving line. Someone led her to her place, near Pat Nixon. Martha spoke to the First Lady, and then, as Martha told it, "She stuck up her nose and didn't speak." It was such an obvious snub even John Mitchell noticed and spoke bitterly of the insult to his wife almost a year later, after the Mitchells had left Washington. "Pat Nixon slighted her," he said.

Martha hid her anger. It was such a gorgeous party, the kind she really liked, that she wasn't going to let *her* ruin Martha's evening or the evening of all those nice people who had turned out to help *her* husband.

John Mitchell and Governor Ronald Reagan spoke, Vikki Carr sang, and gathered around the pool were such celebrities as Charlton Heston, Jack Benny, Zsa Zsa Gabor, Jimmy Stewart, Clint Eastwood and GOP stalwart John Wayne.

Back at the hotel, Martha wanted to talk to John about the snub she'd received, but he was busy meeting with his CREEP deputies, planning ways to contain the Watergate problem, as it turned out later. Martha went to bed, still seething over what she considered lack of gratitude on the part of the First Lady for all the hard work Martha was doing to get Richard Nixon re-elected.

Sunday morning Martha came out into the sitting room to find Fred LaRue and Robert Mardian, with their heads together in hushed conversation. Seeing her, they rushed into the little kitchen where LaRue got on the telephone; Martha heard him trying to find a private plane, saying it was needed for a dire emergency. Soon after, Jeb and Gail Magruder left for Chicago, where a private plane waited to hurry them back to Washington.

The Mitchells checked out of the Beverly Hills Hotel about noon and headed south for Newport Beach. In the car, Martha finally talked to John about the incident of the night before. She told him she didn't see why she had to work herself to death for Richard Nixon when his wife wouldn't speak to her. She reminded John that she'd done everything the Administration had asked her to do; that she was worn out and tired, and she wanted him to get out of politics and take her back to New York where they could live a normal, happy life.

John explained he couldn't leave until after the election, but he promised that if Martha would just hold on for another four and a half months he'd leave politics and practice law, which he said was what he'd always wanted to do.

Once at the beach, the Mitchell party stayed at a plush resort hotel, the Newporter Inn. During the early Nixon Administration it was headquarters for some of the ranking members of the White House staff and government officials when the President stayed at his house in nearby San Clemente. But none of the White House staff was at the Inn this particular weekend since Nixon was in Key Biscayne, Florida.

The Inn had a few villas, each with its private swimming pool. John, Martha and Marty had one, number 355-D, which they shared with Lea Jablonsky and Steve King. The rest of their party was put into nearby rooms.

Something Martha thought peculiar happened soon after the Mitchells arrived at their villa. Everyone disappeared, as if on cue, leaving John and Martha alone. Even Steve and Lea took off, taking Marty with them. The Mitchells sat down to talk in the sitting room, she on one sofa, he on the other. Speaking later of that conversation Martha said, "Those were the last decent words we ever had together." Without telling Martha that he and his aide Fred LaRue, with questionable wisdom, had decided to leave Martha in Newport Beach, John told Martha he realized she was tired and he thought she needed a rest. He suggested that she and Marty stay in California for a few days; he said he'd leave Steve and Lea with them.

Later Mitchell friends would say Martha was left in California to keep her from learning that CREEP security chief James McCord was one of the men who broke into Watergate. This couldn't be true; Martha was free to read the papers, telephone friends and watch television. No one could have believed it possible to keep McCord's involvement from her under the circumstances. A more likely explanation is that Mitchell and LaRue wanted time to work on the cover-up, without Martha underfoot, asking embarrassing questions.

But that Sunday, the thought of swimming and lying in the sun for a few days appealed to Martha. She was exhausted, physically and mentally, from being kept on the road, campaigning for Richard Nixon.

Later that evening the Mitchells and others in the CREEP party, along with Richard Nixon's personal attorney and fund collector for CREEP, Herbert Kalmbach, and Mrs. Kalmbach, left the Inn in a caravan of cars to attend a fund-raising buffet supper at Seven-Up millionairess Mrs. Donald K. Washburn's Newport Beach house.

Like so many Nixon campaign fund-raisers the party was heavy with GOP contributors. Some of the show-business people from the party the night before were there, too, as were Richard Nixon's two brothers, Donald and Edward. Ed Nixon brought with him a recently released Vietnam POW.

Martha talked with Ed, whom she knew and liked. She didn't have the same feeling for Donald, perhaps because John had to spend so much time "taking care" of him. According to Martha, the President had asked John to watch over Donald because he was afraid his brother would do something to embarrass him.

In 1974 Donald Nixon testified at the trial of John Mitchell and former Secretary of Commerce Maurice Stans, when they were charged with conspiracy, obstruction of justice and perjury in connection with a secret campaign contribution from Robert Vesco. He told the court: "John Mitchell is a man that I was delegated—designated that I should talk to him about any matter pertaining to—in other words I never talked to my brother about anything, and John Mitchell was the man that I was assigned to."

John had talked with Martha many times, she said, about the problems with Donald Nixon and revealed it had been necessary to tap his telephone and have government agents follow him to keep tabs on what he was doing. According to Martha, Donald's son, also named Donald, had telephone taps, too. At one time, young Donald lived in California with friends his father called "hippies." Then in 1971 he had gone to work for financier Robert Vesco, whom the Securities and Exchange Commission later branded "one of the world's greatest swindlers." Richard Nixon was instrumental in getting his nephew his job, though columnist Jack Anderson reported that in a letter to a friend, written in 1971, young Donald complained about the job and blamed "the Great God in the White House" for sending him to work for Vesco.

Monday morning, Martha got up and made breakfast for herself and John. There wasn't a kitchen in the Newporter Inn villa, but, as usual, Martha had brought along her traveling coffee pot. She also had oranges and sweet rolls in the refrigerator. When she brought the empty breakfast tray downstairs, Martha noticed Robert Mardian walking through the living room on his way to the pool patio, carrying so many newspapers that she later recalled thinking, "My Lord! What in the world does he want with enough papers to supply New York City?"

As others who were to fly back to Washington arrived—again on the Gulfstream II they'd flown in Friday—they each anxiously grabbed a paper, sat down by the pool and started reading. John came downstairs and everyone left, walking through the back entrance. Martha thought how strange it was that they shuffled out, single file, with their heads down, looking like a bunch of sheep.

She walked out by the pool to get a paper, but there were none left. She sent Steve King out to get one; when he came back with the Los Angeles *Times* she went upstairs where she settled down in the bed, lit a Salem Long and opened her paper. There it was in headlines: An employee of CREEP had been arrested in the Watergate break-in. Martha later told a reporter, "Jesus Christ! I jumped out of bed like a sheet of lightning." Here was someone working for the Committee, arrested while breaking in at the Democratic headquarters. And here she was: (1) a member of the Committee, one of the early members; and (2) her husband was head of CREEP. Yet nobody had mentioned a thing to her; everyone had just flown away without telling her a thing!

She rushed downstairs to ask Steve and Lea what it was all about. She thought their answers were rather vague. Back upstairs she carefully read the whole story and learned for the first time that the day before her husband had issued a statement, which seemed to deny that James McCord, the arrested man, was a full-time CREEP employee.

John Mitchell had said, "We have just learned from news reports that a man identified as employed by our campaign committee was one of five persons arrested at the Democratic National Committee headquarters . . . The person involved is the proprietor of a private security agency who was employed at our committee months ago to assist with the installation of our security system . . . We want to emphasize that this man and the other people involved were not operating either in our behalf or with our consent . . ."

What was going on? John knew perfectly well what Jim McCord did for CREEP. So did Martha.

She dressed and went back to talk to Steve and Lea, who, she felt, knew more than they told. Knowing that John was in flight, Martha called CREEP headquarters and talked to Robert Odle, the director of administration and personnel. He told her it was a horrible thing, but they would take care of the President and her husband the best they could. She called back and talked to Jeb Magruder who said essentially the same thing. They would *take care of the President and her husband!*

Martha paced around the villa, not believing what had happened. Yet it was in the Los Angeles *Times,* and both Odle and Magruder had confirmed it. She called several friends in Washington, trying to get more information. By the time she reached Mitchell, at their Watergate apartment, she was beside herself. John seemed calm and told her that someone was trying to create a problem for CREEP but there was nothing to be concerned about.

She didn't question that John was telling the truth, as he saw it. But it was disturbing that McCord was involved. Was he a double agent? Was he the one trying to discredit CREEP?

Still agitated, Martha picked up a pack of matches to light a cigarette; the whole match clip exploded, severely burning her right hand. A doctor was called and Dr. Clark G. McGaughey, now deceased, came. He dressed her hand, gave her a shot for the pain and wrote a prescription for Phenaphen and codeine tablets. Drowsy from the effects of the shot, Martha went to sleep soon after the doctor left.

Martha found it hard to reconstruct the sequence of the events of the next three days. It all seemed to run together, though she said the *things* that happened were all too clear. They were so vivid that for the rest of her life not a day went by that Martha didn't relive them, over and over again. Many nights she awakened screaming from the nightmare in which she again was in the villa, a prisoner, physically restrained, and given medication against her will. Later her psychiatrist would explain to her that her reactions were similar to those of a soldier who was suffering from "shell shock."

The more Martha tried to find out what was going on, the more frustrated she became. By now, John wasn't taking her calls; the people she did reach brushed off her questions. She became more and more confused. Was breaking into the Democratic headquarters part of a bigger CREEP operation? She had seen the file on Senator Edmund Muskie on Bart Porter's desk, the one with the information gathered from spying on him. There was the $400,000 sent to Alabama when they tried to beat George Wallace in the primaries. (She told Wallace, in 1974, that she'd threatened to bolt the Republican party because of that.) Then, too, John had tried to show her a book filled with what he said were political espionage plans. And how about the meeting in Key Biscayne, when LaRue and Magruder and John were so secretive about campaign plans? Eavesdropping on the intercom she had heard talk about wiretapping and infiltration of Democratic candidates' headquarters.

When Martha went to Dr. McGaughey's office to have her dressing changed (was it Tuesday or Wednesday? Martha couldn't remember), she and the doctor talked at length about the break-in and she told him some of her suspicions about the dirty tricks going on. The more they talked, the more angry she became with John Mitchell and the others at CREEP for not letting her know what was happening. She asked herself, "What am I doing out here?"

Recalling these events later, she said, "I would have taken it. I would have understood it. And they could have left me out there for two months, if they'd been decent and honest with me. Even if I hadn't been a member of the Committee, John owed me some explanation of what was going on."

Martha went back to the villa, prepared to get John on the telephone and give him a piece of her mind. She still couldn't reach him, which only infuriated her more. To top it off, her hand was hurting; the medicine wasn't relieving the pain.

When she wasn't on the phone, trying to reach John or talking to friends, she was pacing up and down, smoking endlessly and drinking Dewar's, her favorite Scotch. Periodically she'd go tell Steve King and Lea Jablonsky about the dirty tricks she knew had been instigated by the Nixon Administration and the Committee, hoping to learn more from them. She kept repeating that she wasn't going to stand for it! Adding to the insult was that nobody had told her that Lawrence O'Brien had announced the Democratic National Committee was suing CREEP and the Watergate burglars for a million dollars. She'd had to hear that on television.

After another unsuccessful call to John (by now it was Thursday afternoon, June 22), Martha reached Fred LaRue at the Mitchells' Watergate apartment. When he told her it was impossible for her to talk to John she gave him a message for her husband: Martha Mitchell was not coming back to Washington, under any condition, unless he left politics *now.* The agreement of Sunday, to wait until after the election, was off. John Mitchell either must leave Washington, at once, or he would never see Martha again.

Before she hung up, Martha told Fred LaRue she was going to call the press to report her ultimatum to John. With that, she called Helen Thomas of UPI; it was about six P.M. She told the wire-service reporter about her burned hand, her dislike for politics, and how she had given her husband an ultimatum to get out of politics, since, as she put it, she was "sick and tired" of the whole operation. At that point, Martha recalled, Steve King rushed into her bedroom, threw her back across the bed and ripped the telephone out of the wall. Evidently LaRue, or someone alerted by him, called the villa to tell Steve King to keep Martha from talking to the press.

Helen reported "the conversation ended abruptly when it appeared someone took away the phone from her hand. She was heard to say, 'You just get away!' " When Helen called back the hotel operator told her, "Mrs. Mitchell is indisposed and cannot talk."

John Mitchell, reached at the Watergate apartment, "expressed amusement at his wife's turning to the phone . . . in her upset," Helen said. And he indicated he didn't mind his wife's going to the press with her troubles. "She's great," John Mitchell told UPI. "That little sweetheart. I love her so much. She gets a little upset about politics, but she loves me and I love her and that's what counts."

Martha's friends questioned John Mitchell's account when they read in the UPI story: "Mitchell said his wife's sister and a secretary [were there] and it was probably one of them who sought to stop her phone call." Martha didn't have a sister.

In her call of June 22, Martha didn't reveal any Nixon Administration secrets, but evidently someone was afraid she would. Hadn't she been ranting for days to Steve King and Lea Jablonsky about dirty tricks? Hadn't she told Fred LaRue about the things she'd tell if John didn't leave Washington immediately? It's obvious someone panicked and told King to *keep Martha quiet.*

The man who gave the order—Mitchell or LaRue or whoever—didn't know how much Martha knew, but there was no doubt as to *how* she knew it: Martha was an incurable eavesdropper. Not only John but others in the Administration knew she shamelessly listened in on his telephone conversations. In his book *Blind Ambition,* John Dean writes that "LaRue had warned me to take extreme care in speaking with Mitchell at home, because Martha had a habit of listening in on the extension. She might call the press." He said the Watergate cover-up conspirators found it necessary to speak to Mitchell in code.

Martha also overheard many of the talks John had with people who came for secret meetings at the Watergate apartment; after John banished her to the second floor, Martha crept halfway down the stairs and listened while perched on the landing. That's where she was the night Richard Nixon came over after midnight, furious with the media, and with John and Nixon friend Charles (Bebe) Rebozo plotted some of the tactics they were going to use to silence, or at least discredit, the national press.

Also, both John and Fred LaRue knew they had to get keys for John's briefcases after it was discovered Martha was going through top-secret papers in them after her husband went to sleep at night.

And surely John Mitchell was aware he'd been indiscreet at times, such as when he'd told her about wiretaps on Administration enemies; and when he'd let her sit in the den with him going through raw FBI files, checking the records of men being considered for appointments. According to Martha, he even discussed with her Mafia involvement in government.

So, through her eavesdropping and rummaging around in John's briefcases, and their husband-to-wife conversations, Martha was privy to a lot of inside government and political information.

After Steve King pulled the telephone out of the wall, in Martha's Newport Beach hotel room, she tried to reach the one in Marty's room. Again, she said, she was thrown aside while the phone was disconnected. Steve then shoved her into her room and slammed the door.

Martha was in serious trouble, but she wasn't sure who was causing it. Was it the Committee? The President? McCord? After all, McCord hired Steve King and King was the one stopping her from talking. She had called reporters hundreds of times before, and nobody had bothered her. It didn't make sense, but she knew that some way she had to get out of the villa.

Only a thin partition separated the balcony off the master bedroom from the one of the next villa. Martha slipped outside onto the balcony, from where she saw two men on the grounds; she recognized them as FBI agents. (Months later, Martha learned that the acting director of the FBI, L. Patrick Gray III, also was staying at the Newporter Inn. FBI agents were in his entourage.) As Martha was trying to climb from one balcony to the other, Steve King ran out and pulled her back inside. She claimed he threw her down and kicked her.

Both John and Martha had FBI protection while he was Attorney General, but Martha knew that they no longer were eligible for protection. Why were the FBI agents outside? She became even more frightened.

Her immediate problem, though, was with Steve King, who stood guard at her door. At one point she asked what his wife would think if she could see what he was doing; Steve answered he guessed she wouldn't like it. By this time Lea and Marty had come back—Martha thought this was the day Marty went to Disneyland, but she wasn't sure. Martha also remembered hearing Lea tell Marty that her mother had gone crazy and would have to be put into an institution. Martha would learn later that the same story was put out by the White House when reporters asked about the California incident.

Martha never understood why the press didn't ask why, if she were crazy, a psychiatrist hadn't been called to take care of her. Another story, detailed at length by columnist Jack Anderson, later went the rounds, saying she was rip-roaring drunk. Again, Martha wondered, if she were in the condition Anderson described, why wasn't she taken care of by a competent doctor? She would say, "You just don't leave a crazy or belligerent drunk woman in the care of a young man without medical experience."

During the next few hours, Martha said, she was batted around, kicked and manhandled in general. The Nixon Administration later tried to brush off Martha's claims as the rantings and ravings of a hysterical woman.

Eventually Martha must have gone to sleep; the next thing she knew it was morning and King no longer was guarding her door. She slipped downstairs, planning to escape, but King spotted her just as she reached a glass door. In the ensuing scuffle, Martha's left hand was cut, so badly that six stitches were required in two fingers.

Martha was sitting up in her room, her hand bleeding—enough to soak four washclothes, she said—when Dr. Dan Romaine Kirkham (asked to take the call by Dr. McGaughey, who was busy in the emergency room) arrived with a nurse. Dr. Kirkham says there were five or six men and a woman secretary in Martha's villa. He adds there was an upstairs and downstairs to the villa and security men were "all over the place."

One of the men told Dr. Kirkham they wanted him to give Martha Mitchell a shot to sedate her. The doctor says he answered, "Look, I'm going to decide whether a shot is given!" When he asked who the men were, he remembers that at least one showed an I.D. card, indicating that he was with the group of security men who "guard the President." The Secret Service? "Yes, as I recall."

Though an FBI spokesman denies there were agents present, Martha said she recognized at least two of the men as FBI agents. Lea Jablonsky told Susan Morrison (John Mitchell's secretary for eight years, including two at the Justice Department) that men from both the Secret Service and the FBI were there.

IN RETROSPECT, DR. KIRKHAM VIEWS THE EVENTS THAT FOLLOWED DIFFERently from his assumption at the time. To him then, Martha was a hysterical woman, upset and bleeding, an alcoholic (he was told she was one) who had been drinking to the point where she was out of control. Martha was calling herself a prisoner, and Dr. Kirkham says he certainly could understand why she was being guarded: "Because you can't let the

Attorney General's wife go out and let everybody know she is an alcoholic."

Today he says, "I think she had worked herself up into quite a state because she realized what it [Watergate] was. I think she knew about it before it came out; she was probably in on the deal somewhat . . . She was ranting and raving . . . about her husband, too . . . They couldn't blow the whole deal. Apparently they knew by now the situation was critical [although] nobody else knew it."

The doctor says Martha wouldn't let him look at her injured hand; Martha said he refused to treat her hand. Both agreed that Dr. Kirkham prepared a sedative (either Valium, Stalazine or Thorazine, he doesn't remember which) and that Martha objected, violently, to having a sedative given to her hypodermically. "She thought I was on their side," he recalls. "She was paranoid about everyone."

To administer the medication, Dr. Kirkham says, it was necessary for at least two or three of the security guards and the secretary to help hold Martha. Martha said, "They pulled down my pants and shot me in the behind." Martha claimed her daughter Marty was a witness to her humiliation; Dr. Kirkham doesn't remember seeing a child while he was in the villa but doesn't rule out that there could have been one.

After they gave her the shot and left, Martha thought maybe if she talked to the doctor and the nurse once more they would understand that she actually was a prisoner and would help her. When she went downstairs, they were near the front door, talking to the guards. She saw this as a chance to escape through the back to the swimming-pool patio.

According to Martha, King saw her dashing toward the door and ran over and slapped her across the room. Dr. Kirkham confirms that Martha tried to escape and was prevented from doing so. "She tried to dash out on several occasions, upstairs and downstairs." He doesn't remember that she was slapped, but he says, "If you are a little lady and some big guy is standing at the door, you are not going to get through the door very easily."

After the doctor left, Lea and King, according to Martha, ordered her to go upstairs, and when she refused they literally carried her up to her bedroom. When Martha asked Lea why she was doing this to her, she said Lea replied, "It's for your own good." They left her upstairs, saying, "You are going to sleep."

But Martha didn't go to sleep. What neither King nor Jablonsky knew was that Martha didn't react normally to all drugs. So instead of putting her to sleep, the shot, combined with the alcohol and codeine pills, agitated her even more. Then, too, Martha said she was so frightened, all the medicine in the world couldn't have put her to sleep. She was in a state of panic over the security guards and that the doctor hadn't believed she was a "political" prisoner, that he had given her a shot against her will and had left her with the very people she'd told him were her jailers.

She was so upset she felt she was going to "jump out of my skin." Thinking if she ate something it might relieve this terrible sensation, she asked for food. Martha claimed she was offered a stale sandwich, left over from the night before. They wouldn't let any food come to the room, she said, because they didn't want the waiters to come in. Nor were maids allowed to clean her room.

Although they wouldn't let her have food, Martha said there was plenty of alcohol, or as she put it, "They plied me with liquor." A doctor who saw Martha often during her last months says, "I'm sure there were some people [involved] in Watergate who wanted her to look crazy . . . and the fact that she did drink was taken advantage of completely . . . If I had wanted to do what they evidently wanted to do, I would have bought her a couple of bottles of booze and given her some pills."

Sometime during this period John Mitchell called, on King's telephone, and asked to speak to his wife. Martha refused to go to the downstairs telephone, but she sent her husband a message: "Tell that bastard I don't want to talk to him."

John then called Herbert Kalmbach and asked him to take over the explosive situation. As a friend of Kalmbach's tells it, Mitchell said, "If you've ever in your life done anything for me, Herb, do this for me now." Mitchell also said he'd arrange for the Mitchells' good friends Peggy and Kenneth Ebbitt to fly from New York the next day to be with Martha.

When Kalmbach arrived at the villa, Martha was pacing up and down, drinking Cokes "like mad" and clutching a bloody cloth in her injured hand, while Marty, looking bewildered, roamed in and out of her mother's room.

Kalmbach called his personal physician, Dr. Donald Martin, and as Martha remembered it, the doctor said she had to go to the hospital. But Kalmbach said she couldn't leave the villa, that someone would have to come to her. After a long argument, the doctor convinced Kalmbach, who insisted that Martha go under his wife's name; he made her promise she would say she was Barbara Kalmbach.

Herb Kalmbach's friend denies that Kalmbach ever resisted having Martha go to the hospital or that he demanded she use any name other than her own. Dr. Martin refuses to confirm or deny either version of the story.

At that point, Martha said, she would have promised anything. The shot had nauseated her, she'd had no food and she was weak. Also, she was confused about what was going on in Washington and with her husband.

She agreed to go as Mrs. Kalmbach. But she told Kalmbach that when she got back she wanted to find a phone re-installed in her room. He promised one would be if she, in turn, promised she wouldn't call anyone in the press. She said she wouldn't. Martha also told him he'd have to get Steve King and Lea Jablonsky out of the villa. He said he would have his two secretaries spend the night with her, and on the way to Hoag Presbyterian Hospital they stopped at Kalmbach's office, where he said he would make the arrangements; he also called John Mitchell to get his permission for Martha to have surgery on her left hand.

He left Martha in the car while he went inside. She thought of trying to get to a telephone, but she realized that anyone seeing her—bloody, dizzy—would think she was "crazy for sure." She sat and waited.

When they walked into the emergency room, who should be there but Dr. McGaughey, who had previously treated her burn. Martha said, "The Mrs. Kalmbach cover was blown before I had a chance to use it."

Martha clutched Kalmbach's hand while the doctor stitched her fingers, and then the two went back to the villa. One of the secretaries was waiting, the other arrived that evening. Steve and Lea had left, taking Marty with them. But the telephones in the upstairs bedrooms had not been reconnected, and, according to Martha, the hotel switchboard operator refused to put outgoing calls through from the phone in King's room.

The next day Barbara Kalmbach came by to stay with Martha while Herb went to the airport to meet Ken and Peggy Ebbitt. Martha said Mrs. Kalmbach tried to use the telephone in the villa, and when she couldn't get a call out she took Martha to her house. Later, the Washington *Post* reported that a security guard at the Newporter Inn said the FBI requested that all incoming and outgoing calls to Mrs. Mitchell's villa be stopped; the FBI denies any involvement.

By the time Kalmbach arrived with Ken and Peggy Ebbitt, Martha had had enough of the Newporter Inn, with its disconnected phones and frightening memories; she wanted to get as far away from it as possible.

But she refused to go to Washington. John was there and she wasn't ready to see him—not yet. It was decided that she would go to Bronxville and stay with the Ebbitts, who, not happy with things as they'd found them at the villa, were quite willing to turn around and fly back to New York. The three took the "Red Eye" flight that night. They left in such a hurry no one thought to tell Kalmbach: he learned about their departure when he called the Inn the next morning.

Something happened on the plane ride back that changed Martha's mind about going to the Ebbitts; she said she didn't remember and they won't discuss it. In any event, Martha went instead to the Westchester Country Club, where she checked into Suite 543 and called UPI to say she'd been held a political prisoner in California.

She said, "I'm leaving him [John] until he decides to leave the campaign. It's horrible to me. I have been through so much, I don't like it. Martha isn't going to stand for it . . . I love my husband very much. But I'm not going to stand for all those dirty things that go on.

"If you could see me, you wouldn't believe it," Martha added, "I'm black and blue. I'm a political prisoner." She said they left her in California "with absolutely no information. They don't want me to talk."

As soon as the story was sent out by the wire service, a swarm of reporters and photographers headed for the Westchester Country Club. Only Marcia Kramer of the New York *Daily News* got through to Martha. As a crime reporter, Marcia says it was her opinion that Martha was a "beaten woman" and that the "incredible" black-and-blue marks on Martha's arms looked like they were a "totally professional job."

Wearing a rumpled, yellow linen pants suit, no makeup and with her hair hanging down her back, Martha paced the floor, chain-smoked and broke down crying on four occasions as she told Marcia she was leaving her husband because of the Watergate incident and other "outrageous and dirty" campaign tactics.

She also said she wanted her husband "out of such dishonest deeds." She wouldn't elaborate on the outrageous and dirty tactics or the dishonest deeds, but she did tell Marcia that she had been told to say the Watergate break-in had nothing to do with anyone at CREEP, which, she said, "was a damn lie."

She claimed she had been beaten and made a prisoner in California by people hired by CREEP to keep her from telling the truth about Watergate and other things. Speaking of politics, she said it was a "cops and robbers game."

To Marcia it was an unbelievable two and a half hours she spent with Martha.

After Marcia's story appeared, it didn't take Mitchell aides long to issue denials: "She has one guard, the same man who goes with her husband and her every place they travel because of the many threats against their lives." And a Mitchell associate told a reporter, "Everyone knows that Mrs. Mitchell has her private personal problems. These are something that only her husband can solve . . . She can be perfectly charming, and then at other times—especially at night—she is not herself. Nobody beat her up, and it's just not true that she ever had five guards."

There was no doubt in Marcia's mind then, nor is there now, but that Martha was telling the truth: "I think she was too upset . . . to be guarded in her remarks or make up stories. At the time I think that because she was so upset she may have said more than she might have otherwise disclosed."

More of the media descended on the country club after the Kramer story. Hundreds of calls came in—from the press wanting any kind of statement, from radio and TV stations seeking interviews, from friends offering help. Although Martha didn't know it at the time, there were two calls from Bebe Rebozo, one through the White House switchboard, the other from Key Biscayne. Martha never knew why he called, but she guessed he wanted to smooth-talk her into keeping quiet about anything she knew that would hurt his good friend Richard Nixon.

There was so much confusion that the club moved Martha two times and eventually placed a security man outside her last suite, number 805. Various club workers were bribed to slip notes under the door, but Martha said the reporters could have saved their money; she didn't receive anything from the media. Neither did she get the telephone messages until more than a year later when she found them in one of John Mitchell's file drawers.

Monday morning, Peggy Ebbitt came over to tell Martha that John was on his way up from Washington; she said she hoped Martha would see him. Martha said she would. John, who'd had a meeting with Nixon before leaving for the country club, broke down and cried when he saw his wife's injuries. It was the first time Martha had seen John cry. She said the tears were streaming down his face and he kept calling her his "poor baby," and telling her how sorry he was for what had been done to her in California. He begged her to try to forget it, to put it out of her mind. At no time did he tell her why it was done or who had approved it.

When John Mitchell entered Martha's suite, the guard outside her door told the press, "They're in there and they're not coming out." They didn't for three days.

During this time Martha never saw anyone alone. Dr. G. Freeman Brooks, a doctor of internal medicine now retired and living in the South, was called to treat Martha's hand, the one with stitches in the fingers. The doctor, who had seen Martha two or three times for minor illnesses when she lived in Rye, New York, says that during his visit they "carried on no conversation, really. I just greeted her, but we didn't talk. Her husband was in the room, he was over in a corner sitting in a chair."

John Mitchell had a hard time convincing Martha that she should come back to Washington; she was adamant about leaving him unless he left the Nixon campaign. Finally he said he would resign as soon as she wanted him to; Martha replied, "That is today." He couldn't get out *that* fast, John explained. First he'd have to find someone to replace him as head of CREEP. He asked Martha to sit down with him and help draw up a list of men capable of taking over the job. When they'd completed the list, John promised he'd submit it to the President as soon as they got back to Washington.

Martha told him another condition to her going back with him was that both Steve King and Lea Jablonsky had to be fired. He assured her they would be. Martha was surprised, months later, to learn that instead of being fired they'd been promoted at CREEP. After the election, both Steve and Lea moved into good jobs in government agencies.

Although Martha always denied it, some sort of bargain apparently was struck in which she promised not to do or say anything, publicly, about dirty tricks and such until after the November election. Several things Martha later said seem to confirm that a deal was made. For instance, a few weeks after she returned to Washington, while talking to me about what had happened to her in California, she said, "I can't tell you everything now, but I will after the election." And soon after the Mitchells moved to New York in September, she started talking about the book she was going to write, a book in which she promised to tell all "after the election."

Thursday morning, John and Martha slipped out the back door, got into an automobile driven by the country-club manager, and went to the Ebbitts' house, in nearby Bronxville. Once they were sure the press hadn't followed them, they got into a chauffeur-driven car and motored to Washington.

"I went back to Washington," Martha explained, "because despite all that had been done to me because of Nixon, I still felt he would make a better President than his Democratic opponent, George McGovern."

That weekend Martha was surprised when John resigned as head of CREEP. He had convinced her it would take quite a while for Mr. President to decide on his successor, but now he said he was leaving at once. In the statement he issued, John said he couldn't devote all of his time and energy to the campaign and "still meet the one obligation which must come first: the happiness and welfare of my wife and daughter."

Martha honestly thought he'd left the campaign because she asked him to until she read, long after John had deserted her, the transcript of the White House tape of June 30, 1972.

According to the transcript prepared by the impeachment inquiry staff of the House Judiciary Committee of experts, from a recording of a meeting among President Nixon, H. R. Haldeman and John N. Mitchell, the following conversation took place:

HALDEMAN: Well, there maybe is another facet. The longer you wait the more risk each hour brings. You run the risk of more stuff, valid or invalid, surfacing on the Watergate caper—type of thing—

MITCHELL: You couldn't possibly do it if you got into a—

HALDEMAN: —the potential problem and then you are stuck—

PRESIDENT: Yes, that's the other thing, if something does come out, but we won't—we hope nothing will. It may not. But there is always the risk.

HALDEMAN: As of now, there is no problem there. As, as of any moment in the future there is at least a potential problem.

PRESIDENT: Well, I'd cut the loss fast. I'd cut it fast. If we're going to do it I'd cut it fast. That's my view, generally speaking. And I wouldn't —I don't think, though, as a matter of fact, I don't think the story, if we, if you put it in human terms—I think the story is, you're positive rather than negative, because as I said as I was preparing to answer for this press conference, I just wrote it out—as I usually do, one way —terribly sensitive *(unintelligible)*. A hell of a lot of people will like that answer. They would. And it'd make anybody else who asked any other question on it look like a selfish son-of-a-bitch, which I thoroughly intended them to look like.

MITCHELL: *(unintelligible)* Westchester Country Club with all the sympathy in the world.

PRESIDENT: That's great. That's great.

MITCHELL: *(unintelligible)* don't let—

HALDEMAN: You taking this route—people won't expect you to—be a surprise.

PRESIDENT: No—if it's a surprise. Otherwise, you're right. It will be tied right to Watergate. *(Unintelligible)* tighten if you wait too long, till it simmers down.

HALDEMAN: You can't if other stuff develops on Watergate. The problem is, it's always potentially the same thing.

PRESIDENT: Well, if it does, don't just hard-line.

HALDEMAN: (unintelligible) that's right. In other words, it'd be hard to hard-line Mitchell's departure under—

PRESIDENT: That's right. You can't do it. I just want it to be handled in a way Martha's not hurt.

MITCHELL: Yeah. Okay.

Martha cried bitterly when she read this conversation between John and Nixon and Haldeman. For the first time she knew what a lot of people had suspected right along. John didn't resign from the campaign for her "happiness and welfare." He left to help with the cover-up.

Chapter Two

THE POPULATION OF PINE BLUFF, ARKANSAS, WAS RIGHT AT EIGHTeen thousand when Martha Elizabeth Beall was born there on Labor Day, September 2, 1918, the daughter of cotton broker George Virgil Beall and Arie Ferguson Beall, a teacher of "elocution." It was a rich town even then, old by its state's standards—around one hundred years at the time —and as Martha was quick to tell you, it was *Southern.*

Martha was fiercely proud of her Southern heritage, and she resented "horribly" that when she first became a Washington celebrity the press gleefully compared her to Lorelei, Anita Loos's dumb-blonde heroine from the wrong side of the tracks of Little Rock, in *Gentlemen Prefer Blondes.* Not so much, Martha said, because of the personal references (she knew she was smarter than *they* thought, and her family, pre-Revolutionary "on both sides," was well-born), but because the comparison implied that Little Rock was as aristocratic and had the same social ambience as Pine Bluff.

As Pine Bluff natives explain it: The Delta, as such, started at Pine Bluff, and a lot of its families were involved in cotton. The city was, and is today, the leading cotton market between Memphis and Dallas. Many of the old families got their wealth from the land. Their plantations, backgrounds and traditions, and way of life were like the Mississippi gentry, whereas Little Rock people were "a breed apart, more Midwestern."

Townsfolk still talk of families of heritage and position, and how Pine Bluff was a part of the *Old* South. They point out that in 1918 it still was an aristocratic little Southern town, "where people entertained very beautifully, very formally, in lovely big houses, with old silver and china—things that had been in the family for generations—and with lots of family retainers in the kitchen." They emphasize that was the kind of atmosphere Martha grew up in.

Although Martha's people were latecomers to Pine Bluff, arriving in the 1880's, they came with impeccable credentials. Calvin M. and Sallie Ferguson, Martha's maternal grandparents, migrated to Arkansas from South Carolina. Sallie Ferguson's mother was a Culp; her family's plantation, in Chester County, recently impoverished by the Civil War, had been in the family since the late 1770's.

Martha always thought her people had received the land directly in a grant from the King of England. Actually, the grant was given to some English noblemen, and Martha's ancestors bought several hundred acres of the land when it was first offered for sale. Another ancestor, a Culp, had the dubious distinction of being the first white woman in South Carolina to be scalped by Indians and live to tell it. The Fergusons, like the Culps of Scotch-Irish ancestry, were affluent pre-Revolutionary landowners who'd been wiped out financially by the Civil War.

Arie Ferguson, Martha's mother, was born at Wylie's Mill, Chester County, on July 15, 1882, shortly before her parents moved to Arkansas with their two children—Arie and her brother, Hartwell Hinton Ferguson, who was three years her senior. When he married, Hinton would cement the Fergusons' position in Pine Bluff society by taking as his bride Nina Smart, a member of one of the city's oldest and finest families.

Sallie Ferguson, a great *raconteuse,* liked to tell her granddaughter Martha about leaving her ancestral home and how the relatives wept as the train pulled out of the station because they feared the Fergusons were going into wild territory, where they'd be killed by Indians and never heard of again.

One of the first, if not *the* first, wholesale grocers in Arkansas, Calvin Ferguson soon built a thriving business, specializing in coffee, tea and fine spices, with branch offices throughout the state. Later the company added a wholesale coffee-roasting business, the Socony Coffee Company.

In 1885 the Fergusons built a large, typically late-Victorian house of white clapboard, at 902 West Fourth Street. "It had all the gingerbread and that jazz," Martha once said of the house where she was born. Much of the furniture in the twenty-room house came from the Culp plantation, where it had been handmade by the slaves. The Ferguson house, still standing on the corner of Fourth and Walnut streets, is now a Martha Mitchell museum.

After Calvin Ferguson died, in 1911, his son Hinton took over the operation of the family business, by then renamed C. M. Ferguson & Son. Sallie Ferguson continued living in the Fourth Street house until her death in 1958 at age ninty-nine. One of Martha's contemporaries remembers Mrs. Ferguson as having been "a lady of the old school, very prim and proper—high-necked dresses and all that kind of stuff. Oh, she was very friendly and had a good sense of humor. But still, she had her place and you had yours."

GEORGE VIRGIL BEALL (PRONOUNCED BELL) WAS BORN IN MISSISSIPPI, ON July 13, 1879. On Martha's birth certificate his birthplace is listed as Vaiden. But when she filed an application for membership in the DAR in 1955, forty years after her mother became a member, Martha named the larger Meridian as the town of her father's birth.

In any event, when he was quite young his parents left Mississippi for Sulphur Springs, Texas. The Bealls, like the Fergusons, had become impoverished by the Civil War. One of Martha's few memories of the Bealls was of visiting them in Sulphur Springs, in a large house next door to the Presbyterian Church, where she loved to play in the attic, especially with the Confederate money Grandmother Beall had transported by trunkload from Mississippi to Texas.

Martha may have been confused about this one memory of her paternal grandparents. A Pine Bluff woman remembers that she and Martha, when five or six years old, found a trunkful of Confederate money the Fergusons had brought to Arkansas. She thinks this, probably, is the money Martha remembered.

It was about 1915 when George Beall came to Pine Bluff, as a representative of the Japan Cotton Trading Company. Not long after, he decided to stay, probably because he'd met and fallen in love with "Miss Arie," the vivacious little elocution teacher who'd weathered an unsuccessful marriage and had a young son, John Quincy Nash, born in 1902. Martha claimed she never was told anything about her mother's first marriage, saying it was "always one of those things that was kind of hush-hush." Pine Bluff townspeople volunteer that Miss Arie lived in

College Park, Georgia, while married to her first husband, a Colonel John Quincy Nash, then Commandant of the Georgia Military Academy. After ten years she divorced him and returned to Pine Bluff with her young son.

"Miss Arie was crazy about Colonel Nash," says a Pine Bluff native. "But he got him a friend on the side and this was sixty years ago and people didn't do those things."

The marriage of Miss Arie and George Beall took place on September 19, 1917. Soon after, he became the representative of Jon. F. Clark & Company, a New Orleans brokerage firm. A 1929 advertisement in the local newspaper encouraged investors to buy and sell their stock and bonds through "Jon. F. Clark & Co.," and noted the firm was a member of the New York Stock Exchange, New York Curb Market, New York Cotton Exchange, New Orleans Cotton Exchange and the Chicago Board of Trade.

George Beall, at one time president of the local cotton exchange, is described by his friend E. A. Bell, a retired cotton broker still living in Pine Bluff, as a happy-go-lucky man, liked by everyone: "I don't know of any enemies George had at all." A heavyset man, about five-feet-ten, with brown eyes and light auburn hair, he was remembered by his daughter as having been handsome, "extremely handsome." Mr. Bell says he thought that when Martha was young she resembled her father, both in looks and in temperament. She also had brown eyes, and as Martha later told a reporter, "I was a redhead. I even had freckles; my hair changed overnight [after she left Pine Bluff]." Mr. Bell remembers that George Beall was a big spender, a free spender, and that Martha got this trait from her father. He adds, "Miss Arie was not that way."

From her father Martha also got her love of gambling. While in school and as an adult, Martha liked to play cards—any kind, but bridge and gin rummy in particular. After she was married to John Mitchell, friends used to tease her about her phenomenal good luck at gambling and accused her of being the daughter of a Mississippi River-boat gambler. George Beall wasn't that, but he liked to speculate and play the stock market and gamble at cards with his friends. Mr. Bell says George liked "to take a chance on anything and there were quite a number of things he went into." Another man who knew George Beall remembers that "he dressed well, was outspoken, smoked incessantly and always had a little reed [cigarette holder] in his mouth." Like her father, Martha liked to dress well, was outspoken and from her early teens smoked constantly.

George Beall adored his daughter and she idolized him. As a small child she loved to cuddle up in his lap and play with his gold pocket watch, covered with marks he said she'd made while teething. Martha remembered that "he petted me and called me his baby. He was very dear to me and very kind to me. He always loved me."

When Martha was older, her father often took her to the cotton and stock exchanges to let her watch the trading, and to teach her how to interpret the mysteries of the Big Board. Her interest in the market carried over into her adult life, when every morning she read the financial pages of the New York *Times* and the *Wall Street Journal.* Martha's father also planned little outings with his daughter. The mother of one of her school friends remembers that George Beall, "that sweet man," often would call when he was taking Martha to a weekend movie, to invite her daughter to go along.

SOON AFTER MARTHA WAS BORN, AT GRANDMOTHER FERGUSON'S, THE Bealls built a large colonial-style house, at 4200 Cherry Street, in a beautiful wooded area out near the Pine Bluff Country Club. George Beall had a small-scale model of the mansion built as a playhouse for Martha. Here she had her own little kitchen, with a stove "that worked," a small piano on which she played simple tunes before she was six—"Jesus Loves Me" was a favorite. She had dolls of all sizes, descriptions and nationalities. One of her favorite games was to line up the dolls and play "Queen." Her choice doll of the moment was "Her Majesty," and all the other dolls curtsied to her.

During this time, Martha's constant playmates were Fannie and Selma Byas, the daughters of Martha's nurse Mary Byas (later Walker) and her husband Johnnie. Fannie (now Fannie Coleman) remembers that Martha was a generous playmate, always willing to share her toys. She also shared her clothes; both Fannie and Selma were married in dresses given to them by Martha.

As much as she loved her playhouse and all of her toys, and having Fannie and Selma to play with, Martha remembered her years at the Cherry Street house as a lonesome period. Because of the difference in their ages, she and her half-brother were not close. And the house was so far out of town that her schoolmates couldn't come to see her unless an adult brought them out and then picked them up.

Occasionally a friend would come to see Martha, and one such visit resulted in her getting the only punishment she ever received from her father. George Beall loved mockingbirds, and for some time he'd been interested in a bird nesting in a bush in front of the Beall house. Martha was about seven or eight years old when she and her little friend pulled the bird's nest out of the bush and destroyed the eggs. It was the first and only time Martha's father spanked her.

Actually, Martha said, she wasn't punished often by Miss Arie either: "I was a shy and bashful child . . . So I seldom did anything to be punished for." Martha always insisted that even as an adult she still was shy and bashful. When asked how this could be true when she was so flamboyant and outspoken, she answered, "This is a camouflage that I have formed, one I use whenever I think it is necessary."

Although most of the people who knew Martha when she was young saw her as a happy-go-lucky, if impulsive, child who had everything she ever wanted, Martha herself described her childhood as not that idealistic: "My mother was seldom home. She was always busy with her many civic clubs and with her pupils. I resented it, horribly.

"I was *so* jealous of these things my mother was doing, because they caused her to leave me all the time; she turned me over to my colored mammy. It aggravated me to the extent I *couldn't stand it*!" All of her life Martha resented not having had more attention from her mother. Recalling that when Miss Arie was dying she'd said to her daughter, "Isn't it strange we have never been friends," Martha cried, "It was *her* fault!"

Martha's feeling of rejection by her mother evidently started at an early age. She was little more than a toddler when she turned to her nurse, Mary Byas, for the love and attention she felt she wasn't getting from her mother. Martha called Mary "Mama," and Mary called Martha "Baby." Even after Martha was the wife of the Attorney General, she still was "Baby" to Mary Walker. A note to Martha in 1970 started, "Baby, we love you . . ." and ended "with all my love, your Mama, Mary B. Walker."

A Pine Bluff woman who knew Martha's mother well says she's sure Miss Arie didn't know that her daughter was calling someone else "Mama": "Miss Arie wouldn't have allowed it!"

"Mary shared everything with me and was always there if I wanted anything," Martha said. When she was small, Martha once told Mary she wished she was her color, and for many years, until she was grown, Martha wouldn't go to a party unless Mary went with her.

It was Mary who took Martha to doctor's appointments, music lessons, the beauty parlor; Martha, according to a friend, was the first girl of her group to have a permanent wave in a beauty parlor. And it was Mary who sat up nights with Martha after her sinus operation. Martha, who was so young she hadn't started school, wouldn't let anyone else nurse her through her illness.

"And," Martha admitted, "Mary picked up after me. I just dropped things all over and Mary was always behind me." Martha dropped things all over for the rest of her life, even when there wasn't a Mary behind her.

After Martha's death, her son Jay Jennings said, "I think this constant love and attention she received from Mary is one of the reasons she desperately needed, and demanded, constant love and attention as an adult. She was used to it. Another reason, perhaps, is that Mom regretted that her mother did not have the time to spend with her and that Miss Arie relegated many of her maternal responsibilities to a nanny, which was very much the accepted Southern practice. Miss Arie had had a nanny; Mom's Grandmother Ferguson had had a nanny. So I think perhaps Mom's desire for attention from others also was motivated by the lack of attention she received from her own mother."

Yet when she herself became a mother, Martha hired a nanny for her son and later a nanny for her daughter Marty Mitchell. Jay has complained, too, about the lack of attention he and Marty got from their mother.

Among the happy memories of her childhood were the times she spent with Sallie Ferguson. Martha loved her grandmother and often said she felt closer to her than she did to her mother: "Grandmother was usually with me where my mother wasn't."

"Her grandmother did an exceptional job of spoiling Martha," according to a Pine Bluff friend. Frances Hall says, "It wasn't Martha's fault that she was strong-willed, self-centered and very spoiled. If her mother said 'no,' then her grandmother said 'yes.' "

UNCHARACTERISTICALLY FOR A WOMAN OF HER DAY, MISS ARIE SPENT LESS time homemaking and mothering than her contemporaries. She was active in the DAR and several other organizations, particularly those concerning the arts. ("She was so literary," Martha complained.) She directed the high school senior play each year, and then there were her many speech and drama pupils.

After Martha's father was no longer there and Miss Arie became the sole support of herself and her daughter, her work load increased. She had a studio at the Woodrow Wilson Junior High School and another at Miss Ferguson's Fourth Street house, where Miss Arie and Martha were living by then. Miss Arie saw pupils at school during school hours and gave private lessons at the house in the late afternoon and often in the evening after supper.

But lessons were apt to be late when given at the house. "Martha was so spoiled!" one pupil explains. "You'd be taking a lesson and poor Miss

Arie was doing her best and Martha would call, from the top of the stairs, 'Mother! You just have to come up and find my clothes!' So your lesson would wait while Miss Arie found the clothes."

But the mother of one of Martha's friends sees it differently: "Martha, that sweet child, couldn't have her friends come to her house if Miss Arie was giving a lesson." Even vacations were often taken in connection with Miss Arie's work. Two or three summers Miss Arie went to Northwestern University to study and took Martha along.

Miss Arie was a brunette who wore her "marcel-waved" hair pulled softly back into a bun. Former pupils talk about how she was the most charming, sweetest, dearest women in the world and affectionately laugh among themselves at the way the bodices of her dresses were constantly wearing out. This came about because Miss Arie was short, and in order to drive she had to push the seat of her big black Studebaker so far forward her large bust rubbed against the steering wheel. They also remember that she could be quite strict.

As a child Martha was pert and pretty and bright, and her proud parents marveled at her ability, at pre-nursery-school age, to memorize and recite any number of nursery rhymes after hearing them only once or twice on her little record player. But there was one "flaw" in the otherwise perfect child. Martha was left-handed. As she explained, being left-handed when she was growing up carried a social stigma. It was *abnormal.* Extreme measures were taken to correct this imagined deficiency in a child.

At mealtime Martha's left hand was tied behind her back, in an effort to force her to eat with her right. And when Martha started school she again was made miserable when there too her left hand was tied behind her back. As she told it: "Here I was, just a child, the only one in the class being subjected to the indignity of having to study with a piece of bedsheet tying her hand behind her back! It made me feel like an outcast; I developed a horrible sense of insecurity and an inferiority complex."

In time Martha started to stutter and her mother gave her hours of instruction to correct it. But for the rest of her life Martha was inclined to stumble over her words when she got emotional. Or afraid. After one of the recurring nightmares she had, following her experience in California, it often was impossible for Martha to speak coherently until someone calmed her.

Both Martha's grandmother and mother had been left-handed. "They were broken and became right-handers," Martha reported. "But they didn't break me!" The only thing Martha learned to use with her right hand was scissors; she wanted to cut paper dolls and there were no special scissors for left-handers.

At the table, with her left hand behind her, Martha simply played with her food and refused to drink the glass of milk, carefully placed on the right side of her plate. She knew she'd get handouts in the kitchen, from the sympathetic help who resented what "they" were doing to that child.

Like many other children who persist in their left-handedness, Martha developed a streak of stubbornness. Or, as those who knew her then tell it, she was a "willful" or "headstrong" child. A childhood friend, Frances Hall, says, "Martha got her way, one way or another," although she quickly adds, "but she was a sweet, nice affectionate person. She was the kind of little girl who always had her arm around you. She just loved people and she was just a sweet child—although she *was* spoiled rotten!"

In addition to being left-handed in a right-handed world, Martha in all probability had another problem: dyslexia. She had many of the classic symptoms of this development syndrome. She had difficulty telling right from left. She transposed numbers. She couldn't spell. She had trouble reading aloud, since she often saw letters or words backwards, and she twisted symbols.

Another aspect of dyslexia is that frequently the child is hyperactive, and sometimes this carries over into adulthood. Martha, according to her former schoolmates, was unusually "high-strung" and full of pep, into everything and always talking. Her late half-brother Quincy Nash said in 1970, "She was a talker. She said what she thought." Even her high-school yearbook has under her picture: *"I love its gentle warble, I love its gentle flow, I love to wind my tongue up, and I love to let it go."*

Anyone who knew Martha well has at least one story that illustrates her apparent symptoms of dyslexia. William Thomas Couch, a former boyfriend, tells with amusement of the day he was in a car with Martha—she was driving—and he told her to turn right at the next corner. "But she turned to the left, and when I asked, 'Can't you tell right from left?' she said the funniest thing. She said, 'I don't have on my wrist watch.' " A dyslexic often uses a "crutch," such as a ring or a watch, always worn on the same side, to remind her, or him, which side of the body is right and which is left.

Her tendency to transpose numbers was one of the reasons Martha had such astronomical telephone bills throughout her life. As one friend puts it: "Martha dialed more wrong numbers than she did right."

A wrong-number conversation, often late at night, might go like this: "May I speak to [Jane Doe] . . . She doesn't? This was her number last week . . . I'm dialing 999-972-3465 . . . This is 3456? Now, this is what happens to me all the time, ever since they started tapping my phones . . . This is Martha Mitchell . . . Yes . . . No, I'm not kidding . . . Well, thanks! I wish you folks out there would complain about what they're doing to my phone . . . (etc., etc.)." Friends who witnessed such calls were dismayed.

Sometimes a person on the other end of the line would turn out to be such a good conversationalist that Martha became a phone-pal, calling back regularly. But she was steadfast in her refusal to give out her number. As she explained to me, "I wouldn't give my number to a *stranger*!"

Her difficulty in reading and in transposing letters and seeing words backwards also helps explain Martha's many malapropisms. For instance, she once told me that when she was going to Stephens College the students could smoke, but only in a special room: "It was a *detergent* and you didn't go, it was too much trouble."

Just as she said *detergent* for *deterrent,* Martha sometimes said *embellished* for *abolished,* or *consolation* for *consultation,* or *alleviate* for *eliminate.*

Her dyslexia, however, did not account for the nicknames she gave people she didn't like. Former New York mayor John Lindsay, for instance, was "Lindsley"; Richard Kleindienst was "Cleandish," and later "Dirtydish"; Senator J. William Fulbright was "Half-bright" or "Quarter-bright"; and Herbert Kalmbach became "Comstock."

Martha's dyslexia also made understandable her unwillingness to read long speeches when the Committee for the Re-Election of the President sent her out campaigning.

Martha would complain that her writers were "no good," that she didn't receive the speeches early enough, or she'd use any number of other excuses. She wanted to make "remarks" only, and she wanted the remarks delivered in time for her to memorize them, just as she had committed to memory the little nursery rhymes while still a preschooler.

If presented with a long speech at the last minute (anything less than forty-eight hours before presentation was the last minute to Martha), she more than likely would discard the speech, flamboyantly, in front of the audience and call for questions from the floor, the way she did at a 1975 Valentine Day forum given by the Junior League of Youngstown, Ohio. The local paper described the incident and reported that Martha, a "vivacious, candid lady . . . fielded questions like a professional." The paper didn't report the emotional shock suffered by the Junior League committee chairmen when they saw their $2,500 speaker casting aside the speech she'd contracted to deliver before their standing-room-only paying audience.

The child Martha never had heard of dyslexia. When she was an adult and I suggested she might be dyslexic, Martha was insulted. Even hearing that such people as Albert Einstein, Nelson Rockefeller, Thomas Edison and Winston Churchill had the same problem, she still wasn't appeased.

Dyslexic children sometimes find themselves up against teachers and/or parents who don't recognize their problem and think they are dumb. After Martha became famous, former teachers and classmates were quoted as saying things like, "Martha [in school] was completely harmless—a real bubblehead." Or, "She was a pretty, happy, empty-headed little girl."

While sometimes appearing stupid to adults who don't recognize their problem, dyslexic children actually are often of superior intellect. So this continual exposure to parents and teachers who don't understand, and to classmates who laugh at their mistakes, often causes dyslexic children to be not only frustrated but aggressive as well. None of her former schoolmates mention it, but Martha often talked about how aggressive she was when in high school.

Although she didn't know about dyslexia, Martha did recognize a limitation in herself and she worked exceedingly hard to compensate for it. For one thing, she *collected* words. When she couldn't recognize or correctly pronounce a word, Martha carefully recorded it in a little notebook. Then she'd look it up in the dictionary and note the correct spelling, pronunciation and meaning.

She started her word collection in the third or fourth grade and her fascination with words continued for the rest of her life. A writer interviewing her in 1970 was surprised when the Attorney General's wife drew three notebooks from her pocket and proudly displayed her latest words. Friends to whom Martha loaned books or magazines often found words underlined and their meanings noted in the margins of the pages. (Later on, her marginal notes were often found to be as interesting as the text. In a book about the Watergate tapes, next to mention of the tape of March 21, 1973, Martha marked, "This was the day John made a deal." Martha insisted John came back from Washington that night and told her he'd made a deal and wouldn't have to go to jail.)

Martha also collected quotations. One quote she read and reread, but never was able to live up to, was one she cut out when she worked in

Washington, in the 1940's: "Always behave as if nothing has happened, no matter what has happened."

ALTHOUGH MARTHA WAS ONLY AN AVERAGE STUDENT SCHOLASTICALLY, she apparently excelled at extracurricular activities. The local newspaper, which recorded the comings and goings of the town's finer families, including their youngest members, mentioned Martha Elizabeth Beall's name often. One fading, yellowing newsclip tells of her singing a solo at the Christmas program staged at Mrs. C. H. Haring's private school, which Martha attended from kindergarten through fifth grade.

Other newspaper stories mention Martha's playing the piano in recitals and acting in plays and pageants. From an early age she was active on the social scene, too. Parents who chaperoned the young people's parties remember that Martha was especially polite to older people. One of her schoolmates says, "My grandmother would speak of Martha as being such a well-mannered young girl. She always took the time to speak to older people."

Hortense Jones, who caters some of Pine Bluff's better parties, and who prepared the food for the reception following Martha's first wedding, was present at many of the children's parties Martha attended. She says Martha was "very dramatic; she liked the stage." But what impressed Hortense most was that Martha didn't forget her friends: "She sent cards to me from all over, to let me know she still remembered me. And every time she came to town to visit, if she didn't see me at any of the parties, she'd telephone to check on me."

Martha had a strong, steady voice, with a good range, and she liked to sing popular songs with her friends. She usually led the group singing at parties, but she hated the voice lessons her mother insisted she take. In fact, she despised all of her after-school lessons—piano, elocution, voice and more.

As she remembered it: "I hated being *forced* to take all of these lessons. I had to sit down and practice piano for an hour every day and I had to play in all the recitals. I just despised it. Later in my life, when I could have been a good pianist, I didn't want any part of it. And my voice—I had to sing every place, every kind of program and in the church choir. My mother wanted me to be an opera singer. I hated it so much I finally tried to ruin my voice by hollering and yelling, deliberately straining my vocal cords."

She said that was why she never gave her daughter Marty lessons of any kind: "I thought when she's ready she'll know it and say so."

Martha took trips with her parents and sometimes with chaperoned groups of girls. One summer she went to Camp Waldemar, in Texas, and in one of her scrapbooks there's a picture of a solemn-faced Martha on horseback. Almost all pictures of the young Martha show her either solemn-faced or with only a hint of a smile. The wide, flashy smile Martha made famous, after her husband became Attorney General, came after she'd had all of her teeth capped, sometime after she met John Mitchell. A Pine Bluff friend says, "Martha's teeth were always skippy (wide-spaced)."

One night, when Martha was about eleven, the comfortable, luxurious life she was used to came to an end. The Bealls' big house on Cherry Street burned to the ground. The fire, which started in an electrical short circuit in a new radio, at first seemed to be confined to the music room. George Beall took his daughter, in her nightgown and robe, to a neighbor's house for the rest of the night. Miss Arie, who was attending a civic meeting, joined her husband and daughter later. Then, in the middle of the night, the house burst into flames and was completely destroyed.

"The fire was so hot," says a Pine Bluff resident, "that all of Miss Arie's sterling silver melted into globs." Also lost with the silver and antique furniture were all their clothes and one of Miss Arie's prize possessions, an autographed photograph of Paderewski, whom she had met and admired.

The fire coincided with the market crash and the start of the Great Depression. The bottom fell out of the cotton business and Jon. F. Clark closed its Pine Bluff office. George Beall, who had lost his own money in the market crash, was out of a job. Like thousands of other men throughout the United States, he couldn't find work.

The Bealls, with their financial situation drastically changed, moved into the Habar Apartments, at 13th and Walnut, and Miss Arie found more girls and boys to teach expression to. Martha saw even less of her mother than she had before, and now she didn't have the big house or the servants either. Only Mary was left and she came only during the day. Although Martha later would talk about her unhappiness at this time, evidently she didn't discuss her feelings with her friends. As far as they knew she was just as happy and full of fun as she'd ever been. But she wasn't. Her house had burned, she had lost her clothes and all the family possessions, her life style had changed completely. Then, too, her mother *worked,* which wasn't true of the other mothers. And unlike the fathers of her friends—who were bankers, doctors, lawyers, landowners—Martha's father had lost his job.

And something else was probably traumatic for Martha. She was moved from Mrs. Haring's to the public school, and she couldn't graduate with the rest of her friends. But since Mrs. Haring's, the only private school in Pine Bluff, went through just the sixth grade, Martha was with her friends at the Woodrow Wilson Junior High School and later at the Pine Bluff High School.

Like other boys and girls of her age, Martha traveled with a group, in her case the sons and daughters of the town's more affluent families. Martha's special friend in the group was William Thomas Couch, a boy she'd held hands with in kindergarten. Martha always said she fell in love with William Thomas in first grade. Later, much later, when she'd get so angry at John Mitchell for deserting her she thought she couldn't stand it, Martha would say, "I have never forgiven myself for not marrying William Thomas. He was sweet and kind and loving; this man wouldn't have done anything to hurt me for anything in the world. He was the kind of man I should have married in the first place, and not a goddamn Yankee!"

William Thomas, called "Sonny" by his classmates, although Martha always used his complete name, took Martha to her first dance when she was eleven or twelve years old. It was all very formal and proper, with Martha in a long, yellow voile dress and William Thomas calling for her in an automobile. The two sat stiffly on the back seat while an adult drove them to and from the party. Later, when they were old enough to drive their own cars, they'd go with friends, to Little Rock to a movie, or they'd drive to Hot Springs, where the Couches had a house on a lake, for a day of boating, water-skiing and swimming. William Thomas's father, Harvey Couch, was a good friend of then President Franklin Roosevelt, and Martha remembered meeting the President on one of his many visits to the Couch house in Hot Springs.

Then William Thomas went away to school, Lawrenceville, a preparatory school in New Jersey. Martha always thought he was sent there because his parents and Miss Arie were afraid their children might elope while still in high school. From Lawrenceville, William Thomas went to Princeton and he and Martha wrote to each other every day. They also dated during vacations. But both started going out with others.

IN SPITE OF THE FACT THAT IT WAS AT THE HEIGHT OF THE DEPRESSION, and her father couldn't find a steady job, Martha's parents still were able to take her to the World's Fair in Chicago in 1933. And as was her habit,

Martha kept a scrapbook in which she pasted or clipped or recorded everything possible about the trip.

Then something happened that was to change Martha's life more than the fire or the Depression. As her father's friend Mr. E. A. Bell recalls: "George fooled around here for a few years, but he couldn't find anything to do. He worked for a while in the Ferguson coffee business, but George was pretty proud and I imagine he didn't like living on his wife. It was the Depression that was his downfall.

"Finally," Mr. Bell says, "George just picked up and left." Without saying a word. Without telling his daughter good-bye.

Martha never talked about her father again. A friend explains, "You see, when he left she *couldn't stand it.* She was so hurt she considered him dead from that time on." Much later, when she became an international celebrity and interviewers asked about her father, Martha said he died when she was so young she couldn't remember anything about him.

Once I challenged her on this, pointing out that she'd said George Beall had given her an automobile, a Ford coupe, when she was fourteen years old. Martha said she didn't want to talk about him, since he had died of a heart attack and she was the one who had discovered him "on the floor, his face all purple, and gasping for breath." And besides, she insisted, she didn't remember him very well, "since he died before I was sixteen."

This wasn't true. George Beall died in Sulphur Springs, Texas, at seven-thirty A.M., October 20, 1943, from a self-inflicted gunshot wound in the head. Martha was twenty-five years old.

Adolescence is recognized today as one of the most emotionally difficult times of anyone's life. When parents part, the children often feel betrayed and sometimes guilty; it's as if they caused the separation. There's also a tremendous feeling of insecurity, a fear that there is no one to take care of them. And often they are left resentful and angry.

The trauma is even more severe when a parent leaves without telling the child good-bye. Without a chance to talk about his feelings with the parent who has left, the adolescent feels more abandoned and unloved.

Martha would experience these feelings again and again for the rest of her life. It was that way in September 1973, when she was deserted by John Mitchell. He too walked out without telling Martha that he was not coming back, never giving her an opportunity to talk over her feelings.

At the time George Beall left, Martha's schoolmates didn't realize the depth of her feeling of abandonment. One says, "I thought she took it very well, she never said anything." Another thought it couldn't have bothered her much since she never mentioned it.

As an adult Martha also tried to avoid talking about unpleasant things. Often she would walk away if someone brought up a disagreeable subject. "And if she couldn't walk away," her son Jay says laughingly, "Mom would squirm a lot." Jay says Martha just wouldn't face up to disagreeable things. "She seemed to feel if she didn't talk about them they would go away."

And if they wouldn't go away, her friends often found themselves called upon to handle Martha's affairs. A problem at Marty's school? A friend was dispatched to talk to the Sisters. Her lawyer wanted her to call? A friend was asked to telephone. A medical report? Again a friend was enlisted, this time to talk to Martha's doctor.

Jay remembers with sadness the time his mother couldn't bring herself to tell him his beloved dog Rusty had died. "I came home one weekend and I asked the help, 'Where's Rusty?' . . . They sat down with me and explained that Rusty was gone. My dog died and my mother never told me. She knew how much I loved my dog and she just didn't know how to approach the subject. She never, until the day she died, told me my dog was dead."

According to Martha's schoolmates she continued to be peppy and vivacious, a teen-ager who was "into everything," "a cut-up," someone who made you forget all your troubles, because she'd "pick you up real quick if you were down." Martha was president of her high school sorority, Delta Beta Sigma, a member of the Glee Club, the Girls' Cotillion Club and the student council.

She also sang in the choir and taught Sunday School at the First Presbyterian Church. Miss Arie had seen to her daughter's religious training, and as an adult Martha's faith ran a great deal deeper than most people knew. She kept a Bible on her nightstand and read it daily. When she traveled, a Bible always was packed in her luggage, and she often carried a purse-size New Testament with her when she left home for only a few hours.

"She was a very religious little old girl," her friend Alleta Saunders says. "For one thing, she carried that little old beat-up Bible with her everywhere. She'd sleep with it, if she were real upset. She put it under her pillow. And she could open it to anything she wanted; she knew her Bible. It was a great comfort to her."

While still in high school, Martha started modeling shoes at the local shoe store. The owner, Jack Eisenkramer, remembers she had a "perfect size 4B" foot and could wear the salesmen's samples. Evidently this is when Martha developed her love for shoes; at the time of her death she had a collection of over two hundred pairs in practically every known color and fabric. Martha always tried to match the color of her shoes to the color at the bottom of her skirts: "It gives a continuation of line." Most were high-heeled, open-toe, sling pumps. Since this shoe didn't stay in style, all of the newer ones had been ordered special from Saks Fifth Avenue.

The big thing for Martha and her high-school friends to do in the evenings and on weekends was to "drag" Main Street, which then meant everybody piled into cars and drove slowly from the court house to the Star Drugstore—some sixteen blocks—where they got out and went inside for a Coke or ice-cream soda and to listen to the jukebox.

Another gathering spot for Martha's crowd was the seventh tee of the local golf course. There, a friend recalls, "We had big parking parties and we 'necked', as it was called then." They also found the vicinity of the seventh tee a safe place to smoke. The youngsters bought their cigarettes, one at a time at a penny each, from a Main Street store. Carrying a whole pack was too dangerous; a parent might discover it.

Martha's former classmates all insist today that nobody in their crowd drank, except for "an occasional rum and Coke, maybe." ("Martha had her first when she was fifteen," William Thomas says.) Yet, a lot of them remember an incident when a drunken boy at a high-school dance cut in on Martha; some of the chaperoning parents discussed helping Martha with the situation, but one mother told them not to worry because Martha knew "how to handle drunks."

Martha was graduated from Pine Bluff High School on Thursday evening, May 27, 1937, along with 168 other students, in ceremonies at the Shrine Temple. Her school yearbook, the *Zebra,* was inscribed with complimentary notes from her classmates, including one from a boy who called her the sweetest girl he'd ever known and vowed his undying love, although he said he knew he didn't have a chance; and another from a boy who wrote, "Martha, you could count your chickens before they hatch."

Chapter Three

MOST OF MARTHA'S GIRL FRIENDS WENT ON TO PRIVATE SCHOOLS in Virginia or New England. In fact, Miss Arie had planned for Martha to go to Virginia, as she had. But Martha ventured on a different course. She felt she had never found herself, she explained later, and it seemed to her that she was not accomplishing what she wanted to accomplish: "I'd had these different things put on me, such as singing and piano, none of which I liked. Suddenly I had the urge to go into dramatics." Actress Maude Adams, then in her sixties, was going to be at Stephens College, a private junior college in Columbia, Missouri, for the first time that year as a professor of drama, and Martha wanted to study under her. In those days Stephens was considered a progressive school; Martha never understood why her mother, a strict disciplinarian and strong supporter of the old rules, allowed her to go.

"Miss Annie" Bridges, mother of Martha's good friend Beverly, remembering the day Martha left for Stephens by train from Little Rock, says she looked "so cute in a little suit and with a small hat on the back of her head." Miss Arie didn't come to see her off, as the other mothers did their daughters, Miss Annie says, and Martha arrived so late she missed her train. But it didn't bother her, as far as anyone could tell. She just got on the next train and shared a bedroom as far as St. Louis with a girl friend who told her mother that Martha cried most of the night because she wasn't going to see William Thomas until Christmas vacation.

At Stephens, Martha lived in Laura Stephens Hall, where she shared a two-bedroom suite with a roommate and two "suitemates." It was the first time she'd been closely associated with Northern girls and it was a revelation: "The difference in the upbringing of Northern girls and Southern girls was amazing. For one thing the Southern girls seemed to be more protected. They were brought up to be ladies, sitting and waiting. And they had everybody helping them; a Southern girl did not have to go in and wash out a pair of stockings."

As for her studies, Martha remembered that the drama students were totally dedicated to Maude Adams ("She got me out of my Southern accent") and to *Chanticleer,* the play they were producing.

Before the year was over, Martha said Maude Adams was encouraging her to go into the theater, and there was some talk of a contract with a touring company. "But my mother wouldn't let me. She thought a nice Southern girl should do one of two things—get married or teach. That's the way it was; we were programmed for marriage. So I thought, 'Shoot, Mother won't let me do what I want to do, so I'll transfer to the University of Arkansas, where at least I can see all of my boyfriends and have fun."

In 1938, Martha took summer courses at the University and enrolled as a full-time student that fall. She was "rushed" by several sororities and pledged Chi Omega.

Martha moved into the Chi Omega house, and the thing she remembered most about the large colonial mansion, with its big pillars in front, was that there was a well-lighted spot on the landing of the front staircase. Martha and her friends sat there at night, after other lights were out, and played bridge until the early morning hours.

She went to sorority and fraternity dances, and she said she played a lot of tennis, including one session with J. William Fulbright, then president of the University of Arkansas (later the U. S. Senator). What she remembered later as the most daring thing she did was to go with groups of her friends up into the hills of Arkansas to buy huge crocks of red wine.

A roommate recalls other daring things: "Martha was the kind who would stay out late and someone else had to slip down and unlock the door for her." The same woman wasn't surprised when Martha married John

Mitchell, a lawyer. She said, "Martha spent most of her time in the law library since she dated so many of the law students."

Every few weeks Martha and groups of her friends took off for one of the intercollegiate dances in another state, where a big name band, such as Tommy Dorsey or Kay Kyser, was playing. At one of these dances, in Jackson, Mississippi, Martha became friends with a Chi Omega sister named Alleta Billips, later Mrs. Charles Saunders. Alleta became one of Martha's most loyal friends. "You know how it is when you meet someone and hit it off right away. That's how it was," Alleta says. It was at Alleta and Charlie Saunders' house, in Greenwood, Mississippi, that Martha hid out from the press during the time John Mitchell was testifying before the Senate Watergate Committee, in 1973.

Someone else Martha met during this period was Clifford H. Kunz, a man who became her most dedicated friend during the last five months of her life. In those days Martha wasn't concerned with national and international conditions the way she was later, Cliff Kunz says. He remembers that she did not make her grades one year and wasn't allowed to live in the Chi Omega house, which was supposed to be a punishment. But Martha took it in stride, since rules at the dormitory where she stayed weren't as rigid, and she discovered she could have more fun there.

"Martha wouldn't date anyone unless he had a car," Cliff Kunz recalls, "and it became a big joke between us. When she married Clyde Jennings [her first husband] I told her I bet he was the only one with a car. Then after she got a divorce, I asked if she left him because he sold his car."

After her sophomore year Martha transferred from the University of Arkansas to the University of Miami, saying the move was necessary because of her allergies. Cliff laughs at this, claiming the grading system was tough then and that "Martha wasn't the only student who transferred for health reasons."

At the University of Miami, Martha had (she said) "just a marvelous time, a great time," going boating, water-skiing and to the hotel night clubs, where she saw the superstars and often met them after their acts. Martha also met a young man she'd see a lot of when she was Mrs. John Mitchell. He was Charles (Bebe) Rebozo. She also met Chicago gangster Al Capone during a time when she was dating Albert Francis (Sonny) Capone, the son of the former gangland leader.

Martha admitted that she ran around with a frivolous bunch in Miami, but she said she balanced that by having as her best friend a Chi Omega sister, Alma Jane Lindgren (now Mrs. Robert McCauley), who belonged to an "intellectual crowd."

Alma Jane, the one sorority sister close to Martha during her final days, remembers one group Martha went with—the one that partied a lot. And she says, "I got the idea that Martha's mother and grandmother sacrificed, financially, to give Martha everything she wanted. They really didn't have as much as Martha had led us to believe."

In later life, too, Martha was inclined to embellish the facts, sometimes dramatically, when they concerned herself, in what seemed to be a desperate need to build up Martha. When talking about her younger days she was the best dancer, she was the most popular girl, she wore the prettiest clothes. After Watergate she was the only one who told the truth. She was the one who saved the country. And as a result she was persecuted more than any woman in the history of the world. When I challenged the latter statement, Martha cried, "Name one woman who was persecuted more, just name one!" "How about Joan of Arc?" "She only burned!"

Martha was alone in the Chi Omega house Sunday, December 7, 1941. She'd stayed behind while the others went out, because it was her habit to listen every Sunday afternoon to the radio broadcast of the Philharmonic. As Alma Jane recalls it: "We came back and Martha was absolutely beside herself. She had heard about the bombing of Pearl Harbor and she was just overwrought. All of us were going with young officers from the Navy Base, and Martha was convinced every one of them would be killed (as it turned out, many were). That is one of my most vivid memories of Martha, of her emotional state that day, how completely she let herself go."

FOR MARTHA, THE FIRST CASUALTY OF THE WAR WAS HER ROMANCE WITH William Thomas. She always said they broke up because she went to Washington, where she met another man and got married. But Martha didn't go to Washington until mid-1945. William Thomas only says, "It was the war." But one who was close to Martha at the time claims that she wanted to get married, and William Thomas, knowing he had to go into the military service, thought it was not the right time for matrimony.

After getting her Bachelor of Arts degree, in February 1942, with a major in History and a minor in English, Martha stayed on in Florida for a few months, working as a substitute teacher. Then she spent the summer in Pine Bluff, where she plunged into the wartime social whirl at nearby Grider Field, an Army Air Corps training station. She and her friends dated the young flight instructors, and there was one in particular Martha liked. Both she and her close friends thought he "would take William Thomas's place."

But the instructor, now an Air Force general living in Virginia, was transferred to a base on the Great Lakes. Soon he sent Martha a letter saying he'd found someone else. Julia McClain, Martha's best friend in Pine Bluff and the wife of a former Grider Field flight instructor, Joseph McClain, says the Air Force officer showed her Martha's reply: "It was so sweet and so sad it just broke your heart."

By September of 1942 Martha was teaching sixth grade in Mobile, Alabama. She hated every minute of it. She went to Mobile because it offered the most money, ninety dollars a month; also because Brinkley Field was there and she knew there'd be a lot of parties and dances. Once in Mobile, she discovered that teaching left little time for after-hours fun. There were meetings with the mothers, PTA, papers to grade, lessons to prepare for the next day. She despised it.

About this time, Martha said, she was offered a job as an airline hostess. In order to take it she had to find someone to take over her teaching contract. "I found a substitute teacher but I had to pay her more than I made from the airlines. And I didn't dare tell my mother I was flying, although I had to get the extra money from her for the substitute teacher. Then on my first flight the plane had to make an emergency landing, in a field. I got everybody off and then I just passed out. That was the end of my flying; I wouldn't go back on. I just figured, being a religious person, that the Good Lord was ag'in' me. The fact that I hadn't told my mother, that I had deceived her, made me feel God was punishing me. I went back and started teaching school!"

Once her teaching contract was fulfilled, Martha went back to Pine Bluff, where along with some of her friends she took a Red Cross training course and received her cap and certificate at exercises on May 12, 1944. She worked full-time as a volunteer aide for several months at Jefferson County Hospital. Helene Johnson Whalen (now Mrs. Arnold H. Johnson of Washington, D. C.) says, "I never shall forget; she came to my house about noon one day, and she was the funniest color. She had just seen twin babies delivered and she was so shook she said, 'I want a drink.' Martha never had seen anything like that before."

By this time Martha had had several traumatic experiences. There was her father's suicide. George Beall lived for two days after he shot himself; Martha and Miss Arie had time to reach Sulphur Springs to be at his bedside when he died. Again, Martha didn't discuss her father or his last days with any of her friends. And only those living in Pine Bluff knew her father had lived until 1943; others thought he'd died when Martha was quite young.

In addition to her father, Martha lost several close friends when they were killed in the war. There was the son of the people who owned the house where Martha stayed the night the Beall mansion burned; the minister's son, a boy Martha "just thought was wonderful"; and a distant cousin who had been her favorite dancing partner from the time they were pre-teen-agers. Then, too, one of her friends had committed suicide by throwing herself out of a moving automobile; and Beverly Bridges, a friend so close she'd sent Martha a whole wardrobe of clothes after the Bealls' house burned down, had died suddenly. Martha had nightmares for years following Beverly's death.

In May 1945, the month Germany surrendered, Martha took a job at the Pine Bluff Arsenal. "Martha was not trained for an office job," Helene Johnson recalls, "but she went out and they made her a receptionist because she had that pretty smile and the cute dimples."

The commanding officer of the Pine Bluff Arsenal, Colonel Augustin M. Prentiss, was transferred to Washington when Martha had been working for him only six weeks. After much coaxing, Martha and Helene Johnson, who also worked at the Arsenal, talked the Colonel into taking them along.

Years later Martha said, "That is the only thing in my life I would have done differently. I would have been all right if I'd never left the South."

Martha was ordered to proceed "on or about 25 July 1945" to her new duty with the legal branch, Office of the Chief Chemical Warfare Service, Gravelly Point, near Washington. Japan surrendered and the war was over on August 14, but Martha stayed with Chemical Warfare (later the Army Chemical Corps) for about a year, working up to the rank of research analyst.

During this period, Martha said, she had her first run-in with the government's General Services Administration; her next would come almost twenty-five years later when, as the wife of the Attorney General, she would spend some $50,000 redecorating her husband's Justice Department office suite.

Her argument with GSA, in 1945, started innocently enough when Martha's boss told her to fix up a place near his office where lunch could be prepared. Instead of asking for the usual coffee maker and hot plate to tuck away in a closet or another available space, Martha requisitioned a whole room and a standard-size sink, stove, refrigerator, and table and chairs. GSA was most upset. After the arguments over her kitchen were over and Martha had won—with the help of her boss—co-workers were so pleased they gave her a kitchen shower and named the room "Martha's Kitchen."

Martha always loved to cook. As a small child she was underfoot in the kitchen so much her parents bought her a little workable stove for her playhouse in order to keep her out of the cook's way. In high school, according to a former home-economics teacher, Martha "made the best biscuits in the whole class." And when she came to Washington as the Attorney General's wife, she gave one of her earliest interviews to a food editor, Marian Burros, then of the Washington *Star.* In the interview Martha said the thing she missed most about coming to Washington was her thousand-dollar electric range in her "left-handed" kitchen in Rye, New York. Martha also revealed she was taking her pressure cooker when the Mitchells left the following week for a Florida vacation. Martha often took kitchenware with her. Once, when she arrived in Washington to co-host a television show, a friend meeting her at the railroad station was shocked to see Martha's maid carrying two huge paper shopping bags stuffed full of pots and pans and kitchen cutlery. Martha explained, "The last time we were here there wasn't a decent pan in that [hotel suite's] kitchen."

Among the men attached to Chemical Warfare when Martha was there was Jacob (Jake) Javits, later a Senator from New York; he told a reporter, in 1973, "I've known Martha for more than twenty years. When I knew her in the war, you couldn't find a fresher, more delightful, brighter girl."

Playwright Charlie MacArthur was another officer at Chemical Warfare; he arranged for Martha and her roommate to go to a Broadway play, giving Martha her first look at New York.

ANOTHER MAN MARTHA MET THEN WOULD BECOME HER FIRST HUSBAND. He was Clyde Jennings, Jr., a likable, easygoing young officer from Lynchburg, Virginia. Years later his son Jay would say he was "what I would call, in every sense of the word, a Virginia gentleman."

The first time Martha and Clyde went out together was on a double date with office friends. Evidently it wasn't love at first sight, because she continued dating other young men for some time after that, going to Washington's then fashionable restaurants (Harvey's, the now-defunct Occidental, and a Russian restaurant she liked because it had balalaika music), the theater, the officers' club and particularly to places where there was dancing.

There were also weekends in New York; one which fell on her birthday was memorable. Martha and some friends were having dinner at the Stork Club when impresario Mike Todd, seated at another table, learned it was Martha's birthday and sent her a cake.

Martha and Clyde became engaged after he'd been out of the country for a few months on a special assignment in the Pacific theater of operations. But they weren't married until after he was discharged from the Army, as a captain, and was in the ladies' purse business as a member of the firm of Surrey Bags, Inc., of New York; before the war he had been general sales manager of another handbag manufacturer.

In August 1946, Martha quit her government job to return to Pine Bluff to prepare for her wedding. She stopped on the way to see Clyde's parents in Lynchburg, where she boasted she'd taken their son away from another girl. In an interview after she became a Watergate heroine, Martha said, "I don't know why I married him. I guess because there was competition for him. He *was* good-looking—and he was a marvelous dancer."

Once in Pine Bluff, there was a steady stream of parties and showers. One was a "something blue" luncheon, which in fact had everything blue —Martha's favorite color. The table linens, flowers and even the food, including the creamed chicken and ice-cream molds, were pale blue. Caterer Hortense Jones says, "It sounds godawful, but it didn't look horrible at all."

Martha probably loved it. She believed in having a motif, usually something to do with color, and carrying it out through the whole party. "Even in food," she once said. "You can do everything with food coloring."

The wedding, remembered as one of the largest and finest Pine Bluff ever had, took place on October 5, 1946, at the old Presbyterian Church, one block from the Ferguson house, where the reception was held. Something happened at the church that stands out in the memories of the guests more than the beauty and romance of the occasion. "It was the comic relief," explains Ray West, Jr., Martha's cousin by marriage. "Mary, who was sort of a family retainer, was straightening Martha's train, and she was so engrossed in doing it that she followed Martha all the way to the altar." Frances Hall remembers, "It was terrible, it was awful. Miss Arie almost had a fit."

Pine Bluff residents recall that they liked Martha's new husband. Miss Annie Bridges notes, "Clyde was charming; he was a sweet boy and he kind of reminded me of William Thomas."

William Thomas attended the wedding; he sat in the very last pew.

THE HONEYMOON WAS A LEISURELY TWO-WEEK AUTOMOBILE TRIP FROM Pine Bluff to New York, with a stop in Lynchburg, where Clyde's mother gave a reception for the newlyweds.

Martha and Clyde lived in Forest Hills, Queens, New York, until after their son was born, on November 2, 1947. Martha later said that the day she returned home from the hospital a bluejay flew on her windowsill, and she impulsively named the baby "Jay." A friend of Martha and Clyde's laughs and says that wasn't the way it happened, that Martha was "putting on" the press when she told the story. It seems that the young parents-to-be agreed that Martha would name the baby if it were a girl and Clyde would name a boy. He selected Clyde Jay Jennings for the baby's name and told hospital authorities of his choice before he told Martha.

Soon after Jay's birth the Jennings family moved to Stuyvesant Town in Manhattan. They lived there until their separation in 1956, a year before they were divorced. The three-bedroom, two-bath apartment was not luxurious, but Jay remembers that it was "in good taste." He also recalls that his mother dressed him "extravagantly—like Little Lord Fauntleroy." When Jay was about six years old he was stricken with polio. He says his only memory of the early stages of his illness is the look of deep concern on his mother's face. When the doctor recommended a warm climate for Jay during his convalescence, Martha encouraged Clyde to rent a house for his family in Coral Gables, Florida. She and Jay spent the winter there, with Clyde coming down for a few days every two to four weeks.

Three things stand out in Jay's mind about the winter in Florida. He started school. His mother bought him his first dog, which he promptly named "Peanut." And he had his foot "almost completely severed" by a neighbor's electric lawn mower.

Martha's former University of Miami classmate Alma Jane, who saw Martha often at the time, laughs when she recalls that when the emergency was over and Martha had Jay safely home from the hospital, "Martha hired a nurse for Jay, called Clyde to get down there to help and then took to her bed." Like many women of the South, Martha often gave in to despair and "took to her bed" during times of crisis.

After Martha and Clyde were divorced, she claimed she knew on her wedding night that the marriage was a mistake; Clyde was quoted as jokingly saying, "After we got married everything was just great, terrific, but then as we were leaving the church . . ." When Martha heard this statement she snapped, "Those are the only true words he ever spoke."

But people who knew them during their eleven-year marriage say things weren't as bad as the two later would have it believed. Martha and Clyde seemed to have a lot in common. They shared a love of the theater and had subscriptions to most first nights. Both Martha and Clyde—a nonsmoker who seldom took a drink—enjoyed the night life New York offered.

And they certainly saw eye-to-eye politically. Both were upset over the 1954 Supreme Court decision that declared segregation in public schools unconstitutional. "She was always conservative," says a man who knew them then. "They never had any differences over that."

Then Clyde's handbag firm failed. As one of his business friends explains it: "Clyde made the mistake of going on his own too soon after the war, and failed. But he was, and is, very well thought of in the business so he got a good position immediately, traveling first for a handbag house and later for Vera (a manufacturer of scarves and blouses)."

When Jay was about seven years old, Martha took a job with the Plymouth Shops, a chain of women's specialty stores in New York: "I sold everything—dresses, gloves. I was just a plain ordinary saleswoman." Apparently she was good at her work and was an assistant buyer before she left. Financially, Martha didn't need to work, but she was bored and restless, with Clyde traveling and Jay in school all day. He went to the expensive Browning School, and like the other mothers and fathers, Martha and Clyde attended the parents' meetings.

Martha resented Clyde's being away from home for weeks at a time. A friend says, "You see, Martha had to have constant love and attention, and if she wasn't getting it she was miserable. So she found being married to Clyde was intolerable, because *he wasn't there.*"

Soon Martha began suspecting that Clyde was being unfaithful to her. There were unpleasant scenes, vigorous spying, private detectives, and charges and denials. Martha knew her marriage was a total failure, but she didn't tell anyone in Pine Bluff, neither her best friends nor her mother, about her difficulties with Clyde. Later she explained her silence by saying she came from a small town "where divorce didn't happen and if it did it was utterly disgusting." She added that people she knew thought "only bad women" got divorces. Yet, her mother had been divorced twice, and according to people in Pine Bluff, she was one of the town's most respected and admired women. Martha said the only reason she stayed with Clyde as long as she did was because of her Southern pride.

Chapter Four

IT ISN'T CLEAR WHEN MARTHA AND JOHN MITCHELL MET, BUT evidently it was sometime before May 1956. In the first week in May of that year Ray West, Jr., moved temporarily to New York. A few days later Martha called to invite him to dinner. Ray remembers that a Cadillac coupe with John Mitchell at the wheel pulled up in front of his building. Ray ran out and jumped in the front seat: "I turned and saw this strange man and I asked Martha, 'Where's Clyde?' She patted me on the knee and said, 'Darlin', there have been some changes in my life; I will explain to you later.' Immediately I shut up."

Martha had met John Mitchell on a blind date arranged by a man also living at Stuyvesant Town. The man, prominent in the television industry, knew Martha was unhappy in her marriage, and for some time he'd been coaxing her to go out with his friend, John Mitchell, who he said was "terribly unhappy and needs cheering up."

Finally, one night Martha and John and the man with his date (not his wife) went to dinner at a Greenwich Village French restaurant. After dinner they had a nightcap at John's *pied-à-terre,* which Martha said was at One Park Avenue. As Martha recalled, John told her that night she was going to be his wife. He also said she would never have to worry about anything again, that he was going to take care of her. "Your problems are my problems," he said.

John Newton Mitchell was born in Detroit, Michigan, on September 5, 1913, where his father was an employee of Wilson & Co., meat packers. When John was five his family moved to Blue Point, Long Island. They moved again, to Jamaica, New York, when he was in his early teens. As a Jamaica High School student he maintained a B-plus average, was captain of the golf team and a hockey star. He played hockey with the Jamaica Hawks while going to Fordham, a Catholic university; after Fordham he went to St. John University's Law School. While still there, he worked at Caldwell & Raymond, an old, established legal firm, and became a partner before he was thirty. John was in his twenties when he married Elizabeth Katherine Shine, a woman one of his friends describes as looking "a great deal like Martha."

By the time John met Martha he was a successful Wall Street lawyer, with Caldwell, Trimble and Mitchell, specializing in municipal bonds. A contemporary once described him as success-oriented, very sure, very certain. A Wall Street lawyer was quoted, in 1970, as having said of John Mitchell: "When you first meet him he may seem cold on the surface—but when you get to know him better you realize that's only the tip of the iceberg."

John Mitchell was of average height and heavyset—as were George Beall, William Thomas Couch and Clyde Jennings. Martha thought he was handsome, "extremely handsome." These were the same words she'd used to describe her father, her former boyfriend and her ex-husband. When she lived in Washington as a Cabinet wife, a writer asked her to name her favorite hero in all history. Martha said her hero was John Mitchell and added, "I recognized my husband at our first meeting for what he eventually proved to be." And she told Judith Michaelson, of the New York *Post*, "He's so tall and handsome . . . if you didn't know him you could walk into a roomful of a hundred people and you would find yourself looking at him."

After their first date, John and Martha saw each other almost every night, often having dinner at a Chinese restaurant in the Village. Both John and Martha were fond of Chinese food, and while living at the Watergate they often had Cantonese food delivered to them from the Moon Palace restaurant.

On May 18, 1956, Clyde moved some of his clothes out of their Stuyvesant Town apartment and left a note saying he'd pick up the rest of his things in June. He also left Martha a bag of fresh oranges and a straw purse. The same day Clyde notified Esso, Diners Club, Bloomingdale's, Altman's, Gimbels, Saks, and other businesses where they had accounts, that he no longer was responsible for his wife's bills. And he stopped the fifty-seven-dollar monthly payments on Martha's Steinway organ.

The two signed a property settlement on July 1, giving Martha, along with other things, the furniture in the apartment and four hundred dollars a month for herself and child support. Clyde also agreed to pay for Jay's private school education, transportation to and from school, tuition for summer camp, and two hundred dollars for Martha to buy a winter coat. And he agreed to pay for life and health insurance.

Martha moved soon after that to a two-bedroom apartment at 45 Gramercy Park, which was on a fenced square in the midst of New York. She furnished it with many of the pieces people would see later at the Mitchells' Watergate apartment, and after that at their Fifth Avenue place—the king-size bed with the red-velvet tufted headboard and two mattresses; the white French Provincial bedroom furniture and the large down-filled sofa covered with pale-blue satin.

According to Martha, John Mitchell "courted" Jay as vigorously as he courted her. And Jay was "crazy" about John Mitchell and urged her to marry him. Martha didn't meet his children, Jack and Jill, until after she and John Mitchell were married.

Early in 1957 Martha moved to Florida to establish the ninety-day residency requirement. In the divorce complaint she claimed Clyde had physically beaten her and that he had other women friends; Clyde denied the charges. A divorce decree was granted on August 1. The property rights were essentially the same as those in the agreement signed the previous July. John Mitchell paid the costs of the divorce, according to Martha.

Jay continued going to Browning School, but he missed the children from the playground at Stuyvesant Town. He remembers spending hours playing alone with his miniature soldiers and other toys. A family friend says that Martha, and later John Mitchell, tried to make up for not spending time with Jay by giving him things. The same thing, the friend says, happened with Marty.

John Mitchell's first wife, Betty, has been reported as having said her husband "just walked in one day and asked for a divorce." Betty Mitchell went to Reno, Nevada, to live at the Biltmore Ranch, where she established the six weeks' residency requirement. She filed a complaint in which she charged her husband with extreme cruelty; he denied the charge. On December 19, 1957, Elizabeth Katherine Shine Mitchell was granted a divorce from John Newton Mitchell.

They had joint custody of their two children, John N. (Jack) Mitchell II, born September 27, 1941, and Jill Elizabeth Mitchell (now Mrs. Edwin C. Reed), born November 29, 1943. The couple's house, all household goods, and the boat and equipment were granted to Betty Mitchell. She also was to receive 35 percent of his gross annual income, this payment to continue even if she remarried, which she did. John Mitchell also was legally bound to carry a six-figure insurance policy with her as the beneficiary. Martha learned of these financial arrangements only after John left her in September 1973.

On December 30, 1957, eleven days after the Mitchell divorce, Martha Beall Jennings, 39, and John Newton Mitchell, 44, were married at Elkton, Maryland, an elopement center some 140 miles from New York. He gave his occupation as attorney; she gave hers as none. Both listed their address 45 Gramercy Park, New York City.

Since Jay Jennings had refused to chose between his father and mother, he lived with Martha but spent six weeks each summer and alternate holidays—Easter, Thanksgiving, Christmas—with Clyde.

FRIENDS OF THE MITCHELLS IN THOSE DAYS THOUGHT JOHN AND MARTHA were blissfully happy. One even felt it was one of the most beautiful marriages he'd ever seen: "John represented a great need for Martha. He had the stability she was seeking. He was a successful man, very well thought of on Wall Street. Then, too, he had wonderful connections; all of this was important to Martha."

She seemed to fulfill a great need for him, too. Recalling that Martha was "cute and feisty and adorable," one friend says Martha made John feel that he was handsome, strong and wise, and that "Martha often would say, in front of John, that she'd married the smartest man in the world. He adored it. Oh! He loved it! John gloated in the love and affection Martha showed him. It was interesting to watch him at a party; he'd stand around, smoking his pipe, never taking his eyes off Martha. He seemed to worship her."

Another says, "You know how Martha was. Sometimes she'd drink too much and get silly and loud-mouthed, and if John saw you looking at her critically, he'd look you coldly in the eye and ask, 'What's wrong with that?' Naturally you'd say, 'Nothing!' "

But many people observed then what Washingtonians were to see later. John Mitchell often treated Martha like a child. Sometimes it was almost as if she were his daughter instead of his wife. He babied her and called her his "little girl," and he indulged her and let her "get by with murder."

"He is a total enigma to me," says a woman who knew the Mitchells during the early years of their marriage. "Because I have seen them together. We would go out to dinner, the four of us [her husband was along]. I remember we would go to the Hawaiian Room at the Hotel Lexington—this would be after Martha and I had been to the theater together that afternoon. And he would say, 'Well, how much money did you spend today?' Of course we were so poor then and I just looked at him in awe. And he would give her wads of bills and say, 'Spend it all; get anything you want.' He was the most generous husband you have ever seen. And he'd ask, 'Isn't she beautiful?' and all that."

"I loved living there," Martha said of their Gramercy Park apartment. "It was the most perfect living I have ever had. We sat on the pouf [the down-filled sofa] every night and drank martinis and talked and talked." She also liked being right in the middle of things—the shops, restaurants, theaters. They had an option to buy the building's penthouse, but when it was vacant John said he wanted to move near a golf course. Jay also wanted to be where he could play outside and where he could ride a bicycle.

The Mitchells started a series of moves and several changes of school for Jay. First they lived briefly in Greenwich, Connecticut. The next move was to West Norwalk, also in Connecticut. It was near the Darien and New Canaan town lines, and since John commuted to New York from the Darien railroad station, Martha always referred to this period as the time when she lived in Darien.

The old Georgian house, with its huge screened porches, was set in twenty-two acres of lush land that had a small river running through it. In the middle of the river, on their property, was a small island with a summer house where Martha often entertained at large, catered, candle-light suppers.

Martha spent months redecorating the house and landscaping the grounds around the swimming pool and terrace she installed. But she missed New York where everything was "so close." And there were times when John was away on business; Martha was lonesome and often unhappy.

Evidently Martha's feelings were known to at least some of their local acquaintances. The Connecticut *Sunday Herald,* reporting about the Mitchells' six years in the area, said, "In their isolated house on Morehouse La., Mrs. Mitchell was bored and lonely. They had only one close neighbor and that family and the Mitchells didn't get along . . ." The paper added that the few people who knew Martha found in her the same odd combination that Washington society discovered: "Both shrewd and scatterbrained, the quick-tongued Southern belle is recalled here as 'an entertaining character.' " In light of John Mitchell's later political activity, the story contained an interesting statement: ". . . oddly enough the Mitchells never registered to vote here."

THE MITCHELLS' ONLY CHILD, MARTHA ELIZABETH MITCHELL, JR., WAS born on January 10, 1961, while they were living near Darien. The last few months of her pregnancy were happy ones for Martha; her doctor insisted she take an apartment in New York to await the delivery. Again she could play bridge and lunch with her friends, and go out to dinner and the theater with John almost every night.

By this time Jay was going to boarding school, the Peekskill Military Academy. Neither Martha nor John Mitchell told Jay, then thirteen, that his mother was expecting a baby. The first he knew about his sister Marty was when he came home from school and saw her in the bassinet.

Jay didn't speak to Martha for days, giving her "the silent treatment" he thought she had given him. Finally, John Mitchell spoke to him about it one night at the dinner table: "I went upstairs and I gave it a long, hard thought and I realized I'd been selfish. I just revised my attitude toward Marty."

Like other children of parents in the Mitchells' milieu, Marty was taken care of by servants. Jay says, "That was the way my mother was raised, and my grandmother, and my great-grandmother, and I don't know how much further back it goes." As a result, Jay feels his mother really didn't spend much time with Marty or with him.

But a Mitchell friend says Martha was a very good mother to Marty when she was little and that "she did all the things a mother should do." Another friend mentions how Martha treated Marty "like a little doll and gave her everything she wanted." And as she had done with Jay when he was younger, Martha dressed Marty lavishly.

Some recall, though, that in the way they indulged Marty, John and Martha seemed more like grandparents than parents. They point out that when Marty was born Martha was forty-two years old, "which is pretty old to have a child," and John was forty-seven.

Organist Rosa Rio, who taught Martha when the Mitchells later lived in Rye, says, "Martha loved that child so. She had a crib brought in and put at the foot of her bed, in her bedroom with John, so she knew little Marty was safe. Marty slept in their room until they went to Washington, because Martha was afraid to leave her alone in her room." Others mention, too, Martha's concern for Marty and claim, "She was pretty protective."

"She took Marty everywhere, even to Europe when she was six and a half," another friend recalls. (Marty wasn't as lucky early in the Nixon Administration when Martha took her to a party at Washington's exclusive Sulgrave Club. "I was distressed when Martha brought the little girl," the hostess recalls. "I had three hundred people, seated at round tables, and we danced. When Martha came through the receiving line she said, 'I brought Marty, she's downstairs with the FBI agent.' And I said, 'I'm sure she will be comfortable there.' ")

NOT LONG AFTER MARTY'S BIRTH, MISS ARIE CAME TO LIVE WITH JOHN AND Martha. A Pine Bluff friend says Martha had a staff of servants, but she felt better about going on trips with John if her mother were there with the baby. And there were a lot of trips—to business-related affairs, such as the annual meeting of the Investment Bankers Association, American Bar Association conventions, the fun vacations at Key Biscayne and the twenty-five-day, 10,224-mile Mediterranean cruise they took in 1964 aboard the RMS *Queen Elizabeth.* It was Martha's first trip abroad (her tales of European travels while in college were only good stories for the press.)

And for Martha, who always had a weight problem, there were the periodic trips to the Greenhouse, an expensive health spa in Texas.

In 1964, Martha and John moved to the affluent suburb of Rye in Westchester County, New York, into a large Georgian-style house (value $250,000) with grounds bordering the seventeenth fairway of the Apawamis Club. The Westchester Country Club was nearby.

Again Martha spent months redecorating. A sorority sister who visited her says the results were "just gorgeous, very elaborate and very extravagant. It was quite ornate, but everything was the best. Martha had theatrical taste."

When they lived in Rye, Martha chauffeured John to the station each morning to catch the eight o'clock commuter train into the city and met him there at 6:05 at night. Sometimes he was able to get in three holes of golf at the Apawamis Club, one of the oldest golf clubs in the country. Martha, who needed to share in all parts of John's life, told him she wanted to learn to play golf so they could both enjoy the sport he loved. He said, "Great," and went right out and bought her a set of golf clubs:

"He bought me all these *right-handed* clubs and when I told him I couldn't do anything right-handed, he told me no one played golf left-handed. So I'd go out to play the last three holes with him and I couldn't do a thing right-handed. After I gave up, I found out that one of the biggest golfers in the country played with left-handed clubs!" Martha said it took her a long time to realize this was a pattern with John, that he often seemed to agree with something she wanted to do but then quietly put obstacles in her way so she couldn't accomplish whatever it was she set out to do.

Following his three holes of golf, John and Martha—continuing the habit which began at Gramercy Park—would settle down before dinner, over drinks, to discuss his day, her day and the state of the world. John listened to Martha's opinions, or at least he gave her the impression that he did: "He told me I had probably one of the most perceptive insights into human nature that he had ever known; he found me very stable in my thoughts. He said I was able to sort the riff from the raff."

Martha and John watched the evening news in the den while dining off trays. A TV tray was the solution Martha had found when John wanted a cozy twosome dinner arrangement, which didn't include her mother.

She was caught in the middle between her mother and John Mitchell, Martha told friends, and finally Miss Arie went back to Pine Bluff, almost a year before her death in December 1967.

There was another situation where Martha felt she was "in the middle." Clyde Jennings stopped the monthly child-support payments he had agreed to in the divorce settlement, after Martha had changed Jay's schools three times in one year—each time losing the prepaid tuition. Martha got a judgment against Clyde for default of payment, but it came through about the time John Mitchell became involved with politics and it never was collected, apparently because John didn't want the ensuing publicity.

Martha said John Mitchell complained to her so much about having to support Jay that finally, a year before Jay graduated from Peekskill, she packed up his clothes and sent him to his father in Lynchburg: "I was determined that I was no longer going to be in the middle between John Mitchell and Clyde Jennings, as to which one was paying for Jay's education." After John deserted her, Martha would lament, "And I gave up my mother and my child for John Mitchell."

IN RYE, MARTHA CONTINUED GIVING LARGE, EXPENSIVE, CATERED PARTIES —always with music and usually with a theme: "Where I come from people try to make their parties different and interesting; not like Washington where every dinner party has the same format. You could cover your eyes and know what every course was going to be."

A party she gave in Rye that didn't receive press attention at the time, but widely reported later, was for Richard Milhous Nixon, who had moved to New York soon after his unsuccessful run for governor of California in 1962 and had joined the Wall Street law firm of Mudge Rose Guthrie and Alexander.

John Mitchell had met Nixon off and on for some years, going back to when Nixon was in Congress. But they didn't actually get to know each other until Nixon moved to New York, where they worked together on projects in which John's firm represented the bond sellers and Nixon's the underwriters.

It both excited and pleased Martha that John was often in contact with Nixon. She hadn't thought much about politics before coming to New York, but a number of her friends there were interested in where the nation was headed, so Martha, too, soon felt strongly about many political issues. And along with many of her friends she thought Nixon could save the country—from Communists, liberals, welfare cheats, crime in the street, permissiveness. John didn't share her political views at first. He was a Kennedy man. In fact, he had been John F. Kennedy's commanding officer during World War II. Martha liked to tell how John always referred to Nixon as "Tricky Dick," and about the night their dinner guests left early because John spoke so vehemently against Nixon. Martha changed John to a Nixon admirer; later she said she regretted it.

Sometime in 1966 John Mitchell was asked to merge his law firm with Nixon's law offices. Martha said she and John talked it over for "what seemed like months" before John decided to make the move, but only after a high-powered sales pitch had been made by Richard Nixon.

Martha was so happy about it, she gave one of her large, splashy parties for Nixon and other senior partners of his firm. The theme was Southern, and she called her friend Alleta in Mississippi for suggestions and for her corn-pudding recipe. About forty guests dined on Southern fried chicken, country ham, beaten biscuits and other dishes typical of the South. Martha had a small orchestra to play for dancing, and when the musicians took a break Richard Nixon played the piano. It was a good party, Martha remembered, even if she didn't particularly take to Pat Nixon; Martha found her "aloof and cold."

A lot was written later about the close social relationship between the Mitchells and Nixons. According to Martha, the only time the Nixons were in the Mitchells' Rye house was at the one dinner. Martha was in the Nixons' Fifth Avenue apartment once, for a Christmas party the Nixons gave for members of the firm.

Caldwell Trimble & Mitchell merged with Nixon Mudge Rose Guthrie and Alexander on January 1, 1967. After Watergate, John Mitchell said he believed the merger was the "one mistake" of his life.

Within a few weeks after the two law firms merged, John Mitchell was actively working toward getting the 1968 Republican presidential nomination for Richard Nixon. This came about, with Martha's encouragement, after a small secret dinner meeting at the Plaza Hotel, where some of Richard Nixon's closest friends and supporters met to discuss financing a campaign. John called Martha the day of the dinner and asked her to come into town to attend something so secret he wouldn't reveal what it was over the telephone. She drove in alone from Rye and met John at the Fifth Avenue apartment of New York-based investment banker Maurice Stans and his wife, Kathleen. Stans had been finance chairman for Nixon's losing race for governor of California, and before that he'd been director of the budget in the Eisenhower Administration.

After cocktails at the apartment, the group walked the few blocks to the Plaza Hotel, where they slipped through a side door and rode a back elevator to an upstairs private dining room. More Nixon supporters joined them there.

After dinner when the talk turned to business, Martha was shocked to hear the men say Nixon didn't have a chance but since he was insisting he was going to run, they'd have to go along with him. Martha kept quiet at the dinner, but she had a lot to tell John as she drove home to Rye. (Martha always drove their car since John complained that his old World War II hip injury made it too painful for him to drive.) Martha told him that while listening to the men talk she'd felt they'd been saying prayers over a dead body. It infuriated her. She said she thought it was a disgrace for these men, who were supposed to be loyal Nixonites, to sit there and say he couldn't win. Such talk, she told John, made her sick at her stomach, and she for one was going to do everything in her power to see that this man won. She encouraged John to help, too, using some of the arguments she'd used to make him take to Richard Nixon in the first place.

Martha never knew whether it was due to her arguments or whether John planned to do it anyway, but soon he was putting together several state organizations for Nixon. Then one evening, over their before-dinner Scotches, he told Martha that Nixon wanted him to run the Midwestern part of the campaign. He asked if that were O.K. with her. "Then I made a mistake, a horrible mistake," Martha said. "I said, 'If you're going into politics, go all the way or else forget it. Don't fool around with state activities; run the whole show.' "

After Mitchell became campaign manager, people would speculate on why Nixon picked a nonpolitical Wall Street lawyer for such a position. Mitchell told a friend, "It was a natural. I'd been dealing with municipal and state bonds for thirty years and I knew every politician in the country, from the courthouse clerk on up."

MARTHA THOUGHT JOHN WOULD BE A BRILLIANT CAMPAIGN MANAGER. Naturally she expected to help, especially with the social functions every campaign requires. Martha always loved giving parties and having people around; she mentally started planning the kinds of entertainment she'd give for people important to the campaign. It didn't happen that way. Martha wasn't asked to become involved in any part of it. But what really hacked her was that she wasn't even asked to see the Nixon campaign headquarters.

John Mitchell was away from home for days at a time; when he came back to Rye, it was usually late at night. Martha missed the before-dinner drinks and discussions with her husband. She also missed meeting him in town for occasional dinners and a play. Finally she became so frustrated at having John away so much, and at being excluded from all campaign activities, she packed up and took Marty to Europe, on the RMS *Queen Mary.* They stayed five weeks before sailing home on the SS *France.* Midway in the trip, John flew to Scotland to spend some time with them and to pacify Martha.

But later that year, when Miss Arie had a stroke and Martha had to rush to Pine Bluff, John was too busy with Nixon business to go with her. He came later, though, after she called and demanded that he do so. Even then he was on the telephone, night and day, taking care of campaign business. It was so disturbing that they couldn't stay at the comfortable house of Martha's relatives, the Ray West Seniors; they had to move to a hotel. Martha didn't like it. She felt John should be concerned with her problems, not Nixon's.

Meanwhile back in Rye, little Marty wasn't happy either. She missed her parents so much she had gone to bed with a fever; Martha and John had to go home, leaving Miss Arie in the hospital. A month later, on December 26, Miss Arie died, at age eighty-five. Since Marty still was sick, Martha didn't go to her mother's funeral.

The firm, Nixon Guthrie Mudge Rose Alexander and Mitchell, sent flowers; neither Pat Nixon nor any other partner's wife called or came to see her, Martha said. She was hurt and she was angry, particularly at the wife of the man she felt was taking John Mitchell away from her.

It reached a point where her husband was staying in town so often he took rooms in a New York hotel. This left Martha alone in Rye, answering the constantly ringing telephones. In spite of the fact that John had two fully staffed offices—one at the law firm and the other at campaign headquarters—people still called day and night trying to reach him at home.

When Martha answered the telephone, most of the time there would be a woman on the other end of the line. No matter how many times John explained that the women were calling on campaign business, Martha was not convinced. She came to believe that it was a woman, or more likely women—and not politics—keeping John away from home. She was particularly suspicious of two prominent Republican women working for Richard Nixon's nomination, and later election.

There was one caller, though, who became one of Martha's Watergate neighbors and bridge-playing pals after the Mitchells moved to Washington. She was Anna Chennault, the Chinese-born widow of World War II Flying Tiger hero, Claire Chennault.

Mrs. Chennault called John frequently during the 1968 campaign and transition period, but Martha didn't know the nature of her business with him—other than that it concerned Nixon—until after John was Attorney General. Then Mrs. Chennault poured out the whole story to Martha one day when she was angry with the Nixon Administration for ignoring her and for not asking her to the White House for one of the many presidential parties.

Martha said Anna Chennault told her she was a good friend of many South Vietnamese politicians and also of the Vietnamese ambassador to the United States, Bui Diem, who also was the South Vietnamese representative to the Paris Peace Conference. Anna Chennault told her, Martha said, that she had worked closely with the Nixon people during 1968 and had arranged for Richard Nixon to meet with a high-ranking Vietnamese official. As a result of her labors, Anna Chennault said, the peace talks in Paris had been delayed, helping Nixon to defeat Hubert Humphrey.

In an interview with Aaron Latham, which appeared in the October 1977 *Esquire,* the late Hubert Humphrey said, "Nixon undoubtedly had Anna Chennault telling Thieu—that thieving, conniving leader of South Vietnam—'Don't come to the conference table in Paris.' I had reason to believe that Madame Chennault was representing Nixon, but I couldn't prove it. . . .

"My information was that Madame Chennault was telling Thieu and Ky that Nixon was going to win. That there was no sense in South Vietnamese's turning up in Paris. That a new Administration would be coming into power. We had information from the White House that indicated this was going on."

Martha said Anna Chennault told her Richard Nixon met with Thieu or with Bui Diem. Martha didn't remember which one, but she thought the Vietnamese official seen by Nixon was Thieu. She clearly recalled that Anna Chennault brought to the Mitchell apartment, as proof of the meeting, a large folder containing letters and documents. Martha reported to John how angry Anna Chennault was with the Administration for ignoring her. Then Martha turned the folder over to him. He told her to "stay out of it."

Evidently Mrs. Chennault was complaining to others at the same time. Peter Flanigan, an assistant to the President, sent John Mitchell a memo on October 2, 1969, in which he said, "I have had it reported indirectly that Anna Chenault [sic] is unhappy because she has not been recognized by the Administration. Since you had the liaison (if it can be called that) with this good lady I'd like your suggestions as to whether we should take some action to recognize her . . ."

Soon after her visit to Martha, Mrs. Chennault was invited to a dinner at the White House. Then on June 25, 1970 she was appointed by Secretary of State William P. Rogers to the one-hundred-member U.S. National Commission for UNESCO. On March 1, 1972, she was appointed to a slate of Republican-convention delegates pledged to President Nixon in the D. C. presidential primary on May 2. And on January 20, 1973, she was appointed to a three-year term on the Woman's Advisory Committee of the Federal Aviation Administration.

THE LONGER MARTHA SAT IN RYE, ALONE, FEELING NEGLECTED AND PUT upon and drinking Scotch by herself, the more upset she became. When John did come home, she berated him for leaving his wife and child. She told him Nixon was not only taking him away from his family but away from his law firm as well, since he was so busy with the campaign he didn't have time to see what was happening at the office.

John wouldn't listen. Martha repeatedly called his two offices to complain to his staff. Susan Morrison, John Mitchell's secretary, says the first she remembers that Martha was a "problem" to the office staff was during the 1968 campaign. "Up to that point she didn't make demands."

Martha also telephoned friends, seeking sympathy, even begging Alleta Saunders to come North to visit her, saying she was alone and afraid. Finally Martha telephoned a lawyer, Henry Rothblatt, later the first defense attorney for the four Floridians who broke into Watergate. Martha told him to start divorce proceedings against John Mitchell. She said she would name two prominent Republican women as correspondents.

Even this threat, an obvious cry for attention, didn't bring John Mitchell running home. The more distressed and abandoned Martha felt, the more she sought comfort in the bottle, until finally she was in such a state a friend talked her into entering Craig House, a psychiatric hospital in Beacon, New York, with an environment Martha called more social than medical, and where some of its wealthy patients came to "dry out." It would be the first of many hospital trips alcohol would cause Martha to make, either to Craig House or to the VIP wing of the Walter Reed Army Medical Center.

It's hard to pinpoint just when alcohol became a problem for Martha. Like others with the same difficulty, she was unbelievably clever at hiding her drinking. Many friends of longstanding didn't know about it until her last years. They're the ones who're apt to blame it on her coming to Washington, claiming that nothing in Martha's background had prepared her for the national spotlight, which she just didn't know how to handle. Or they blame Watergate, asking, "After what they did to her in California why wouldn't she drink?"

Julia McClain, perhaps Martha's best friend in Pine Bluff, is among those who think Martha started her heavy drinking while John was Attorney General: "I don't think that she could cope with the life that she had after she got to Washington. And I think she really fell apart after she found out that John was involved in Watergate."

Others remember that alcohol created friction during her first marriage, and one friend thinks she started drinking heavily when she was a secretary in Washington following World War II: "Martha liked to go have a good time and if that [drinking] was part of it that is what she would do. Remember, wartime Washington was quite a place."

As for Martha, she wouldn't discuss it at all, except to vehemently deny she had a problem. But she must have thought about it a lot. She read everything she could get her hands on about Marilyn Monroe and Judy Garland, two women who also combined alcohol and drugs, as Martha would later. She also carefully read every article that came to her attention involving alcoholics. Once when I mentioned a story in a magazine about a woman with a drinking problem, Martha glared and shouted, "I've already read it!"

And she did complain sometimes, when feeling depressed: "I don't understand it. A few drinks used to make me so happy, but they don't anymore."

Although Martha drank to excess, her son and many of her long-time friends, even some of her own doctors, do not believe she was an alcoholic. And when the Mitchells were in Washington, some wouldn't admit that she drank at all. One close associate of John Mitchell's was led to believe that Martha was a "severe menopausal case."

Sometime after she married John Mitchell, Martha developed gastrointestinal problems—diverticulitis by her account, although this seems not to have been confirmed by medical tests. Then she drank to kill the pain. Somewhere along the way a doctor gave her Valium or Librium or another of the depressant drugs, and the combination of alcohol and pills aggravated her problems.

Now Martha was in Craig House. John was all involved in politics with Richard Nixon. And she was threatening a divorce she didn't want at all.

Once Nixon was safely elected, if only by a 500,000 popular-vote margin, he asked his campaign manager and several top staff members to come with him to Key Biscayne to celebrate the victory. John Mitchell declined, saying he had to take care of personal business; he headed for Craig House. Even there Martha didn't have John's undivided attention; while he was visiting her, Richard Nixon telephoned John several times.

Later Martha told her lawyer and friends that John Mitchell changed her mind about the divorce "with his sweet talk and patriotic speeches." Her husband convinced Martha that Nixon was the only one who could save the United States from going down the drain. He also persuaded Martha that he needed her, with her superior insight into human nature, to help him pick the new Cabinet. He told her the President-elect wanted his two old friends William Rogers and Melvin Laird in the Cabinet, but it was up to Mitchell to find the rest. Martha couldn't wait to check herself out of Craig House; she told the hospital staff it was important to get her out in a hurry because she was "holding up the selection of Nixon's Cabinet."

MARTHA WENT ALMOST DIRECTLY FROM CRAIG HOUSE TO FLORIDA WITH John for the Investment Bankers Association convention, where John, instead of attending all the meetings and social events as he usually did, was constantly on the telephone, talking to the men he and Nixon hoped would be in the new President's Cabinet. This time, though, Martha wasn't upset,as she'd been with his telephoning in Pine Bluff when her mother was dying; now she was helping. She placed calls, kept records and in general served as John's secretary. For Martha it was wonderful and exciting to be working with John, to be in the middle of the political action at last.

It was discouraging, however, to find so many men turning down the Cabinet offers made by John and others. She couldn't understand how anyone would refuse to serve his country, especially in time of crisis, which she believed described the condition of the United States in 1968. John couldn't understand either; at one point he almost gave up. "How do you get people to staff the government when they turn it down?" he despaired.

David Rockefeller refused to become Secretary of the Treasury; John's friend David Kennedy, a Chicago banker, took the job only after John called him two times. Maurice Stans desperately wanted Treasury and refused for some time to take anything else; eventually Peter Flanigan and John Mitchell talked him into taking Commerce. Walter Hickel and George Romney had to be persuaded into taking Interior and Housing and Urban Development, respectively, which they both later regretted doing. Robert Finch refused Attorney General but accepted Health, Education and Welfare.

Arthur Burns accepted the position of counselor to the President only after being promised he'd be moved to the Federal Reserve Board as soon as there was an opening. Nelson Rockefeller didn't want to be in the Cabinet, as Martha remembered, and neither did Pennsylvania Governor William Scranton or Senator Henry (Scoop) Jackson. Senator Hubert Humphrey refused to accept the United Nations ambassadorship.

Fortunately, enough men were found in time for John to announce to reporters on December 6 that Richard Nixon would name his Cabinet the following week. Mitchell also said he would not be one of those appointed, adding that he hoped his name would remain on the Nixon Mudge Rose Guthrie Alexander and Mitchell letterhead "forever."

He did not get his wish. Richard Nixon nominated his campaign manager for the post of Attorney General. Martha wholeheartedly approved. John Mitchell told many people then, and later, that he didn't want to go to Washington. All he wanted to do was stay in New York and practice law, which was what the top advisors in the campaign thought he was going to do. Pat Buchanan, a Nixon White House aide, one who'd been with the 1968 campaign, says, "A number of people said almost as doctrine that Mitchell either would not be offered a Cabinet job or would not take one because of the Martha situation. Everyone was conversant with it, after her many phone calls to headquarters. So it was a bit of a surprise when he took the Attorney General job." He adds, "I guess one would have to believe they [Nixon and Mitchell] thought the problem was containable."

Mitchell's former secretary Susan Morrison thinks John Mitchell accepted the Cabinet post thinking that while Martha was busy having her own life in the Capital he could enjoy a challenging job. According to Sue, Mitchell thought "being a Cabinet wife would give Martha everything [she] desired. And it did, with one exception—John Mitchell. She needed *him.* She was tremendously insecure and she had this great dependency on him; all the rest of it wasn't enough."

Others familiar with the situation say that Mitchell went to Washington because Nixon was insecure and had grown to depend upon him. Nixon believed that he couldn't have won the Presidency without Mitchell. Ray West tells a story which seems to confirm this: "I was sitting next to George Romney, the former governor of Michigan, at a dinner one night at the State Department. When he found out I was Martha's cousin he said, 'Well, you are part of the Mitchell *but for* family.' I asked what he meant and he said, 'The President is always telling us *but for* Mitchell none of us would be here.' "

Chapter Five

ALTHOUGH SHE WOULD DENY IT LATER, MARTHA ACTUALLY looked forward to going to Washington. The newly elected President had talked at length with her about the importance of the role her husband, John Mitchell, would be playing in the Nixon Administration. He'd discussed, too, how she was going to take an active part in his plans to "turn the country around."

Of course, he'd scared the wits out of her when he said John Mitchell as Attorney General would wage such a vigorous fight against organized crime the lives of the whole Mitchell family would be in danger, so much so he was ordering FBI protection not only for John but for Martha and the Mitchells' eight-year-old daughter, Marty. It would be the first time in history, Nixon explained, that the wife and child of a U.S. Attorney General would have the FBI guarding them around the clock.

The opportunity to save the country from radicals, or what she'd later term "liberal Communists," clearly outweighed the dangers, as far as Martha was concerned. She was a conservative, to such a degree her amused friends joked that, politically, Martha was slightly to the right of Attila the Hun. Martha thought Richard Nixon really meant what he said about swinging the country back to the Right. She also believed he actually had a secret plan to end what she called "that miserable war in Vietnam." Martha for some time had been advising friends with sons of draft age to slip them over the border to Canada.

While having their before-dinner drinks, Martha and John often discussed the terrible condition the country was in; they thought the United States was so close to becoming Communist they even talked of moving to Switzerland.

A Mitchell friend of longstanding says, "Martha just felt the country was being sold down the river, so to speak, by the liberals . . . And, in fact, John Mitchell still to this day is convinced that the reason the Nixon Administration fell was because of a concerted plot by the liberal element in this country to bring him and Nixon down because of their stand against crime and big labor and all that stuff."

THE MONTHS BETWEEN JOHN MITCHELL'S SELECTION AS ATTORNEY GENeral and Inaugural Week were probably the busiest of Martha's life. She had to sell the house in Rye, find an apartment in Washington, select a school for Marty and buy a complete new wardrobe—with special attention paid to clothes suitable for a Cabinet wife to wear during the Inaugural festivities. Alleta Saunders remembers the first time she went to the Mitchells' Watergate apartment; how proud Martha was to show Alleta closet after closet, overflowing with new dresses, suits, coats and the proper accessories. "You see," Alleta says, "John had never turned her loose on clothes before."

But first there was a trip to Washington with John. Once the Cabinet was selected, President-elect Nixon decided to introduce all of the nominees on December 11 at the same time at an elaborately staged extravaganza, televised on prime time. Martha thought it set the tone for the whole Nixon Administration, which in her opinion became "nothing but a P.R. operation, a Madison Avenue proposition."

In television-m.c. fashion, Richard Nixon introduced the obviously embarrassed Cabinet nominees who, it was evident, were not used to carnival-type exposure. The President-elect noted that he had picked "Big Men" for his Administration. He added he wasn't going to have a Cabinet made up of Yes Men, and claimed "everyone is an independent figure."

The independence Nixon promised his Cabinet was short-lived. On January 4, 1969, seventeen days before he became President, Richard Nixon taped, for Bob Haldeman, his ideas about staffing the various government agencies and departments.

Nixon noted that he didn't think Cabinet officers had been adequately informed that their selection for undersecretaries had to be approved by him. But he didn't want to hear about recommendations until they had been cleared first with transition team members, John Mitchell, Bryce Harlow and Peter Flanigan.

The President-elect said he already was upset with his nominee for Secretary of Transportation, John Volpe, because he'd publicly mentioned wanting a particular man on his staff before John Mitchell knew about it.

About the same time, the President-elect also had some thoughts on the staffing of his Vice-President's office. Nixon said he wanted all discussion of Spiro Agnew's staff to go through a committee with John Mitchell presiding. In other words, Vice-President Agnew wasn't free to get his own people.

THE MORNING AFTER INTRODUCING HIS CABINET, THE PRESIDENT-ELECT called a meeting of his Cabinet nominees and their wives. Martha only remembered three things about that historic gathering, which was a "first," Nixon pointed out, since wives never had attended such a meeting.

First, Nixon said, he was starting a precedent by having wives attend Cabinet meetings. Martha thought this was an excellent idea. Unfortunately, after having the wives cleared for security and making a great media event of it when they later attended a White House meeting, Nixon abandoned the idea. "They told us they had a new Cabinet table and there wasn't room for us anymore," Martha explained.

Second, he wanted the wives to be active in their own way, both for the good of the country and for the good of the Administration. Again, Martha approved. Immediately she started thinking up things the wives could do; some of her ideas would alienate her from the women who, she claimed, at the beginning of the Administration were like "sorority sisters."

Third, Nixon hoped they would remember his unfortunate experience with the press. He warned everyone: Don't trust the press, don't have anything to do with the press, the press is the enemy. He was so vehement about this that at first Martha was afraid to be in the same room with a member of the Fourth Estate.

For the next several weeks Martha became a commuter between Washington and Rye. She bought a $150,000 duplex in the $70-million Watergate apartment complex. And as usual when redecorating a new home, Martha proceeded with reckless abandon. She tore up the flooring, replacing it with marble in the entrance hall and parquet in the other downstairs rooms. The walls were painted her favorite Wedgewood blue, and she replaced a contemporary stairway with a more traditional one.

Since it would be a month or two before the Mitchells could move into the Watergate, Martha rented an apartment at the Shoreham Hotel. John moved to Washington first, and when it was time for Marty to start school, at the Stone Ridge Country Day School in suburban Maryland, Martha moved her daughter and the maid to the Shoreham. Although Martha was a Presbyterian she always sent Marty to Catholic schools because she felt "there has been no discipline of children" in public schools since before World War II, and "the Roman Catholics are about the only ones that have discipline."

The FBI took Marty to and from school, so Martha didn't have that worry—she could continue commuting, coming to the capitol only for what she called the official "command performances."

One night while Martha still was in Rye, supervising the packing and deciding what to put in storage and what to send to Washington, there was a robbery up the street. Martha vividly recalled the gun shots and the police chase "all over the golf course with searchlights—police were everywhere." She called the FBI in New York and said, "Look here, if my husband is going to head the Justice Department, and if Richard Nixon says I am to have FBI protection, I have a perfect right to have someone out here now!" She added that she thought it was "ridiculous to have to go through all of this by myself." Immediately the FBI sent agents, who guarded her until she moved to Washington, where the local FBI men took over.

The public wasn't aware of the protection until late 1969, when Martha confided to someone at a party that she had a "bodyguard" because she was afraid in Washington. After considerable backing and filling the Justice Department confirmed to columnist Maxine Cheshire that the Mitchells had a "security coordinator." Even then the full extent of the Mitchell protection wasn't known; the FBI accompanied the Mitchells everywhere, both in the United States and abroad.

In August 1970, John and Martha flew to St. Louis in a government plane for an American Bar Association meeting. FBI agents accompanied them, as did a *Life* magazine photographer and reporter. As usual when they went out of town, they were met by local FBI with government cars.

When *Life*'s cover story came out on October 2, Martha was upset. She felt the magazine painted her position in Washington in an unfair light when it said the price of her flamboyance had been her friendships and that she had no close friends in Washington. Others were less concerned about Martha's feelings than they were about the pictures showing an FBI agent helping her iron a dress in the hotel suite and later snipping a loose thread from the back of her bodice.

Then in November, *Time* reported that the Mitchells' FBI agents' duties "frequently extend beyond what J. Edgar Hoover presumably has in mind. Recently, on a maid's day off, Agent Frank Illig helped out by serving Marty her breakfast in bed . . ." This upset more taxpaying readers.

Had a magazine's photographer and reporter followed Martha and Marty and their FBI agents in 1971 while they were touring England, Switzerland, Italy and Greece, their readers would have been even more distressed at the FBI's role.

By prearrangement, Martha met her Washington couturier Philip Robertson and his wife Mary in Florence for what later was described as a hectic and harassing day of shopping. The harassment was provided by various groups of American students who recognized Martha and asked for her autograph, taking away from valuable shopping time. Even so, she managed to spend over $10,000 before catching a six P.M. train for Rome.

Martha had arrived in Florence from Venice the evening before with Marty, her friends Ken and Peggy Ebbitt, and two FBI agents. Everyone went along while Martha and Philip selected fabric for two evening gowns he would design and make for her.

Martha fell in love with two pieces of material priced at approximately seventy-five dollars per yard. Marty, then ten, objected strenuously, telling her mother the fabrics were too expensive, pleading with her not to spend "all this money on clothes," and reminding Martha that Daddy wouldn't be Attorney General much longer and she should not throw their money away. Martha bought fourteen yards.

She asked one FBI agent to pay for the fabric while she moved on with her entourage and the other agent. This leapfrogging of agents (one paying and one guarding) continued through a multitude of shops, where Martha bought gloves, purses, linens—place mats, napkins, tablecloths, handkerchiefs—negligees for John's daughter and daughter-in-law, and silver. Martha was walking down the street when she spotted an epergne in a silver-shop window. "I want that," she said, and walked into the store. The epergne was just over $4,000; she took it.

The only break from shopping came when the group stopped for lunch, after which the Ebbitts left to go back to the Excelsior Hotel to pack. The agents tried to get Martha to go back to the hotel, too, but she refused. "They both were trying to get her to leave," Philip recalls. "Finally one turned to me at five-fifteen and said, 'We've got to get back to the hotel, the train leaves at six o'clock. She hasn't packed and she has twenty-four pieces of luggage to get to the train station.' "

Martha always traveled with everything she possibly would need and more. In addition to four or five times too many clothes, Martha took her pillow, Marty's pillow (when she was with her), an electric coffee maker and a three-pound can of coffee, since "nobody makes good coffee anymore"; a plastic bag full of oranges, a fruit juicer and her favorite paring knife, because she wouldn't start the day without a large tumbler of freshly squeezed orange juice; and among other various and sundry things a thermal pitcher for her nightstand.

Not only were the FBI agents responsible for Martha's twenty-four pieces of luggage, but there were Marty's three, the Ebbitts' ten, and their own, for a total of forty-three. In Venice they'd had to hire an extra gondola to haul the things down the Grand Canal.

WHEN THE MITCHELLS FIRST CAME TO WASHINGTON IT SEEMED TO MARTHA the President couldn't do enough for them. There were rides on Air Force One, trips to Camp David (the Presidential retreat in the nearby Catoctin Mountains of Maryland), use of Presidential yachts for entertaining, telephones with direct lines to the White House switchboard, where superefficient operators would place calls to anyone, anywhere in the world. All free, of course.

In the early days of the Administration, notices of the many perquisites of high office poured out of the White House almost daily. Use of the Executive Mansion tennis courts was extended to the new President's Cabinet, as was the barber shop, set up in the basement of the West Wing —open one to six P.M., Tuesday and Thursdays, "or later if required." For a Cabinet member so burdened with work he couldn't get away from his desk, the White House barber went to his office. Then there were the White House church services, an innovation of Nixon's, allowing him to worship under his own roof. The Cabinet was invited to bring guests— "Just call the [social secretary] and give names"—providing them, at no cost, with a status way to entertain.

Martha took full advantage of this; she brought friends from Arkansas and New York plus, at different times, her maids, chauffeurs and the families of the FBI agents guarding the Mitchells.

John and Martha were offered the use of the President's boxes at Kennedy Center functions, the horse show and other events, if the Nixons weren't using them, which they seldom were. And John's name was put on an honorary membership list for the White House Staff Mess, Washington's most exclusive restaurant, located in the basement of the West Wing of the Executive Mansion. He could bring Martha or other guests for an excellent meal, cooked and served by Navy stewards, and subsidized by the taxpayers. It also was possible, with a little finagling, to get the White House Filipino stewards to work afterhours at home parties.

The White House swimming pool was open to the Cabinet, too, but this privilege was extended only to men. Suits had to be worn: "Bring your own and take it with you after swimming." This perk was short-lived, though. In order to keep the press from seeing visitors entering and leaving White House offices, a new, more isolated press room was constructed over and around the old swimming pool.

Since President Nixon had ruled that his family and Cabinet, for "security" reasons, could not fly in commercial planes, a whole fleet of military aircraft was at their disposal. There was a choice of several types of planes, from VC-6 King Airs at $90 per hour to VC-137 Boeing 707s at $914 per hour. The charge was for flying time only, waiting on the ground was free. Naturally, the Cabinet officer did not pay the fee himself; the tab was picked up by his department or bureau.

Actually, some of the perks started even before the new Cabinet was sworn in. Back in December 1968, notice went out that Cabinet members and their families could receive free medical attention from Dr. Walter Tkach, an Army doctor Nixon had selected as the White House physician. Once he set up office, on the lower floor of the Executive Mansion, and had a full staff, Dr. Tkach's medical services, including house calls, were available on a grander scale.

Dr. Tkach often was called to the Mitchells' Watergate apartment. Just as she had panicked when Jay had polio and when he cut his foot in Florida, Martha became frantic whenever Marty was ill; she always insisted the child have medical attention *immediately.* The White House physician also came to the apartment to take care of Martha during her recurring attacks of diverticulitis. Another doctor familiar with the situation says Dr. Tkach felt it was better for him, personally, to make the house calls to attend Martha: "He thought if she had private care, it might expose her to unpleasant publicity."

Once the Cabinet and the sub-Cabinet were sworn in, the full facilities of various service hospitals were available—for a modest fee. The Mitchells, along with most of the others, chose to go to Walter Reed Army Medical Center, which had an elegant VIP wing. As Martha recalled, it was called VIP Sixth Ward; "I love the name, I get tickled everytime I say it!"

The medical services offered at Walter Reed were considered so excellent, Martha said, that in 1972 the then Secretary of Commerce Maurice Stans refused to resign his post to take over as finance chairman of CREEP until President Nixon assured him that Stans's wife Kathleen could continue as a patient at the Army hospital. (Jack Anderson reported on July 3, 1973, that Mrs. Stans had spent the last four months of 1972 in Walter Reed, "then came back for another nineteen days in January 1973. She returned again from May 8 to 22.")

Although the original notices had said medical services were available to the Cabinet and the sub-Cabinet, as was customary in other Administrations, President Nixon freely granted permission for others he favored to use the service hospitals. For instance, when his personal secretary Rose Mary Woods became ill in San Clemente, California, Richard Nixon had her transported back to Washington by military aircraft and entered in the Bethesda Naval Medical Center Hospital, where she was a patient for a week, staying in a room in the luxurious Presidential Suite.

"President Nixon thought anything that belonged to the government was his," Martha explained. "So, when anybody needed anything Nixon gave it to them—if they were in good graces at the time." Bebe Rebozo was treated like a member of the family, according to Martha: "Whatever Bebe wanted, Bebe got . . . The government protected Bebe's yacht all year round, although Nixon was on it only occasionally . . . That was the way Nixon operated. And he always gave the impression that anyone on his side—they had to be on his side, of course—would get all the crowns of glory that could ever come into being."

Martha admitted that she enjoyed the "crowns," and one that delighted her the most was the use, rent free, of a beautiful house at Key Biscayne, on Harbor Avenue. Only a short block or so from the Nixon compound, the house had a swimming pool and faced the bay. It was owned by Bebe Rebozo or his bank, according to Martha, but it was managed by the General Services Administration: "Everything that went wrong at the house was paid for by the U.S. government, which was GSA. The swimming pool was cleaned by GSA maintenance men and any broken appliances were repaired by them."

The house was tied in with the White House communications system, so it was used only by high-level Nixon people. This was the house the Mitchells were staying in when he allegedly gave his consent to the campaign dirty-tricks package, the one resulting in the Watergate break-in. Martha said she heard the discussion of the plans over the house intercom system.

Another perk of the high office Martha enjoyed to the fullest was her diplomatic passport, which allowed her to whisk through customs without a suitcase being opened or a question asked.

Martha also had a privilege not afforded other Cabinet wives. Just as he'd promised the night he told her he was going after the Mafia, Richard Nixon saw to it that Martha had her own government-owned car and a chauffeur. Other Cabinet wives could use an automobile out of the government car pool when on official business, but Martha's chauffeur-driven black Mercury sedan was for her exclusive use, twenty-four hours a day. She could dispatch it on personal errands, and often did. And, according to a former Justice Department employee, the chauffeur sometime doubled as a houseman—he vacuumed the carpets in the Mitchell apartment.

When this special car arrangement became known, some two-and-a-half years later, a surprised General Services Administration official said, "Those cars are supposed to be for official use only, not for Cabinet wives." Then it was discovered the car had been authorized by the White House Office of Management and Budget, and no more was heard from GSA.

Taxpayers, though, let it be known they were outraged to find themselves paying over $10,000 a year for a Cabinet wife's transportation. Martha gave up the government car, in January 1972, two months after the ruckus started, but not before she had arranged for another car and driver, paid for by the Committee for the Re-Election of the President. Martha simply told CREEP officials she wouldn't campaign anymore unless they provided her this convenience.

RICHARD NIXON LOVED CAMP DAVID; DURING HIS FIRST FOUR YEARS IN office he went there 117 times, one trip lasting almost two weeks. At first the President frequently took the Mitchells with him when he went to the Catoctin retreat. "The cottages at Camp David looked very rustic on the outside," Martha recalled. "But when you got inside they were the most lush things you have ever seen. Nixon did this; they were rustic before. He had all of them redecorated, and he had two cottages built for Tricia and Julie—those were decorated according to their taste.

"And although there was a huge, pretty swimming pool, Nixon had his own heated pool built. [At a cost of $150,000 to the taxpayers.] It was right by his cottage; he wouldn't go to the big one because the staff used it." In the summer of 1970, two young Marines sneaked a swim in Nixon's pool and narrowly escaped court-martial.

Only a thirty-minute helicopter ride from the White House, Camp David, according to a notice sent the Cabinet, had accommodations for twenty-four guests ("eight in single rooms and sixteen in double rooms") in cabins with such names as Witchhazel, Dogwood, Maple and Birch.

When not asked to dine with the First Family, guests in the other cabins (actually large one- or two-bedroom suites) ate at Laurel or had room service. Cooks and stewards were provided by the White House mess staff; the service was excellent.

The Mitchells usually had dinner with the President, which Martha liked, except the President loved red wines and she couldn't stand them. He was forever pressing the reds on her, saying, "You must try this, it's delicious."

Usually she went along with him and drank the red wine, but one night at Camp David, she said, she just couldn't do it. When the President turned to talk to his dinner partner on the left, Martha poured her wine in her water glass and put it under the table by her feet.

Most evenings when they were dinner guests of the Nixons, the Mitchells watched a movie with their host. It amused Martha that John Mitchell, who "absolutely hated" movies, had to sit through film after film with the President. Fortunately, John and Martha weren't at Camp David the weekend the Nixon family saw seven movies. But John Mitchell was in on several showings of Nixon's favorite film, *Patton,* in the White House theater. "John would come home," Martha recalled, "and say, 'If I have to watch that damn *Patton* again, I'll resign.' "

Martha wasn't much for outdoor sports, but she loved going to Camp David and being privy to the "inside" conversation. This was different from the campaign, when she'd been left out of everything. Now she was there when the President and John, and almost always Bebe Rebozo, discussed what had to be done to stop the "enemy."

It was at Camp David, Martha said, during one of the informal conferences between the President, John and Bebe that she first realized, "Any man or group controlling the White House and the Justice Department can control the whole United States; there is no way to stop them."

The evening at Camp David that Martha recalled most clearly was the night Nixon selected the movie *Dr. Zhivago* for his guests to see after dinner. "John and I had been talking for weeks about how the Russians were taking over this country," Martha said. "So when I saw the beginning of the picture it upset me so I thought I couldn't stand it; that was what I thought was happening here. So I got up and left. I went to the President's room, stretched out on his bed and read the TV guide, the only book in the room. When they came looking for me I was asleep."

She laughed and added, "I don't think we were invited back many times, if at all, after that!" As she was to discover, the privilege of going to Camp David wasn't the only perk the Mitchells would lose.

"It reminded you of a king and his court, the kings we studied about in school," Martha remembered. "King Richard gave and King Richard took away! There was all the in-fighting, too, among the *Princes, Dukes* and *Earls.*"

Martha was convinced that Nixon thought of himself as King. As examples of this she pointed to the trumpeters, with the banners draped on their elongated trumpets, that he installed to announce his appearances; and the fancy Student Prince-type uniforms he had the White House police dress in for ceremonial occasions, until public laughter forced him to stop the practice.

Martha enjoyed giving formal dinner parties aboard the ninety-nine-foot presidential yacht *Sequoia,* where a Navy crew of fourteen made entertaining elegant and easy—not to mention inexpensive. All Martha had to do was plan her guest list. The Justice Department secretary sent the invitations and received the acceptances. The dinner was selected from ten sample "sit-down" menus prepared by the *Sequoia* chef.

When the Mitchells were told the *Sequoia* was no longer available to them, Martha was unhappy. But not as unhappy as she was when she was barred from Air Force One in September 1970, after she told a press pool the war in Vietnam "stinks!"

The Mitchells were coming back from California with the Nixons when Martha became bored with the other passengers in the VIP section (John was with the President in his quarters). She went back to play gin rummy and bridge with the press, and she was there when Press Secretary Ron Ziegler strolled back. The reporters asked for news; Ron said he didn't have anything to tell them. Martha volunteered to give them something to print, and she did.

After stating her opinion of the war, Martha added that "if it weren't for [Senator] Fulbright, we'd be out of it." The Senator kept the war going, Martha said, because "he wants to promote himself."

Soon John Mitchell came looking for Martha and was asked if he'd like to know what his wife had to say. He answered, "Heavens, no! I might jump out the window!"

The Mitchells didn't know Martha was barred from the plane until several weeks after her remark. They were going to Florida at the same time the President was heading that way, and John called the White House to ask for a ride. He learned he was welcome but Martha was not. Martha said John was angry, but he didn't seem to stay mad for long.

When the President and his Attorney General flew south for the dedication of the Arkansas River Navigation System on June 5, 1971, Martha already was there. Naturally, Martha thought she would fly home with John. But the minute the dedication ceremony was over, Martha was whisked out to the airport and put aboard the back-up plane. Without saying a word to Martha, John got on Air Force One with the President. "I was so embarrassed and so ashamed, I just sat huddled in my seat, hoping no one I knew would see me," Martha remembered. She also claimed, "I never forgave John for that."

Neither did she take her ban quietly. "I just found out every time the plane was going someplace and then I annoyed the *hell* out of them! I'd have my secretary or my scheduling man call the White House and insist I had to fly on Air Force One in order to keep a campaign commitment." What was puzzling was how she knew every time the plane was leaving; it was suspected she had spies in the White House. Martha didn't need a spy. She received her information directly from the President; when he called John, Martha eavesdropped on the phone calls.

Chapter Six

MARTHA LEARNED QUICKLY THAT RICHARD NIXON COULDN'T stand criticism of any kind, and anyone who opposed him in any way was the "enemy." He was especially sensitive to anything the media said against him. "He hated the press," Martha said. "It was an obsession with him."

The minute something was written that put him in a bad light, Martha noticed that Nixon started the wheels in motion: "It was like a big campaign, with each worker having a particular phase of it as his responsibility. For instance, they seemed to have people who did nothing except notify these little groups of people, all over the country, when they wanted letters and telegrams sent to editors.

"Other people had the responsibility to contact reporters on *our side* to leak contradictory stories, some of them outright lies. There was a whole bunch of columnists and reporters and television people who would use anything the Administration fed them."

Some of these members of the media not only passed on to their readers and listeners the Nixon leaks but they in turn fed information to the Administration. In late 1971 an ultraconservative columnist warned the Attorney General he had heard the "enemy" had some information which could be embarrassing to Mitchell, "namely that you gave orders not to prosecute RF, notwithstanding that you have an airtight income-tax case against him . . . [I] thought I ought not to delay in advising you of it . . ." ("RF" is not identified.)

It seemed to Martha that John was constantly plotting against the media with the President and/or Bebe at Camp David, Key Biscayne or San Clemente. Or he was on the phone with them, mapping ways to control and discredit this or that long-time Nixon foe. When he wasn't talking with one of them he was speaking on the same subject with Bob Haldeman, John Ehrlichman, other White House aides or people at the Justice Department.

Two or three months after Nixon took office, Henry Kissinger, then presidential adviser on national security, joined those calling John to complain about the press.

"I swear to God to you that there was never a night that passed that Mitchell didn't talk to Kissinger," Martha told Donnie Radcliffe of the Washington *Post* in June 1974. One of the things precipitating Kissinger's anger with the media was a New York *Times* story by William Beecher in May 1969, reporting secret B-52 bombing raids on Cambodia.

"Kissinger just had fits: he kept insisting John *had* to find the source of the leaks and do whatever was necessary to stop them," Martha said. "Many times John was mad when he hung up and he'd turn away from the phone in exasperation and explode, 'That man is crazy!' "

Eventually, leaks about the Cambodian raids and other secret actions of the White House led President Nixon to order wiretaps on the home telephones of seventeen White House aides, government officials and newsmen.

Although Henry Kissinger has denied under oath that he instigated the wiretaps, Martha always thought it was his insistence that something be done that led to the electronic surveillance. A memo left by J. Edgar Hoover also seems to point to Kissinger. Dated May 9, 1969, it notes that Kissinger called the FBI director from Key Biscayne, complaining about the William Beecher story of the B-52 bombing raids, "which is extraordinarily damaging and uses secret information. Dr. Kissinger said they wonder whether I could make a major effort to find out where that came from. I said I would."

Others in the media, not revealing White House secrets, also had their telephones tapped at various times. Martha said John told her a television newscaster was under surveillance because he was suspected of being a Communist, but eventually Martha thought this untrue. The man was a close family friend of the Kennedys, and Martha felt that by tapping him the Administration was keeping tabs on what Senator Edward Kennedy was up to: "Mr. President just hated the Kennedys. He even wanted to change the name of Kennedy Center but found out he couldn't."

Although many in the Nixon Administration have denied that Martha "knew anything," she must have known about the wiretaps. She told me sometime in late 1970 or early 1971, "Winnie, be careful what you say on your telephone."

DURING THE WATERGATE HEARINGS SENATOR LOWELL WEICKER MADE PUBlic thirty-four documents that illustrated how the Nixon Administration was trying to control the press. Among them were sample letters drafted in the office of White House speech writer Pat Buchanan to be sent to various parts of the country: "To the Editor: The best proof yet of the allegations of Vice President Agnew about the nation's news media was their incredibly arrogant performance before the entire nation last Thursday night. Who in the hell elected these people to stand up and read off their insults to the President of the United States and then ask that he comment?" Or, "To the Editor: . . . when will you people realize that he was elected President and he is entitled to the respect of that office no matter what you people think about him?"

One of the victims of a White House-inspired letter campaign, according to Martha, was Dan Rather of CBS: "The Administration just loved ABC and Howard K. Smith. But it couldn't stand CBS, especially Walter Cronkite, Dan Rather and Daniel Schorr.

"It just killed the Administration that Dan Rather broadcast from the White House lawn [with the Mansion in the background]. Nixon thought the White House was *his* and he didn't want this man he couldn't stand using it as a backdrop. They tried to keep Dan off the lawn, or said they were going to, but I guess they couldn't. So they started a letter, phonecall and so-forth campaign against him. John even asked me to call CBS and complain about Dan, which I did." (In a tearful telephone call in 1974, Martha apologized to Dan Rather.)

Daniel Schorr irritated the White House so much that Haldeman ordered an FBI investigation of him. When the network complained about government agents interviewing Schorr's co-workers and friends, the White House put out a completely false story to the effect that the check was necessary because it was considering Schorr for a government job. Someone even got J. Edgar Hoover to back up the lie. During the

Watergate hearings Bob Haldeman admitted the story was false.

As for Walter Cronkite, the White House tried to discredit him whenever possible, and Martha did her bit to help. In a July 1971 article in *Ladies' Home Journal,* titled "Martha Mitchell: People I'd Love to Phone," she said she wanted to call the CBS anchorman because "Cronkite twists the news so much I want to ask him 'why?' Then I'll needle him and say that I want to come advise him before he goes on the air . . ."

John and the President and the others talked a lot about what they would do to various radio and television newsmen—and they carried out many of their threats—but the "big thing," Martha said, was reserved for the stations. They would lose their licenses. She thought it was a "Hitler-run operation."

"The Administration started a whole siege against the Washington *Post,* " she continued, referring to the time friends of the Administration formed four groups in Florida to challenge the licenses of two television stations—one in Miami, the other in Jacksonville—owned by the Washington Post Company. The challenges later were withdrawn, probably because the political ties of the group had been exposed. When then President Ford testified before a House Judiciary Subcommittee on October 17, 1974, he supplied the lawmakers with a memorandum, prepared by the Watergate Special Prosecutor's office, saying that one of the criminal charges that might have been brought against Nixon had he not been pardoned included possible complicity in the filing of challenges to the licenses of the two Florida television stations owned by the *Post.* This was only one among ten areas of possible criminal activity by Nixon under investigation.

The Administration desperately tried to control the press, Martha said, because without it the P.R. operation to improve the image of the President would fail. Martha insisted, "It didn't mean a who-happy to them what anything or anybody was; it was how that thing or that person looked to the public, the voting public."

It seemed to Martha that the only reason Special Counsel to the President Richard Moore was in the White House was "to protect the President by counteracting anything said by these people who came out against Nixon in any way, shape or form. It was the Administration's habit to deny, deny, deny. Even if the story they were denying were absolutely true they would call it 'false and irresponsible' or 'distorted and unfair' or some such thing, if the story was not favorable to Nixon.

"Another thing Mr. President did against the media," Martha recalled, "was to send Vice-President Agnew out to stir up hatred of the press. But Ted (as Agnew was called by his friends) didn't always like what he was doing. He even had to say what Nixon's speech writers wrote for him. I remember more than once, when Ted and Judy [Mrs. Agnew] and John and I were together, the Vice-President was furious about what they were making him do. One evening, I think it was when we were having dinner at their Sheraton Park apartment, he even threatened to resign; John had to talk him out of it."

To discredit or intimidate the press, Martha said, the Administration often used the Internal Revenue Service or another agency to find out embarrassing things about individuals. Then Nixon people would use the information "to straighten them out."

Not everyone gave in to Administration pressure, though. At a time when the chief investigative reporter of a nationally known paper was digging into and writing about things embarrassing to the Administration, the paper's publisher happened to drop by John Mitchell's office at the Justice Department, where the Attorney General spoke to him about the "criminal record" of the investigative reporter.

The next week John Mitchell received a letter from the publisher in which he said he took the reference to a criminal record as a veiled threat. He also said he had told his investigative reporter about Mitchell's disclosure and enclosed the reporter's written reply to the charge. As it turned out, the reporter was a former military intelligence officer who, while investigating a criminal case, was booked into a jail to "spy" on a suspect. The fact that he was a military intelligence officer apparently was recorded along with the information that he had been in jail. The publisher had been told only about a "criminal record."

John Mitchell spent so much time trying to disarm the press that Martha finally cried in exasperation, "Why aren't you doing your work; why aren't you taking care of your law and order?"

Her husband explained that the press was so hostile to Nixon it was making it impossible for him to run the country; therefore the Administration either had to get the press on its side or discredit it so no one would believe it. She said he did such a good job of "brainwashing" her, she felt sorry for Mr. President.

SOON MARTHA DISCOVERED HARASSMENT WASN'T LIMITED TO THE NEWS media. People who demonstrated against the White House angered Richard Nixon so much that John W. Dean, then Counsel to the President, asked the Justice Department in December 1971 if legislation could be enacted to "establish a Washington counterpart to Hyde Park, London, using a location on the Mall or elsewhere."

White House enemies even included members of the President's own party. Martha said the Administration tried "to get rid of" the then Minority Leader Senator Hugh Scott because the White House thought he was not showing enough active interest in the President's programs. At the same time, the White House wasn't getting along well with then Representative Gerald Ford, since he "was not on our side, he was following along on Scott's coattails." But the Nixon people "were able to turn around" Scott and Ford. Ford became such a loyal supporter he even launched an unsuccessful attempt to get Justice William O. Douglas off the Supreme Court after he was told how important the Justice's departure was to the Nixon Administration.

When Republican Senator Charles Goodell refused to approve Nixon's stand on Vietnam, the White House started a successful campaign to defeat him at the polls. Martha was sent up to New York as a campaign attraction to a dinner to help his opponent, James Buckley.

There also was an ongoing campaign to "eliminate" all liberal politicians—Republican or Democrat. John Mitchell once told Martha he had put out so much money defeating them in campaigns he couldn't even remember the amount spent.

Sometimes, if the Administration thought a Democratic candidate would be more helpful, it put money into his campaign, even if it meant defeating a Republican. For instance, when Nixon's former Postmaster General Winton ("Red") Blount ran against Senator John Sparkman, Nixon wrote a complimentary letter to the incumbent Sparkman, which managed to find its way into print. Martha saw Red Blount and his wife Mary Katherine in Alabama in 1974, and it was obvious to her that he still was hurt over the treatment he had received from his former boss.

In 1971 Martha accepted an invitation from a nonpartisan group of Washingtonians to attend a fund-raiser in the garden of the Sheraton-Carlton, for Republican W. Thatcher Longstreth, a Philadelphia blue blood who was running for mayor of that city against Democrat Frank Rizzo, Philadelphia's "tough cop." When John Mitchell heard Martha was planning to go to the party, he forbade her to go. The Nixon Administration wanted Frank Rizzo to win, even though he was a Democrat.

After Watergate, Martha repeatedly tried to warn Republicans that Richard Nixon had deserted them. No one believed her. So the night she found, in a file cabinet after John left her, an EYES ONLY memorandum from the President to John Mitchell that proved she was telling the truth, Martha was on the telephone for hours, calling the offices of Senator Hugh Scott, Senator Robert Dole (later President Ford's running mate in the 1976 campaign), former Nixon Cabinet officer Rogers C. B. Morton, and other men important in the Republican party. It's unknown how many she reached.

The memorandum, dated June 6, 1972, eleven days before the Watergate break-in, reads:

This memorandum is for your information and guidance, and the contents and observations should . . . not [be] attributed to me since some rather sensitive political matters are contained in it. In talking to John Connally he has decided within the last two weeks that McGovern will probably be nominated . . . [Connally] made one point very strongly with which I totally agree. To put it in perspective it is necessary for me to point out that one of the major mistakes we made in 1960 was to allow Republicans, particularly in the Southern states, to control the Nixon organization and also to be out front in the Nixon effort. Their interest, of course, was to use the Presidential campaign for the purpose of building the Republican party in their states. . . . We avoided it in a state like California only because Bob Finch was totally aware of the California problems and saw to it that we ran a campaign that did not cut out the Independents and Democrats.

Connally's admonition is that as we see the inevitability now for a McGovern nomination we must "leave the door open" for Democrats and Independents not only to join us but to have positions of real leadership in the Nixon campaign. . . . Every state is to be examined with a merciless and impartial eye as to what people in that state we need in order to carry it. Generally speaking, you will find that what we need are prominent Democrats and Independents who will join our cause and if possible who will take positions of leadership in it. In California one of the reasons we probably have less of a chance in 1972 than we had in 1960 and 1968 is the fact that Reagan and the regular Republicans will insist on running the campaign. This will make it a walking disaster and the same is true of Texas and all the Southern states as well as some of the other states, including states like Pennsylvania where we need prominent Democrats. For example, Rizzo is infinitely more important to us in Pennsylvania than Scott or Schweiker. Ways have got to be found to allow Rizzo to be out in front if he is willing to do so.

The purpose of this memo is simply to make sure that an examination is made of the state's situation with only one view in mind—what men and women can do us the most good in getting us the votes we need—the votes of Independents and Democrats? . . . This does not mean that the Republican organization should be cut out—it does mean that we should avoid identifying too closely with

Republican candidates who are weaker than we are or with Republican organizations that are in ill repute . . .

The McGovern strategy is becoming very clear now that he believes that he has the nomination wrapped up. His going to the Governors' conference for the purpose of "clarifying" his stand on amnesty, marijuana, abortion and welfare is a case in point. I know there are those who will say that he can't get away with it any more than Goldwater was able to get away with it when he tried to enlist Republican governors in Cleveland in 1964. There are two very significant differences, McGovern is more clear and less principled than Goldwater and will say anything in order to win. And second, McGovern will have about 100 percent support from the media in his effort to clean himself up so that he can beat us in the final. This points up the necessity at this time to get *Democrats* and *Independents,* not Republicans, to nail McGovern on the left side of the road which his record so clearly identifies him with . . .

MARTHA FOUND THE ADMINISTRATION JUST AS EAGER TO HELP ITS FRIENDS as it was to harm its enemies. Sometimes it seemed to her that Nixon and those around him went out of their way to do favors for anyone who was "for us."

Some of the ways the Administration helped its friends were:

- While still Attorney General, Ramsey Clark initiated an FBI investigation of twenty-one Nixon-Agnew fund-raising committees that were late filing reports of money raised and spent in the 1968 campaign. A little over two months after Nixon took office, Walter Pincus and Jan Krause, writing in the Washington *Post,* noted that the inquiry begun by Clark of the Republican campaign committees "appears to have been halted, according to informed sources." The same day the article appeared, the Attorney General received a copy, along with a memo from his aide, Kevin Phillips, saying that "Rosthal [the federal elections unit chief] says that nobody except Kossack [deputy assistant attorney general, Criminal Division] and himself know about the memo calling off the FBI. He says that there are no leaks."
- The U.S. Attorney's office in New York asked the FBI to conduct a preliminary investigation into the alleged violation of the civil rights of protesting students by construction workers during an encounter on May 8, 1970, after the American Civil Liberties Union charged that police failed to provide adequate protection for the students. The ACLU furnished a list of witnesses it wanted interviewed by the FBI. The White House sent Attorney General John Mitchell a memo,

written by Tom Charles Huston to Ehrlichman, Haldeman, Harry Dent and Charles Colson: "I would strongly recommend that the Justice Department decline to authorize the investigation . . . it is questionable whether the civil rights of the protesting students were any more violated than those of countless thousands who have previously been on the receiving end of student demonstrations. . . . The actions of the construction workers in N.Y. City were only symbolic of the deep-seated resentment against protesting students which is characteristic of the blue-collar elements. Any Federal move against these workers or the New York City Police Department will only add fuel to the flames of resentment and redirect it from the protesting kids to the Administration."

Typed on the bottom of the page, in another typeface, but unsigned, was "I suggest that someone turn Jerris Leonard [assistant attorney general, Civil Rights Division] off before this matter gets out of hand."

- Good friends of the Administration felt free to write the Attorney General to suggest campaign donations in return for aid at the Federal Trade Commission. One of the papers Martha found in John's files, which she tried to turn over to either the Senate Watergate Committee or the Special Prosecutor's office, and in desperation gave to Bob Woodward of the Washington *Post,* was a letter from Elmer Holmes Bobst.

  The largest stockholder of Warner-Lambert Pharmaceutical Co. and honorary chairman of its board, Bobst is the man President Nixon called his "honorary father." At one time he established a trust fund for Nixon's daughter, Tricia Nixon Cox.

In the letter, dated October 13, 1971, Bobst first suggested the names of two federal court judges for appointments to the Supreme Court. Then he added:

> I take this opportunity of mentioning that the FTC situation has not altered significantly. The lower echelon seems to have a complete hold on the show to the extent that the top 5 appear to be not much more than puppets. I might say that one of my close friends interested in the case mentioned that if there was any evidence of a more favorable attitude on the part of the tops, he would come up with 100,000 for the ![sic]72 fray. I, too, have already committed myself for that amount—although it probably will be considerably increased when the battle begins.

With kindest regards to your ever active bride, who is not afraid to speak out, and best to you.

Sincerely,
Elmer

Someone had underlined, in ink, the words "he would come up with 100,000 for the !72 fray."

According to the *Post*, the "situation" Bobst mentioned was an FTC challenge of a merger between Warner-Lambert Pharmaceutical Co. and Parke, Davis, Inc.

Although she later would become the nation's most vocal critic of Nixon and his Administration's "dirty tricks," Martha sat by silently while the Administration spun its web, ensnaring facts and people.

Why?

This is a question she eventually would ask herself over and over. But at the time, John had her thoroughly convinced that the deceitful things being done were necessary to either turn off or turn around the liberals and radicals who were selling the country "down the drain." So, although she questioned the method used to neutralize or outflank the enemy, Martha was willing to go along with it to save the United States. As she said at the time, "When we lived in Rye we thought the government was deceiving the people; now I know it *has* to deceive the people."

Actually, Martha was always convinced that some of the dirty tricks accomplished what she thought they set out to do. Several months after Watergate she told me she still believed a statement she made during the early stages of the campaign: "Now I see things turning around—the Supreme Court, the drop in violence, the winding down of the war in Vietnam. The riots have stopped, the people who thought demonstrations would work found out that they didn't. We don't see people tearing down government buildings anymore. That's because of President Nixon and my husband."

Late one night, in 1972, Martha, who was then living in New York, telephoned me. Her first words were, "Now, I want you to explain to me —and tell the truth—*what did they do wrong?*"

"They got caught," I answered and laughed.

"I'm serious!" Martha snapped. "What did they do wrong? They didn't do anything that hasn't been done before. Other Administrations wiretapped and used the IRS and everything else."

When I tried to explain that the Nixon White House seemed to be more devious and more corrupt than normally was the case, Martha interrupted: "But that isn't true. John Connally told the President the Democrats had done as many things as the Republicans and consequently Nixon had nothing to worry about. Connally said he had the proof and he'd produce it. I heard John and the President talking about it over the phone. They said everyone will be exonerated, because John Connally said they shouldn't worry about Watergate since it all had been done by the Democrats so damn many times.

"That's a quote!"

Chapter Seven

INCREDIBLE AS IT SEEMS TODAY, MARTHA LIVED A RELATIVELY private life the first ten months her husband was Attorney General. It wasn't until November 21, 1969, when she went on the *CBS Morning News* and talked about "liberal Communists" among antiwar demonstrators that she became a national celebrity, and eventually something of a folk heroine.

Not that Martha lived the life of a recluse those first months. She went to official White House parties, embassy galas, the "little sit-down dinners" for which Washington is famous, plus innumerable charity affairs. But the press made only passing notice of her presence.

It didn't mention any of the outrageous outbursts, candid remarks, Martha-isms or outspokenness it would make so much of later. No one called her "Martha the Mouth" or "Martha the Lip." In fact, the press didn't call her Martha at all. When her name appeared on a guest list she was "Mrs. John Mitchell, wife of the Attorney General." (In late October 1969, Perle Mesta gave a dinner for the Mitchells, and the Washington *Star* noted: "Saturday night it was Attorney General John Mitchell's turn to be the Mesta man of the hour and he and Mrs. Mitchell took it with great grace.")

Even her flamboyant clothing, her outmoded shoes and her spectacular hair-dos seemed to have been editorially ignored, too, except for one writer's criticism of the shade of her "brassy" blond hair. And although Martha told friends she was furious about this, she didn't telephone anyone in the press to complain.

How could an open, candid, uninhibited, gregarious, vivacious woman live in the same city, attend the same newsworthy events, with the world's most inquisitive and aggressive press, without being quoted, described or at least noticed?

The answer seems to be that during this time Martha was taking seriously Richard Nixon's advice about the press; she was staying away from it as much as possible.

Naturally, Martha met many reporters during this period, and she discovered to her surprise that some of them seemed like nice people. But she didn't dare trust a one, not after the things Mr. President had warned the Cabinet wives about, such as, "We all have skeletons in our closets . . . the press is going to be after all of you."

So Martha kept her distance from the press, only occasionally exchanging more than the pleasantries, and then only with reporters from publications John thought were *safe*.

She gave a loving-little-wife interview in early October to the Chicago *Tribune*, and followed it up a week later with a husband-wife interview with Vera Glaser and Malvina Stephenson for the Knight Newspaper Syndicate.

The Glaser-Stephenson article didn't stir up unusual interest in Martha, although it should have alerted the media that she wasn't the ordinary, run-of-the-mill Cabinet wife. When discussing the President's close friend Bebe Rebozo, Martha described him as "extremely intelligent, but you would never know it just sitting down socially with him. That's why the President likes him."

As for the President himself, she said, "He has a marvelous sense of humor, a dry wit something like my husband . . . everything they say is funny, but you have to be able to pick it up, to be in time."

When talking about her husband she observed, "Yes, he's tough. I wouldn't want him any other way." Later Martha said her husband was "so sweet and tender—how can he be top cop if he doesn't seem hard-boiled?"

Martha made minor news of sorts two days before her newsmaking CBS show when newswoman Helene Melzer, then with the *Wall Street Journal*, revealed that Mrs. Mitchell was allergic to marijuana. The story was picked up by papers around the country, not because it was shocking, as many of her later doings would be, but because it was amusing. (One paper reported that the Attorney General's wife "had a reaction to pot.") Martha, while visiting the Bureau of Narcotics with a group of Justice Department wives, sniffed burning marijuana leaves to see if they had a distinctive odor. She wound up with puffy eyes and swollen cheeks and required medical treatment.

While the pot tempest in a teapot was still bubbling, Martha was reaping Administration ire for her candor on the *CBS Morning News,* which was taped a few days after the November 13–15 Moratorium. "I got myself in a heck of a mess," she confessed a few days after the show was aired. But she refused to take blame for being on the show in the first place. Nixon's communications director Herb Klein was responsible for that, she insisted. But Herb says the first he knew about the program was when "a lady called from Baltimore and asked had I seen Martha Mitchell on CBS." Herb hadn't seen the interview, but he immediately had the tape run so he could view it.

According to Marion Goldin (later a producer of CBS's *60 Minutes,* but then with the *Morning News*), the very day she called the Attorney General's office to ask for an interview Martha herself called back. Following several conversations, Martha and Marion made the arrangements. Marion says, "As far as I could determine, no middleman was involved." But of course one was: until after Watergate Martha didn't do any interviews—newspaper, magazine, radio or television—that were not cleared with someone—John, the White House communications' office, others in the Administration, her press secretary (the short time she had one) or later with a member of the Committee for the Re-Election of the President.

The CBS interview, aired by coincidence on the same day the Senate rejected the Supreme Court nomination of Judge Clement Haynsworth, Jr., probably was cleared in John's own public-relations office. Or perhaps his press aide called Klein's office and received an O.K. without Herb knowing about it. In any event, someone approved and Martha dashed back early from a Florida vacation to keep her appointment for the taping with CBS correspondent Marya McLaughlin.

Marya is a knowledgeable, tough interviewer; she also is a charming, friendly, warm person. Martha immediately felt comfortable with her, so much so she sat in front of the cameras with Marya and had an animated girl-to-girl chat in which she gossiped away as freely as she would have with a friendly next-door neighbor.

Among other things, Martha revealed that her husband had looked out of a Justice Department window at the antiwar demonstration and said "it looked like the Russian Revolution going on."

She also said, "I don't think the average American realizes how desperate it is when a group of demonstrators, not peaceful demonstrators but the very liberal Communists, move into Washington. This place could become a complete fortress," she added. "You could have every building in Washington burned down. It could be a great, great catastrophe. And this is the thing I worried about way before I came to Washington, knowing the liberal element in this country is so, so against us. As my husband has said many times, some of the liberals in this country, he'd like to take them and change them for the Russian Communists."

As soon as Herb Klein finished listening to a rerun of the CBS tape, he telephoned John Mitchell at the Justice Department. Martha's remarks, Herb said, "put a bad aspect as to how we were handling the demonstrators." Mitchell, who hadn't seen the broadcast, agreed. He suggested that Herb Klein talk directly to Martha about it. Herb wasn't surprised at Mitchell's suggestion: "On almost all occasions he would not want to deal with Martha on anything that would be a problem of a public-relations nature, and he would suggest that I talk to her about it directly."

When Herb called Martha, he told her she had to consider what the impression was, that "she was the wife of a Cabinet officer." (He says he thought Martha was doing some harm, that there was a tendency of McCarthyism in some of the statements she made, "in particular when she would say her husband also thought that.")

Herb and Martha had what he believed to be a "very rational discussion about it, and she agreed that she would check with me on other occasions." Martha saw it another way; in her opinion Herb was unusually stern with her, and it upset her when he said she wasn't to talk to anyone in the press again without his permission.

Martha's cousin from Pine Bluff, Ray West, who was at the apartment with Martha when John Mitchell came home, says Martha was apprehensive about how John was going to take it. "Not that she said she was worried, but I had that feeling. But when he came in—the FBI was with him—he went over to her and said 'my little baby' or something like that, and put his arms around her . . . She was very relieved when he made light of it, when she realized she hadn't made him as mad as she thought she might have."

Martha awakened the next morning to the sound of her own voice on radio. John Mitchell always slept with a radio earplug in his ear; he told Martha the constant chatter helped him sleep. That morning, when he heard the partial replay of Martha's interview, he rolled over, held the speaker plug to her ear and laughed uproariously.

As the days went on, Martha would recall later, "Holy hell broke loose." Her remarks were discussed on radio and television, people wrote letters to the editor. Some Republicans disclaimed her. And more horrible, John seemed to side against her. He told the press he'd be happy to change her expression "liberals" for "violence-prone militant radicals."

Martha was devastated. For days she wouldn't go out to face people. One evening she sent John off without her to a State Department dinner she'd been anxious to attend. She asked Ray West to go in her place, saying, "If the press cornered me and started needling me, I might blow up and say something I shouldn't."

Jay, who was attending the Virginia Military Institute, received a call from his mother, saying she needed him. "Mom was very upset," Jay recalls, "because she thought they had tricked her [in the CBS interview], that it was supposed to be about cooking and they had asked hard questions."

This was the first time Martha had spoken with her son for almost a year. After Jay went to live with his father at the end of his junior year at Peekskill, he and Martha were estranged for some time, apparently because Martha thought Jay was taking his father's "side." They had a short reconciliation, though, which ended in late 1968, when, as Jay tells it, he and his mother had a "falling out" during one of his visits to Rye.

Although Jay won't pinpoint the time of the falling out, a friend suggests it probably took place the day a newsmagazine photographer came to Rye to take a picture of Richard Nixon's Attorney General-designate and his family. Jay didn't know a picture was to be taken, so he suspected nothing when John Mitchell sent him on several errands—enough to keep him away for about two hours. When Jay returned to the house, Marty ran to tell him the exciting news: a man from a magazine had taken a picture of her with Mommie and Daddy.

But now, in answer to her cry for help, Jay went to see his mother in Washington. She was cheered by his visit, as she was cheered by something else that happened at the same time.

John Mitchell discussed Martha's depression with Richard Nixon, who sent her a handwritten letter on his pale-green presidential stationery:

Dear Martha,

Don't let the critics get you down—Just remember they are not after you —or John—but me—I appreciate deeply the loyalty and courage you and John have consistently demonstrated.

We'll come out on top in the end.

RN

"That letter is what gave me the courage to go on," Martha told me a few months later.

Soon after receiving the letter, Martha went off to Florida for another investment bankers' conference. There she was with old friends, and the "mess" she'd created in Washington seemed far away. Though he let her talk freely with old friends, it was reported that John Mitchell kept his wife away from the press, that in fact he didn't let her show up at any event where reporters were present.

John was one of the conference's speakers, as he'd often been in the past. He got his biggest laugh when he said it wasn't true that he'd forbidden Martha to give any more interviews. "We have a full understanding in the family," he said. "She can go on television any time at all; she can say anything to the newspapers. There's just one limitation that I've placed on her; she is to do it in Swahili."

WHILE STILL IN FLORIDA, MARTHA LEARNED THAT A REPERCUSSION OF HER CBS appearance was the revelation to the press that several weeks earlier she had lobbied for Senate confirmation of a judge Richard Nixon had nominated for a Supreme Court appointment.

This came about in mid-August, after Richard Nixon had nominated Judge Clement Haynsworth, Jr., a fourth-generation South Carolinian, for the Supreme Court seat vacated by Justice Abe Fortas. (Fortas resigned after it was revealed he had accepted a $20,000 fee from a foundation controlled by the family of a man under investigation by the Securities and Exchange Commission.)

The nomination, as expected, didn't sit well with liberals and civil rights activists who thought the Judge had a go-slow attitude on integration, or with labor leaders who didn't like what they felt was an anti-labor stand. But unexpected was the charge that the Judge had not disqualified himself from a trial involving a union and a firm that did business with a company in which Haynsworth had an interest. After that disclosure the American Bar Association, which originally supported the nomination, decided it would take another look at his qualifications. By this time several Republican senators had joined the Democrats in refusing to vote for Haynsworth's confirmation.

The hearings continued through September and October and into November. Richard Nixon refused to withdraw the nomination; he was said to be convinced that "they" (liberals and the "Eastern establishment press") would attack all his appointments to the Court. John Mitchell agreed with the President and was quite vocal at home about his feelings.

It was in this atmosphere that John turned to his wife one evening and suggested that since she was a Southerner and had influential friends in her home state she should get on the telephone and tell them to put pressure on Arkansas Senator J. William Fulbright to vote for Haynsworth's confirmation.

Martha was every bit as upset as John and Mr. President over the way the nomination was going. To her, the senators' criticism of Judge Haynsworth was nothing but a "deliberate slap" at the South. Martha had read the FBI files and other information on Judge Haynsworth; in her opinion he was an excellent choice. Also, she had gone with John to meet the Haynsworths at a judiciary meeting at the Homestead in Hot Springs, Virginia, where she had taken an immediate liking to the couple, especially "Miss Dorothy," the Judge's charming wife. As far as Martha could see, there was no logical reason for the Senate to be dragging its feet on the nomination.

After John's suggestion she didn't waste a minute before getting on the telephone to her Arkansas friends. The more people she talked with, the madder she got; she started making local calls to Senate wives and aides. This went on for several days.

At the time, none of her calls were reported to the press. But now, in December, Martha's penalty for calling attention to herself on CBS news was that the political wives, who traditionally stay away from public controversy, were talking.

Isabelle Shelton, of the Washington *Star,* interviewed several of them and reported that

- Martha had threatened some Senate wives and staffers that she would "go on national television and defeat" the senators in their own campaigns for re-election if they voted against the Judge.
- One outraged Senate wife described the language used by the Attorney General's wife as "vile and nasty." (As Martha's friends well knew,

when she was drinking and angry her language often was of the barnyard variety.)

- Senator Fulbright told friends his wife was "so mad" (after her call from Martha) that he was afraid Mrs. Fulbright "was going to have a heart attack."
- ". . . the wives, all politically knowledgeable, were particularly affronted by the amateurishness of Mrs. Mitchell's performance . . . When the Attorney General's wife threatened Mrs. Fulbright with a television campaign against her husband—who had just won re-election the previous November to a six-year-term—Betty Fulbright is said to have responded icily: 'You'll have to wait five years.' "

When the story about Martha's lobbying came out, a former Mitchell aide recalls that at first "everybody in the Justice Department thought the roof was going to fall in. Here was the wife of a Cabinet officer in a Republican Administration attacking the chairman of the Senate Foreign Relations Committee, a Democrat, that they had to do business with. But so many people wrote in saying 'terrific, Martha,' the White House realized that what had happened to Agnew was happening here."

Martha wasn't upset over the unfavorable publicity about her calling the Senate wives, as she'd been after the Moratorium uproar. This time she'd done only what John had asked her to do. Also, the President had followed up his letter with a phone call in which he told her to keep it up, she was doing fine. And an overwhelming number of letters and telegrams (99.9 percent in her favor, she said) was pouring in at the Justice Department. There were dozens of requests for speeches, too, and the press was after her for interviews. It was annoying, though, that John wouldn't let her return the press calls.

THE FIRST CHANCE THE PRESS HAD TO TALK TO MARTHA, FOLLOWING HER CBS appearance and the report on her lobbying Senate wives, came in mid-December when the Mitchells went to a dinner party at the George Town Club given by Robert Keith Gray, who had been secretary of the Cabinet in the Eisenhower Administration. Former First Lady Mamie Eisenhower was there, too, but none of the local papers mentioned that fact until several lines down in their stories. It was the Mitchells' evening as far as the press was concerned, although Secretary of Defense Melvin Laird and his wife were the honored guests.

The Washington *Star* reported that John Mitchell said, "Anything my wife does is fine with me," then proceeded to do all the talking.

Martha laughed a lot and told the Washington *Post,* "I always try to create a little fun wherever I go."

After the newspaper stories about the dinner appeared, there were even more requests for interviews. None was granted; the press was told that Mrs. Mitchell would not be available until after the holidays. A *Star* columnist had a chance to ask Martha if she'd been ordered to keep quiet and was told, "You are kidding! I will say anything I want to say. I happen to be a free citizen." The *Star* reported Martha thought "the only way to handle all the publicity and jokes at her expense is to laugh the whole thing off."

Privately Martha wasn't laughing. Again she was upset and confused because she was in the middle of another brouhaha over something she'd said, this time while discussing life in Washington with a *Time* magazine writer. Martha had called it a "comedown" from her life in Rye, New York. She claimed, "We'll be happy to go back and make some money." In an interview with the Los Angeles *Times,* John Mitchell defended her: "I really doubt that she ever said that. She's never had a particular interest in money because she's never had a lack of it. I think she's perfectly willing to accept life in Washington, but she did have to leave her home, her friends, her way of life in Rye."

But Martha *was* complaining about money, despite what John was telling the press. Privately she was heard to express her dissatisfaction with her husband's government salary compared with the income from his law firm. John Mitchell wasn't sympathetic. "You're the one who wanted to come to Washington," he said. "So don't tell me there's not enough money."

A few months later Martha publicly said, "After taxes, what is sixty thousand dollars [his government salary]? Only about thirty-five thousand that we can live on, which is nothing."

It wasn't just having less money and being criticized for the things she said that were making Martha unhappy. There were other reasons, too. Her Pine Bluff friend Julia McClain says Martha wrote her on January 14, 1970, about being in "this Washington imprisonment" where she no longer was allowed to be an individual. Martha expressed her concern about the country and said that John Mitchell had said to her only the night before that "We are fighting—fighting for the survival of this country—and if we don't succeed we may as well cash in our chips and get out."

Martha wrote about the "nasty, dirty, messy operation" of the government and wondered how the country had survived. She also said John had told her that he'd learned the week before about a civil rights group hiring detectives and writers to follow Martha in an effort to find out something about her that could be used to discredit her. She said she had been followed for months and didn't know it.

Eventually Martha decided that writers were not trying to do an article to discredit her. She thought John made up the story to keep her afraid of the press, as she'd been ever since Nixon's first warning. Had she been friendly with reporters she would have been uncontrollable, the way she was later. But now, completely believing John, she was frightened and talked only to interviewers approved by John or Herb Klein's White House office.

In an approved interview, with Betty Beale in the Washington *Star,* Martha said, "I was mortified that I had been thrust into the public eye so vividly . . . this is from the bottom of my heart—I have never been so embarrassed."

But she added, "I think if I had been a man who had made the comments I did, it would not have made the back page . . . Because wives are usually not outspoken. And because women are supposed to keep their mouths shut and not say anything and not think anything and not do anything except be a social butterfly.

"Women have not reached the age of maturity themselves. They have not reached the stage where women will take up for other women and until that day arrives we are going to be in the same situation as we are now."

In answer to a question, she said her comments didn't hurt the Nixon Administration or her husband "in the slightest. I think most people realize that I am politically naïve and what I am saying represents my own viewpoint."

As for the Communists, she said there were two kinds in the country, "Marxists who will take over America in a peaceful way, and the element who are trying to overthrow the government by force." Then, although she had said her statements represented her own viewpoint, Martha commented on her remarks about the Communists: "People don't realize when I say this I am not just speaking off the top of my head. I have basis for such a statement."

A FEW DAYS AFTER HER INTERVIEW WITH BETTY, DEMONSTRATORS marched on the Watergate apartment complex in protest of the conspiracy trial of the Chicago Seven. Hundreds of policemen, firing tear gas and making 145 arrests, kept most of the demonstrators away, but more than a hundred got within sight of Martha's apartment. She was terrified. Later she would tell the Washington *Star,* "What makes it so absurd is that they are tried for their activities outside the Democratic convention which had nothing to do with us."

Not long after the protest march to the Watergate, it was reported that the individual rights and responsibilities section of the American Bar Association had decided to investigate the Chicago Seven trial and Judge Julius Hoffman's contempt judgments. The ABA's contemplated action so incensed Richard Nixon that he had Bob Haldeman notify his Attorney General: "The President wants you to know that he will resign publicly from the American Bar Association if they decide to go after Judge Hoffman as was indicated as a possibility in the news today."

Sometimes the lengths to which the Attorney General went to control Martha's exposure to the media were amazing and amusing to some of the members. Marlene Cimmons of the Los Angeles *Times* was surprised one day when a Justice Department spokesman told her, "I'm sorry. I can't get you in to see Mrs. Mitchell. How about the Attorney General instead?" Marlene said "fine" and the busy Attorney General took time out to talk at length with her about his wife.

Curious as to why Martha wasn't doing her own talking, Marlene asked the Attorney General about it. He explained, "Right now she has so many problems, she just wants a little time to reassess the situation . . ." He insisted, "She hasn't stopped talking to reporters. She talks to them when she sees them at social events." Then he indicated he had some reservations about Martha's calls to the Senate wives. But he didn't reveal he was the one who first suggested that Martha make calls for the Haynsworth confirmation.

Neither did he ever admit that he put Martha up to almost all of her early outbursts. Instead, he always managed to create the impression that he was an unfortunate but compassionate man saddled with a slightly flaky wife whom he adored too much to suppress. Martha didn't see it that way. She claimed that it was at John's request that she made most of the calls that turned out to be controversial.

Former Nixon White House aide Clark Mollenhoff confirms that Martha was not the "unguided missile" her husband wanted people to believe. When he wrote a memo to Bob Haldeman saying, "All the things you are trying to do around here . . . are going to come undone unless Martha Mitchell holds her tongue," Bob Haldeman replied, "She's the best thing we've got going for us to keep the conservatives pacified." As Clark explains it: Martha first came to the attention of the general public during a period when the White House was "getting criticism on things that Kissinger was doing, and on some of Moynihan's activities [which had] little flutters over to the Left that also were designed for political purposes. So Haldeman and Ehrlichman felt—and Nixon and Mitchell agreed—that Martha's comments represented a balancing factor on the Right, but one with which they would not be held necessarily accountable. They felt because she was a woman she would not be subjected to the kind of attacks that Mitchell would if he were making such comments as Attorney General.

"So they used her for a long time, even in the campaign in 1972, until the Watergate scandal broke. Then they wanted no part of this woman who said what she thought and had it come through as the truth."

"A lot of her antics—if that's what you call them—were programed, absolutely," says Junie Dankworth, a member of Martha's staff at CREEP. "Martha told me a lot of the time she was told what to do and she did it.

"And I asked her one time about those dumb telephone calls. I said, 'Martha, why do you call people at that hour?' Do you know what she said? She said, 'John Mitchell says that's the time when you get their attention.' "

Still, Herb Klein insists, "They used her as they would any other prominent figure as a campaigner."

But few campaigners are treated as a prize product and packaged and presented to the public the way Martha was. Even her code name had Madison Avenue connotations. It was "The Account," an advertising term for client or customer.

While Bob Haldeman, a former account executive for J. Walter Thompson advertising agency, apparently was the first to recognize Martha's potential as an unofficial spokesman for the Administration, the decision to use her in this capacity seems to have had the approval of Richard Nixon, John Ehrlichman and John Mitchell.

The question is, Why would John Mitchell join in this scheme to exploit his wife? It is especially puzzling in light of remarks he made to Ray West shortly after Martha made her statements on the *CBS Morning News.* At that time John said he had to "protect" Martha, since all of the adulation and attention might "hurt" her. He was particularly concerned about the press and said he was afraid Martha might not know how to handle it. His feeling then, according to Ray, was that Martha had gotten in over her head and it was up to him to take care of her.

John Mitchell knew his wife was totally unprepared for the rough and tumble life of a controversial Washington celebrity. He was aware of her feelings of insecurity and that she was high-strung and had a drinking problem. It was obvious she was a poor risk for overexposure to the limelight. (After his wife's death, John Mitchell told someone the tragedy of Martha was that she "just couldn't handle Washington.") Yet he went along with the full-scale "selling" of Martha, which started in April 1970.

Again, why? Herb Klein says, "I think he thought she was enjoying it . . . And it made up for the fact that he was gone long hours and frequently days. So it made things more peaceful for him."

Martha was surprised one evening when John told her she'd been right, her mail should be answered and not thrown in the wastebasket, as he'd first told her. And the press calls ought to be returned. He suggested she should have a press secretary. Herb Klein might know of someone, John said. Martha hurried to call the White House communications office before John could change his mind.

Herb knew that two of his press friends, Bill and Kay Woestendieck, recently had arrived in Washington, where Bill had become the first editor of *Newsroom,* a new program on public-television station WETA. Kay, an excellent newspaperwoman and former women's editor of the Houston *Post,* though still getting settled in a new house, was available for a job.

When Herb talked to her about being Martha Mitchell's press secretary, Kay said she wanted to think it over. One night, several weeks later, Herb took her to see Martha. A slender, soft-voiced blonde, Kay was intelligent and articulate and had a marvelous sense of humor; Martha took to her right away. Kay liked Martha, too. She found her outgoing, sharp and spunky. And she wasn't intimidated by her, as many of Martha's future secretaries would be. Or as Herb Klein puts it: "Kay was able to speak up if she thought Martha was going off on a screwball idea."

It was agreed that Kay would go to the Justice Department the next morning to look over Martha's correspondence files and to check the requests for press interviews.

The night Martha and Kay met was Wednesday, April 8. That day Nixon-nominee Judge G. Harrold Carswell—like Judge Haynsworth before him—had been rejected by the Senate to fill the still-vacant Supreme Court seat. And that night, two hours after midnight, Martha would make her famous telephone call to the Arkansas *Gazette*, demanding that it crucify Senator William Fulbright.

Judge Carswell was a strict constructionist Southerner. He had been recommended for the nomination by John Mitchell, who first heard of him when Warren Burger, shortly before his appointment as Chief Justice of the Supreme Court, suggested Carswell to the Attorney General as one of three judges "who might warrant consideration for appointment or promotion on their professional qualities." Burger noted that "Carswell was the youngest U.S. Attorney appointed in the Eisenhower Administration and one of the very able ones."

John sat up night after night going through Judge Carswell's records; he didn't want a surprise like the one that developed into a conflict-of-interest charge against Judge Haynsworth.

"My God! This man is too good to be true. He has the most perfect record!" Martha remembered John saying to her one night as he passed the Carswell FBI files to her. She read them and also was excited over the idea of having him represent the South on the Supreme Court.

But Judge Carswell soon was in more trouble than Clement Haynsworth had been. He was opposed by colleagues on the Fifth Circuit U.S. Court, and there were disclosures about his alleged past prejudice toward blacks. Finally, he too was rejected.

A few months later, when a reporter asked Martha that if John had checked the Judge's records so carefully how could he have missed the white supremacy speech Carswell had made several years earlier, she answered, "How many people in the Senate and the Congress would not have held the same viewpoint in those years?" She added that she, too, might have felt the same way then: "But hasn't everything changed in the last ten and twenty-two years? Are you going to be prejudiced against me because my grandparents had slaves?"

Richard Nixon was outraged that his second nominee had been turned down. He asked John Mitchell to join him on the *Sequoia.* And together they cruised down the Potomac, plotting how to strike back. When John arrived back home he was still smoldering over the rejection of Judge Carswell. He told Martha that Mr. President wasn't going to let them get by with this.

(The next afternoon Richard Nixon accused the Senate of "vicious assaults" on the intelligence, honesty and character of Judges Haynsworth and Carswell. He said he would not nominate another Southerner and "let him be subjected to the kind of malicious character assassination accorded" the two Dixie jurists.)

That night after John retired, Martha called the Arkansas *Gazette.* The call was not made on the spur of the moment; she had planned to telephone the paper back in November, if Senator Fulbright had voted against the Haynsworth nomination. Since he didn't she waited to see what he'd do the next time around. Now she knew. Fulbright had voted against Carswell.

Martha picked up the telephone—and called the wrong Arkansas newspaper. As Herb Klein tells it: Martha wanted to call the more conservative Little Rock paper, the one that had supported Richard Nixon. But because the paper's name was Arkansas *Democrat,* which Martha thought described its politics, she called the Arkansas *Gazette,* a paper Herb describes as "very ardent, liberal Democratic."

Martha told the *Gazette* she wanted a letter to the editor printed in the paper. Then she gave her name. "Instead of taking my letter," she complained, "they got all excited. They even *taped* the call, which John said was against the law. So the Justice Department went all-out to keep them from printing exactly what I had to say."

According to John Woodruff, the reporter who took Martha's call and wrote three stories about it, the telephone rang in the newsroom about 1:03 A.M., Arkansas time: "It was about three minutes after deadline so one of the editors yelled jokingly, 'Don't answer it!' But I picked up the phone." At first he didn't believe it was Martha Mitchell, but just in case it was, he borrowed a tape recorder and plugged it in "for protection and to be sure that I got her quotes correctly."

The conversation lasted over an hour (at one point they were disconnected but Martha called back), with Martha occasionally laughing, sometime sobbing. Shortly after two o'clock (three in Washington) John Woodruff told Martha, "Mrs. Mitchell, we are not going to get anything in if I don't hang up and get working on it."

Earlier he'd told her he would have to call back to verify that she indeed was Mrs. Mitchell. Martha gave him a telephone number. But when he called the number, a White House operator answered and refused to connect him with the Mitchell apartment. A few minutes later Martha called back and asked, "What happened to you?"

The reporter explained that it was impossible for him to verify the story, therefore it couldn't be used. With that Martha gave yet another number—after first making him swear he would never use it again or give it to anyone else. It, too, was a White House number, but this time the call was put through.

Martha said John heard the phone ring and that's when he found out she had called the *Gazette.* But her husband told a reporter he first heard about the call on the radio that morning: "I just laughed and laughed and laughed. She got mad at me."

At first Martha denied she had called the *Gazette,* claiming it was the other way around, that the paper had called her. "We had the tape," John Woodruff says, "and on it she clearly stated, 'The reason I called you was to get a letter to the editor.' When people called up saying 'but she says *you* called her,' we told them we had it on tape."

After the wire services put out the story about the tape, a former aide to Mitchell says, "The Attorney General, needless to say, was upset. He was *upset*!" John Mitchell told the aide to get in touch with the *Gazette*. "We did not have the ability to stop the thing," the aide says, "so the best thing was to keep it low key and not wave any big sticks. It was their tape and they could dump it if they wanted to."

There was a lot of talk, in more than one call, about how concerned Mrs. Mitchell was about the tape and how embarrassed she would be if it were used. Both parties agreed they didn't want that to happen.

John Woodruff admits, "I was really terrified about having this tape . . . A couple of days after she called, and after [she had admitted she *had* called], I turned it on in my apartment, alone, and played the whole thing and kind of chuckled here and there. Then I erased it."

In Woodruff's story Martha was quoted as having said, among other things, that Senator Fulbright's vote against Judge Carswell "makes me so damn mad I can't stand it. He [Fulbright] could have done a great deal for the whole state . . . I want you to crucify Fulbright and that's it." Telephones started ringing—at the Justice Department, the White House and the Watergate-complex switchboard. In an apparent effort to justify why she was qualified to be a spokesman for Arkansas, Martha told a reporter that her family "started the state of Arkansas, practically . . . when my grandmother and grandfather went to Arkansas they thought the Indians were going to kill them before they arrived. . . ."

When Senator Fulbright was told of the call to the *Gazette* he said, "Mrs. Mitchell has become a kind of character around here." He mentioned that Martha had been living outside the state of Arkansas for twenty to thirty years and was more of a New Yorker than an Arkansan. Mrs. Fulbright observed, "She's quite an unstable one, isn't she, calling a newspaper long distance at two or three in the morning?" Martha's answer to Mrs. Fulbright was ". . . whose business is it, anyway, when I called? The paper was open all night!"

John Mitchell said, "I love her, that's all I have to say." Later he would tell Nan Robertson of the New York *Times*, "What else can I do, but let her speak? She has no inclination to be quiet. She's not politically motivated, she's just saying what she feels."

By now Kay Woestendieck was handling the press calls. A story went out that Attorney General John Mitchell had hurriedly hired a press secretary for his outspoken wife "as an aftermath of her latest verbal foray into public print."

Within two days there were 115 requests for interviews. Soon the volume of mail increased to four hundred pieces a day, "fifteen-to-one" in Martha's favor, Kay said. One of the first telegrams was from Mrs. Harrold Carswell: "You are one hell of a gal and we love you . . . Virginia."

A month later a clipping service delivered thousands of items (an average of 175 per day) mentioning Martha's name. She was offered a movie contract, her own TV show and a by-line on a syndicated column. She was made the butt of jokes, with both comedians and politicians delivering the lines.

Among the best was one delivered by Liz Carpenter before a luncheon group: "I tried to be a member of the Silent Majority but I felt like Martha Mitchell with a mouthful of Novocain."

MARTHA AND KAY SET UP AN OFFICE IN THE MITCHELLS' TURQUOISE-BLUE breakfast room, with its Formica table and fish tank and potted plants, and tackled the cartons of mail while trying to answer the five constantly ringing telephones. When Kay was busy at something else, Martha cheerfully answered Kay's phone, taking messages as "Mrs. Woestendieck's secretary."

After the two talked over the press requests, Kay would call Herb Klein. He says, "Kay filled me in . . . and we would talk over some of the areas that they were working on."

Sometimes Martha herself called Herb with an idea he felt "would not be good from a public point of view." Then he'd talk to Mitchell about it. But Herb says, "I never could get John to face up to her on any of these things . . . he always preferred that I do it."

Kay scheduled Martha for her first interview on April 13; by the 29th she'd talked at length with fourteen writers. (Perhaps it's coincidental, but only two months before Martha was launched on her media blitz, Bob Haldeman sent a memo to Jeb Magruder—then an assistant to Herb Klein—telling him to find ways of mobilizing the nation's Silent Majority; he suggested pounding the magazines and the networks in counteraction "against negative Administration coverage." He added: "Concentrate this on the few places that count, which would be NBC, *Time, Newsweek* and *Life,* the New York *Times* and the Washington *Post.* Don't waste your fire on other things." Before the year was out, Martha had an interview in every publication Haldeman mentioned.)

Martha had something quotable for each of her interviewers. First off, she said she didn't believe in that "no-comment business," claiming everyone in public life had a responsibility to the American public and shouldn't say "no comment" unless he or she had no opinions.

Martha had opinions on everything. In her distinctly Southern drawl, with her brown eyes either flashing in anger or twinkling and full of mischief, Martha took out after educators, politicians, radicals, fashion designers and hairdressers (they voted her the "worst-tressed" woman in America). No one was spared. She even complained about a heating plant polluting the air outside her Watergate apartment; never mind that it was supplying heat to the White House and her husband's office at the Justice Department. She called for wage, price and rent controls when the Administration was dead set against them. She lobbied for a woman on the Supreme Court. And she declared that "the Vietnam war stinks!"—at a time when the President was desperately trying to justify it.

She said if it were in her power she'd eliminate politicians: "I don't think they are representative of themselves or of the people. What irks me, what I abhor, is the cloakroom bit. Here they are, elected from a district and they trade off this for that. It's not in the interest of the people they are representing. It seems to me that once these elected officials are in the political arena they immediately latch onto the idea that they are presidential material and they look for national attention. Few people can stand prosperity.

"Anytime you get somebody marching in the streets," she said, "it's catering to revolution . . . My family worked for everything we had . . . now these jerks come along and try to give it to the Communists."

Discussing integration, she claimed, "I've never said I was against desegregation. It should have started right after the Civil War. But when they're desegregating I don't see why they should single out the South. The South has been imposed on long enough. It's the orphan of the nation. I think even states should have equal rights. That's my personal Southern strategy and the only Southern strategy there is."

After the Supreme Court had rejected the arguments of the Justice Department against desegregation by busing, Martha told the Washington *Star*, "The Supreme Court should be abolished. We should extinguish the Supreme Court. We have no youth on the Court, no Southerners, no women—just nine old men. I have never been so furious. Nine old men should not overturn the tradition of America."

She clarified the meaning of the word "crucify" by telling reporters:

"It's a little Southern word . . . Crucify is just an idiomatic saying—like someone saying, 'Oh, I could *kill* you.' "

Universities should solve their own problems, Martha said, "instead of casting them on the public and on law-enforcement officials . . . those who dissent are a small minority and the faculty and Board of Regents could handle them."

At the time the Administration thought the media was encouraging the Viet Cong to drag its feet at the peace table, Martha took to the phone and told a reporter the press's "indiscreet judgment . . . may result in complete suppression of the press, in which event it has caused its own death."

She had a lot to say about the press—often in the middle of an interview. She claimed, "The thing that's made the greatest impact on me is the realization that the media has such powers. It can make or break someone in a matter of hours, just as it can build a person up. It's frightening and it terrifies me." A reporter was told, "Being interviewed is like having a physical examination, only mentally."

Interviewers who let their own animosity come through in their stories irritated and confused her: "Reporters come here to interview me, knowing in advance the type of stories they are going to write. I can tell by the questions they ask, the way they immediately try to put me on the defensive." She once left a two-and-a-half-hour interview pale and shaken, declaring she'd been "plucked to the soul."

Her frank and forthright statements, often delivered over the telephone late at night, made her the most talked about, written about, adored or hated, praised or maligned, admired or ridiculed Cabinet wife in the history of the United States.

She also became the only Cabinet wife ever voted one of the ten most-admired women in the world, and the only one to have the Gallup Poll discover that her name was recognized by 76 percent of the American people. "No woman in public life has achieved so quickly the national awareness of Martha Mitchell," solemnly reported the American Institute of Public Opinion.

Thousands of admirers saw her as something of a national heroine. Her critics thought her a scatterbrain, overstimulated and loud-mouthed. Those who didn't know what to think were just grateful to find a live-wire *enfant terrible* in such a dull Administration.

An outspoken Cabinet wife was amazing enough, but a free-speaking *conservative* Cabinet wife was unprecedented. Traditionally, political wives have kept quiet and let their husbands do the talking on any subject more issue-oriented than food or fashion. But here was Martha Mitchell, wife of a Republican Attorney General, refusing to fit in the mold. Neither would she be intimidated by those who thought she should. "I've never analyzed what a Cabinet wife is, so I have continued to be Martha and I shall continue to be Martha," she declared.

The blond, gregarious and impulsive Martha loved her public role and admitted, with an impish grin, that she liked to stir things up and to do devilish things. Although she claimed she was genuinely puzzled by all the fuss over "little ol' me."

Martha even tried to make light of her dour, pipe-smoking husband, claiming he was cute and soft and cuddly. (When he heard this description of the Attorney General, a Mitchell friend said, "I always knew you were soft, John, but I didn't know you were cuddly.") The tense, publicly proper President wasn't left out either. Martha told a national television audience that she found Richard Nixon "sexy." On NBC's *Not For Women Only,* Martha burbled, "I think President Nixon is probably one of the sexiest men in the country. He is cute. He is adorable. He has a great sense of humor and he is just—well, he is my man. . . ." The President said he found her spunky and then urged her to "give 'em hell!"

When cartoonists made her a favorite and frequent subject, Martha laughed at their caricaturing as heartily as anyone else and made every effort to get the originals for her collection. She claimed she didn't mind if the country laughed at her expense: "It's fun taking a serious problem and trying to make it light, to inject a little bit of comedy into our trials and tribulations. I just hope it [the humor] pulls the country together so we can go forward." Besides, she pointed out, the things she did caused excitement and awakened people: "The country needs awakening."

Middle America loved her. The Silent Majority embraced her as its own. Martha had struck a cord with all these people by saying in public the same things she and John had been saying for years, in the den before dinner over those glasses of Scotch. Liberal permissiveness—in the courts, the schools, the Congress, and especially in the press—was selling the United States down the drain to Communists. Every time she took off after justices, educators, senators and representatives, reporters and newscasters, her mail increased a hundredfold.

Nobody was more surprised than members of the Nixon Administration. Former Nixon speech writer Pat Buchanan says, "Frankly it was a mild startlement among us in the White House and elsewhere when she suddenly became a folk hero and became number eight, or whatever it was, on the list of most-admired women in the world. There was general amazement and astonishment that this was happening."

Particularly amazing was the reaction of students and other young people to Martha. They thought she was great. Pat Buchanan thinks they liked her because "she was candid and she would cut loose with her views without regard to what people thought of them. That has great appeal to kids, whether they agree with her or not."

It was put another way by a weeping college freshman attending Martha's funeral. When asked why she was distraught over the death of a woman who spoke out so forcefully against students' dress, sex code and drug use—among other things—the Sweet Briar student Piper Dankworth answered, "Because she was honest; she let it all hang out."

Chapter Eight

MARTHA'S STRAIGHTFORWARD, OUTSPOKEN APPROACH TO POlitical life was not appreciated by all Republicans. One woman announced, "I'm just embarrassed out of my socks that she's in my party!" And there were others so irritated at the amount of coverage Martha was receiving they looked for ulterior motives on the part of the press. One high-placed official's wife told a friend she thought all the fuss over Martha was a deliberate anti-establishment plot by the press to make the Nixon Administration look foolish.

The reason was more simple. The press wrote about Martha because she couldn't be ignored. She was good copy—some thought the *only* copy. Martha was forthright. She had spunk. And most reporters agreed with a little old lady who, after standing in a line for hours to meet Martha, declared, "She is the only one in the lot who's got any gumption!"

A Southern belle, albeit fading, Martha's manner of dress was as colorful as her speech and now received as much press coverage as her statements. Reported in detail were her spectacular hairdos—accomplished with the aid of hair pieces, sometimes two at a time; her vintage high-heeled, open-toed, sling-back pumps; and dangling earrings and bangle bracelets. Recorded, too, was her taste in clothes, which ran to ruffles and bows and full-skirted gowns, one which she herself dubbed "Mah 'Gone-with-the-Wind' Dress."

Martha's flamboyant clothes were not accidental or "poor taste" choices, as some people thought. They were deliberate attention-getters. Her friend Pat Mosbacher, wife of former Chief of Protocol Emil Mosbacher, recalls with amusement the time Martha told her she bought her clothes at a discount house in New York: "Martha laughed and said nobody else would wear the things she wore, so the racks always were full of the things she liked."

As much as Martha liked to dress up, she didn't let high fashion get in her way. For instance, she said of her shoes, "They may be dated but men love them." And when the midi was *de rigueur,* she bought one, wore it around the apartment (John asked if it were a new nightgown), decided it made her look "frumpy and dumpy," and discarded it. Her skirt lengths stayed just at the knee. Another time, Martha bought a see-through blouse but kept it hidden away. No one would have known a thing about it if Martha hadn't mentioned she had one after Senator Edward Kennedy's wife Joan—who, like Martha, knew a headline when she saw one—wore a see-through blouse (revealing a dainty blue brassiere), wet-look skirt and black boots to a White House luncheon.

Martha was one of Joan Kennedy's ardent admirers, and nothing pleased her more than having someone tell her "you look like Joan." There was a resemblance, although Martha was older, by eighteen years, and rounder. Martha read all the articles and books written about Joan and often pointed out that the two shared the same birthday and that both were blondes and played the piano. She never mentioned that they also had identity problems and both had been treated in expensive institutions for their drinking habits.

JUST AS THERE WERE REPUBLICANS IRRITATED AT THE AMOUNT OF COVERAGE Martha received, there were others disturbed by the reporting they thought was slanted—in Martha's favor. For instance, William Safire in his book, *Before the Fall,* claims the press "in a kindness rarely extended celebrities, protected her . . ." He adds, "Martha got away with murder, if there were any press 'conspiracy,' it was in the way the press corps gentled Martha along . . ."

Bill Safire's premise isn't borne out by the articles written about her at the time. They show that the media before Watergate was often rough with Martha, that it reported her as she was, warts and all:

- A news magazine pointed out that a Washington socialite had said Martha was "grotesque. She is not attractive physically, socially, intellectually. If she weren't the Attorney General's wife, she wouldn't get the time of day."
- Reporters disclosed that Martha had called her childhood nurse, then living in Arkansas, her "colored mammy." (When her interviewer looked surprised she added, "I can't get over saying 'colored.' I said it all my life. All the Negroes seem to resent it and I don't know why.") And after Martha left a social event with the Jewish wife of an important Jewish Republican and naïvely asked, "Aren't you glad to get away from all those Jews?" it was reported nationally. *Women's Wear Daily* printed Martha's rebuttal: "There was no witness at all and I don't see how they could print anything that is so unfounded."
- Her taste in food, fashion and furnishings was criticized constantly. Reporter/author Myra MacPherson wrote: "She walks tilted slightly forward because of the shoes—high, pencil-thin spikes, 'pearlized' leather, open-toes, sling-backed . . . her legs are still slim, but two recent diets have failed to conquer waistline bulges . . . [she is a] fifty-one-year-old former small-town Arkansas girl . . . dressed in a blue-and-white checked two-piece dress with white loop trim around the sleeves, sparkly buttons down the front, elephant earrings, a very blond fall halfway to her shoulder blades, a white bow, an elephant pin, a gold bracelet, pinkish-purple nail polish and lipstick to match."

That's hardly gentle treatment or letting Martha get "away with murder."

Although Safire felt then, and claims he does now, that Martha was treated with kindness, some of her friends thought the press manipulated and used Martha while she was in Washington.

"The press didn't use me," Martha vehemently denied. "The only one who used me was the Nixon Administration."

She insisted, "*I* used the press!" Evidently Kay Woestendieck agrees; she told a columnist in July 1972 that Martha was "very shrewd and intelligent. She learned fast how to use the press."

The fact is, Martha and the press used each other; at the time it worked out very well. But it wasn't in Martha's nature to admit she'd been *had* by a bunch of women reporters. Just as it wasn't the disposition of some of the reporters to concede they'd been used by a politically naïve newcomer to the Washington scene, particularly one many considered a loud-mouthed, slightly wacky blonde from Arkansas.

Not long after Martha accidentally made headlines for her appearance on the *CBS Morning News,* she called one of her phone pals, Hal Gould, a Washington man-about-town and author of the column "Hal's Hunches." "I've learned how people get their names in the society columns," Martha enthusiastically reported. "They give the reporters a quote. From now on, darlin', I'm going to quote 'em to death."

From then on Martha got off enough quotable remarks to guarantee her name being mentioned more than any other Administration wife's. And as one newspaper put it, she was "able to say the most outrageous things and be forgiven on grounds of invincible naïveté. [Her remarks] were as tough as Agnewisms, but a lot more entertaining."

"She always would run over to you at a party and say something outrageous, something that was too flashy to ignore," says Washington *Post* columnist Judith Martin. Judy tells of the time she was sent to cover Martha's appearance at a church bazaar: "When I arrived Martha was just very quietly talking to people. I stayed over at the side and watched her. Any number of people asked me, 'Don't you want to talk to her . . . shouldn't we tell her you are here?' I said, 'No' and kept out of sight." Martha never knew a member of the press was there, and according to Judy, "She didn't go into her act, which she would have if she had seen me. She was very clever in knowing how to manipulate this [getting attention] and we played right in her hands."

I'D NEVER SEEN MARTHA MITCHELL BEFORE THE DAY I WENT TO THE Watergate apartment to outline for the Attorney General's wife what was involved in an "in-depth" *Look* interview—the first such media exposure for her. While researching her, though, I'd discovered we'd attended some of the same White House parties. How could I have missed this vivacious, talkative woman? This puzzled me for several months, until just before she left Washington when Martha told me about her early fear of the press and how it came about.

(Other reporters would ask themselves the same question after Martha's first outbursts about liberal Communists and such. Her performance sent many writers scurrying to newspaper libraries and to their own files. Elizabeth Shelton, of the Washington *Post,* says, "Although Martha Mitchell was at several things I covered, there was nothing in my notes about her. And the only thing I could remember was that she was a blonde.")

My get-acquainted session with Martha went along fine; as she said, we were *simpatico.* We were of the same generation, I was born in a

Southern town even smaller than Pine Bluff, our roots were similar in many ways. And to top it off, I'd named my only child Martha Elizabeth.

The *Look* interview was spread over a five-week period, in seventeen sessions (some beginning before breakfast and ending after an embassy dinner), and included innumerable telephone conversations. It was the first of many articles I would write about Martha.

When Black Star photographer Fred Ward went over to discuss his assignment for the *Look* article, things were even more congenial than they'd been the day I met her. Fred is handsome, charming and a native Alabaman. Martha thought he was great; for the next five weeks she played her Southern-belle role to the hilt and flirted with him outrageously.

Fred recalls, "I think in many ways she used the press. The day she decided to pop in on John Mitchell in his office, for instance. There was no reason whatsoever for doing that, other than she knew it would be something good for us, for our story."

The visit to the Attorney General's office took place one day after we'd gone to a luncheon with Martha at the National Arboretum. That was the day she got the idea that Cabinet people should have elegant government housing in a protected compound. Martha thought the Arboretum grounds would be a nice place for such an enclosure: "They have so many acres, they could spare some." When her suggestion appeared in the *Look* article, she was deluged with unfavorable mail from infuriated taxpayers and tree lovers.

After the luncheon we visited an antique shop and had started back to Martha's apartment—in her government car with the driver and an FBI agent—when suddenly she told the driver to change course, saying, "We're going to drop in and surprise John." As much as Fred and I wanted the story and picture of a wife popping in on a Cabinet member, unannounced and accompanied by a reporter and a photographer, we both protested.

She insisted and in we walked. Secretaries in the outer office wanted to alert him, but Martha stopped them. The Attorney General was at his desk being interviewed by a man from the New York *Post,* who looked more surprised by the interruption than the Attorney General did. We were introduced and had exchanged a few pleasantries when Martha turned to Fred and asked, "Did you get a good picture?" He said he did, and out we went.

When I asked, "Won't he be furious with you?" she smiled and answered, "Of course not. These things I do are the only fun that poor man has." A good friend of John Mitchell's saw it a different way. He says, "We always thought she did these [unexpected and startling] things to get even with him." Even for what, he was asked? He didn't explain.

The same day we went to see John Mitchell she took us on a tour of the Attorney General's offices, including a private dining room and kitchen, to show us her redecorating project. This was before it was publicly known that Martha was spending over $50,000 of the taxpayer's money for the remodeling job. The cost didn't include furnishings or the expensive china, crystal, silver and Greenwald linens. Then we went outside, with an entourage of unhappy Justice Department people in tow, so she could show them how she wanted the trees and shrubs trimmed or replanted.

One morning later that year, columnist Myra MacPherson reported that Martha had had government painters working a four-to-midnight shift the night before, repainting corridors leading to the Attorney General's office, in order to have the area freshened up in time for the President's visit that day to sign an anticrime bill. About a week later, Jack Anderson reported that Martha had not only spent over $50,000 refurbishing the Attorney General's office but had put out another $50,000 to spruce up the greenery outside.

Martha denied everything. She said that she had saved the government money by taking an appropriation that "was there to spend" and finding ways to "stretch the dollar." The General Services Administration, the agency responsible for doing the redecorating, was instructed to back her up in the denial.

Now that John Mitchell is no longer a threat and GSA feels more free to speak, a man familiar with the situation declares, "Mrs. Mitchell did *not* save money; she just went crazy at that building." According to this man, who asks to remain anonymous, the corridors were repainted and light fixtures refurbished in time for the President's visit, at a cost of $24,000, because "she was pushing it."

John Mitchell seemed to approve everything she was doing; as far as it is known, he made no effort to stop her. Perhaps he felt the expenditures were so insignificant they didn't matter when compared to the monies being spent by Richard Nixon on his private properties.

(Martha started refurbishing the Justice Department after her first visit as a Cabinet wife to Florida, where she saw the vast amount of work GSA was doing on Nixon's private property at Key Biscayne. A few months later she would see even more being spent on his estate at San Clemente, California.)

When a Jack Anderson column appeared describing the inside and outside refurbishings of the Justice Department, an irate taxpayer in California sent Martha sixty pounds of steer manure. A few days after it arrived, the Department called GSA to come get it, giving enterprising GSA employees an opportunity to divide some of the manure into glass test tubes, mount the tubes on wooden plaques with copies of the Anderson column laminated on the back and label each plaque, "Martha's B.S." The plaques were distributed to those employees of GSA, the Justice Department and the FBI who had working relationships with the Attorney General's wife.

With all the decorating of the Justice Department, there was one room Martha didn't do a thing to improve. On a mezzanine-like level of the Attorney General's private office there was a little bedroom, reached by slipping through a secret panel in the woodwork and climbing a circular stairway. Martha evidently decided John didn't need a little room outfitted with a daybed; she used the space as a catchall storage place for dozens of pictures, cartoons and portraits of herself.

While doing the *Look* article, Fred and I found Martha unusually cooperative. There were no restrictions on the types of pictures Fred could take, which was refreshing in image-conscious political Washington, where 90 percent of the officials scream if their pictures are taken with a drink in hand. (A picture Fred took which has been reproduced over and over again was one of Martha at the beauty parlor, sitting under a drier while having a pedicure and manicure.)

Nor was I told that anything I heard or saw was "off the record." And one day when I asked a question about her mail, Martha answered, "Why don't you just open it and see for yourself." From then on when I was waiting for Martha to dress, or while she was busy with other things, I often sat, unsupervised, opening the Attorney General's wife's mail. Occasionally there would be a letter containing what seemed to be a genuine threat, and once I opened one written in blood.

I was surprised at the number of letters that came addressed "Martha Mitchell, Washington." Junie Dankworth laughs when she recalls a letter Martha received while at CREEP that was addressed only "Martha Mitchell." As Junie recalls it: "A woman in Grosse Point, Michigan, had left an envelope for her laundry woman, whose name was Martha Mitchell. Someone saw it on the hall table, put a stamp on it and sent it off. I couldn't understand why this Grosse Point woman was sending Martha money, so I telephoned her. She was more surprised than we were to learn where her laundry-woman's money was."

Although Martha was friendly and open and warm we soon saw that her attitude toward us changed completely whenever we were with her in an official situation, such as at a White House function or an embassy dinner, or even when she was with people she had known while living in Rye. As Fred puts it: "One minute she was extremely friendly and the next moment she seemed to forget she had ever seen us."

Martha didn't limit her off-again-on-again friendships to the press, as we first had thought since this was at the height of Spiro Agnew's "effete snob" period. Junie Dankworth and others had the same experience with her. "She was your very best friend one minute and the next she didn't know you," Junie recalls. Other times she might *know* you but relegate you to a subservient role, without your knowledge. Such as the time Martha didn't want to travel alone to Ohio, where she had a speaking engagement, and talked Junie into going with her. Once there, Junie learned Martha had told everyone that Junie was her *secretary.*

It's unclear why Martha did this. One reporter thinks it was because she was so insecure she couldn't admit she was friendly with "anyone below Cabinet rank." Others, more likely right, believe Martha was taking her cue from the White House. She'd watched "Mr. President" and Pat Nixon during public appearances. She'd observed their imperial manner. She'd seen the retinue—made up of friends, staff, press and hangers-on—following in their wake. To Martha, a newcomer to official Washington and one who desperately wanted to do the *right* thing, this probably seemed to be the role the wife of Nixon's closest adviser should be playing, too.

MARTHA'S HAPPINESS AT HAVING A PRESS SECRETARY WAS SHORT-LIVED; KAY Woestendieck worked only two months for her. Eight days after Kay started work, her husband Bill was fired from his $50,000-a-year job at WETA-TV. The station claimed Kay's job with Martha created a "conflict of interest" for Bill; four regular guest editors on his *Newsroom* program quit in protest.

Martha was distraught. Quiet, softspoken Kay had been an excellent press secretary to the volatile Martha. She not only steered Martha through dozens of interviews, and organized her home office, but Kay seemed to understand Martha's moods and was able to handle them with good humor and without a lot of fuss. The two months Kay was with Martha were probably the best of Martha's Washington experience.

In early June, Hank M. Greenspun, the publisher of the Las Vegas *Sun,* called a press conference in Washington to announce that Bill Woestendieck had been named editor and publisher of Greenspun's newly acquired Colorado Springs *Sun.* Martha had lunch with Greenspun and his wife and the Woestendiecks before the press conference, where she was supposed to read a prepared statement in which she called Kay an "invaluable aide and good friend." But Martha became so upset at losing Kay she had to leave before declaring her friendship and admiration.

One afternoon about a month before she left, Kay called and said she wanted to come see me. We sat and talked about Martha's need for a press secretary/friend, and it was obvious Kay was checking to see if I would take the job. When I realized this, I said something for which Martha never quite forgave me. I told Kay I couldn't afford to take a job with Martha Mitchell.

Misunderstanding my meaning, Kay assured me the salary would be "right." Then I explained that as a White House correspondent who had to cover both Democrats and Republicans, I couldn't afford to work with anyone in either political party.

I didn't know Kay had told Martha I couldn't afford to work for her until four years later. Martha asked me to accompany her to Canada, where she was to tape a television show. All expenses were paid by the station, including a limousine in Washington and in Toronto, and a two-bedroom, two-bath, $150-a-day hotel suite. Once we were installed in the suite, Martha turned to me and said, "And you told Kay Woestendieck you couldn't afford to be associated with Martha Mitchell!"

At the time Kay talked with me, I'd told her that although I couldn't work for Martha, I'd be glad to help Martha in any way I could, as a friend. After that I was one of the people Martha called often—sometimes for advice or help with a problem, other times just to chat. Her gossip about Administration figures was so fascinating I begged her to keep a diary. When Martha protested she couldn't write, I told her to make believe she was writing a friend, but not to worry about spelling or punctuation. A few days later she called to report, "I started my diary! But I didn't write a friend. It's to 'Dear Heart,' because everything I do comes from the heart."

Martha said she'd written about Secretary of State William Rogers calling that morning to say that Robert Finch had been "pushed out" as Secretary of Health, Education and Welfare and moved to the White House. John Mitchell hadn't known about the move until Rogers called. She was sorry for Bob Finch and wrote that he probably wouldn't be at the White House very long, since some people there thought he was "weak."

She also had written about William Rogers hating Henry Kissinger because he got in Rogers's way. But Martha thought someone should point out that Richard Nixon was his own Secretary of State; she couldn't see why the press didn't understand this.

Martha's opinion of the State Department wasn't high, so she discussed in her diary how it was full of hypocrites and no-goods left over from so many years of Democratic rule. But she wasn't pleased with the Nixon Administration either, saying she thought the President was catering to too many people in an effort to win all sides, which she said was not possible. She thought he was appearing immature.

Discussing the Cabinet, Martha said the only men in it who were true to Nixon were John, Maurice Stans and Secretary of Labor George Shultz. Martha noted that she didn't believe her husband knew what he was doing when he sat in that Florida hotel room and picked the rest of the Cabinet. She also expressed wonder that Nixon *et al.*, ever won the election.

Unfortunately, Martha's one letter to "Dear Heart" was the only one she ever wrote.

MARTHA HAD AN INSATIABLE APPETITE FOR INFORMATION ABOUT WHO-Was-Who in Washington and how people became important enough to rate constant mention in the local society columns. She showed little interest in "Old Society" or official wives. Martha wanted to know how to get *her* name in the papers, not as Mrs. John N. Mitchell, wife of the Attorney General, but as *Martha Mitchell,* a woman with an identity of her own—like an Alice Longworth or a Perle Mesta, a Gwen Cafritz or a Barbara Howar.

She asked my advice, and I suggested that since Perle Mesta was a friend of Martha's she might study how Perle always had something to say that could be reported; how she saw that the press covered her parties; and how she even entertained for the press. The first party Perle gave when she returned to the United States after being Minister to Luxembourg was an elegant dinner and dance for members of the Women's National Press Club (now integrated and called the Washington Press Club).

After that Martha saw that she always had something quotable to say when a working reporter was around. She entertained for various reporters —perhaps at a coffee at her Watergate apartment, or a luncheon in the Attorney General's private dining room at the Justice Department. And she saw that the press was invited to all of her parties and was present when she attended public events.

Once when Martha went to Winchester, Virginia, to help the campaign of a Republican who was running for the House of Representatives, Martha took three press women along with her in her limousine. On the way to Winchester she was chatty and amusing, and once there she made hard news, deliberately. She walked across the street to the campaign headquarters of Senator Harry F. Byrd, Jr., who was running for re-election as an Independent, leaving a supporter of the Republican candidate angrily screaming that she couldn't do that!

Undaunted by the woman's outburst, Martha called over her shoulder that "the Byrds are my good friends and I want him re-elected . . ." After the election, which Byrd won, Martha told a newswoman that the Independent Senator Byrd was "with us."

One time Martha sought advice was when she wanted to know the best way to get something in the paper "in a hurry." She said she'd been telling syndicated columnist Betty Beale a lot of things for her column, but now she was "mad" at Betty, and Martha wanted to call someone else.

Betty Beale was one of Martha's first press friends. Martha called Betty as frequently as six times a day and often told her, "Betty, you're my best friend in Washington." But when Martha, after becoming a household word, started calling Betty and demanding that she put in the column things Betty didn't think should be there, Betty acted like all newsmen who "cover the Hill; they don't pay attention to what is told them when it is said from drunkenness or whatever . . . Martha was mad for publicity." Betty pauses and adds, "Maybe she thought that was the only identity she had."

So Martha was "mad" at Betty and she was looking for someone to get her remarks "out immediately." I explained that the only way to get a story published instantly was to call one of the wire services. No matter what time of day or night an item is put on the wire, I said, there'll be a paper somewhere in the world that will still be able to meet its deadline.

Martha knew Isabelle Hall, then the UPI correspondent covering the Justice Department. She decided Isabelle would be her primary phone-pal in the press. Of course there were others, but Martha usually called them in answer to their requests.

It was Isabelle whom Martha called one weekend from the pale-blue telephone in her bathroom, "so John won't hear me talking to you." John was upset over a story Kandy Stroud had written about him in *Women's Wear Daily,* quoting the Attorney General as saying educators were the "stupid bastards" who are ruining our educational institutions, and that

Henry Kissinger, head of the National Security Council, was "an egocentric maniac."

Martha told Isabelle the story was "ridiculous." She denied John had made either of the quoted remarks. Then she gave her own views about professors and educators: "They are totally responsible for the sins of our children. These are people that are destroying our country. It makes me sick at my stomach. They're a bunch of sidewalk diplomats that don't know the score . . . they don't have any right to talk."

"I thought everything she said was mouthing him," Isabelle says of Martha's calls. "She was saying what he wanted to say; she was like a little puppet on a string. But she was enjoying it. It put her in the limelight and Martha liked being on covers of magazines."

Martha *did* mouth John almost totally at first, but it's doubtful she was echoing him on September 1971, when she talked to Isabelle and poured out her advice to American women, after President Nixon appealed to Cabinet wives to speak out in support of his economic policies. "Go out and spend your money and enjoy yourself," Martha counseled.

"I liked Martha, awfully well," Isabelle recalls. "We were pretty good friends at one point." Why didn't they stay good friends? Isabelle laughs and answers, "Because I stopped writing everything she called me about. It's as simple as that."

Martha switched to another UPI reporter, Helen Thomas, and it was Helen she called from California, on June 22, 1972, when she had the telephone torn out of her hand and then ripped out of the wall.

Chapter Nine

"THE ONLY FRIENDS I HAVE IN WASHINGTON ARE MEMBERS OF THE press," Martha told an interviewer in late 1970. That wasn't totally true, but it probably seemed so to Martha. By this time most of the Cabinet wives were giving her a wide berth. Martha was in disfavor at the White House, barred from Air Force One and denied access to the *Sequoia.* And Old Washington—the established Washington society—never had accepted her.

Martha said she didn't care, claiming she found the media more interesting and knowledgeable. "Although I never quite understood the Washington press corps," Martha later said in a *McCall's* magazine article, "I always enjoyed going to anything given or attended by its members. I found them the most intelligent, the most perceptive of all the people I met in Washington."

She always insisted that the press gave the best parties. She went to many of them and her presence guaranteed a good story for the press; in some cases the fact that she didn't show up was a story in itself. Such was the party which would become known as the Great Grits Affair—a John Mitchell/FBI-inspired misunderstanding as ridiculous as its name.

One night while in a nostalgic mood over the South and things

Southern, two former North Carolinians—New York *Times* reporter Marjorie Hunter and the late John Colie, a Washington interior decorator —organized The National Hominy Grits Foundation (TNHGF). John Colie was named president; Maggie Hunter held all other offices. They declared the aims of the foundation to be furthering the use of grits "by making it the national food, as eagles are the national bird; and to have Congress declare a day a year National Grits Day, sort of like National Pickle Week."

Soon John and Maggie's displaced Southern friends—many members of the media—were joining in the fun and becoming members of TNHGF. A grits party, where each member would bring either a favorite grits dish or a food complementing grits, was planned for Washington members. When Martha heard about it, she wanted to come; she promised to cook her version of fried grits.

The nearer it came to party night, the more elaborate were the plans. John Colie managed to get bolts of Jim Dandy grits bag material, and put the employees of his decorating and upholstering shop to work running up aprons for the women, ties for the men and jackets for the waiters. He also had a sunbonnet made for Martha, since by now it had been decided to crown her Miss Grits of 1972.

But CREEP booked Martha into a large GOP fund-raiser, to be held the very night of the grits party. (Martha always thought it was deliberate, in order to keep her from fraternizing with the press.) She was so unhappy at missing the party that TNHGF members agreed to change the date —to the night of February 8, 1972, at John Colie's townhouse, renamed "Hominy Hall" for the occasion.

The day of the party John Colie sent his crew of workmen to his house to transform it into a true Hominy Hall. His silk damask draperies were taken down and replaced with Jim Dandy grits curtains; dining-room chair seats and table were covered with the same gaudy material, as were various pillows in the drawing room. As Marian Burros, then food editor of the Washington *Star*, wrote later, "somehow it all blended in with his rare eighteenth-century porcelains."

In the middle of all the redecorating confusion, the FBI arrived to check out Hominy Hall. They took a quick look around and went back to the Justice Department to report to the Attorney General. That evening Martha was told she couldn't go to the party because the press, and her good friends in it, had set her up for an orgy to embarrass the Nixon re-election campaign. She was informed that there was no Hominy Hall, only an apartment, and it was a mess, with cartons on the floor and no curtains at the windows; and that the FBI had telephoned Marian Burros and she'd said she was not going to a grits party. Marian, who did go to the party and brought a *Star* photographer with her, later denied ever telling the FBI she was not going to the party.

No one told Martha that the host's stepson was with the Secret Service, on the Vice-President Agnew detail, or that John Colie was well known as the decorator of some of the better homes in Washington. Both facts surely were known by John Mitchell and the FBI. Neither was she informed that two of the dinner guests would be officials of the National Trust for Historic Preservation, or that the Trust had loaned Mrs. Woodrow Wilson's mortar and pestle for a dining-room centerpiece. The *Star* article explained the connection was appropriate since "the second Mrs. Woodrow Wilson [partook of] corn, in solid or liquid form, every day of her life." And if John Mitchell knew it, he didn't let Martha know that Senator Herman Talmadge's wife, who couldn't come to the dinner, had sent over a country ham from her Georgia farm; or that Mrs. Hale Boggs (now Congresswoman Lindy Boggs) had dropped off a large dish of her baked grits with cheese and a serving dish of New Orleans' famous grillades.

To Martha, the revelations were proof that Nixon had been right about the press all along. Less than an hour before the first guests were scheduled to arrive at the party, Martha had her secretary call to say that due to unexpected circumstances, Mrs. Mitchell would not be there.

It wasn't until a week later, when the *Star* article and pictures appeared, that Martha realized she had been lied to. And she knew why; it was to keep her away from her friends in the press.

The grits fiasco temporarily served its purpose. It kept Martha away from her friends for some time—not because she distrusted the press, but because she was so embarrassed by the circumstances that made her miss the party she didn't know what to say.

MARTHA'S CONTACTS WITH THE PRESS WEREN'T LIMITED TO REPORTERS based in Washington. She had many phone-pals scattered throughout the United States. One she called often, at his Los Angeles office, was Lloyd Shearer of *Parade*, the "Sunday Newspaper Magazine." In addition to his own by-line articles, Lloyd writes "Personality Parade" under the *nom de plume* Walter Scott.

"She'd call me regularly," Lloyd recalls. "And she'd say, 'Walter'—she always called me Walter—'I have a great story for you!' " He laughs, recalling the time Martha telephoned to say she'd won the daily double at the Laurel Race Course. " 'Isn't that a good story, Walter,' she said. And I said, 'yes, it is.' " But when she called after Watergate her stories were more serious and contained more news. "She was furious then," Lloyd says.

Another reporter who became a telephone confidant following Watergate was Bob Woodward, of the Woodward/Bernstein team. She first met him when, as a new reporter for the Washington *Post*, he covered her air-pollution complaint against the plant supplying heat to the White House and the Justice Department. Following Watergate, Martha talked with Woodward often enough for the Washington *Star*'s "EAR" column to speculate that Deep Throat, the principal informant in *All The President's Men*, was more than the one mysterious man Woodward and Bernstein claimed him to be, and to suggest that Martha was part of a composite Deep Throat. Then, according to what Martha told me, she invited both Bob Woodward and Carl Bernstein to come see her at her Fifth Avenue apartment, after John left. She also said she had made available to them papers from John Mitchell's files.

Once Martha discovered press people weren't the villains Richard Nixon and John Mitchell had led her to believe, she made every effort to meet as many of them as possible. Martha claimed it was because she desperately wanted the press and the Administration "to get together." They had to stop fighting each other, she said, or the country wouldn't survive.

At her request she accompanied me to the American Designers' press showings, in June 1970, and delighted two hundred fashion editors and writers beyond their expectations. One wrote that the editors found Martha "far more appealing than expected, a woman who is simply being herself regardless of her husband's position."

Martha accepted an invitation from Katharine Graham to lunch in the Washington *Post* publisher's private dining room. *Post* employees still laugh at the *faux pas* made by Mrs. Graham when she personally took Martha on a tour of the newspaper plant and led her through an unmarked door—right into a men's room.

Later, Martha went to a *Post* employees' dinner at the home of managing editor Eugene Patterson, now managing editor of the St. Petersburg *Times* in Florida, and according to him "charmed the 'enemies' among whom she was completely at home, though the Attorney General appeared a little sweaty in the powder-blue blazer and powder-blue matching pipe in which she had outfitted him."

JUST AS SHE HAD CHARMED THE FASHION EDITORS AND THE *Post* NEWS staff, Martha enchanted the British press when she went to London to meet the Queen. Martha first learned she was to see Queen Elizabeth—at a Buckingham Palace garden party—when the Attorney General's office called to tell her the various things the Mitchells would be doing while in London for the second session of the 1971 American Bar Association convention.

Ladies' Home Journal asked me to go to London with Martha to write an article about the event. Martha had never had a national magazine follow her all the way to Europe. That was pretty heady stuff and she admitted it. The next day she called to say John was just as pleased as she was about the article. Both, she said, would give their fullest cooperation.

As it turned out, this was another one of the times when John Mitchell led his wife to believe he was solidly behind her in a project when, in fact, he secretly was putting stumbling blocks in her way.

But Martha wouldn't know that until later. Now she was happily, if frantically, getting ready for the trip. First, there were clothes to buy—for herself and for Marty. Martha had to plan a wardrobe not only for her many public appearances in London but for trips to Switzerland, Italy and Greece.

For the party at Buckingham Palace, Martha bought a dress designed by Allen Davidsen for Jo Ellen Couture. It had a pale-apricot Ban-lon jersey bodice and white silk organza skirt, with what the designer called a "cuff" on the hem. Martha called it a flounce. Around the top of the cuff and running from it to the waist were bands of French ribbon in apricot, yellow and green. With it Martha carried a yellow silk purse, dyed to match the French ribbon, with a gold chain. (Martha was irritated with the press for reporting the purse was "plastic.") Her shoes were white silk—high-heeled, sling-back, of course. Her only jewelry was a flower-shaped pin of topaz and brilliants, and matching earrings. Her wide-brim, high-crown, apricot organdy hat was copied from one she had in her closet. To top off the outfit, she carried a custom-made yellow organza parasol.

Following Martha's death, when John Mitchell was disposing of her extensive wardrobe, the "Queen Costume," as Martha dubbed it, was one of only two of her mother's dresses that Marty Mitchell would choose to keep; the other was the evening dress Martha wore to both of Richard Nixon's inaugurals.

Martha wore the Queen Costume first to Tricia Nixon's wedding in the White House rose garden. A close Republican friend of the Nixons claims the White House was "furious" with Martha for wearing the eye-catching costume. "Everyone there thought it was a deliberate effort on her part to steal the limelight from Tricia," he says.

Not long before we were to leave for London—Martha on the *Queen Elizabeth 2* and I by air—Martha called to say she was going to the State Department for a briefing on the countries she would visit. As Martha said, before she went anywhere she always tried "to find out in advance what could be expected to happen and what part, if any, I was expected to play." Since I'd be writing about the London phase she asked if I'd like to go along. I did.

When we arrived at State, two foreign-service officers—armed with briefing books and hundreds of statistics—were waiting. Martha's opening sentence was, "Tell me about meeting the Queen."

She was told, "The rules for meeting the Queen are fairly basic and simple. There is a reception line, as there is at most occasions, only this one is in reverse; the guests line up and the Queen moves along." The Queen always starts the conversation, one of the officers said, "and the first time you answer her you call her 'Your Majesty.' After that you address her as 'Ma'am.' "

He emphasized that no one speaks to the Queen until spoken to, and then one discusses only those subjects introduced by Her Majesty. Martha wasn't happy about that. She'd spent hours, many of them on the phone with me, deciding what she'd talk about to the Queen. Since she was sailing on the *QE 2* she thought she could mention that and add that the Captain of the ship had been the skipper of the *Queen Mary* when she and Marty sailed on it in 1967. Marty came down with the mumps during the crossing, and the Captain had put both of them in quarantine.

She also had decided she'd tell Her Majesty about the time Martha met Prince Philip, in New York, when he was the guest of honor at the Pilgrims' Dinner. After the dinner, Martha, then Governor Nelson Rockefeller and his wife Happy, and Britain's ambassador to the United States John Freeman and his wife Catherine went up to the Prince's hotel suite. They were there for more than an hour; Martha found the Prince "absolutely charming and fascinating." She also was fascinated when she went to the bathroom to see that a servant had prepared Prince Philip's gold toothbrush for a nightly brushing; he'd squeezed the paste neatly along the bristles.

Martha asked the State Department men about curtsying and was told some Americans did and others didn't at a garden party, which after all wasn't the same as being presented at Court.

Then she was given a briefing book that contained maps and other information about Great Britain, including its history, political and economic situations, and its foreign policy.

She received the same type of briefing about Switzerland and Italy. Martha asked about the Mafia and quickly was told that Italy is "absolutely opposed to any organized criminal activity, no matter what name it is called."

One of the officers talked about Greece and "the very sensitive political situation there," noting that the State Department hoped "trips like yours don't weaken" Greek-American relations. There were safe subjects she could discuss though, he said, and started to tell her what they were. Martha stopped him cold; she declared, "My husband says I can say anything I want to!"

He turned pale, then paler when Martha continued: "John doesn't agree with the Secretary trying to stop people from going to Greece. So if I hurt Mr. Rogers's ideas about Greece, that's too bad."

The man recovered enough to advise Martha not to eat "the shellfish, there are high incidents of hepatitis."

As we left the State Department I told her, "Martha, you aren't going to see very much of Greece."

She assured me that no one would *dare* restrict her visit, that "John wouldn't stand for it." But when she returned from Greece, Martha called and said, "You were right. I was controlled every minute I was there." She laughed as she recalled how she and her party (Marty, the Ebbitts and the FBI agents) were whisked aboard a luxurious yacht ("the one the Greek King escaped in") the morning after arriving, for a cruise of the Greek Isles, and were kept there until the afternoon before going back to Italy. They got back to Athens just in time for an embassy dinner in Martha's honor.

Both nights they were in Athens they stayed at the American Embassy, where all phone calls to her were screened. There never was an opportunity for the Greek press to get near Martha.

The Mitchells sailed for England on July 8. Martha talked to reporters before embarking and praised the American Bar Association for turning down a resolution calling for the United States to end the war in Vietnam. She told the press that "no one outside the government can tell the government what to do. It is ridiculous." She added, "I don't care who it is. Those who try to do it are sidewalk diplomats."

Discussing the protocol of her upcoming meeting with the Queen, Martha said, "The Queen must speak first," and confessed, "I'll probably have to be gagged for the first time." In the privacy of their deluxe suite, John Mitchell told Martha the Queen probably would cancel her invitation after hearing what she'd told the press.

When I arrived in London two days before the garden party and ten hours ahead of Martha, I immediately called the Palace press office about my press invitation, which the British Embassy had arranged for before I left Washington. I was told that the American Embassy was handling my invitation. This puzzled me; it wasn't like the British to let a foreign embassy handle its press arrangements.

The American Embassy told me that the ambassador had a limited number of invitations to the garden party, and of course he had so many obligations they were sure I'd understand there weren't enough invitations to go around. No matter how much I explained that I wasn't a guest of the ambassador but a member of the working press trying to cover a party, it didn't change the situation. Other calls to various British press offices didn't either. From these conversations, though, I learned it wasn't the British keeping me away from Buckingham Palace.

Martha enlisted John's aid in trying to get credentials for me. He reported back that the Queen *never* allowed the press at her parties. (The first thing Martha said to me after the party was, "That garden was crawling with press. Someone lied to John!") Thinking the magazine article would be cancelled, Martha was almost in tears. Although I assured her there *would* be a story, that being barred from an event was an everyday occurrence for a Washington reporter, she still doubted it could be done.

The afternoon before the party, I went to the Mitchells' Hilton Hotel suite to be there when Robert Scott, Chief of Protocol at the American Embassy, came to brief Martha and John on Palace protocol. He started with a history of the royal garden parties. They began with Queen Victoria, he said, when she found she had many relatives and friends she couldn't manage to meet on a one-to-one basis. Now, the parties were no longer merely gatherings of blue bloods. The Queen sometimes stays at the party for only forty-five minutes, Scott said; at other times she's there for the two hours the party usually lasts. In any case, no one leaves until the Queen does.

Martha was anxious to know what to do about her white gloves when she met the Queen. Did she take off only the right? Both? Neither? Scott, who had received his information straight from the Palace protocol office, said, "The Palace prefers that you have both gloves on when meeting the Queen. However, if you have taken off your gloves to eat or drink, do not try to put them back on." The bad thing, according to the Palace, was to be fumbling with one's gloves while being introduced to the Queen. Whether she curtsied or not was up to Martha. Some Americans did, others chose not to.

The Mitchells also talked to Scott about their invitation to the garden party, which had been hand-delivered to their hotel suite. In the one envelope there were eight separate enclosures—a treasure trove of information. There were two red cards which would get John and Martha into the Royal Tea Tent Enclosure (better known as the Royal Tent), where the Queen comes for her own tea and cakes, and where she talks at greater length to her guests. More than five hundred Americans went to Buckingham Palace the day the Mitchells were there, but the only ones Martha saw in the Royal Tent were Chief Justice and Mrs. Burger, Justice and Mrs. Byron White and former Justice and Mrs. Tom Clark.

Scott ended his briefing with a few remarks about protocol inside the Royal Tent. Then he added, "It's really quite simple; you won't have any problems."

John Mitchell quipped, "You don't know my wife!"

Martha and I talked the morning of the garden party and she said she wasn't feeling well. But I didn't realize how sick she was until I arrived at the Mitchell suite with a photographer, about an hour before she was to leave for Buckingham Palace.

Martha was still in a negligee, sitting on the side of her bed, drinking a thick green medicine out of the bottle. She said it was for diverticulitis. Later I'd learn the medicine, which contained a narcotic, was prescribed by her doctor to calm intestinal spasms.

She stood up and immediately doubled over with pain. Knowing how much it meant to her to meet the Queen, and thinking she wasn't going to be able to go, I cried, "Oh, Martha! How terrible. You'll never make it."

Martha thought I was upset at the prospect of missing the *Ladies' Home Journal* story; she threw me an indignant look, declared, "I promised you I'd do this, and I will!" and stomped off into the bathroom to put on her makeup.

Even with such determination, she had to stop every five minutes or so to rest and take more medicine. Finally she was dressed, and we went into the sitting room where the photographer was waiting.

Everyone was ready except John Mitchell. He wasn't there, and the FBI agent claimed he didn't know where he was. I told the photographer to go ahead and get Martha's picture, there wasn't time to look for her husband.

The photographer snapped on the lights—and blew all of the fuses in the Mitchell suite. Martha went into the bedroom to take more green medicine, while we debated what to do.

The only thing we could do was go across the street into Hyde Park. As we dashed down the street to an underpass which would take us into the Park, I noticed that Martha obviously was having abdominal pain. But she didn't complain. It was the first time I was aware of this quality in Martha. She often complained bitterly before, and almost always after doing something she was committed to do. But once it was time to do it—appear on a TV show, pose for a picture, make a few remarks, or whatever—she took hold and did whatever had to be done.

The day before, thinking Martha would be my only source of information about the garden party, I'd spent an hour coaching her on what was important to remember. Now, realizing that she wasn't physically up to doing it by herself, I thought how lucky we were that I'd found someone else to cover the party, too. My friend Anne Schmidt, a Washington correspondent for the Denver *Post,* who was at the ABA meeting with her lawyer husband, Richard, had offered to cover everything for me except what went on inside the Royal Tent.

The previous afternoon, Anne had taken me to the Hilton suite of the new ABA president Leon Jaworski, Houston lawyer, friend of Lyndon Baines Johnson and breeder of champion quarter horses. I'd asked to meet him since I presumed he would be one of those the Queen would talk to at Buckingham Palace.

When I told Martha I'd talked to Leon Jaworski and his wife Janet, she looked surprised and asked, "Why did you do that? They aren't important."

"He's the new president of the American Bar Association!" I reminded her. "That makes him important."

"Well, John says he isn't," Martha declared. "And he isn't the one John wanted to be president." Three years later, Leon Jaworski, as Watergate Special Prosecutor, headed the office that gathered the incriminating evidence that sent John Mitchell to prison.

When we got back from Hyde Park to the Hilton, John Mitchell was sitting in the car in front of the hotel. He refused to step out so the photographer could get a picture of him with Martha.

WHEN THE MITCHELLS CAME BACK FROM THE GARDEN PARTY, JOHN Mitchell walked into the suite, tipped his hat at a rakish angle, did a little dance step toward Marty, and recited the Old English nursery rhyme, "Pussy cat, pussy cat, Where have you been? I've been to London, to look at the Queen."

Martha went into the bedroom to get out of her Queen's dress. She had an appointment at the hotel beauty parlor to get her hair done for the dinner to be given that night by Lloyd's of London.

I asked John Mitchell what he'd done with his top hat. Earlier he'd complained that he didn't see why he had to have the "damn top hat" since he couldn't wear it. No man keeps his head covered in the presence of the Queen, so the hats are in hand more often than on the head. He said, "I was there with my hat and my heart in hand. The hat for the Queen. My heart for my poor wife who had to stand so long her feet were hurting."

Martha came out of the bedroom, dressed casually in slacks and blouse, and we started for the beauty parlor, where because of limited time I would have my only chance that day to "debrief" her. As we were going out the door, John Mitchell said something that I felt was a threat. He warned me, "Don't you write anything to embarrass the Queen!" (Evidently, it wasn't unusual for John Mitchell to threaten the press. Two Washington newswomen say that when they obtained information about Martha and Clyde Jenning's divorce proceedings, John Mitchell learned about it. He called them to his Justice Department office, where he proceeded to tell them both would be barred from covering the White House or the Justice Department if they dared print one word about the divorce.)

Surprisingly, Martha turned out to be a most observant reporter. She was able to describe in minute detail such things as the condition of the Palace garden's green turf ("so thick your heels don't sink into it"), the Queen's dress—and was even able to draw a picture of her diamond-and-pearl pin with another diamond hanging from it; and items on the Royal Tea Table. But as attractive as it looked, and as hungry as she was, Martha didn't eat a bite or drink a sip. She didn't want to take off her gloves "and be fumbling with them" when she met the Queen.

Queen Elizabeth and Prince Philip came out a few minutes after four, Martha said, looking impressive and very royal as they stood at the top of the terrace steps while the band played "God Save the Queen." Martha laughed when she told me about the band, saying she first thought it was playing "God Bless America" in honor of the ABA guests.

From what Martha and Anne said, the garden party was a fascinating performance which seemed casual, but actually wasn't. Everything had been meticulously arranged. For instance, a few guests who'd been selected in advance stood at designated spots and the Queen stopped to chat with them for a minute or two. She had been thoroughly briefed about everyone she'd meet. And my hunch was right; she stopped to talk to Leon Jaworski and his wife Janet.

While the Queen was strolling down the passageway, John and Martha mingled with the other guests. Martha said she introduced herself to several, "the way I would have at a party in America," all the while making her way to the Royal Tent.

Queen Elizabeth had been out in the garden for more than an hour when she came into the tent and headed for one end of the tea table with a lady-in-waiting. The two stood there alone while the Queen drank two cups of tea and ate something. Martha thought, "She looks just the way I feel after standing in a receiving line and shaking hundreds of hands. She wants to be alone a few minutes and relax."

When Martha met the Queen she created something of a sensation; she didn't curtsy. It was reported that Martha Mitchell, wife of the Attorney General of the United States, *refused* to curtsy to Queen Elizabeth because she did not feel an American should bow to a foreign monarch. (Martha always felt that no one would have cared had it not been for the fact that Mrs. Warren Burger did curtsy, drawing attention to the fact that Martha did not.)

Martha was still telling me her impressions of the Queen and her party when we got on the elevator to take her back from the beauty parlor to their suite. But our conversation stopped when Chief Justice Burger got on the same elevator. He told Martha one of the things he'd been doing in London was taking a look at their courtrooms. They were smaller and had room for fewer spectators than the U. S. courts, he said, adding that he was going to ask GSA to investigate and see if the U. S. courtrooms couldn't be designed with less space for the general public.

Martha and I parted, with the understanding that we'd talk the next day. She'd agreed to have her by-line on the article with mine, and it was important for us to discuss what was in it.

But the next morning she decided to go shopping at the Silver Vaults. She bought thousands of dollars' worth of what she called her "heirloom silver," including a tea service, which she decided was too valuable to ship. It was carried, by the FBI agents, from England to Switzerland, Italy, Greece and back to America.

That afternoon, in her suite, Martha entertained a select group of the British media at tea.

A British reporter wrote, "The invitation brought the biggest turnout of journalists (mostly male) so far for any of the events of the American Bar Convention which has attracted 12,000 U. S. lawyers and their families here for a week of professional work and social pleasures."

It was obvious the press hadn't come to suite 2714 for tea; no one sat down and no one touched any of the little sandwiches or rich pastries. Neither had it come for tea-party conversation. The questions were tough; many of them seemed to surprise Martha. But true to her rule of always having a comment, she answered questions on such subjects as the President's trip to China, the Pentagon Papers, America's young people and the Black Panthers.

An American Embassy press officer winced several times at Martha's answers. He seemed especially uncomfortable when she categorically stated that John Mitchell was going down in history as the greatest Attorney General the United States ever had, and added, "It's the first time the Justice Department has ever been concerned with justice." Evidently Martha wasn't alone in thinking John Mitchell was an outstanding Attorney General. When he resigned the office to run CREEP, Chief Justice Warren Burger wrote to tell him if he could live down the "horrible mistake of May 21, 1969 (the day Burger was nominated to be Chief Justice, at John Mitchell's suggestion), you will rank with the strong men who have held the great office of Attorney General."

The British, who, like American Southerners, love and appreciate eccentricity, were intrigued with Martha, and they liked the blithe way she presented her forthright, if not always well-thought-out, opinions. The *Evening Standard* declared that life in London would be "a lot less dull if we had Martha on the Westminster scene."

After a round of social activity Martha got sick with diverticulitis and was in bed for four days, requiring the care of a doctor. I had seen her at various parties, but there hadn't been an opportunity to talk about the article.

Finally, in one of our many telephone conversations, she said, "You don't have to talk to me. Just write anything you want to." Martha would do this with later articles carrying our double by-lines. At first I thought she was terribly naïve. Later I wondered if she weren't terribly smart. It's difficult to be unkind to someone who trusts you completely.

Many reporters and TV commentators felt this way about the telephone calls Martha made to them after John left her. As one well-known columnist says, "I know it wasn't good journalism, but I found myself *protecting* her. She'd call and talk to me as one friend to another; I couldn't write the things she said when I knew they weren't in her best interest."

Chapter Ten

MARTHA HAD BEEN ECSTATIC WHEN RICHARD NIXON SAID HE wanted the wives to be active, working members of his Cabinet. After all those months of being ignored during the 1968 campaign, she was more than ready to play a meaningful role in the new Administration. So, as she put it, she came to Washington just full of ideas. Unfortunately, not all Cabinet wives were as enthusiastic as Martha; some even resented it when she prodded them into participating in projects she suggested.

One wife, complaining off the record to newswoman Vera Glaser, said she had called Martha to say she didn't want to take part in a particular program, "but Martha is someone you don't say 'no' to. This is part of the problem; she gets emotional. Anyway, I wound up saying I would do it."

Martha didn't realize until later that her messianic zeal for what she termed "helping both the country and the Administration" wasn't shared by everyone. She forged ahead, looking for meaningful things the wives could do.

In her search for projects, Martha turned up so many a newswoman dubbed her the Administration's "original idea girl." And one of her programs was so successful a White House aide called to ask if she'd mind their saying it was the President's idea.

Shortly after she arrived in Washington it became clear to Martha that neither she nor the other Cabinet wives could be helpful to the Administration unless they became better informed about the government and how it worked. As she told it, she "dreamed up" the idea of having the wives visit each Cabinet-level department or agency, to tour the facilities and to be briefed—either by the Cabinet officer himself, or another high-ranking official. The know-your-own-government series started with a tour of the State Department, sponsored by Mrs. William P. Rogers, the ranking Cabinet wife. Martha followed with a luncheon in the Attorney General's private dining room at the Justice Department. John made a speech and J. Edgar Hoover talked about the rising crime rate.

When the White House wanted the President to take credit for the visits, Martha told the aide she wouldn't mind. But she did, and she angrily told John, "If I've got to think for him he might as well get out of the damn White House!" She wasn't satisfied with John's explanation that Nixon was the important one, not members of his Cabinet or their families. It added to her fury when she read, in the Washington *Star,* reporter Barbara Kober's coverage of the visit to the Department of Commerce. Barbara wrote that the excursion was "part of President Nixon's program to acquaint the women with and involve them in federal government."

Martha's plans for the wives didn't stop at Washington's city limits. When Richard Nixon spent the late summer of 1969 at San Clemente and took some of his Cabinet and their families with him, Martha arranged for the wives to take a tour of Universal Studios. Universal sent an elegantly outfitted mobile home, with a fully stocked bar, to whisk the women to Hollywood. One later said, "We enjoyed our ride almost as much as the studio." Another was so pleased she praised Martha for her "Brownie leader" qualities.

It's ironic that Martha's efforts in the early part of the Administration seem forgotten now by some former Nixon aides. In fact, one high White House official, reflecting on the early Martha, says, "I think she really wasn't interested in the other Cabinet wives and pretty rarely participated in their own affairs . . . She was more interested in what men had to say and in talking to them. Women didn't interest her much."

Not all of Martha's ideas were as readily accepted as the department visits and the studio tour. She tried, unsuccessfully, to set up a monthly press conference for the wives. And she didn't get anywhere with a suggestion for a "clearing house" where all social engagements for Cabinet wives would be kept. One reason she thought this was necessary was because she felt a lot of worthy charity events were not getting the assistance they deserved. She complained, in 1970, "Sometimes we all show up at the same thing when I know there are other events that same day where the appearance of one of us would help."

When Martha asked for a secretary to the Cabinet wives, with duties patterned on those of the secretary to the Cabinet, someone suggested that the Republican National Committee furnish the secretary. But Martha didn't want that, claiming, "A Cabinet wife should be nonpolitical. We are serving our country."

She thought the United States had gone overboard with the word "politics." She told a reporter, "I've got news for you. If more people thought of our country before they thought of politics we'd be more united."

When Martha first started making her public statements, top Administration wives were shocked and embarrassed but not unduly alarmed, since, as one wife said, "Most people in the Administration keep thinking she will burn herself out." Martha continued with her outbursts, though, and some of the wives' embarrassment turned to anger. They were especially irate when Martha's remarks involved them.

To alleviate their financial burden, Martha suggested that America's top designers provide Cabinet wives with clothes, the way French *haute couturiers* do for some of their public officials' wives. It was a suggestion not well received by either the garment industry or other Administration wives. Mrs. Nixon said she'd be happy to accept things for the White House but not for herself. "It's illegal," snapped Adele Rogers who, like her husband, was a lawyer.

The wives talked among themselves about this unprecedented Cabinet wife, whom one called a strange American phenomenon. "Most of us are not publicity seekers and we simply can't understand why someone would seek it like Martha does," she told a friend.

It's true Martha loved publicity. It's also true that Martha sometimes was blamed for seeking it when she hadn't. For instance, Bob Haldeman's wife Jo, in a *Ladies' Home Journal* article, said, ". . . Martha enjoyed the attention. Once she was visiting across the street from our house. Our youngest daughter, Ann, happened to be selling lemonade. When Martha heard about it, she came over and bought a glass of lemonade. But she also brought a photographer with her. Naturally, she got her picture in the evening paper."

That isn't an accurate account of what happened. One day Martha went to a small tea in Maryland; I rode out with her, in her government car.

A Washington *Star* photographer wanted Martha to let him get a picture of her "across the street where some kid is selling lemonade." Martha said she would. After the picture was taken, the child said her name was Ann Haldeman and that her father worked at the White House. I asked Martha, "Did you hear that?" "Yes," she said, "and I'll hear about it after this picture comes out."

WHEN MARTHA FIRST STARTED HER OUTBURSTS, THE WIVES THOUGHT someone would speak to John about his wife. But they lost hope of that happening when, to their surprise, the President himself publicly egged her on. Even the East Wing of the White House was dismayed at the President's encouragement.

Helen Smith, Pat Nixon's press secretary, says the First Lady and her staff thought the Attorney General's wife would be silenced after the lobbying calls. "But then we picked up the paper one morning, and saw that the President had told her to 'Give 'em hell.' That was quite a shock."

There came a time when even the President became concerned. A Cabinet wife confided to Vera Glaser that the President turned to her husband and "completely out of the blue, in the middle of another conversation, asked, 'What are we going to do with Martha Mitchell?' "

But by then it was too late to do anything. Her constituency was too large. "It is amazing the attraction she has for many," a puzzled wife said privately. "When we were at the reception the President and Mrs. Nixon gave for legislators, at San Clemente, half or more of the people who went through the line said, 'Martha we think you are great.' And about a quarter of them were saying, 'Keep it up girl, we are for you.' "

Another wife talks today, with some annoyance, about the way Martha constantly did things to get attention, and not just when the press was around. She remembers when some Cabinet officers had to meet secretly with a top-level man from another government, and it was most important, she said, that no one know he was in Washington. For utmost privacy the meeting was held in the seclusion of one Cabinet member's house. The servants had been sent home and the wife finished and served the dinner. "The men were in the drawing room, having the meeting after dinner, and the wives kept out of the way in another room. But Martha wandered off somewhere and came back downstairs wearing a hula skirt. She danced into the room where the men were meeting and wouldn't leave. John Mitchell didn't say a word; he just let her do it."

Although she never saw John Mitchell indicate to Martha in any way his displeasure with her remarks or actions, a Cabinet wife remembers well the night at a large banquet when one of Martha's antics brought out John's sardonic sense of humor. She said as each VIP guest entered the darkened ballroom a spotlight was put on him or her; the name was announced, and the VIP walked to an assigned seat: "I remember when Martha came in she was wearing a luxurious fur coat, some kind of light color, and when she got to her chair she just let the coat slip off her shoulders and fall right on the floor. My husband was near her and I thought, 'If he picks up that coat I will kill him!' (He didn't.) But the interesting thing is that the Attorney General, who was near me, watched her performance and said, 'There she is, Minsky's finest!' I didn't know what he meant, but when I told [my husband] he thought it was hilarious."

This woman admits that she didn't like Martha. Then she laughs and confesses, "Oh, I suspect maybe there was a little tinge of jealousy, too. We'd come from communities where we were sort of *it,* and then in Washington we weren't anybody. Our husbands were and we weren't."

"I liked her," says Mrs. George Shultz, whose husband was Secretary of Labor. She recalls the way Martha "had us doing things together," and how pleased she was with the education in government she got as a result of Martha's getting the wives to visit all the departments. She adds, "I thought she was very good."

Mrs. George Romney was quick to defend Martha during the time their husbands were in the Cabinet together. After the criticism following Martha's call to Mrs. Fulbright, Mrs. Romney told me, "Martha wasn't arm-twisting. She was pouring out her heart about something that meant a lot to her. She thought she was talking to a friend."

Another Administration wife who had fond memories of Martha is Pat Mosbacher, wife of Nixon's first Chief of Protocol. The two worked closely on several projects, and since the Mitchells and Mosbachers lived at the Watergate, they often shared a limousine in the evenings when both couples were attending the same party, which was about twice each week.

Sometimes the Mosbachers would stop in at the Mitchells' for a nightcap. According to Pat, those would be "very interesting evenings, fascinating, really, hearing him talk about what he could talk about." Did he speak freely in front of Martha? "Oh, yes. And in those days nothing seemed to rattle him that she did."

When the Mitchells moved to New York, Martha and Pat continued their friendship. But Pat laughs when she recalls how difficult it was to stay in touch with Martha. "She would call to give me her new number and then it would be changed the next week so there was no way I could reach her." Pat would have to wait for Martha to call again with the new number.

"Martha was a very good friend to me," Pat recalls. "I always found her willing and cheerful. She had a good sense of humor; when that big grin went on and those eyes sparkled, there was a lot of machinery behind it." She also says Martha had a "fantastic memory; she had total recall. She could recall, word for word, months later, something she'd heard at a party."

Martha's various projects for the Cabinet wives developed gradually, simply because she didn't know what the President wanted the wives to do. John wasn't any help; he was too busy running the Justice Department, making plans for the 1972 campaign (Martha always insisted that John started working on Nixon's re-election the day he was sworn into office) and being Richard Nixon's lawyer. John Mitchell continually talked about being the *President's* lawyer; he persisted in this claim even after the media repeatedly pointed out to him that the Attorney General of the United States is supposed to represent all the people, not one individual.

In fact, not only did John not help Martha find a project but he was quick to veto a worthy one she found for herself. Through Mrs. Potter Stewart, Martha heard about the Friends of the Juvenile Court, a nonprofit organization that helps find jobs for fourteen- and fifteen-year-old "first offenders." John forbade Martha to work with the Friends, saying that the organization was "too political." Apparently he based his judgment on the fact that one of its members was Mrs. Ramsey Clark, wife of the Democrat who preceded John Mitchell as Attorney General.

Martha sought help from various White House aides, calling one or the other of them daily. At the time, an aide told a friend that Martha "really is crying out for guidance, but nobody will give it to her."

Her most frequent contact at the White House in the early months was John Whitaker, who was Secretary to the Cabinet. Herb Klein also received frequent calls and at one point arranged for Jeb Magruder to help Martha. And Charlotte Butterfield recalls that Martha often called her husband, Alexander Butterfield, a Haldeman aide who later revealed the existence of the White House tapes.

Charlotte Butterfield was another Administration wife who liked Martha. "I felt I understood her," she says. "I had a feeling for her, her situation as a small-town girl with feelings of inadequacy, her anxieties in a new situation. When she came to Washington some jolting adjustments had to be made."

Many people who met Martha socially during the early months of 1969 recall she was seeking advice from almost everyone she met. Bob Gray, who talked to her often, says, "She thought she could make a contribution to John's career and to the Administration. And she seemed to take both assignments personally."

At one point Martha became interested in launching a national program to help educate teen-agers and parents about the dangers of drugs. When she couldn't get it going as a Cabinet wives' project, she adopted it as her own, saying she was determined to promote it because "drugs have been pushed under the rug too long and because one night at a party I was dancing with a good friend when he told me that his thirteen-year-old daughter was on heroin. He was frantic. He hadn't even told his wife." Her determination to do something about drug abuse was strengthened when another friend's son had a tragic reaction to a mind-altering drug.

Martha was outraged and made her feelings known publicly when anthropologist Margaret Mead called for lenience toward marijuana use and asked for a ban only for those under sixteen. And Martha proudly reported to the press Marty's reaction when she learned one of the Beatles was on drugs: "I walked into Marty's room and found her stomping with all her might on her Beatles records. She has loved the Beatles. I said, 'Marty, what's the matter?' She told me that she had found out that one of them had taken dope and she wanted no more to do with them. I was so proud of her."

Martha threw herself wholeheartedly into the drug program. She organized a drug-abuse symposium at the State Department (after her request to have it at the White House was turned down; the First Lady also refused her invitation to attend). She conferred with the Smithsonian Institution about a planned drug exhibit, recruited other Justice Department wives and led them through the FBI's drug exhibits, and went to New York to check out the Beth Israel Medical Center's drug program, where she talked to addicts and former addicts about the merits of methadone in drug treatment.

When Martha had to abandon the program, a White House aide told a reporter, "It just fell through the cracks," leaving the impression that Martha had lost interest.

Actually, Martha had to give up the program because she didn't have time to devote to it. John and the White House thought it more important for Martha to attend Republican affairs; by this time they had discovered she was one of their better drawing cards and that her presence at any event guaranteed it would be a sell-out.

IRONICALLY IT WAS MARTHA'S LAST IDEA FOR THE CABINET WIVES THAT, in her words, got her into "a heck of a mess." Before the program was over several wives were openly hostile, and First Lady Pat Nixon was completely alienated.

It all started innocently enough when Pat Mosbacher told Martha that needlepoint seat covers were needed for some of the dining-room chairs in Blair House, the President's guest quarters across the street from the White House. Martha suggested the Nixon Cabinet wives should contribute them; she and Pat thought each woman should do her husband's seal of office.

Martha checked with the Cabinet wives and thought that everyone agreed to produce and donate a seat cover. Mrs. Nixon was to do the Presidential seal; Mrs. Agnew the Vice-President's. Martha found a New York designer to paint the seals on canvas and to select the yarn for each one.

Later it was discovered it was against tradition for anyone to sit on an official government seal, but by then the project was so far along, it was decided the needlepoint seals could be framed and hung as pictures. Martha invited Pat Nixon, Judy Agnew and all the Cabinet wives to a luncheon at Blair House to receive their needlepoint kits.

Martha spent days working on the details of the luncheon—the menu, the guest list (Mrs. Nixon, all of the Cabinet wives and Pat Mosbacher; Mrs. Agnew was out of town) and especially press arrangements. She had seen the press clippings from the previous Administration's involvement in Blair House, when the Democratic wives had received tremendous media coverage for their work. Martha seemed to take it as a personal challenge to see that the Republicans fared as well, if not better.

She talked to me several times about press coverage. I told her to have a "pool" reporter for the luncheon itself and a small group of newswomen in for cocktails before lunch. I suggested she have Scripps-Howard columnist Wauhillau LaHay as pool reporter, since she knew more about needlepoint than the rest of us.

Then, three days before the luncheon, while giving out the First Lady's schedule, Pat Nixon's press secretary, Connie Stuart, announced that her boss would attend a luncheon at Blair House as the guest of

"Cabinet wives and Mrs. Agnew." She did not mention that the Attorney General's wife was the luncheon hostess.

When she heard about Connie's announcement, Martha felt she had been deliberately and publicly "put down" by Connie. Martha had had earlier run-ins with Connie and for some time the two had been feuding; Martha thought the press secretary was not delivering her messages to Pat Nixon.

Martha stewed over the insult all that day and the next, and discussed it over the phone numerous times with friends. By the second evening she was so upset she called Isabelle Shelton, of the Washington *Star,* and charged, "Connie is trying to get rid of me, to kill me, because I announced to the press that I called her at five A.M." Sometime before the Blair House incident Martha had told reporters she made a predawn call to Connie "to get her attention."

Continuing her complaint to Isabelle, Martha said that someone had "disinvited" her pool reporter, and a member of the First Lady's press staff had been substituted. Accusing Connie of trying to take over press arrangements for her private luncheon, she asked, "How can she take over my party? This is my party; I'm giving it; I'm paying for it."

Connie denied she had "disinvited" Wauhillau. A Justice Department spokesman said Mrs. LaHay had "voluntarily withdrawn as a guest." Wauhillau indignantly denied the allegation. Martha continued to believe Connie was the culprit.

When her guests arrived for the luncheon, Martha still was sizzling. While Mrs. Nixon chatted with the other wives, Martha talked to the press, telling them that Connie "probably gives me more trouble than she gives you." When asked about her statement that Connie was out to get her, Martha said, "It is a really hazardous situation."

It was more hazardous than Martha knew at the time. Many of the wives were understandably furious with Martha for airing the official family's wash in public; they thought the feud with Connie was petty, not to mention embarrassing. Then, too, some of them were irritated when they discovered the needlepoint kits were costing about seventy dollars each. A few at first refused to pay their share. "Who do they think is going to pay for them?" Martha demanded to know. "This is each wife's contribution to Blair House!"

The next problem arose when it was discovered the designs were painted on petit-point canvas, making the working so tedious many wives had to give up and farm out their seals to friends. Wauhillau did the Justice Department seal; Martha was so grateful she gave a luncheon in

Wauhillau's honor in John's private dining room and presented her with a large silver shell engraved with the Attorney General's seal.

It was more than a year before all of the seals were completed and framed. Once they were in place on the stair wall between the first and second floors, Martha and Pat Mosbacher invited Mrs. Nixon, Mrs. Agnew and all of the wives to Blair House for tea and an unveiling of their handiwork. Before they set the date, the hostesses checked with the White House to be sure there wasn't a conflict with the First Lady's schedule.

But a day or two before the tea, Martha was told that Pat Nixon wouldn't attend. Martha telephoned the First Lady to ask her to change her mind; Pat still refused to go to the tea. Then Martha called several White House aides, including John Ehrlichman, to demand that Pat attend; she explained that the First Lady and Mrs. Agnew were the guests of honor; that columnists already had announced that Pat would be there, and that the party was a *group* activity. When this failed to get an acceptance from the First Lady, Martha telephoned Bebe Rebozo, in Key Biscayne, and insisted that he contact the President and tell him to intervene.

Pat Nixon went to the tea.

The proper Pat and the quixotic Martha never did manage to get along. Martha found the First Lady "mechanical," claiming, "You could go out and build a woman like Pat Nixon." And the volatile Martha, so spontaneous in her emotions and reactions, must have been appalling to Pat Nixon, the perfect political wife who remained unruffled and seemingly unperturbed come what may.

Although a hint of Pat Nixon's feelings came out to reporters in May 1971. Asked about Martha's outspokenness, the First Lady said, "This is a free country, and I'm not going to criticize someone for what they say. As for myself, I only talk on subjects on which I am really informed."

That afternoon at Blair House, Pat and Martha, both of whom had wanted careers in the theater at one point in their lives, put on award-winning performances. The First Lady joked and laughed with reporters and discussed at length her upcoming trip to the People's Republic of China. Even Martha grudgingly admitted later that she'd never seen Pat so "fluid and gracious." Martha, too, was chatty and gay and flashed her deep dimples a lot. But she couldn't resist a put-down of the First Lady. After hearing from reporters that Pat was discussing the China trip,

Martha said *she* wouldn't go to a Communist country, adding that she'd get her "Chinese food at home."

The Blair House affair didn't ruin Pat and Martha's friendship, since none ever had existed. It only ended for the two any future pretense of cordiality.

Chapter Eleven

MARTHA'S OPINIONS AND ASIDES ON EVERYTHING AND EVERYbody from the Supreme Court ("eradicate it") to anthropologist Margaret Mead ("she caused a lot of trouble, she advocated taking drugs and early marriages") brought her thousands of telegrams and letters, most of them favorable, ranging from pleas that she run for President to a suggestion from a Republican on Long Island that "Madam Attorney General" should resign. An Ohio admirer saw her as the only voice crying out in the wilderness of a nation where even its lawmakers had "sold out for a vote." But to a woman in Pasadena, California, Martha was "a pitiful, prating, mincing, giggling, illiterate child-woman."

As Martha read a particularly hateful letter she often wailed, "I can't understand why the liberals are so against me. Here I am, doing *their* thing, trying to have some freedom of speech and they want to take it away."

Mail from "liberals" was usually heavy after Martha said something outrageous, such as suggesting that singer Carol Feraci be "torn limb from limb" after the young girl, performing at the White House, pulled from her bra a banner denouncing the Vietnam war. John whisked Martha away from the party almost as fast as the Secret Service sequestered Miss

Feraci for questioning in the downstairs library. Ironically, Martha blasted Carol Feraci not because the singer was against the Vietnam war—Martha was, too—but because she chose the White House as a forum for her protest.

It would be hard to overestimate the importance Martha attached to her mail. To her it was "proof" that what she was doing and saying was right. Martha hadn't been surprised that the press and the "liberals" criticized her remarks—and even her personal appearance. But she couldn't understand, and didn't until the day she died, why members of the Nixon Administration would find fault with her for saying in public the things they knew the President was saying in private. Not that any of her critics said anything to her personally. But others told her. They even let her know that "the girls" [Tricia and Julie] were furious that Martha was stealing the limelight from their mother, the First Lady.

"Sometimes," Martha later said, "my mail was the only thing that kept me going." She felt the same way, after Watergate, when hundreds of people wrote to tell her she was doing the right thing when she talked of dirty tricks and a President who *knew.*

When she was in Washington, a great number of people wrote asking for help with their personal problems or wanting her to champion causes. This was so, Martha said during a 1970 interview, because "Washington has been too far away from the people for so many years they have no contact here." She faithfully read their letters and telegrams and tried to help them through the government red tape—the red tape she herself hated so much—by telephoning the head of the bureau or agency involved with the particular problem.

"You see," she gleefully explained when we were doing the *Look* interview, "they don't know if it is just little ol' Martha calling or if it is the Attorney General, or maybe the President himself who wants the matter taken care of!"

In July 1970, Martha received a letter from Mrs. James R. Hoffa, wife of the former president of the two-million-member International Brotherhood of Teamsters. After reading the five-page handwritten appeal for help in freeing her husband from prison, Martha wrote Mrs. Hoffa, telling her the letter had touched both her heart and mind, and assuring her that she, Martha, understood Mrs. Hoffa's "sickening frustrations." At the time Martha thought she did. Later she said she really didn't know what sickening frustrations were until after Watergate, when she found *herself* in what she felt was a hopeless, no-win situation.

When John heard Martha had written Mrs. Hoffa, he forbade her to have any further contact with the wife of the former Teamster boss. Naturally, Martha thought it was because the Nixon Administration felt Hoffa *should* be in prison and that it wouldn't do anything to set him free. But two days before Christmas 1971, only four months after the U. S. Parole Board had turned down Hoffa's parole application for the third time, President Nixon pardoned James Hoffa. Martha was shocked—and confused. If they were going to pardon this man, why was John angry with her for writing to his wife? In her mind, Martha went over and over everything she had seen or heard about Hoffa. Finally, she thought she had the answer.

Martha figured John didn't want her to get mixed up in anything he and the White House were working on for fear the press might find out and upset their apple cart. At the time the Attorney General was secretly courting Frank Fitzsimmons, who had become president of the Teamsters' union after Hoffa's conviction. Martha had no idea, then, that there was a connection between Fitzsimmons and Hoffa's future pardon. She just thought it odd that when Fitzsimmons was coming to the Mitchells' Watergate apartment, John asked her to dress up and be ready to meet him; usually when her husband had secret meetings at the apartment—which he often did—he made her stay upstairs. When Fitzsimmons arrived, Martha went down and talked for ten or fifteen minutes to the man John had told her was the only one in organized labor on the side of Nixon.

John Mitchell and Fitzsimmons had a long meeting that first afternoon, and after that John often came home and said he'd seen Fitzsimmons, or sometimes that Fitzsimmons had been over to see Mr. President.

The Administration had to court Fitzsimmons, Martha said, because he could deliver Teamster votes to Nixon in 1972. Later, John boasted to her that Fitzsimmons also delivered quite a lot of money to the Nixon re-election kitty. Before he disappeared in July 1975, James Hoffa accused the Teamsters of giving more to the Nixon campaign than it had reported. He said part of the money came from Las Vegas gambling interests. Fitzsimmons branded Hoffa's remarks as "damn lies."

During the time John was meeting with Fitzsimmons, Martha said, he was making a lot of phone calls to Murray Chotiner (a long-time political friend of Richard Nixon's and special counsel to the President in 1970) and to John Ehrlichman to talk about Hoffa. John Mitchell also had meetings and phone conversations with John Dean and U.S. Pardon Attorney Lawrence H. Traylor about the Teamsters' past president. Later, when William Saxbe was Attorney General, he ordered Traylor not to answer any questions about his talks with John Mitchell concerning Fitzsimmons and Hoffa.

A right-wing publisher, friendly toward Hoffa, learned about John Mitchell's meeting with Fitzsimmons and wrote him, saying that the vice-presidents of the Teamsters were unanimous in their support of the Democratic party. He added that Mitchell's deal with Fitzsimmons was not going to get the Republicans anything. But he noted that members of the union were devoted to Hoffa and would follow him if he were out of prison and suggested that they vote Republican.

So it seemed that Fitzsimmons couldn't deliver anything from the Teamsters as long as James Hoffa was in jail; only his pardon would get the votes. But a pardon would put Hoffa back as head of the Teamsters. This would never do because Fitzsimmons, not Hoffa, was the Administration's friend. A deal was finally worked out, in which Hoffa got out of prison but was not to engage in union activities until 1980.

In March 1974, Hoffa filed a suit seeking to have the ban on his union activities declared illegal. John Dean, in a deposition taken by James Hoffa's attorneys, said he originated the idea of a restriction on Hoffa's pardon while talking with John Mitchell. In his deposition before the same attorneys, Lawrence Traylor testified that it was the first time in his five years at the Justice Department that an employment condition of this type had been added to a pardon.

WHEN HER MAIL FIRST BECAME HEAVY (UP TO FOUR HUNDRED PIECES A day), Martha asked John for more help in answering it. It was impossible for the one secretary provided her by the Justice Department to handle such a volume. John suggested she dump the letters in the nearest wastebasket. Martha later said, "His answer infuriated me. First, because it wasn't the kind of reply he would have made before becoming involved in politics. Second, because he wasn't helping me to do something that had to be done. I felt that if the public wanted something of me, if there were questions they wanted me to answer, I was going to answer them —that's why I was in Washington."

For some time she tried to take care of the mail with just the one assistant. Sitting in her breakfast room, smoking Salem Longs and drinking Cokes, she carefully read each letter, making notes for answer on all with return addresses, which most of the hate letters didn't have. A lot of the poison-pen mail was written in red ink—sometimes in blood—and a large part of it came without stamps. Martha always paid the postage. Some of the hate mail was so threatening it was turned over to the FBI.

Often Martha took stacks of mail with her to read in her chauffeured car on the way to a party. And it wasn't unusual for her to show other guests a purse stuffed with mail, or for her to discuss the letters' contents. One day she came to a benefit fashion show and cheerfully produced an anonymous letter containing bumper stickers urging "Impeach Martha Mitchell." And a friend remembers the day Martha arrived at a State Department luncheon furious about something in one of the letters she was carrying. It involved a serviceman in Vietnam, and Martha declared, "It makes me so damn mad I'm going to call Mel Laird [then Secretary of Defense] right now and tell him about it!" Off she went, out of the room in search of a phone.

Eventually Martha talked to Rogers C. B. Morton, then chairman of the Republican National Committee, about her problem with the mail. He immediately assigned two women from the Committee to help. (The first two weeks they answered a backlog of two thousand letters.) This worked beautifully, until Robert Dole replaced Morton as chairman; then Martha was told there was no one available. She never knew why. Finally, she was given an office at CREEP, with secretaries and volunteer help.

But Martha still insisted on reading her mail and often a letter would send her flying to the telephone. One day a letter arrived from a disillusioned Republican couple in Seattle, Washington, explaining why—given Nixon's performance on Vietnam—they couldn't vote for his re-election. Martha told volunteer Junie Dankworth to "get these people on the phone." Martha talked to the couple for several minutes. When she hung up, Martha walked out of her private office, slapped the Seattle letter on Junie's desk, grinned and said, "Chalk up two more votes for Nixon!"

Martha didn't do all of her corresponding with strangers. Raised in the Southern tradition of letter writing, she kept in touch with old school friends with long, handwritten, detailed reports of her life in Washington. Following the 1969 Inaugural, she wrote her former Pine Bluff friend Helene Johnson Whalen that it was fun "putting Pine Bluff on the map; it should have been there a long time ago." Helene recalls with affectionate amusement that Martha was "so tickled to be writing on White House stationery."

Although at first John had told Martha to throw her mail in the wastebasket, there came a time when he was unusually interested in the people writing to her. Martha didn't find out about it until much later, but certain letters that were not threatening were turned over to the FBI to check out the people who had written them. She didn't know how they were selected, but after the writers had been investigated, the FBI reports were delivered to John under the classification, "Individuals in Communication with Mrs. Martha Mitchell."

After Martha made a remark that she'd help anyone get a one-way ticket to Cuba if he didn't like the U.S.A., she received a flood of mail. One was from a student at a Southern college who wrote asking Martha to please furnish more details about her offer to help any dissatisfied citizen get to Cuba. There was nothing threatening about his letter; in fact, he was quite complimentary. But the FBI checked out the student anyway and learned nothing other than he was studying law.

In with other letters she never saw were some interview requests. One from the Canadian Broadcasting Corporation had a little note attached, asking "Should Mrs. M do?" John Mitchell had penned on the note, "How many votes are there in Canada?"

Another practice Martha wasn't aware of was sending form letters with John Mitchell's rubber-stamped signature thanking people for writing to Martha. She never knew why some of her mail was answered by John.

Mail from young people was especially cherished by Martha. She claimed she related to them, that she understood them. An amazing number of them wrote her, particularly after it was reported she had said "the Vietnam war stinks." Typical of hundreds of letters she received from college students was one from a twenty-two-year-old self-styled "protester-flower child." The girl wrote that she had believed Martha was "part of that establishment who believe in the insanity of power mongering, of nationalism over humanism, and I rather thought you a nut . . ." But she continued, "I've come to believe that you are a free thinker, a lover of life, and a beautiful person. I'm rather sorry I ever felt otherwise. I just want to tell you that you're really okay and together. Keep laughing, loving and enjoying life . . ."

She received many invitations from campuses to come speak; she was eager to do it. There were a lot of things she wanted to say to young people, including, "Don't think the world is coming to an end; every generation has a generation gap, this has existed since the beginning of time." She wanted them to know their turn would come, and in the meantime they should pursue their studies, because the smarter they became the better equipped they would be to handle the problems of the country.

But John wouldn't let her go on the campuses, claiming it would be too dangerous. Since Martha didn't believe him, she took every opportunity she could to see students on her own.

Washington man-about-town Bob Gray remembers walking into the George Town Club one noon and seeing Martha seated at a table with three young men: "She called me over and said, 'Bob, I want you to meet my friends.' But she didn't know their names. It turned out they were college students who had written her a letter saying they wanted to meet her. She agreed to it and took them to lunch. They couldn't help her in the slightest and there never was a word about it in the papers. But she did it. It seemed to me to be commendable."

In the rare interviews Jay Jennings gives about his mother he always emphasizes these good things Martha did. And that was what he wanted to talk about when we met one evening for dinner. He told me he thought his mother's greatest attribute was "her definite concern with and for other people." He spoke, with some bitterness, about this facet of her personality having been more or less ignored by the media.

Actually, Martha's public-service roles weren't overlooked at the time; the Washington press regularly wrote about Martha's involvement in charitable and civic affairs. Gwen Dobson, then women's editor of the Washington *Star,* wrote in early 1972 that there wasn't a charity appeal in the city that Martha ignored: "She will pose, sip tea, taste preview menus, dance, speak Swahili or simply make the appearance. To the recollection of the press, Martha has never let anyone down."

Washington hostess Jane De Graff claims, "I never met a woman who put as much emotionally of herself, as much caring, into any project she was involved with." And one of the FBI agents who guarded Martha remembers that Martha was "overjoyed" to appear at the various charity events. "It wasn't a duty or a chore for her," he says.

MARTHA OFTEN AMAZED PEOPLE WITH HER ENTHUSIASTIC RESPONSES TO their requests for help. Such was the case when she was asked for assistance with the annual benefit given by Marty's school, Stone Ridge Country Day School of the Sacred Heart. Martha arranged for the benefit to be a coffee at historic Anderson House, where one mother confided to the press, "Normally we have about one hundred mothers at the party. Thanks to Martha Mitchell's generosity—she's paying for the whole affair —there are more than three hundred here and everything we're taking in [five dollars per head] is for the school's building fund." Another mother added, "We never had it so good—thanks to Martha Mitchell."

The Daughters of the American Revolution could always depend on Martha's participation in their programs. She was proud of her family's long association with the DAR and she often told interviewers about starting "The Good Wives River Chapter" of the DAR in Darien, Connecticut. She enjoyed going to DAR functions, and it both annoyed and angered her that John belittled the organization and refused to go with her to its events. The only time he went was when "Mr. President asked John to represent him at something the DAR gave."

Not only was Martha a Cabinet wife who "never let anyone down" but she was a publicity chairman's dream; Martha was game for anything. The charities she touted weren't publicized with sterile pictures of a woman behind a teapot.

While helping with a telethon for Children's Hospital, Martha donned a Santa Claus costume and let a photographer take action shots of her putting on Santa's snow-white wig. Once in Santa's suit, Martha took her place in front of the cameras and stayed for an hour, instead of the scheduled ten minutes, sometimes using four telephones at a time to answer such questions as, "What do you feed your reindeer?" Without hesitating a second, Martha replied, "Claus food."

When she was asked to help get advance publicity for a match at the Potomac Polo Club to raise money for a Heartmobile, Martha—in borrowed britches, boots and pith helmet—posed astride a horse that, according to the *Star*, she approached in the ninety-degree heat "with caution, trepidation, courage and a great amount of good-sportsmanship, after first asking a committee chairman, 'Are you sure you want me to do this?' "

But all of Martha's good deeds weren't publicity stunts. For example, the public knew nothing about a young Nigerian girl Martha sponsored as an immigrant to the United States until Martha accidentally ran into the mathematics student at a restaurant where the girl was working as a part-time waitress.

And it was months before the press knew that Martha was trying to get back to the United States an American woman's two children, who had been kidnapped by their Greek father and taken to his homeland. Martha told Gwen Dobson shortly before Watergate, "That's a tough one since we have no [extradition] agreement with Greece. But I'll get them home some way or another." Unfortunately John was out of Washington before she could complete the job. But even after she'd moved to New York, the children's mother wrote to thank Martha for giving her the courage to take the custody fight to the Greek courts.

Martha didn't limit her good deeds to Washington programs and projects; she went all over the United States helping worthy causes. And often if she couldn't attend an event in person she donated a "Luncheon with" or "Dinner with" Martha Mitchell for an auction item or door prize. One such luncheon was donated to the Little Rock [Arkansas] Art Center's benefit auction. Robert Hickman, a young insurance salesman, and his wife Ann paid $110 for the privilege of eating with Martha. They got a bargain. Martha paid off with a luncheon at Blair House, where the Hickmans ate with such luminaries as the Attorney General of the United States, the Chief of Protocol and his wife, various congressmen and the mayor of Little Rock. Martha never had met the mayor and wasn't aware he was a Democrat when she called to invite him.

Another luncheon donated by Martha got her into an unexpected controversy. Martha agreed to have lunch with the highest bidder of a George Washington University scholarship auction, never dreaming that a twenty-year-old sophomore journalism student, with red beard and long blond hair curling over his collar, would bid the highest (one hundred dollars) in order to get a publishable interview.

A month of negotiations between the student, Jan Bridge, and a Justice Department aide followed. Jan claimed the aide gave him a "hard time" and at one point said he thought his phone was tapped. The aide denied both allegations. Finally Martha and Kay Woestendieck had lunch with Jan at the Mitchell's Watergate apartment. The outcome was surprising.

Martha so charmed Jan that he came away her fan. "I thought she'd be like a vulture—I thought she would be very cold, nasty, biting, but she was very, very warm," Jan told waiting reporters. Then he added a surprising observation about the wife of Richard Nixon's Attorney General, "She is one of the very few adults I've met in the last few years who gives a damn about youth—pro or con."

PERHAPS MARTHA DIDN'T CONSIDER GOOD WORKS A DUTY OR A CHORE because so many of the fund-raising events she attended were the types of parties she adored. "I'm probably the only person who's a member of official Washington who will say this: I like charity balls," Martha told me once. She thought the balls were the best parties given in Washington. She liked the fact they they lasted "a while," instead of ending around ten P.M., as most Washington seated dinners do.

Martha once said she wasn't right for Washington and Washington wasn't right for her, adding that the main reason might have been that Washington "operates on a set of rules of etiquette that goes by the name of 'protocol,' whereas I was brought up on a completely different set of principles known as 'good manners.' "

Washington journalist-author Hope Miller remembers Martha talking to her about protocol soon after the 1969 Inaugural: "She was saying how silly it was in Washington that people who were ranking guests had to leave parties before other people did. And I said everybody can't go to the door at the same time! You need to have some kind of ranking; it simplifies things . . . And Martha said, 'We still think it's silly that we've got to leave the party first before anybody can go home.' "

Martha had firm and positive reasons why she didn't like protocol. "For example," she said, "it dictates that a guest's position at the dinner table is determined by her or his rank. The higher the rank, the closer the guest is to the head of the table (or, by tradition, nearer the salt). Your hosts couldn't care less if this arrangement puts you next to your worst enemy."

One time protocol *did* put Martha next to a hostile fellow Arkansan. When the Mitchells went to the French Embassy dinner for President Pompidou she was seated beside Senator J. William Fulbright. This was soon after Martha had telephoned Betty Fulbright about the Supreme Court nominee vote. The senior Senator from Martha's home state, usually a polite and proper gentleman, sat next to Martha all evening and didn't say one word to her.

The first time Martha was embarrassingly aware of protocol was when, a few weeks after arriving in Washington, she went to a "ladies' luncheon" and stayed on and on, wondering when the other women were going to leave. "I stood on one foot and then the other," she said, "getting more and more nervous about getting home before my little girl came home from school." Finally, Mrs. Everett Dirksen whispered in her ear: "Nobody can leave until you do—you're the ranking guest."

Martha admitted, though, that protocol wasn't all bad: "It often got me seated next to some of my favorite dinner partners—Bill Rogers, Mel Laird, Elliot Richardson, Bill Brock. Bill Rogers, then Secretary of State and my first choice of a man-to-dine-by, is intelligent, amusing and always good company."

She thought that Elliot Richardson was a great conversationalist, "although Elliot did talk a little highfalutin occasionally." And that "if one can believe his publicity, Henry Kissinger is an ideal dinner partner. I like Henry, and John thought he was intelligent, but I've never been able to fathom what other women apparently see in him. As far as I'm concerned, I couldn't even *understand* him. With that accent, it kept me busy translating everything he said."

But Martha loved talking with Patrick Moynihan, because he "had the greatest sense of humor." Evidently he liked her, too. He once ended a letter to John Mitchell, "My love to Martha, who was always kindness itself to me. *And* the nearest thing I could find to a Democrat at those Cabinet dinners!"

Martha also said, "Maybe one reason that I was never taken seriously in Washington—no woman is—is it's a man's town. Probably the thing that hacked me most about protocol was that the man, who is supposed to be the protector of the woman he is married to, was always the one who was catered to."

Another sore point with Martha was the way the sexes were segregated following dinner: "At many parties, whether private or at an embassy or whatever, the men went off by themselves for cordials and cigars and the women went to another room . . . This aggravated me so much I told John Mitchell, 'I'm not going off again to a party where I'm shoved into another room, to discuss tea-party subjects, while you sit downstairs with a bunch of men and discuss politics or whatever it is you discuss.' "

Martha also put her foot down about going to large dinners where her husband sat on the dais and she was seated at a table "with a bunch of women." She told John Mitchell that if they couldn't sit together, she'd stay home.

Protocol wasn't the only reason Martha didn't like Washington social life. It "irritated the hell out" of her that the private get-togethers of Administration people were always working sessions where the men talked business even *before* dinner. "I remember one night at the Peter Flanigans'," Martha said, "when the men were on the sun porch for cocktails and the women sat in the living room in their beautiful gowns, lined up like dolls in a museum. I thought, 'We're nothing but window dressing!'

"The same separation of the sexes before dinner (as well as after) took place at the home of Chief Justice and Mrs. Warren Burger. The women sat on the patio while the men were inside talking business. That night at the table, when I asked for an ashtray so I could have a cigarette, Burger gave me a lecture on the health hazards of smoking. After we ate I went outside in the woods to smoke while they had coffee."

Although Martha occasionally tried to put a little fun into these parties, her behavior on the regular Washington party rounds seems to have been above reproach.

"I never saw her do anything that was not, shall we say, ladylike. Never anything out of line," says Hope Miller, who saw Martha at many parties.

But another observer of the Washington scene volunteers that she can't say the same about John Mitchell. One night when socialite-philanthropist Rose Saul Zalles gave a dinner party for the Mitchells at the 1925

F Street Club, John Mitchell stood up after dinner to toast his hostess. But first he told what the Washington *Post* reported as "a couple of tired old locker-room jokes." After the jokes there was some nervous laughter, and the woman remembers that "the gentleman sitting next to me, who was big with the Republicans, said, 'I'm awfully sorry for John Mitchell. I think he must be dead drunk.' "

Not all of Martha's defenders are women. "I saw her a lot," says a Republican gentleman whose first political appointment was during the Eisenhower Administration, "and she struck me as a hell of a good wife for a guy in his position. She conducted herself as a good Southern wife would in terms of public attitude to her husband."

He recalls one night after a private dinner party when the guests went to the drawing room for liqueur and demitasse: "Then Mitchell just took over the conversation. He was pontificating and no one else could get in a word. It was like the Sermon on the Mount. He, with that goddamn pipe, just acted like what he said was the *ultimate pronouncement.* And she sat quietly, she really did, and I distinctly remember feeling sorry for the poor woman having to put up with this."

Because Martha wanted "more than anything for this country to become a family with the rest of the world," she tried to go to every embassy party or benefit she was invited to. She made many friends among the foreign community, though most embassies were a disappointment to her because they had what she called "the predictable social format." Martha said, "It always seemed so stupid to me to go to the various embassies and find them trying to be just alike in food and service. Why don't people stick to the ethnic bit? Let the Italians serve Italian food and have Italian entertainment. Let the Germans act like Germans, the French like French, the Spanish like Spanish, and so on. Our ambassadors abroad should concentrate on American foods, wines and entertainment, too. That way we could all learn a lot about other people . . .

"One hears so much about the 'little' Washington dinner party," Martha continued. "How chic it is. How stimulating. Don't believe it. Although most of the dinners are for only eight or ten, the rules are as rigidly followed as they would be at a White House state function. . . .

"That isn't my idea of fun or friendliness or hospitality—or of anything smacking of *human* society. I thought society was one thing, and Washington society turned out to be something else. I guess that was my problem."

Bob Gray puts it another way: "I think Martha was knowledgeable and sophisticated in the standard of Pine Bluff, Arkansas. And she expected the same consistencies of friendship, the same standards of performance and reliability of commitments here that [she expected there]."

Another long-time observer of the Washington scene agrees that Martha's Southern background contributed to her problems in Washington. "I have found that Southern women are different, and it has helped me in understanding my mother," says Scottie Smith, the daughter of Zelda Fitzgerald.

Scottie says that Zelda was not prepared for living in the North without her beloved family and old friends surrounding her, since "in the South, life was so cozy and full of love that it formed a cocoon . . .

"Southern women of my mother's generation, and of Martha's generation, had a 'belle' complex," Scottie continues. "When Martha was growing up women were taught that there is only one thing you are supposed to be in this world and that is charming. That's all that matters."

Unfortunately in the case of many women, just sitting around and being charming led to what Scottie calls an "on-stage" syndrome. "When Martha was young," she explains, "she probably got off these little funny remarks and everyone said, 'Isn't she cute!' So all of her life she kept acting out the cute child that everybody laughs at, the darling of the group.

"Washington probably is the staidest place in the world, in many ways," Scottie continues. "Everybody is on view, and on tip-toe and watching themselves every minute. So Martha appeared in a town which is made up of people who have an opposite attitude from hers toward how you behave in public. What she did was so completely against the grain of everything that Washington had been about for so long that people were just dazed. They thought she was Alice in Wonderland."

Martha had another trait of Southern womanhood, one which has been described by the great Southern poet James Dickey. He said, "They are very loving and affectionate, but they really think their men are dependent on them. If their man is brilliant, they think he's brilliant because they helped him be brilliant. Basically, they think their men are weak, and could never have gotten anywhere without their help."

Martha sincerely felt John Mitchell achieved his social status because of her. Like Dickey's Southern woman, Martha thought her man was weak and that his downfall came when he no longer accepted her help.

Chapter Twelve

DISENCHANTMENT WITH THE NIXON ADMINISTRATION CAME early for Martha. And long before it was generally known, she was not saying the same things about it in private that she was saying in public.

"The first inkling I got that Martha was not in accord with Nixon," says a woman who asks to remain anonymous, "came at a dinner Anna Chennault gave for bigwigs of the Republican party—this would have been in 1970, probably late summer—I believe the heads of two large aircraft companies were there—and high-ranking Pentagon brass.

"We were seated at round tables and Martha was at one, beside Bob Gray, with John seated at the next table. Their backs were to each other. When the toasts started, one of the military men who had just returned from Vietnam told how the young kids there—teen-agers, fourteen and fifteen years old—were putting on American uniforms and fighting with the American soldiers. Martha began crying out loud, sobbing. She said, 'We ought to get out, we ought to get out. We have no business there.' The man just stopped, taken aback. Bob Gray put his hand on Martha's shoulder and started patting her. But she kept on sobbing and saying, 'We ought to get out, we have no business there.' "

"Martha got real mad and she threw her napkin down on the table," Bob Gray recalls. "She sat there just fuming. Then as someone would say something she didn't like, she'd start making comments. First just between us and then to our table, and then really for the whole room. She had a debating society going right there. She was terribly upset about [the Vietnam talk].

"And I remember it was when a high-ranking military guy was talking that she said things like, 'That's a lie, that's a lie,' and he heard. It was so loud eventually he had to acknowledge her interruptions. He told her, 'Madam, I've got this opinion and you have yours.' It was embarrassing."

Still later, when another man started talking about Nixon's election, Martha cried, "It was a sad day; I wish he'd never been elected."

There were many reasons why Martha became disenchanted early with the Nixon Administration: Nixon hadn't ended the war as he'd led her to believe he would; his White House was spending more time "getting" its enemies than fighting crime in the streets; welfare still was a mess; and as she noted in her one "Dear Heart" letter, she was beginning to wonder if Nixon and his aides were capable of running the government.

But one of the principal reasons Martha was unhappy was because she thought the Nixon Administration was taking John away from her, in the way Clyde Jennings's salesman job had taken *him* away when they were married. Again she felt deserted, unwanted and left out.

Martha had come to Washington expecting to work with John and to help him make the United States a better country. Now it wasn't working out that way. Many evenings when John and Martha had plans to go out, the President would call to say he was going to have dinner on the *Sequoia* and he wanted John Mitchell to accompany him. It didn't matter that Martha was already dressed for a party; neither did it matter that a hostess was left without two of her guests.

"Many were the times when Richard Nixon asked John Mitchell to take off and go to Florida with him," Martha said. "Once John told me that there was a 'very crucial meeting,' but I learned later they were vacationing on Robert Abplanalp's island in the Bahamas. It hurt me tremendously."

On the nights when John was home there wasn't any free time for the two to share. There were phone calls from the President and his senior aides complaining about media criticism and how to counteract it. "Then there were the calls or visits from disgruntled Cabinet members and people with government agencies. As Washington observers have pointed out, the President would have little to do with most of the Cabinet, except at Cabinet meetings. Very often these people complained to John Mitchell and he tried to appease them.

"Even Rose Mary Woods, who had been Nixon's loyal personal secretary since his Senate days, came to our Watergate apartment to cry over the treatment she was getting from Bob Haldeman." John Mitchell talked her out of quitting.

John Mitchell not only had to appease people in the Administration, he also had to fire them. Richard Nixon, who couldn't stand confrontations, insisted that his Attorney General do the firing when the Administration wanted to oust someone in government. John Mitchell didn't relish having to be the President's hatchet man. He complained bitterly.

Martha told the Washington *Post* in 1974, "Mitchell used to come home and say, 'Why the hell do I have to fire them?' "

Her husband was on the phone so much, Martha said, that Marty complained. "He was supposed to help her with her math lessons, but many nights Marty sat and waited for her father until ten or eleven o'clock before she could complete her lessons and go to bed. She cried and cried over it, and even wrote in her diary that she didn't get enough attention to make her happy."

Marty became shy and withdrawn. Perhaps because, as Ray West says, "Marty did not have a normal childhood. But I don't suppose you can blame Martha and John for that," Ray continues. "It was just the circumstances of who they were and the lives they lived."

Sue Morrison, John Mitchell's secretary, used to feel sorry for Marty: "She couldn't even take a walk, she might be kidnapped—and that got to be a phobia."

Marty resented, too, the time her mother spent going to parties. It didn't matter to her that most of them were official functions, considered as extensions of her father's position in the Administration. During one period Marty would cling to her mother as her parents were going out the door and beg her to stay home.

Martha tried to make up in other ways for the lack of attention she could give Marty. Piper Dankworth, daughter of CREEP aide Junie Dankworth, remembers how Martha always was planning things for Marty, such as having Piper, who is four years older than Marty, go shopping with her—just the two girls and the chauffeur. Once, when Marty wanted a "different" birthday party, Martha asked Junie and Piper to help her plan a slumber party. They got a movie from the American Film Institute and they served hamburgers and hot dogs. The next day all the little girls took a tour of the FBI and posed for pictures with an agent.

BOTH JOHN AND MARTHA ENJOYED REPEATING TO FRIENDS A REMARK Richard Nixon made to John not too long after the first Inaugural. "You be President and I'll be Secretary of State." There were times when Martha thought he must have been serious.

Once when complaining about John's devotion to his job, Martha said, "Our weekends weren't safe from the interference, either. No matter what we planned it seemed the President had other arrangements for John, and the President's arrangements always took priority.

"If I did go on an out-of-town trip with John," Martha continued, "the President still monopolized his time. One summer when he was spending a month or two at the Western White House in San Clemente, he suggested that John and I take a house near his. We did, and we were constantly having to make appearances. For instance, the President would decide at four o'clock in the afternoon that he wanted some people in for dinner. Then he'd call John and say that we must come over, too. There was never any thought of refusing."

It was during that summer in San Clemente that Martha had her first inkling that there were people at the White House who were jealous of John Mitchell's closeness to the President. A relative of Bob Haldeman's who was in the real estate business handled the rental of the houses used by the Mitchells, Secretary of State and Mrs. William P. Rogers, and Henry Kissinger, then Nixon's adviser on national security. The Mitchells' house, Martha said, was the only one without a private swimming pool; she thought the absence of a pool was a deliberate slap at the Mitchells by Bob Haldeman.

The first day the Mitchells were in San Clemente, Richard Nixon drove over to their house in a golf cart. (GSA, with taxpayers' money, bought six electric golf carts, at two thousand dollars each, for the Nixon compound.) He asked how they liked the house. When he heard that they didn't have a pool, the President invited them to use his, anytime. But John Mitchell put his foot down and forbade Martha and Marty to use it; they went swimming in Rose Mary Wood's pool, but Martha wasn't happy about it.

Martha, who by her own admission couldn't stand having anyone tell her what to do and what not to do, had another reason for being unhappy with Nixon's White House—it sometimes exercised control over her social life.

The opening of the Kennedy Center for the Performing Arts was one of those times. Martha had been looking forward to being there for all the glamour and excitement. The Kennedys—Rose and Eunice, Teddy and Joan, Ethel and five of her eleven children—would be there, along with just about everybody else of importance in Washington. And Leonard Bernstein's "Mass," composed at the request of Jackie Kennedy Onassis, would be performed for the first time.

Then John came home one evening and said they weren't going. The President didn't want them there, he claimed, because "Mass" contained things that were sacrilegious. After reading the reviews, Martha realized there wasn't anything in "Mass" to have kept the President and the Mitchells away. She continued to be puzzled as to why she couldn't have gone, but she thought she knew why Richard Nixon stayed home: he didn't want to compete with the Kennedys for attention.

That may have been part of Nixon's reason for staying away, but there was another. Jack Anderson reported that the White House had been warned that Bernstein planned to sneak a peace message into "Mass." As it turned out, Anderson said, "Bernstein's Mass contained only one line that could be interpreted as antiwar—*Dona Nobis Pecem,* or 'Give Us Peace.' "

One of Martha's disillusionments with the Administration came when it encouraged Lenore Romney, wife of Secretary of Housing and Urban Development George Romney, to run against Senator Philip A. Hart, a Democrat, in the 1970 elections. Once she was running, the White House ignored the race. Martha said this was because Richard Nixon didn't want women in government anymore than he wanted one on the Supreme Court. She also felt she had been used in the game he was playing—telling the public he was trying to find a woman for the Court when he had no intentions of appointing one. John had asked Martha to help find a woman jurist, and then he led her to believe a woman actually was being nominated. This caused her public embarrassment when it was reported that Martha had told a friend, "I know for a fact a woman will be nominated, and that's *inside* information."

The night after the Supreme Court nomination of Lewis Powell was announced, Martha got her revenge. When she and John arrived at a banquet of the National Federation of Republican Women, he got a big round of applause; Martha got a standing ovation. Then while he ate dinner, Martha autographed hundreds of menus. As the Washington *Post* reported: "Women stood five and six deep in front of Mrs. Mitchell, twenty to thirty crowded up before her at a time, eager to grasp her hand, talk to her and get her to sign her name."

Although Martha strongly felt more women should be in the courts, in the Congress and in top-level government jobs, she had mixed feelings about the role of women in today's society. On the one hand she was very female—a Southern female who wanted men to indulge her and above all "take care of her." On the other, she hated the notion that because she was a woman she was supposed to shut up and smile, as enigmatically, if possible, as the Mona Lisa or Pat Nixon.

She was vehemently against the Equal Rights Amendment because she felt it would take away from women many of the rights they now have under the law, that it would force women out of the homes into the labor force. Yet she firmly believed that something should be done for women in business, where she said they were not treated as equals "especially in their pay checks."

Martha also felt that women should have the rights of the First Amendment. She told Myra MacPherson of the Washington *Post,* "I'm a perfect example of a woman discriminated against. If I were a man and say what I say, nobody in the world would pay one iota of attention to me."

But she often took out after liberation women for the way she thought most of them dressed—no bras, tight jeans, low (or no) heels, and casual, "natural" hair styles. "I just wonder how they have any respect for themselves," she said.

THE PEAK OF MARTHA'S PRE-WATERGATE DISENCHANTMENT WITH THE Nixon Administration came when John Mitchell had to give up his Cabinet post as Attorney General to head the Committee for the Re-Election of the President.

Martha knew the job of campaign manager didn't hold the clout of a Cabinet post. Neither did it hold the rank. The move for John was a demotion, for both of the Mitchells. It also meant loss of Cabinet-rank perks—and invitations. A former Justice Department aide to John Mitchell says, "Pat Nixon couldn't stand Martha and neither could Adele Rogers. The minute John Mitchell was no longer in the Cabinet, Pat and Adele cut them off every list."

Martha fought the move for weeks. There's no record that John Mitchell tried to stay at the Justice Department, although he told a reporter five days before he resigned, "Hell, no, I may be fired but I'm not going to resign."

In the meantime, Martha tried to talk Richard Kleindienst into running CREEP. (Kleindienst replaced Mitchell as Attorney General, but not before a lot of in-fighting; John Ehrlichman wanted the job, but

Mitchell insisted on having Kleindienst take over.) She also tried to get Robert Mardian to help her stop the move. Both men assured her it was not their decision to make. Martha couldn't understand why John couldn't run the campaign from Justice, claiming, "He's been running it from there ever since CREEP started."

Martha declared, "They can't do this. What will our friends think? We gave up everything to come here to help Mr. President and the country; now they want to cast us off. I won't stand for it!" She was worried, too, about losing her FBI protection.

Finally Martha appealed to Bebe Rebozo, in the hope that he could solve the problem, as he had done so many times in the past. Bebe persuaded her there was no use fighting it; John was going to be campaign manager whether she liked it or not.

The strategy was for Richard Nixon to stay in the White House, busy being President, and not go out into the rough and tumble of a heated campaign. According to Bebe and others with whom she talked, John Mitchell was the only one who could keep Richard Nixon in the White House, where he couldn't make any *faux pas*: "Each one of them told me the same thing; they didn't want Richard Nixon out of the White House during the campaign because he would go out and make a damn fool out of himself."

Bebe also assured her, she said, that she wouldn't have to go through what she went through during the 1968 campaign, when John was away day and night, leaving her alone at home: "He said they had in book form everything that was going to happen in the election. He said it was down to a tee." This is the book Martha later told interviewers was the one outlining, among other things, dirty campaign tricks.

So John Mitchell resigned. Florine Plater, one of the Mitchells' maids, remembers that Martha was so upset her two secretaries had to come stay with her. "It's the only time I ever saw her that way," Florine says.

"It just breaks my heart," Martha publicly announced.

A few days after the resignation, the Mitchells went to Florida, although Martha had wanted to go to the Caribbean. They stayed in Bebe's house, the one where they'd vacationed so many times before. Martha was surprised to see that others involved in the campaign also were in Key Biscayne and that they spent most of their waking hours at the house with John Mitchell.

Martha was so upset over having all the extra men around that she called her Washington office in tears, declaring she wasn't going to spend her vacation cleaning up after a bunch of "clowns." Finally someone called to have the maid, Julia Carter, sent down to run the house.

Another thing Martha objected to was having Jack Caulfield "sitting around the swimming pool, in his bathing trunks, with his gun at his side." John C. Caulfield, a former New York detective, was John Mitchell's first CREEP security guard.

But Martha was even more upset when Caulfield had to leave in a hurry because of a problem in Washington and turned his gun over to Fred LaRue. "It frightened me out of my wits," Martha told me soon after Watergate. "My God, this man had killed his own father in a hunting accident and that jerk gave him his gun!" (Frederick Cheney LaRue, a Mississippi oil heir, shot and killed his father, Ike Parsons LaRue, Sr., in a Canadian duck-hunting accident in 1957.)

One of the visitors to the house was Jeb Magruder, who arrived with a stack of campaign option papers for John Mitchell to see. Among them was an outline for an intelligence operation which included electronic surveillance. John Mitchell, Fred LaRue and Jeb Magruder went over the papers and all three have different versions of what happened. John Mitchell says he refused the plan outright. LaRue testified that Mitchell said, "This is not something we have to decide now." Magruder says Mitchell okayed the plans. And Martha, who was listening on the kitchen intercom, said, "There was no question *if* they were doing the dirty tricks, only the amount of money to be spent. They used terms like categories: how much to spend on people, on wiretapping, and other various and sundry things. They also discussed who was in charge of what, who would do this and who would do that."

BEFORE THE MITCHELLS LEFT FOR FLORIDA, JOHN HAD TOLD BOB Haldeman that he didn't want his White House telephone removed while they were away.

His request was ignored. When the Mitchells returned, the telephone was gone, and John, since he didn't have their private numbers, was unable to telephone 90 percent of the people he wanted to reach. In the past, the White House switchboard had placed the calls.

Just before she left Washington, in the fall of 1972, Martha still was seething over the insult to her husband. She claimed that Nixon crony Murray Chotiner, who by now had left government, still had a White House telephone, as did Bebe Rebozo. She added that she'd never seen John "as mad in his life" as he was when he discovered the telephone was missing.

Chapter Thirteen

By the time John Mitchell resigned as Attorney General on March 1, 1972, and took over running the Committee for the Re-Election of the President, Martha had been with CREEP for almost a year.

She'd had working space at 1701 Pennsylvania Avenue since shortly after CREEP opened a small but unpublicized office there in May 1971. Martha also had received help from two White House aides, Jeb Magruder and Bart Porter, for several weeks before that. And CREEP had hired Martha a secretary, Lea Jablonsky, who worked out of the Mitchell apartment until Martha's second-floor office was ready.

When John Mitchell told Jeb Magruder, in March 1971, that Jeb was to set up the Committee, he also asked him to help Martha with her volume of mail and requests for appearances and interviews. According to Magruder, Mitchell said, "She needs professional guidance. She can help the Administration, if she's used properly. So I wish you'd give her a hand."

Magruder wasn't pleased. Later he wrote, "Managing Martha was not part of my game plan." He quickly assigned one of his assistants, Bart Porter, to take over the responsibility. Martha went to the White House to meet with the two men and came away ecstatic. I remember her calling to say that "at last" she had capable help to assist and guide her.

Martha was especially glad to have someone who would tell her which to accept of the scores of invitations she received each week. During this period Martha lived in fear of doing something wrong—something that would embarrass the Administration, her husband or herself.

But now, she said, her worries were over. She had someone who'd guide her in the right direction.

She was wrong about that.

Shortly after CREEP opened its offices, someone there approved Martha's endorsement and support of the conservative Young Americans for Freedom's "Project Appreciation" drive to raise funds for Appreciation Kits for wounded Vietnam veterans.

Evidently no one checked into just *how* conservative the YAF was. Less than a month after Martha's endorsement, the organization voted to oppose President Nixon's re-election, set up a $750,000 fund drive to challenge his nomination as the GOP presidential candidate, and was strongly critical of his welfare-reform package, his proposed trip to mainland China and his ninety-day wage-price freeze.

To make matters worse, YAF sent fund-raising letters bearing Martha's name to 250,000 people. The letters told of the proposed kits, which would contain such items as after-shave lotion, dominoes and toothpaste. They didn't mention that several publications critical of President Nixon would also be included in the packages. The YAF's Washington address was on the envelope with Martha's name, but the letterhead gave only her Watergate address.

Of course, the press learned of the letters and wrote about Martha's endorsement of an organization that had voted to oppose Nixon's re-election. The fact that her husband would run the campaign wasn't overlooked. Through no fault of her own, Martha again was in what she called "a heck of a mess."

Soon after the fund-raising letter was mailed, Junie Dankworth came to work in Martha's office. A long-time Republican and wife of Navy Captain Theodore Dankworth, Junie had been a volunteer for Richard Nixon since 1952. In 1960 she helped staff his campaign office in Coronado, California. Junie was working as a volunteer at the White House when a Nixon aide asked if she would please go to CREEP to put Martha's office in order. As Martha said at the time, everyone helping her was young and inexperienced in political campaigns. With her volume of mail and 150 invitations a week, Martha needed someone politically knowledgeable.

Junie remembers how shocked she was, the first day she went to work, to see in Martha's office files "drawers full of money, cash money and checks, hundreds of dollars—even one check, I think for $550, from Elmer Bobst, the man Tricia and Julie called 'Uncle.' "

Martha's office wasn't the only place at CREEP where money was handled in a cavalier manner. One day when Junie went to the finance office—where millions of dollars were gathered and disbursed under the direction of former Secretary of Commerce Maurice Stans—she walked into the incoming-mail room, where she saw young people, "just kids, opening the letters with the money—a lot of it cash. I was appalled. There was no one supervising them. They could have pocketed thousands and no one would have known."

The money in Martha's file drawers had been donated in response to the YAF fund-raising letter. Not knowing what to do with it, Junie went to Bart Porter to ask for guidance: "He acted like I'd unearthed a dead rat! He didn't want to have anything to do with it. Neither did anyone else. So I returned all of the money to the people who'd sent it."

Just as she'd been wrong in thinking the CREEP staff would protect her from making embarrassing mistakes, Martha was wrong in thinking Bart Porter would devote full time to her affairs. One day she walked into his office, unannounced, and saw on his desk information a CREEP spy had gathered on the then Democratic front runner for the presidential nomination, Edmund Muskie: "They knew everything Muskie was doing, from the time he got up in the morning until he went to bed at night." She added indignantly, "Here Bart was, supposed to be taking care of me and he was doing dirty tricks!" Martha asked Jeb Magruder to find someone who could devote his full time to her affairs.

Martha probably knew earlier about a concentrated effort to stop Senator Muskie from getting the Democratic nomination. In March 1971, at a time when Muskie was running several points ahead of Nixon in the polls, Martha made a bet with a friend of ours—giving her five-to-one odds—that Muskie would not be the Democratic presidential candidate. I asked Martha how she could be so reckless, pointing out Muskie's top position in the polls. "Muskie isn't going to get it," Martha stated firmly. "I *know,* Winnie. I can't tell you how I know, but it won't be Muskie."

Of course she was right. The White House's concerted campaign of dirty tricks against Muskie succeeded. He didn't get his party's nomination.

WRITING ABOUT MARTHA IN HIS BOOK, *An American Life,* JEB Magruder said the policy at CREEP was to present Martha "as a personality but never as a spokesman on matters of substance." Yet every time Martha was booked into any kind of event, she was coached on what to say about such subjects as busing, environment, the economy, welfare, ITT and women's liberation. Briefing papers on these subjects were delivered to her almost daily.

When it was charged that the Justice Department, under her husband, agreed to settle an antitrust suit against ITT out of court in return for a $400,000 contribution to the Republican party, Martha was told to say, "I am aware of the charges. I consider them irresponsible. All this political hokum is the result of claims by a sensation-seeking political gossip columnist and a purported memorandum written by an unfortunate woman (ITT lobbyist Dita Beard) who is critically ill in a hospital. Her own lawyers say she has ridiculed these preposterous claims. They ought to stop wasting the taxpayers' money and get down to business."

When asked about the economy, Martha was to reply: "I think the President's bold move on the economy was designed to start letting charity and prosperity begin at home. You know, I believe that Uncle Sam —some countries think he is Uncle Sugar—has recognized the fact that we better start taking care of our own people first. And I think that it would be well for our allies around the world to do the same thing. I don't mean to become isolationists, no sir, I mean just what I said earlier—charity and prosperity begin at home."

Martha chafed at the long, involved answers she was supposed to make to issue-oriented questions. But she loved delivering the laugh-getting one-liners prepared for her before some appearances. Professional comedians and writers, from all over the country, loyal to the Republican cause, contributed Martha's one-liners. When she needed amusing material for a particular event, the usual procedure was for Martha, or one of her assistants, to pick up the telephone and call one of her sources.

Paul Keyes, a good friend of Richard Nixon's and producer of the hit television show *Laugh-In*, was one Martha called often. He met Martha at Nixon's first Inaugural, Paul Keyes says. Then he saw her at many White House functions, including Tricia's wedding. And while Martha was at CREEP, she flew to California to appear on *Laugh-In*.

"We had a lot of fun with her on *Laugh-In*," he recalls. "We gave her straight-to-the-camera jokes. I remember in one Martha said, 'John and I have the perfect arrangement. He runs the Attorney General's office and I run the rest of the country.'

"I thought she was a very vibrant, vital lady," he adds. "Martha was an original. We all are *trying to be* originals; Martha *was.*"

The more appearances Martha made, the more she was in demand. A CREEP scheduling man revealed to me—confidentially and off the record—that requests for Martha were second only to those for the President: "They want her before Vice-President Agnew or the First Lady." He added, incredulously, "When she goes to one of these functions the people scream and yell and want to *touch* her! She's a celebrity like a movie star."

Martha's appeal as a Nixon campaign money-maker wasn't limited to Middle Americans, as many people thought. She also did well with affluent and social Republicans. One event starring Martha—a chic party in Palm Beach, Florida, in early 1972—brought in some $100,000 from such contributors as Winthrop Aldrich, Mrs. Ogden Phipps, Mrs. Joseph A. Neff and Mrs. Harvey Gibson.

In spite of her popularity on the campaign trail, CREEP aides "just hated her," according to Junie Dankworth. "They treated her terribly. I asked someone—I don't remember who it was—'Why did you give her an office?' And they said—and I never told Martha this—'She has to be watched.' In other words, 'We have to control her.'

"I got into a hassle with them. I said, 'I don't understand. She's doing a marvelous job for the Administration. I haven't seen where she's made one misstep.' And she had fantastic ideas; but they wouldn't let her follow through."

Soon after her conversation with the unnamed CREEP aide, Junie was told she was no longer needed in that office and they had hired a young man to handle all of Martha's campaign business. She was asked to take a position in the finance office, which she refused.

A few days later Martha, who was out on a campaign trip, called Junie at home to ask why she wasn't at the office. "All hell broke loose when she found out what had happened," Junie recalls. "She blew sky high." Before hanging up Martha made Junie promise she'd come back.

So again Junie was on Martha's staff. To show her appreciation, Martha sent her CREEP chauffeur to Junie's house, in Arlington, Virginia, to bring her to work every morning and to take her home in the evening.

LONG AFTER THE ELECTION MARTHA ASKED JUNIE IF SHE THOUGHT STUMBLING blocks deliberately had been put in her way. "I had to tell her I thought there had been," Junie says.

In addition to creating problems for Martha, CREEP was scheduling her too heavily, Junie says, adding, "She was bone-tired. At the last she didn't even see her husband often. They had separate schedules and it was just 'hello–good-bye, I'll be seeing you.' "

Yet in a television interview with David Frost, in September 1977, Richard Nixon said, "If it hadn't been for Martha, there'd have been no Watergate, because John wasn't mindin' the store." Claiming that Martha had mental and emotional problems, Nixon said, "John was practically out of his mind about Martha in the spring of 1972. He was letting Magruder and all these boys, these kids, these nuts, run this thing."

Newspaper clips and CREEP schedules for the spring of 1972 don't bear out Nixon's statement. During this period Martha was carrying the heaviest campaign schedule of anyone at CREEP. In April, for instance, Martha made four out-of-town campaign trips—to New York, Indiana, Illinois and Virginia. During the days in-between when she was in Washington she attended eight events in the Washington area, and she entertained at home at one cocktail party and one dinner (this at John's request for Washington *Post* publisher Katharine Graham.)

Then in May she made trips to Michigan, New York, Nebraska and Pennsylvania, in addition to attending seven functions in the Washington region. She was still at it in June, right up to the day before she left for California. Martha's last solo appearance before the Watergate break-in was on the fifteenth of June, when she was the guest of honor at a Flag Day Gala, where the sponsoring Washington Host Lions Club presented her with the 1972 Distinguished Citizen's Award. In her acceptance speech Martha noted that "despite some of the bad things, this is still the greatest nation in the world . . . I defy anybody to prove otherwise." Martha continued to believe this as long as she lived. A flag-waving patriot, Martha used to say, "There's nothing wrong with America—except those jerks in Washington who're trying to run it!"

If Martha were so mentally and emotionally disturbed that her husband "was practically out of his mind," as Nixon said, it hardly seems possible that she could have maintained such a grueling schedule.

In his book, *The Ends of Power,* Bob Haldeman also discusses John Mitchell's problems with Martha in the spring of 1972: "There is no doubt that Mitchell was preoccupied by Martha's problems in those days. He was actually afraid she might jump off the balcony and would not allow her to be left alone. I have been at meetings where Mitchell would receive a call that whoever was then with Martha had to leave, and Mitchell would quit the meeting—no matter how important—in order to rush home and be with his wife." What Bob Haldeman doesn't say is that John Mitchell sometimes rushed home *after* Watergate, after Martha's experience in California. Martha herself spoke of having to call John home from the office, after California, saying she was terrified at the thought of being alone.

Martha complained bitterly about her heavy schedules. Once she cried out to Junie, "How did I ever get myself into this?" But, with few exceptions, she went everywhere they asked her to go.

It's true she once missed a large and important luncheon given by a group of Republican women. But Martha thought she had a good reason for staying away. The night before she'd learned that one of the Republican women Martha had planned to name in her threatened divorce suit in 1968 also would attend the luncheon.

Another time, Martha skipped an out-of-town event at the last minute although she had gone to that city especially for the party. This time she was upset with the Defense Department. First, they had sent her son Jay to Vietnam, which she thought was done only because he was her son; then, when she hadn't heard from him for several weeks, the Defense Department wouldn't tell her where he was. She learned his whereabouts only after a television crew found him and filmed an interview.

Later, when the Associated Press caught up with Jay in Vietnam, he still seemed displeased about all the furor. Jay said he would like people to "treat me just like any other lieutenant. But when they find out who I am I get static from the things she says . . . [But] that's the way mothers are. I try to understand that my mother is as worried about me as other mothers are worried about their sons in Vietnam."

MARTHA'S FIRST CREEP OFFICE WAS A SMALL CUBICLE THAT SHE DEscribed to the Washington *Star* as being so tiny that once when she spilled a cup of coffee she and her two secretaries almost drowned. Next she was moved into two rooms, on the same second floor, which hardly had space enough for three desks and her ever-growing number of file cabinets.

Then Martha was given a plush, two-room suite on the eleventh floor —one room with windows, a luxury missing in her other two offices. To decorate the rooms, Martha brought from her Watergate apartment bric-a-brac, paintings, original cartoons of herself, and a red, white and blue French telephone given to her when she appeared on the Dinah Shore TV show. Later Martha sent the phone to Bebe Rebozo to install on his yacht for President Nixon's use, an act of generosity she lived to regret.

A few days before she moved to the eleventh floor, Martha gleefully told me, "I'm getting a carpet on the floor and my name on the door!"

She got the carpet—yellow and burnt-orange and deep-piled—but her name was never on the door. Neither was it on the directory of CREEP offices, nor on any CREEP staff roster.

This infuriated Martha. She thought she should be recognized as a legitimate member of the Committee, which she was. Martha said she was led to believe it was because she was a woman and there weren't any women in the top echelon of CREEP.

Then she read in a local newspaper that Rita Hauser, an attractive New York attorney and then delegate to the United Nations, was being named as John Mitchell's deputy at CREEP. Martha threatened to quit. She refused to go to fund-raisers or any other type of campaign activity if Rita Hauser got the number-two spot when Martha couldn't even get her name in the staff roster or on her door. Rita Hauser did not become a member of the Committee.

Although Martha had been thrilled at first with her new suite, she soon felt they'd moved her there to get her away from the main activity. She told Junie, "They have sent me to Siberia." Her suspicions about being banished were confirmed when she learned that one of her secretaries (by now she had three) was supposed to call CREEP to let them know anytime Martha was headed that way. Martha never believed she was being guarded for her own good. Nor did she believe that the electronic eye outside her door, which revealed on closed-circuit television everyone coming and going from her office, was there for her protection. She thought it was a way of spying on her.

The electronic eye didn't last long, though. Another tenant on the eleventh floor had Russians as business clients. "The first day the Russians saw the eye," Junie Dankworth says, "they thought it was there watching them and they had a fit. The eye was removed."

Sometimes Martha was able to slip away from her secretaries and visit the CREEP offices unannounced. She said it was on one such visit that she saw on Jeb Magruder's desk the outline for the dirty tricks CREEP planned to use during the campaign. The detailed outline, later called the "Gemstone File," was burned by Jeb Magruder a few days after the Watergate break-in. He testified that he asked John Mitchell what to do with it and that the former Attorney General suggested, "Maybe you ought to have a little fire at your house tonight."

Publicly, Martha was giving the impression that CREEP was just one big happy family and that there was nothing she enjoyed more than bringing in votes and money for Mr. President. As she put it, she was "being a good little girl and doing everything they asked me to."

For the next three and a half months, Martha continued her rugged campaign schedule, publicly smiling and waving and praising Richard Nixon, although behind the scenes she was being what CREEP aides called "difficult." Junie puts it another way: "She started acting up." Martha said it was deliberate, that she was trying to "annoy the hell out of them" the way they were annoying her.

She made demands. She threatened. And she got her way.

Then came the trip to California, the Watergate break-in, her harrowing experience in the Newport Beach villa, the hurried flight to the Westchester Country Club, and the reconciliation, of sorts, with John Mitchell.

Martha came back to Washington disillusioned with politics, afraid of the power of the Presidency and angry with a lot of people—including her husband. Two years later she would confess, "I never forgave John Mitchell for what he let them do to me in California."

It isn't known what arguments or promises John Mitchell made to get Martha to come back to Washington, or to keep her from talking until after Richard Nixon was safely re-elected in November. But again, Martha was the "good little girl." She did what she was asked to do. She kept their secrets.

AT THE TIME OF THE WATERGATE BREAK-IN, MARTHA WAS SCHEDULED TO appear at three or more campaign functions each week until Election Day in November, and as a "star" and top fund-raiser attraction, she was booked into only large affairs scattered throughout the country.

This created a tremendous problem for those trying to convince the public that the break-in was a "third-rate burglary," as Ron Ziegler, White House Press Secretary, termed it, instead of a little political espionage involving CREEP. If Martha continued to campaign, she would be asked about Watergate, and it would be impossible to control her answers. Even if she didn't campaign, Martha might get on the phone again and talk to reporters about "dirty tricks." It was evident that a way had to be found to discredit Martha if they were going to keep the public from believing anything she said.

Martha's credibility was ruined in two ways: (1) The media and political insiders, and through them the world, were told that Martha was a "sick woman" whose rantings and ravings could not be taken seriously; (2) word was passed around that Martha didn't know anything anyway. Who would be dumb enough to reveal important information to a bubble-headed, talkative blonde?

A magazine correspondent recalls that a "trusted" White House news source confidentially revealed that Martha had "gone bonkers." From one of Mrs. Nixon's staff another writer heard how Martha had been "in a mental institution before they came to Washington and poor John doesn't know what to do with her now," the implication being Martha was fit to be committed. And a member of the Nixon family suggested to me, "Why don't you call the institution she was in? She hallucinates, you know."

Of course, Martha had been in Craig House. But her doctor there, Wallace Vogt, says Martha never hallucinated. Was she crazy? Indeed not, he says, and states positively that he never saw any signs that Martha was psychotic.

Dr. Klaus Mayer, the doctor who treated Martha and saw her almost daily during her final illness, says the same thing. And when asked if Martha were normal mentally he answers, "Oh, God, yes! She was a character, but she was normal."

The story that Martha knew nothing was spoon-fed to some of Washington's respected columnists, who reported it in good faith. There were those in the Administration, however, who realized that—through her eavesdropping and rummaging around in John's briefcases, and her husband-to-wife conversations—Martha was privy to a lot of inside government and political information. But once her credibility was in question people wouldn't believe a thing she said. Eventually she became a twentieth-century Cassandra, roaming the countryside, being interviewed by the press, showing up on radio and television shows, telling her story over and over and not being believed.

Therefore it isn't surprising that when the Senate Select Committee on Presidential Campaign Activities convened in 1973 it wouldn't call Martha Mitchell to testify, even though she sent word she'd reveal any number of Nixon Administration dirty tricks, plus throw in heretofore unknown information about Mafia involvement within government—in both past and present Administrations.

Still later, the Special Prosecutor's office, supposedly eagerly running down every lead about the misdoings of the Nixon Administration, repeatedly refused Martha's offer to turn over politically sensitive papers she had taken from her husband's files. Finally, in desperation she invited the Washington *Post* to come pick up a handful of the revealing documents. Soon titillating scoops appeared in the pages of the *Post.* Even that didn't help establish Martha's credibility; the *Post* didn't reveal its source.

This omission annoyed Martha to the point where, in her words, she could "hardly stand it." Just as she hardly could stand it, and was alternately irritated, hurt and puzzled, that no one in the press thoroughly investigated her having been held prisoner, restrained and sedated in California. Even when, in 1974, the doctor who administered the sedative confirmed that government agents had been involved in restraining her (just as Martha had said all along), there was no mass investigation or indignation. In fact, one columnist went so far as to write that while Martha, in truth, *had* been subjected to these indignities, it was done "for her own good."

ONCE BACK IN WASHINGTON FROM THE WESTCHESTER COUNTRY CLUB, Martha virtually became a recluse. She claimed it was her own decision to stay sequestered in her Watergate apartment, explaining she was ashamed to see people because having her husband involved in something like Watergate was such a terrible thing for her.

But Martha soon realized her self-imposed exile was a mistake, or as she put it, "I played right into their hands." With her out of sight and off the telephone, it made more believable such news dispatches as, "In Cabinet circles the word is out that pressure has taken a toll on Martha's nerves, that she has a severe personal problem."

Bonnie Angelo of *Time* magazine says that one of the White House insiders "laid on me and I dutifully put it in the magazine as 'this is the way it really is,' that Martha obviously was cracking up and that John Mitchell loved her so much he knew the only way for him to save her life was for him to quit [as head of CREEP]. They gave me that whole song and dance and I bought it."

Bonnie wasn't alone; others "bought it," too. In a July 4 editorial, the Washington *Daily News* noted that many people thought it admirable that John Mitchell would consider the interests of his family over politics, adding, "Whatever one thinks of John Mitchell it's apparent that . . . nothing in his public life became him like the leaving it."

Even Pat Nixon added to the gossip about Martha's mental health—over a month after Martha returned from the Westchester Country Club, and after close Mitchell friends knew Martha was out and about. During a meeting with a group of women reporters, on August 8, 1972, in the yellow Oval Room of the White House, the First Lady was asked, "We all felt that Martha Mitchell was interested in politics . . . do you feel sorry now [that she cannot participate]?" Pat Nixon replied, "Well, I hear it was from exhaustion, because she had been doing a great deal."

Martha was beside herself when she heard of the remark. She demanded to know why one of the reporters hadn't asked Pat Nixon, "What kind of flowers did you send to this sick woman who is the wife of the President's closest friend?"

It was another sore point with Martha that although people from all over the country—strangers for the most part—were flooding the apartment with flowers, none had been received from the White House or CREEP. Yet they were the ones talking about her being sick. And taking their cue from the White House, others in the Administration didn't send flowers or call her either.

The only one from the Executive Mansion to talk to Martha was President Nixon, who called John Mitchell the day after he resigned from CREEP to talk about "personal things," and during the conversation John had put Martha on the phone. The White House announced that Nixon had made the call to express his "understanding of Mr. Mitchell's decision."

In addition to talk of Martha's mental condition, there were rumors then, and they still persist, that she was kept prisoner in her apartment, with a uniformed nurse in attendance.

The rumor of her imprisonment probably started with Martha herself when she called a reporter, the day after John's resignation, to ask a question. She said at the time that she still was a political prisoner and that she couldn't talk long since she was calling "surreptitiously." Later Martha explained that in calling herself a prisoner she didn't mean she was *physically* restrained, but that political events had imprisoned her.

As for the uniformed nurses in attendance, this rumor started, or at least was kept alive, when a columnist, appearing on NBC, said in July she had knocked at the Mitchells' apartment and a nurse came to the door: "She asked who was there and I said 'a friend,' and she said she [Martha] is asleep and cannot be disturbed . . . It was two-thirty in the afternoon—and I insisted she open the door and take a note. And you could hear—she had three keys on a chain on her belt—and she unlocked all these locks, and you could hear the clank, clank, clank . . . and here is this huge woman in white uniform and white stockings, who won't let me in, and I left a note . . ."

About a year later Julia Carter, the Mitchells' maid, told me that *she* had opened the door that day, and she angrily denied that Martha had had a nurse in attendance, or that she, Julia, had any keys on a chain on her belt: "I had one key and it was in my pocket!"

WHILE THE TALK ABOUT MARTHA'S "BREAKDOWN," "EXHAUSTION," OR worse was supposedly keeping her incapacitated, Martha was busy finding an apartment in New York and getting Marty enrolled in a new school —Sacred Heart, at Ninety-first Street and Fifth Avenue.

Martha told me in July about her plans to move to New York and why she wasn't going back to Rye: "Never at any time did I plan on returning to the suburbs. I'd had enough of the commuting bit—taking my husband to the station every morning, picking him up every night, fighting the traffic into the city every time I wanted to shop or go out to dinner or go to the theater. I love the theater, I love the arts and I never could get where I wanted to go when I lived in Rye before."

She said she'd limited herself to a certain twelve-block area on Fifth Avenue, which would put them in walking distance of Marty's school. The size and style of the apartment, she told me later, was determined by John Mitchell's dream: "My husband's greatest desire was to build the biggest law firm in the country. He loves his law and he would rather practice law than do anything else. In order to help him build the biggest firm, I had to have the equipment and the facilities to entertain the people from all over the world he would be dealing with in his office."

Throughout the last of July and early August Martha called often—sometimes from her Watergate apartment, other times from New York —to give me progress reports. On August 4 she was bubbling over with news. She'd had her first taxi ride in four years and "with all that screening I felt like I was in a police van." She hadn't known that New York cab drivers, in an effort to discourage holdups, had installed barriers between the driver and the passenger seats. She also was shocked by the increased taxi fares and laughingly said she felt like she was making re-entry into the real world.

In one call Martha said that Marty was in New York with her and would be going to Europe, to the Olympics, with a family with seven children. Martha said she wasn't happy about having Marty so far away but that she'd been "talked into" letting her go. The father of the family, she said, was a man John knew on Wall Street, William Simon, a senior partner with Salomon Brothers, one of the country's largest investment banking houses. According to Martha, William Simon was "just dying to get into government." Later that year, Richard Nixon named William Simon his Deputy Secretary of the Treasury; eventually he moved up to become Secretary.

In May 1973, after John Mitchell had been indicted in the Robert Vesco influence-peddling case, William Simon was one of many Nixon Administration officials who wrote the former Attorney General offering help. Another who wrote to reaffirm his friendship was then Attorney General Richard Kleindienst, whose handwritten words of comfort were penned on the stationery of the Attorney General of the United States.

Martha told me, in another of her calls, that the Mitchells had sold their Watergate apartment to Senator Russell B. Long, but wouldn't have to vacate it until fall. Martha was upset about the sale, claiming that the sale price was ridiculously low. Martha later told Junie Dankworth that she couldn't understand why John let Senator Long have the apartment for so little and that she was puzzled as to why John was being that kind to Russell Long. In a *New York* magazine interview, in late 1974, Martha told of another kindness to Senator Long. According to the article, "She mentioned that the Nixon Administration had bailed him [Long] out of hot water when he had some trouble with the IRS over income-tax difficulties in Louisiana."

On August 11, the day after Marty sailed for the Olympics, Martha said she'd found her dream house, the place she expected to spend the rest of her life. It was an apartment at 1030 Fifth Avenue, on the corner of Eighty-fourth Street and kitty-corner from the Metropolitan Museum of Art. "It is my kind of charm," Martha said. Later John Mitchell would say it reminded him of the Taj Mahal.

The apartment did indeed have all the ingredients to give a woman from the South, with antebellum tastes, visions of a Tara in the sky. Nineteen-foot ceilings, carved marble mantels, massive rooms with hand-done crown moldings, decorative panels in bas-relief, walnut herringbone parquet floors. And space—100 by 50 feet, covering a whole floor in a fifteen-story, early twentieth-century building facing Central Park.

During this period of preparing to move to New York, Martha seemed happy, and her friends hoped she was going to be able to put Washington and politics behind her. Evidently there was no worry about the Watergate break-in or the consequences it might have on John Mitchell or the Nixon Administration. She had been reassured about that when she overheard a conversation John had with the President about Watergate. John had told Richard Nixon they were going to pull the thing through and that everybody would be exonerated.

Of course it was disturbing to have the CREEP finance chairman Maurice Stans come to the Watergate apartment so often to talk to John about things they tried to keep from her. But John assured her that Stans's problems had nothing to do with Watergate; he explained that Stans was in trouble because a large amount of money, some two or three million, was missing from the campaign funds. And the Washington *Post* had reported that a $25,000 campaign check given to Stans had been deposited in the bank account of one of the Watergate burglers.

Then came the Republican National Convention and the events

leading up to it. John was still in politics as a consultant to CREEP. Until the White House tapes were released Martha thought John was helping the campaign only because she gave her consent. As she told it, when Richard Nixon called the Mitchell apartment the day after they returned from the Westchester Country Club, John told him that Martha was all right and everything was just great between them. Then he asked the President if he wanted "to speak to my girl." Martha took the phone.

Recalling the conversation two years later in an interview with Donnie Radcliffe in the Washington *Post,* Martha said, "Nixon was telling me stories had broken all around the country that Mitchell was no longer there (CREEP) and he didn't know what he was going to do without Mitchell.

"I said—and here is Martha, the loving wife who gives everything—I said, 'Mr. President, I will allow John to take an advisory job . . . with the Committee.' "

Martha soon learned an advisory job can be just as time-consuming as full-time employment. John was working harder for CREEP than he had when he headed it. And now he wanted to go to the convention in Miami Beach.

But Martha was *persona non grata* with the Administration. The Mitchells had been told this privately, and Anne Armstrong, vice-chairman of the convention, had made it clear publicly on July 18 when she told UPI, "We have no plans whatsoever [for Mrs. Mitchell to take part in the convention activities]."

John kept bringing up the subject of the convention until finally Martha picked up the phone and called Bebe Rebozo. She told him she would stay on Key Biscayne instead of Miami Beach, where a suite had been reserved for John Mitchell at the convention headquarters hotel. Martha promised Bebe she wouldn't let anyone know she was in Florida. Bebe told her there was no way they were going to let her anywhere near the convention.

Since John would not go without Martha, the Mitchells stayed at their Watergate apartment and watched the proceedings on television. There was no official mention from the convention floor of Martha, nor of John Mitchell for that matter. It wasn't like the Democratic convention the month before when Martha received five-sixths of a vote from the Maryland delegation for the Democratic vice-presidential nomination.

The Republicans kept Martha away from the convention, but they couldn't keep her out of the news. Every day there was something about her in the papers or on radio or television. But the first to so upset Martha that she took action was a Maxine Cheshire column reporting that conservative writer Victor Lasky, during a discussion about Martha, had noted that "mental illness is no laughing matter."

Martha demanded that John call Victor Lasky and force him to publicly retract his statements. Two weeks later the Washington *Post* printed a letter from Victor Lasky in which he said, "The implication that, in a dinner conversation with Maxine Cheshire, I suggested that Martha was mentally ill is absolutely false. I never said the things Miss Cheshire attributes to me . . . what I did say was that I resented the 'Free Martha' buttons so evident at the Democratic convention. I thought they were demeaning . . ."

His letter didn't satisfy Martha. She was still angry with Victor Lasky for discussing her with a reporter at all. In the first place, Martha said, Victor Lasky was on CREEP's payroll, although this wasn't known at the time. And Victor and his wife were Watergate neighbors of the Mitchells; they had been in the Mitchells' apartment many times. When it was revealed in CREEP campaign funding reports in 1974 that Lasky had received $20,000 for unspecified work, he said the payment was for ghost-writing speeches for Martha.

He wrote the remarks Martha made about a month before Watergate at the Brookdale Hospital Medical Center of Brooklyn, when she said she'd been asked for her views about who Richard Nixon's running mate should be that year: "I've been giving a great deal of consideration to recommending that he run with his beautiful daughter, Julie Eisenhower. That way, it would be a Nixon–Eisenhower ticket and they could bill it as 'All in the Family.' "

Martha had barely calmed down from the column about Lasky's remarks before another Maxine Cheshire story appeared. In this one she said Clark MacGregor, who had replaced John Mitchell as head of CREEP, "is saying that Martha Mitchell is expected to accompany her husband to Miami today."

Maxine continued, "Mrs. Mitchell might still cancel out, as she has done so many times in recent months when she was scheduled to appear at Republican events . . ."

Martha was beside herself. Here were the Republicans, who had refused to let her come to Florida, telling the press she was expected and then insinuating that she, Martha, might cancel out! She picked up the telephone and called the Washington *Post* and other papers, saying "When I said I was through with politics, I meant it. I meant it a thousand percent. All I'm trying to do is lead a quiet life, the life of a private citizen . . . I am tired of all this speculation and innuendo and would very much like to be left alone."

The media reported Martha's calls in detail. On the same day her remarks were quoted, William Eaton of the Chicago *Daily News* wrote, "John N. Mitchell, former Attorney General who is said to be President Nixon's political mentor, is the forgotten man at the Republican convention."

Chapter Fourteen

SINCE RETURNING FROM THE WESTCHESTER COUNTRY CLUB, MARTHA hadn't talked to anyone in the media about her California experience or about dirty tricks. Then on Sunday, September 10, a question and answer about Martha appeared in *Parade* magazine, in Walter Scott's "Personality Parade."

A reader asked if Steve King, "in charge of security for the Committee to Re-elect the President," was the man who threw Martha on the bed, in California, and gave her an injection? It was the first time the name Steve King had been mentioned in connection with the California incident.

According to Walter Scott's answer, Steve King indeed was in California, but he did not inject Martha "in the upper extremity of her thigh." The answer continued: "If in fact Mrs. Mitchell was 'needled' by anyone, and she has always been a scrupulously truthful woman, it is safe to assume that she was injected by a physician or nurse qualified to do so. Steve King says he is not."

The minute Martha finished reading the item, she sat down and wrote Walter Scott a five-page letter that six weeks later was printed in *Parade* in its entirety.

In the letter Martha said she was coming out of her "self-imposed retirement to set a few facts straight." She claimed it was Steve King who "not only dealt me the most horrible experience I have ever had—but inflicted bodily harm upon me." After going into detail about her California experience, she said, "The doctor and all the rest of them should have been arrested . . ." In conclusion she wrote, "This is just to set part of the record straight. I refuse to let these lies be told."

One thing Martha didn't mention in her letter was that she had learned for the first time, while reading the item, that Steve King was now in charge of security at CREEP. Although one of the conditions of her coming back to Washington with John had been that Steve King and Lea Jablonsky be fired, one of the last things John Mitchell did before resigning as head of CREEP was to promote Steve King. Lea Jablonsky also received a promotion—but Martha wouldn't know about that until later. Lea was made head of CREEP's Young Voters for the President office.

When Martha called me that Sunday afternoon to read me the letter she had just written, I was in my office working with Clare Crawford (then on the staff of the Washington *Star*) on an article we were writing together for *Washingtonian* magazine. Martha wouldn't talk to Clare, but when I relayed Clare's request to use the story Martha was telling me, she said, "Do anything you want to with it, Winnie."

Clare wrote the story and when it appeared the next day the press again descended on the Watergate. Martha called to say reporters were downstairs in the lobby, notes requesting interviews were arriving at her door and there was a reporter in the hall outside the Mitchells' apartment who had been there for hours. "I understand from the management she bribed a maintenance man to get in," Martha said.

At Martha's suggestion, I went over to join her "in prison." Although we'd talked by phone dozens of times it was the first I'd seen her since she'd gone to California. She'd lost weight—she said ten pounds—and she was quite pale. But she looked trim rather than drawn in her white pants and yellow-and-white sleeveless overblouse. She laughed when I told her, "Tragedy becomes you."

THE MITCHELLS WERE MOVING TO NEW YORK THE NEXT DAY, BUT NOT TO their new apartment. It wouldn't be available until late October, but Republican J. Willard Marriott had generously given them the temporary use of a luxurious suite at the Essex House, on Central Park South.

As we went about the Watergate apartment while Martha packed the things she'd take to New York (everything else would be left at the

Watergate until October), she seemed to be in a happy mood and was obviously delighted to be leaving Washington. She told me, "I woke up at five this morning and said, 'Goodie, goodie, I'm leaving' . . . In New York I think I'll go into local politics—I think that'll take care of Lindsley" (New York Mayor John Lindsay, whom she detested). And when I asked if she were going to write a book, her eyes twinkled mischievously as she said, "You bet! I'm going to tell it all."

The telephone rang often while I was there, and most of the calls were about uniforms and school arrangements for Marty, who was downstairs saying good-bye to the staff of her favorite bookstore. Marty was a constant reader, and one of her greatest pleasures at the Watergate was to have her mother give her money to spend downstairs at the bookstore. I went with her one day when none of the FBI agents were there. (Marty couldn't go outside the apartment alone, because, as she often reminded her mother, "Somebody might kidnap me!") I was surprised at Marty's selection of books; they indicated a reading level far advanced for her age. Martha took credit, claiming, "I taught her to read when she was three years old."

Martha and Marty left Washington on September 13, traveling in a private compartment of a Miami-to-New York train. The Mitchells' suitcases and boxes of personal belongings were piled into Martha's 1968 blue Mercury station wagon, which was driven to New York by a CREEP chauffeur.

John didn't go with them. He told Martha he would be tied up with business matters for a few days. According to evidence later presented by the Senate Judiciary Committee on the impeachment inquiry, John Mitchell was busy working on the Watergate cover-up during this period. Only a few days before Martha left, he had met with John Dean and Jeb Magruder. When Magruder outlined the false story he planned to tell the Watergate grand jury about the meetings he had with Mitchell, Dean and Gordon Liddy in January and February of 1972, John Mitchell listened and did not express any disagreement. So Magruder went before the grand jury and testified falsely. The day after his meeting with Magruder and Dean, John Mitchell testified before the Watergate grand jury and swore he didn't have previous knowledge of illegal CREEP political intelligence operations or about Gordon Liddy's intelligence-gathering activities.

AFTER SHE MOVED TO NEW YORK, MARTHA BECAME LESS SOLITARY. IN HER telephone calls she talked about how happy she was, and although there were daily revelations about Watergate and related matters, they didn't seem to bother her too much.

We talked about CREEP's $2.5-million countersuit against the Democrats and Maurice Stans's $5-million libel suit against Larry O'Brien, in which he claimed O'Brien had "falsely" and "maliciously" accused him of "criminal acts." On September 11 the Democrats had changed their complaint in their break-in suit, adding the names of Liddy, White House consultant E. Howard Hunt, CREEP treasurer Hugh Sloan and Stans, and increasing damages to $3.2 million. Martha said she had a lot of background on the two suits and promised, "I'll tell you about *that* later."

When the federal grand jury indicted only Liddy and Hunt and the five men arrested in the break-in, Martha wasn't surprised. John had told her in advance the indictments would be limited to these seven men. He also told her that with the indictments, Watergate was over.

The first few weeks she was in New York, most of Martha's conversations were about her new-found freedom and what she was doing with it. She dashed around the city looking at tiles and fabrics and kitchen equipment for the apartment. She lunched with friends at New York's chic restaurants. And in the evening she went out with John to private parties.

But the White House had to show that Martha was back on Richard Nixon's team. Only then could it stop worrying about her constituency. At John's insistence, she went to a big Republican fund-raising dinner. He promised her it would be the last political event he'd ever ask her to attend.

The Mitchells sat at the head table, to the right of the podium. The Nixons, who hadn't seen Martha since the California incident, were to the left. At the party's end, when everyone stood to leave, a swarm of people surged toward Martha, some turning over chairs on the way. The President and First Lady were being ushered to the exit when one of Nixon's aides saw the people stretching up and across the table to shake hands with Martha and to hand her their programs to autograph. Pat Nixon continued out the exit, but an aide said something to Richard Nixon and he turned, walked to Martha's end of the table and started shaking hands with the crowd. An Associated Press picture of the moment shows an exuberant, laughing Martha, grasping hands while a somber-faced and apparently unhappy President stands nearby. It became one of Martha's favorite pictures.

It was a surprise to Martha to find that in New York she could go to public places without having people "make a fuss." Neither was she bothered often by the press. Bob Woodward, of the Washington *Post,* did find his way to suite 710 one morning and knocked on the door about the time the maids arrived. Martha answered the knock, and although she wouldn't let Woodward in, she talked to him for fifteen minutes while the vacuum cleaners buzzed in the background.

Had Bob Woodward knocked on her door a few days later Martha probably wouldn't have been so cordial. That morning, October 5, the Washington *Post* reported that John Mitchell had controlled a secret fund which was used "to finance widespread intelligence-gathering operations against the Democrats . . . Beginning in the spring of 1971, almost a year before he left the Justice Department . . . Mitchell personally approved withdrawals from the fund. . . ." The article also identified Maurice Stans and Jeb Magruder as two of four others "later authorized to approve payments from the secret fund."

The *Post* had reached John Mitchell the night before and reported that he said, "All that crap, you're putting it in the paper? It's all been denied, Jesus. Katie Graham . . . is gonna get caught in a big fat wringer if that's published. Good Christ. That's the most sickening thing I've ever heard."

The *Post* said the fund, which fluctuated between $70,000 and $350,000, was kept in Maurice Stans's safe. It quoted a spokesman for the General Accounting Office as saying "the fund contained $350,000 as of May 25, and was possibly illegal because receipts and expenditures were not publicly reported for a six-week period after the new disclosure law took effect on April 7."

DURING THE FIRST WEEKS AT THE ESSEX HOUSE, MARTHA HAD THOUGHT John was happy, except for his irritation over what he told her was the unpleasant situation at his office. The senior partners of the firm couldn't have been nicer. They saw to it that he had his former office back, although another lawyer had to move out to make it available. And an office was found for Sandy Hobbs, the secretary he brought from Washington.

But there were younger lawyers in the firm who didn't take kindly to his return. "Things were tense on account of Watergate," Sandy says. "A few people were bitter and not nice."

Martha contrasted John's treatment to that afforded Richard Nixon. She said his former office was standing empty, kept as a "shrine." It was furnished as it had been when Nixon was a senior member of the firm, and the present partners loved to walk by the door with a client and say *this* is Richard Nixon's office. Special clients were taken into the room for cocktails.

John Mitchell became so disgusted with the office situation that at one point, Martha said, he talked of leaving the firm. He certainly had enough offers of places to go. One of Wall Street's largest investment banking firms wanted him to take an executive position. Another tempting offer came from Texas multimillionaire Ross Perot, whose company is the Electronic Data Systems.

Until she saw the *Post* story about the secret fund, on October 5, Martha had no idea that John's irritation was related to anything other than the office situation. He'd thoroughly convinced her all the flap about Watergate was just campaign propaganda, and all the commotion would die down after the election.

But the story in the *Post* was disturbing. She'd eavesdropped on the Key Biscayne meeting where they'd discussed ways to spend some of the money. If the Washington *Post* had this information, John couldn't be as relaxed as he'd seemed. Martha thought she knew now what all of those telephone conversations were about "every night, every night," with John Dean and others from the White House and CREEP.

The next time she called, her first question was, "Winnie, is John in trouble?" And the next day, when I called her from the airport before leaving on a vacation trip to Russia, Martha sounded worried and depressed. John was in Washington and wouldn't be home that night. "And I can't even call you," she complained. "You'll be on that goddamn plane."

My plane was still on the ground when Martha called Clare Crawford to say she was considering suing CREEP since two of its employees "beat me up in California." She asked Clare to "pursue as fast as possible . . . why the re-election committee continues to maintain those two characters [Steve King and Lea Jablonsky] . . ."

Clare wrote that during the conversation Martha apparently shooed Marty out of the room, saying, "I'm not going to make your father mad. I don't care whether your daddy is pleased or not—I've had it."

A few days later, Vera Glaser and Malvina Stephenson, in their syndicated column, "Offbeat Washington," quoted many people as having praised Steve King. The reporters claimed the list of King's admirers was headed by "Martha's husband, John."

Also about this time Martha learned, from a former CREEP secretary, that a member of Mrs. Nixon's staff was spreading rumors about Martha's mental health.

Martha insisted something be done to counteract the White House gossip and the column praising King. A few days later, CREEP issued a statement: "The Committee for the Re-Election of the President deeply appreciated the generous assistance of Mrs. Mitchell in helping to re-elect President Nixon . . . Mrs. Mitchell has made several personal appearances in recent weeks and participated in numerous interviews which we believe remove any doubt about her physical and emotional health. The rumors to the contrary should be taken for what they are—outrageous gossip . . ."

There were other stories at that time, too, which displeased Martha. Maxine Cheshire revealed that Tom Wince, "the driver who also doubles as Mrs. Mitchell's bodyguard and butler, is still on the payroll of the Committee . . ." Maxine was unable to determine who paid for the car, leased from the Ford Motor Company at an annual rental of one thousand dollars.

In any event, the Mitchells had the car until sometime after Nixon's re-election, when they bought another leased car and hired their own chauffeur-bodyguard, a man named Zolton Komadi, who said he fled his native Hungary during the 1954 uprisings.

When I returned from Russia, Martha's mood was about the same as when I left three weeks before. She still was worried and depressed. There were a number of disturbing new Watergate developments, she said. But first she wanted to tell me, "Don't you ever again go someplace where I can't call you!" She repeatedly had tried to reach me in Russia, and during at least one telephone call had had "a fight" with the Intourist bureau.

Martha seemed to be bothered most that day by the Senate's interest in the break-in. On October 12, Senator Edward Kennedy, as chairman of the Judiciary Subcommittee on Administrative Practices and Procedures, had ordered a preliminary inquiry into Watergate, and on October 20, Senator Henry Jackson called for the creation of a twelve-man bipartisan committee to investigate Watergate.

During one of our many conversations, Martha said she'd be in Washington within a few days to move her furniture from the Watergate apartment.

Soon after dinner on November 1, my telephone rang. It was Martha. "Winnie, come help me," she screamed. "Please help me!"

"Where are you?"

"The Watergate. Hurry!"

I heard her shout at someone, "Yes! I called Winnie and she's coming over!"

The phone went dead.

My husband, Navy Captain John Benjamin McLendon, drove me to the Mitchells' apartment. I went up alone and John Mitchell answered the door. He looked terribly annoyed. With his uncombed hair and flushed face, his white dress shirt opened at the neck and the tail partly out, he also looked like he'd been in a brawl. The shirt was wet, too. But I couldn't tell if it were from perspiration or if something had been thrown at him.

I asked, "Where's Martha?" He answered by calling to her, "Your *friend* is here."

Martha, her face tear-stained and blotched, walked down the stairs, wearing slacks and a rumpled sleeveless overblouse that didn't hide large red marks on her arms.

"Well, I'll leave 'you two girls' alone," John Mitchell said, sarcastically, before stomping up the steps.

Martha said, "Thank you, Winnie, for coming," and started to cry. Only then did I see that one of her front teeth was out. She led the way to the breakfast room and sat down at the bright-blue table.

"Martha," I said, "before we talk, I want to call Bennie to come up. He's in the lobby. He'll sit in the living room; he won't hear what we're saying."

"Good," she said, "I'm glad he's here."

When I let Bennie in the door I whispered, "I don't know what's going on. But I'm afraid to be here without you."

Martha and I sat in the breakfast room, talking, sometimes crying, for almost four hours. I'd never before seen a woman who said she'd been roughed up. It upset me so much that at one point Martha had to comfort *me.*

I wanted to get her out of there, to our house or someplace else where she'd be safe. But Martha said no, he'd go to sleep soon and she'd be all right. "Just stay with me until I knew he's sound asleep," she said.

Shouldn't she at least go to a dentist about her tooth?

"The tooth isn't *out,*" she explained. "It's the cap he knocked off. All of my teeth are capped. John Mitchell didn't like my teeth from the day he met me. He made me have them capped."

After a while, when both of us could talk calmly, she said she was "scared to death" they were going to commit her to an institution. After what had happened to her in California, she was convinced a President and those around him could do anything they wanted to to anybody; no one was safe.

Why would anyone want to do such a thing to her? "Because I know *so* much, Winnie," she answered. She promised to tell me more "after the election."

But would her husband let them do anything like that to her?

Martha looked at me for a long time before she answered with the greatest sadness in her voice: "John was behind everything that happened to me in California." That, she added, was why she was so frightened of him when the fight started that night.

If she were afraid of her husband, why did she come back to Washington? Why was she staying with him now?

"I have to. I have to," she insisted.

Several months later she'd tell me she stayed because "I've never had any faith in myself. I've never felt I could make it alone."

I was shocked, although I don't suppose I should have been. Martha's feelings of insecurity certainly were well known to me, as they were to others in Washington.

Off and on that night as we talked, Martha reached for her blue push-button telephone and called a friend in suburban New York. The friend was not home. I got the impression it wasn't the first time Martha had called this woman, late at night, when she was troubled.

After one of her unsuccessful calls, Martha turned to me and said, "I want you to make me a promise, Winnie. Anytime you don't hear from me for a full day, I want you to start looking for me. If you can't find me, don't ask John where I am." She gave me the name of a friend to call, saying, "If she doesn't know where I am, phone the police and then tell the press."

I remember thinking, as I watched Martha, that she looked like a woman without hope, one who was going on only because it was something that had to be done. I couldn't believe this was the same vivacious, smiling Martha who with a flash of her dimples and a wave of her hand could captivate rooms full of people.

As we talked, Martha reviewed what had happened in California. She also touched on many facets of the Mitchells' relationship with Richard Nixon. It was as if by going over and over in detail the seven years they'd known this man she could find the answer to what had gone wrong for her. "I did everything to help, everything," she cried. "They never asked me to do a thing that I didn't do it."

It was almost midnight when Martha said she was "all right now," and that I should go home. I thought Bennie and I should stay with her, but she insisted we go. She'd be in town another day or two, she said, and she'd appreciate it if I'd come back the next day to be with her while she finished packing and when the movers came. I promised I would and left.

A few hours later, alone and afraid, Martha went to Union Station and boarded a train for New York. She wore dark glasses and her blond hair was wrapped in a silk scarf. She kept her lips pressed tightly together so no one could see the missing tooth. In New York she was met by friends and taken to the Essex House.

When she called, soon after arriving at the hotel, her only explanation for the sudden change in plans was, "I had to get out." She didn't talk about the incident of the night before for nine months.

THE DAY AFTER RICHARD NIXON'S LANDSLIDE VICTORY, I MET MARTHA AT 1030 Fifth Avenue so she could show me her new apartment. Martha still wasn't her usual exuberant self, but she said John was ecstatic. People were calling from all over, congratulating him on another successful campaign. Letters would pour in for days. Among those who wrote John Mitchell was Chief Justice Warren Burger, who noted that John's candidate had done well and facetiously asked what was wrong with his people in Massachusetts. (Senator George McGovern, the Democratic presidential candidate, carried only Massachussetts and the District of Columbia.)

Workmen were swarming all over the apartment, and as we picked our way around them, Martha showed me how extensive her redecorating would be. Since I was doing an article for *Ladies' Home Journal* about the apartment, I would periodically go to New York to see it in various stages of renovation.

Reporters heard little from or about Martha during this period. She was too busy to make many phone calls to them. But on one of their rare nights out a photographer spotted the Mitchells dining with friends, at the Sign of the Dove restaurant, and took their picture. Martha noted at the time that redecorating an apartment was "just madness, like starting in housekeeping again."

By this time the Essex House was saying it needed suite 710 and was asking the Mitchells when they'd be moving to their apartment. And John was becoming irritable. He'd been upset about something since shortly after the election. Martha said, "Until then he was living in a fool's paradise." Martha wouldn't know the reason for John's sudden change in mood until after the Senate Watergate Hearings got under way.

According to testimony by John Dean, John Mitchell, Fred LaRue and Dean met in Mitchell's Washington law office on July 18 to discuss "the need for support money in exchange for the silence" of the original Watergate defendants.

After much scrambling around, several hundred thousand dollars were raised and paid to the men. But now that the election was over, the demands for money were getting greater.

So was the pressure on the defendants. James McCord testified that in late November Dorothy Hunt, wife of defendant Howard Hunt, told him there would be no more money "unless you fellows agree to plead guilty and take executive clemency . . . and keep your mouths shut." Eight days after she talked to McCord, Dorothy Hunt was killed in an airline crash; in her purse was $10,000 in $100 bills.

During one of Howard Hunt's demands, which he spelled out in a memorandum, he set a deadline of November 25 for what he called "the close of business." In order to guarantee the defendants' silence, the cover-up conspirators would have to pay each of the seven a salary, plus money for their families, incidentals and lawyers' fees. This, of course, could go on for years.

On Thanksgiving, two days before Hunt's deadline, John Mitchell was worried enough to telephone John Dean and suggest that the defendants' current demands should be paid out of a $350,000 slush fund Bob Haldeman had at the White House. The money was "loaned" to the hush-money fund-raisers and paid to the defendants.

In addition to worrying about the hush money, John Mitchell was upset over his position, vis-à-vis his co-conspirators at the White House. At one point he complained to Martha that he was "out and those jerks are still in and they are the ones who were doing all the dirty tricks."

On December 19, Martha called to say they were leaving the Essex House and going to Key Biscayne, where they'd stay in the house Bebe owned until the new apartment was ready.

The Mitchells came back to New York on January 8, the day the Watergate break-in criminal trial opened in Judge John Sirica's court.

Chapter Fifteen

MARTHA RETURNED FROM HER FLORIDA VACATION RELAXED AND rested. She also came back confident that she was "home free." The Watergate problem, as far as she knew, was over. That's what John told her, and he certainly hadn't seemed worried while in Key Biscayne.

Now she could finish decorating the apartment and get down to the serious business of helping John build his "biggest law firm in the country."

But first, less than two weeks away, there was the second Inaugural of Richard Nixon. John insisted that Martha attend; gone was his promise, made before the pre-election fund-raising dinner, that it would be the last thing she'd ever have to do involving the Nixons. She said she'd go to the Inaugural, but only after he'd given his word that this effort on Nixon's behalf really would be her last.

In her early January calls, there was discussion of the Watergate defendants—five had entered guilty pleas, but McCord and Liddy pleaded not guilty. Martha thought it would be "funny if those two get off and the others go to jail." Originally the four Cubans entered a plea of not guilty. But suddenly they changed to guilty, against the advice of their lawyer Henry Rothblatt. When he wouldn't consent to the new plea, they fired him. Martha showed special interest in this aspect of the case because Henry Rothblatt had been her lawyer in 1968, when she was thinking about leaving John Mitchell. After John left her in 1973 Henry would be her lawyer again.

Martha had a lot to say about Alfred Baldwin, the former FBI agent who monitored the phone calls of the Democrats at the Howard Johnson Motor Hotel across the street from DNC headquarters. Baldwin had come forward to tell everything he knew about the Watergate break-in, but Martha wasn't putting much faith in anything he said.

Al Baldwin, she recalled, was one of a succession of "jerks," six in all, hired by James McCord to guard her. None were any good, she insisted, and in her opinion Baldwin was the worse of the lot: "One time, in Michigan, he led me right into the middle of a demonstration." (In her deposition for the DNC–CREEP suits, Martha said, "Al Baldwin is probably the most gauche character I have ever met in my whole life . . . [at the Waldorf Astoria hotel] Mr. Baldwin proceeded to take off his shoes and socks and walk around in front of everybody in New York City barefoot. Not only that, but Mr. Baldwin had the disposition of trying to get himself into every conversation. He made no bones about telling me that he was a Democrat, that he had Democratic friends.

"I said, 'Well, that's all right. I've been a Democrat, too, you know.' I mean it doesn't make any difference to me."

And Martha and I talked about a phone call John had made, while Attorney General, to the U.S. Embassy in Switzerland on behalf of American businessman Robert Vesco. The call, according to a Washington *Star* article by John Polk, was placed "within hours after Vesco was arrested and jailed on a business complaint in Geneva."

"Routinely," the article continued, "the State Department handles all contacts when an American citizen is arrested abroad. A government source here said it 'would be extremely rare' for a high-ranking official outside State—such as the Attorney General—to contact the embassy directly." The *Star* noted that Vesco was a significant campaign supporter of Nixon and had given $25,000 in 1968 and $50,000 in 1972. It would be more than a month before reporters learned that Vesco also had contributed an unreported $200,000 at a time when he was a key figure in a Securities and Exchange Commission investigation. In May, John Mitchell and Maurice Stans would be indicted on charges of perjury and obstruction in connection with the $200,000 campaign donation, which was given in cash—all in one-hundred-dollar bills.

The Associated Press reported in 1975 that John Mitchell used a CIA agent in efforts to free Robert Vesco. The agent "told the chief of Swiss intelligence on Dec. 1, 1971, 'that there was unusual interest in higher U.S. government circles, including Attorney General Mitchell, in this case and that we hoped that Vesco would be released on his own recognizance today,' according to a memo, stamped *Confidential,* that was shown to AP."

In January, when the story broke about John calling the embassy in Switzerland, Martha didn't see anything unusual about it. John often called people in government to help friends in trouble. In fact, she later said, he *invited* requests from friends who wanted help. In a late 1974 article in *Ladies' Home Journal,* while discussing how politics ruined her marriage, Martha said, "In addition to everything else, John Mitchell began to take on Nixon's traits. For instance, we would be having dinner with long-standing friends, and all of a sudden Mitchell would ask these people what he could do for them, for their children, or for their relatives. He did this especially if a child was in the Army or Navy or with the Civil Service. This was a trait Nixon picked up in his early experience in politics: do a political favor for someone and guarantee his vote. I disliked what I considered to be hypocritical 'kindness.' "

Most of our talks, in early January, were about the Inaugural and her wardrobe for it. For her last Nixon Administration appearance Martha decided to wear the same clothes she'd worn to the first; each event of the three-day Inaugural festivities would find Martha Mitchell in the same gown, shoes, purse, jewels, and coat—some cloth, others mink—she had worn to the corresponding event four years earlier. She worked for days coordinating the various outfits. She swore me to secrecy about her plan, saying she wanted to surprise her press friends. Unfortunately she didn't get to tell any of them about her second-time-around wardrobe, since John Mitchell insisted she keep a low profile and that she limit her exchanges with the press to mere pleasantries.

If she were nervous about seeing Administration people she hadn't seen for six months, Martha didn't show it. She looked confident and radiant as she swept in and out of parties, smiling, waving.

Five hundred university students, lined up on the sidewalk to watch celebrities, cheered when Martha arrived at the exclusive F Street Club, where Henry and Christina Ford were giving the Inaugural's most brilliant private party. At the Inaugural Ball the crush around the Mitchells' thousand-dollar VIP box was so dense Martha couldn't see the dancers. And everyone who could get close enough—including Henry Kissinger—hugged and kissed her.

She seemed to be having a marvelous time everywhere she went, but when she called from New York the night she got home, Martha said she was "mad as hell" at the Nixon Administration for the treatment it had given the Mitchells.

Not only were the Mitchells not asked to the regular Inaugural events, Martha complained, but they weren't asked to sit in the President's reviewing stand for the Inaugural Parade—a courtesy extended to his other former Cabinet members. The Mitchells had to watch the parade from the Mudge Rose Guthrie and Alexander Washington law offices on Pennsylvania Avenue. The worse thing, though, in her opinion, was that the Mitchells were excluded from the White House church services that morning, while their Cabinet contemporaries had been invited.

Yet on the press releases I had, the Mitchells were listed among the guests the Nixons were expecting for the church services. And on a seating plan of the presidential reviewing stand, there were two seats set aside for former Attorney General and Mrs. Mitchell.

Martha, not knowing about the press release, naturally blamed the White House for the snubs. Later her suspicions were directed toward her husband.

MARTHA AND JOHN'S SOCIAL LIFE APPARENTLY WAS UNAFFECTED BY THE frequent revelations about Watergate—many seeming to involve John Mitchell. In late January, they went to a dinner party at Bernard (Bunny) Lasker's, where Martha saw Imelda Marcos, wife of Philippine President Ferdinand E. Marcos. (Bernard J. Lasker, former chairman of the New York Stock Exchange, is a close personal friend of both Richard Nixon and Spiro Agnew.) Martha knew Mrs. Marcos from her visits to Washington and had seen her Inaugural week at the Henry Ford party. Martha liked Mrs. Marcos a lot and the feeling evidently was shared; Martha had a beautiful seven-piece set of Philippine rattan furniture, which was a gift from the Marcoses.

One of Mrs. Marcos's aides telephoned later to ask if Mrs. Marcos could call on Martha. But John, who didn't want anyone coming to the apartment, answered the telephone and said the Mitchells would be out of town. The same day John Mitchell also said no when Aristotle Onassis wanted to come over to talk to him. The two secretly were working on a $500 million "deal," Martha said, involving Onassis's oil tankers. The Greek shipping tycoon wanted to talk to John Mitchell, but not at his law office, where he would be recognized. John Mitchell suggested meeting at Onassis's apartment, a block away, but Onassis vetoed that, saying there was press outside. The two finally met at one of Onassis's offices.

The Lasker party was one of many private and unpublicized gatherings John and Martha had attended since returning to New York. The William Simonses were among the people they saw, as were Governor Nelson Rockefeller and his wife Happy. The Mitchells went to dinner at the Rockefellers' Fifth Avenue apartment, where, according to Martha, he said he was going to run for the presidency in 1976 and wanted John Mitchell to run his campaign. Of course, that was when he thought Richard Nixon would be completing eight years in the White House and the field would be open for Republican candidates.

Not long after the Inaugural, Martha started complaining that John was uncommunicative. Later she'd say he had been irritable and drinking heavily. His mood and drinking would worsen until, as she told Clare Crawford for *People* magazine in 1974, "He wouldn't go out. He ate at his desk. He let his hair grow and wouldn't shave. He wanted me to cut his hair. Finally, I got a non-English-speaking barber to come in. John didn't want to see anyone. He wouldn't give me my phone calls. He'd say I was out. And if I answered he'd listen. He was drinking and taking tranquilizers. There were nights our daughter Marty and I had to drag him to bed."

Some friends of John Mitchell's said Martha was transferring her own symptoms and condition to him. But during this time close Mitchell associates noted his unaccustomed depression and whispered among themselves that they feared a disastrous outcome.

By late January several things had happened to cause John Mitchell to worry.

Howard Hunt was demanding more money and executive clemency.

The New York *Times* revealed that at least four of the defendants were still being paid and that campaign contributions totaling $900,000 could not be accounted for by CREEP.

All efforts to get James McCord to change his plea to guilty were failing; he even rejected an offer of executive clemency.

Judge Sirica was not satisfied that the full Watergate story had been disclosed and publicly stated that he hoped the Senate Watergate Committee would be "granted power by Congress by a broad enough resolution to get to the bottom of what happened in this case."

Pretrial depositions in the DNC civil suit, which had been sealed on September 21, were released. They suggested that John Mitchell knew in advance about CREEP's intelligence-gathering activities.

And the Senate voted 70–0 to establish a select committee to investigate the Watergate break-in.

The desperation of the men trying to contain Watergate, by buying the silence of the original defendants, is demonstrated in a conversation President Nixon had with John Dean on March 21, 1973. According to a tape of their discussion, Dean told Nixon about Hunt's latest demands. The President said, "For Christ's sakes, get the money." Watergate grand jury documents, later released, indicate that arrangements to pay Howard Hunt apparently were made at once, after Bob Haldeman telephoned John Mitchell.

By the time I went to New York on February 12, to have another look at the apartment-decorating progress, Martha was so upset over the continuing developments she wouldn't even leave the apartment for fear she'd be recognized and asked about Watergate. We had planned to go together to several fabric and carpet houses—I, too, was redecorating my apartment—but I wound up going alone, in her chauffeur-driven car, armed with her swatches and paint samples and small pieces of wallpaper, along with mine.

Once I got back to Washington, her calls were to discuss Watergate more than to talk about redecorating. And she didn't ask anymore if John were in trouble. She wanted to know, "What's going to happen to John? What's going to happen to me?"

The more worried she became, the more enraged Martha was with the White House, "the cause of all our troubles." It was in this mood that she called one morning at seven o'clock, so riled she hardly could speak. Martha said her former CREEP secretary Kris Forsberg wanted to work at the White House in the office of counselor Anne Armstrong but had been denied the job because of her connection with Martha. Yet Anne Armstrong had hired as her liaison assistant with women's groups Jill Ruckelshaus, whom Martha disliked intensely.

She seethed over it all day; that night she called Helen Thomas to say, "I'm going to tell you something I resent like hell. I resent that Jill Ruckelshaus is in the White House with Anne Armstrong and all her liberal ideas." Martha said her husband even turned off the television when Jill Ruckelshaus appeared on the screen.

The next day L. Patrick Gray III, acting director of the Federal Bureau of Investigation, told a Senate committee that FBI agents wanted to question Martha during their Watergate investigation because of news reports that she had said she was going to "tell all" in a book. "But Mr. Mitchell said that Mrs. Mitchell's stories and the things that were in the press were not so, and we were not going to interview Mrs. Mitchell. There was no need to interview Mrs. Mitchell and that was that." He added that as a "courtesy" the agents didn't question her.

Martha said Gray's testimony was a "goddamn lie" and if anyone wanted to question her they could. Two weeks later, she was still angry at Gray and said she'd always thought he was a "flimsy little nothing" and had tried to tell John and the President. But, she claimed, they were "training" him to take over from J. Edgar Hoover: "They wanted someone who would do what they wanted him to do. Mr. Hoover had never done what anyone wanted him to do."

Five days later, Gray said he had erred when he said John Mitchell blocked questioning of Martha. He "didn't have all the facts," Gray claimed, adding that Mitchell offered to have Martha come to Washington but the agents said it wasn't necessary.

The day after Gray's testimony, Martha and Marty sailed for the Caribbean, on the MS *Victoria,* with Kris Forsberg and her mother.

Martha would return to more problems than she had left. First there was a Jack Anderson column claiming that confidential ITT documents contradicted "the sworn testimony of former Attorney General John Mitchell before the Senate Judiciary Committee a year ago."

Anderson said Mitchell's testimony was at odds with the documents when he told a Senate Judiciary Committee that when he met in his offices with an ITT executive he did not discuss the Justice Department's antitrust case against ITT designed to force it to divest itself of the $2 billion Hartford Fire Insurance Company. He also swore under oath that "The President has never talked to me about any antitrust case that was in the department." Yet, according to Anderson, the documents reported that Mitchell told the executive "that Nixon was not opposed" to the merger the Justice Department was suing to stop.

John Mitchell denied everything in the Anderson column. But Martha remembered that when they lived at the Watergate she had heard John talking many times about ITT with Haldeman and Ehrlichman and others at the White House and Justice. She was worried.

Two days later, switching from ITT to Vesco, Jack Anderson claimed that John Mitchell had set up a meeting with the chairman of SEC and Robert Vesco immediately after the $200,000 campaign contribution was delivered.

Martha had a little comic relief, though, during this time of accusations and denials. On February 23, Martha's neighbors Steve and Jean Smith had given, in their apartment a few floors above Martha, a square dance to celebrate the birthday of Jean's brother, Senator Edward Kennedy, and Martha gleefully reported to me how she had put her head out the window to watch the press, waiting below to see all the Kennedys and Kennedy friends arriving for the party. At the time, the media still was trying to find out where the Mitchells had settled once they left the Essex House. Martha thought it terribly funny that she was looking out her window without being recognized. She also laughed about the condition of the building's elevators, which were "full of straw," since the Smiths had brought in bales of hay, along with one or two barnyard animals, to give an authentic atmosphere to the square dance.

THE SEVEN WATERGATE DEFENDANTS APPEARED BEFORE JUDGE SIRICA FOR sentencing on March 23. The sixty-nine-year-old Judge, whose heavy sentencing had earned him the name of "maximum John," imposed thirty-five years on Howard Hunt; forty each for the four Cubans, and six years, eight months to twenty years for Gordon Liddy.

He postponed sentencing James McCord after reading in open court a letter in which McCord explained to the Judge the reason for his not having answered questions posed to him from the Judge through his probation officer. McCord added:

"Be that as it may, in the interest of justice, and in the interest of restoring faith in the criminal justice system, which faith has been severely damaged in this case, I will state the following to you at this time which I hope may be of help to you in meting out justice in this case:

1. There was political pressure applied to the defendants to plead guilty and remain silent.
2. Perjury occurred during the trial in matters highly material to the very structure, orientation, and impact of the government's case, and to the motivation and intent of the defendants.
3. Others involved in the Watergate operation were not identified during the trial, when they could have been by those testifying.
4. The Watergate operation was not a CIA operation. The Cubans may have been misled by others in believing that it was a CIA operation. I know for a fact that it was not.

McCord also said, "Following sentence, I would appreciate the opportunity to talk with you privately in chambers. Since I cannot feel confident in talking with an FBI agent, in testifying before a grand jury whose U.S. attorneys work for the Department of Justice, or in talking with other government representatives, such a discussion with you would be of assistance to me."

James McCord's letter was a devastating development for the Watergate cover-up conspirators. And although he didn't name names, Martha knew it was only time before the other shoe would drop.

"I can't conceive what he's talking about," John Mitchell told the Washington *Star* when asked about McCord's statement that "others involved in the Watergate operations were not identified during the trial." John Mitchell added that a CREEP legal-staff investigation "showed that there wasn't anyone involved."

Publicly Martha didn't say anything for several days; privately she was telling a lot, particularly the day after she read a Washington *Post* story saying Martha "knew and liked McCord very much."

"I didn't trust him the first time I met him," she declared in one of several calls that day. "And I told the Committee how I felt. I even asked the FBI to please check on him for me."

Martha also said she suspected McCord of acting as a "double agent," and she was quite sure he tapped the telephones in the Mitchells' Watergate apartment. Later I'd learn that John Mitchell had planted the idea that McCord was a double agent when Martha called him from California about James McCord's arrest.

She not only didn't trust McCord, but she thought he was incompetent at his job: "During the whole time the FBI was protecting me, I had a total of four agents. But I had six security guards in the few months he was supplying them. He couldn't have found six more unsuitable people if he had tried for a hundred years."

Martha changed her mind about James McCord after John Mitchell left her; by then she considered any enemy of the Administration to be a friend of hers. At Martha's request, Junie Dankworth arranged a meeting at her house between Jim McCord and Martha during the 1974 Christmas holidays. Junie says the two greeted each other with an affectionate embrace before settling down for a four-hour conversation.

It was an animated talk, covering a variety of subjects. "My first question," Martha recalled, "was, 'Why did you all enter the Democratic Committee and tap the phones?' And he said, 'Because they had a feeling that the Communists were financing the Democratic Committee.' "

Martha also wanted to know how he could have placed a tape "from left to right" on the Watergate building door the night of the break-in. A security guard, Frank Wills, discovered the tape placed (to keep the door from automatically locking) in a horizontal position, instead of perpendicular so it couldn't be seen. "And Jim said, 'I would never tape a door like that.' He said he didn't do it, that somebody else had found out they were in there and they had been down and changed the tape. Jim denied 100 percent that he placed the tape that way."

McCord claimed he'd been sold a "bill of goods" by CREEP. He blamed "Magruder, Liddy and Company." And he said Mitchell had approved everything he had done, insisting that Mitchell had said yes, go ahead with it.

Two days after Judge Sirica read McCord's letter in court, I went to New York. For the next four days Martha and I talked, about Watergate and related matters, for hours at a time—at her apartment and by telephone.

One of the first things she told me was that she was frightened; again she asked me to come looking for her if "you hear I'm sick or can't talk." She added, "Somebody might try to shut me up."

She feared for John, too, since she'd learned that the White House was trying to make John "the goat" of Watergate. She wouldn't say how she'd heard this. Several months later Martha admitted she'd received the information through eavesdropping when a *Newsweek* writer, "a very good friend of John's," called to alert John that in its upcoming issue the magazine would have an article quoting a White House source as saying John could be the scapegoat.

Martha said she wasn't going to let them sacrifice John. "I'll name names and I don't give a who-happy who gets hurt," she declared. "I'm going to clean my skirts and I'm going to clean his."

SOME OF THE THINGS SHE WANTED TO TELL, ACCORDING TO MARTHA, couldn't be revealed in public. But she was afraid to talk to the Justice Department since it was headed by Richard Kleindienst. Martha claimed he was "on their side," meaning the White House's. She didn't know where to go with her information—even some things "involving national security that I can't talk about, now."

But she wanted to tell part of what she knew within the next few days. She asked me to write it, because she didn't want "some damn paper saying, 'Martha called.' " I said I'd do it for the New York *Times,* since the day before I left Washington, Bill Blair of the *Times'* Washington Bureau had asked if I would interview Martha for them.

Martha wanted to work out in her mind just what she wanted to say for the *Times*; we decided to meet the next day to put the story together. But at five o'clock Martha called to say the story couldn't wait until tomorrow, it had to go out *now*! She wouldn't say why.

Perhaps someone had reported to John Mitchell, and Martha had eavesdropped, about an eleven-ten A.M. meeting that day among the President, Haldeman and Ehrlichman. The three were discussing John Mitchell when Haldeman said, ". . . The more O'Brien [CREEP lawyer Paul O'Brien] thinks about it, the more it bothers him with all he knows, to see all the people getting whacked around in order to keep the thing from focusing on John Mitchell, when inevitably it is going to end up doing that anyway . . ."

Martha had made notes of exactly what she wanted to say for the *Times*: Someone was trying to make John "the goat." She was afraid for him and for herself; she compared her fear to that she felt when she was thrown to the floor and stuck with a hypodermic needle in California. Herbert Kalmbach, the President's personal lawyer, "was very much involved" in what happened to her in California, as were two FBI agents. And "McCord probably bugged our apartment. In fact, I'm sure of that. We were bugged in Rye for sure, and these men, not the FBI, came with their little gadgets and found them. That was sometime in 1968."

When Martha hung up, I let our dinner hostess know I'd be late, then I called the *Times.*

The next day the ringing telephone awakened me at seven-forty A.M. It was Martha. Outraged! The article was in the paper, with everything I'd turned in. But without my knowledge something had been added—a sentence saying, "Mrs. Mitchell telephoned the New York *Times.*"

"That is a goddamn lie and you know it, and they know it," she shouted. "They called *you.*"

It's indisputable that Martha made hundreds of telephone calls on her own. But a large portion of those one read about in the papers, or heard of on the airways, was not instigated by Martha. When John Mitchell was Attorney General, reporters would call his office and leave messages, requesting that Martha call. Sometimes she did, and more often than not the resulting story would read, "Martha called." The same thing happened when she had her own secretaries to take messages—or in New York, both at the Essex House and on Fifth Avenue, where bellmen constantly slipped notes under her door from the press, begging her to call. Some reporters sent flowers with their requests and usually got replies. Martha loved fresh flowers, particularly roses. And one ingenious reporter sent telegrams reading something to the effect: "Please call me. I have important information for you." Martha, whose curiosity knew no bounds, couldn't resist those.

Martha and I had one good laugh, though, the day the *Times* article appeared. As usual we checked and discussed our horoscopes for the day. Mine read, ". . . an unusual friend may make for a really mixed-up situation this morning." Hers was just as accurate, although not as funny: "Do your best this morning to deal with instability and chaotic conditions in economics and at home. Your mate or others may be uncommunicative . . ."

FOR MARTHA IT SEEMED THAT EACH DAY BROUGHT A REVELATION MORE disturbing than the last. The same day the *Times* story came out, James McCord appeared in secret session before the Ervin Committee and said Gordon Liddy told him about a meeting in February 1972, in John Mitchell's office at the Justice Department, where the bugging was planned. He said John Mitchell specifically authorized money for Watergate.

The information was leaked and appeared in the next day's papers. The same morning the *Wall Street Journal* reported that more and more Republican politicians, some on the Hill, were blaming John Mitchell for Watergate.

Later that day, John Mitchell released his reply to McCord's latest accusations: "I deeply resent the slanderous and false statement about me concerning the Watergate matter as being based on hearsay and leaked out of the Ervin Committee. I have previously denied any prior knowledge of, or involvement in, the Watergate affair and I again reaffirm such denials."

During one of my conversations with Martha, John got on the telephone and said all of McCord's testimony was hearsay, that he hadn't seen McCord on a regular basis (as McCord had testified), and how shocking it was that secret testimony would be leaked.

In another call, Martha had a different problem to report. As a result of our *Times* article, the FBI had informed John that Martha had to testify before their agents. On April 3 she was questioned in her apartment by three FBI men. She had asked me to be there, but John had said no. His secretary Sandy Hobbs and a friend from Bronxville sat in during the questioning.

Martha said the interview left her surprised and puzzled. There were too many questions left unasked. And the ones asked weren't the right ones.

She had always thought the FBI was the greatest law-enforcement agency on earth; J. Edgar Hoover was Martha's hero. And she'd admired and respected the agents who protected her in Washington, although she sometimes had bitter battles with them. But as a man with the Justice Department puts it: "She got mad and there were some good fights [between Martha and the agents]. But [we] always treated Mrs. Mitchell with great deference."

During Martha's calls the first two weeks in April, she was sounding more and more frantic. She was upset over the reports John was receiving about White House meetings at which there was a great deal of discussion about making him step forward to take the blame for Watergate. Martha never told who was leaking the information to John.

On the night of April 13, Martha called at eleven-thirty and talked for an hour. At two A.M. she called again; that conversation also lasted an hour. She had called the White House, she said, and told them "to get this over with or I'm going to get the whole Administration over with."

Did her husband know about her call? "No," she said, "but he gets a lot of surprises . . . I may be dead on account of it, Winnie, dead in the gutter. But I'm screaming loud and clear. I'm not going to let them pin this on John." If John would not save himself, she would.

In an editorial the day after she died, Martha's hometown newspaper wrote about this underappreciated aspect of Southern women. "They don't stay up on a pedestal, not in a crisis," according to the Pine Bluff *Commercial.* "When the menfolk are defeated or cowed, they come down to do battle. That business about the retiring Southern lady is a well-cultivated convention that may have its charm. But whether it was fighting against lynching long ago, or more recently, keeping the schools open in Little Rock, Southern women played their part: the leading part." The editorial continued: "It can be a lonely road." It was for Martha.

Martha fought not only for John but to hold on to the high standard of living the marriage gave her. She saw the whole thing crumbling, John's law practice going down the drain, no money coming in, and she worried for herself and her daughter. She responded in the only way she knew how.

Later Martha tried to get John to plea bargain, to seek immunity from prosecution in return for evidence. He refused. Their arguments over this became so frequent and violent that he finally stopped speaking to Martha at all.

Martha telephoned early on April 14. John had been called to the White House. The President wanted to see him. Why would the President call him to come to Washington on Saturday morning? What was going on? Had I heard anything on the news?

Then she called in tears. She'd telephoned the White House to ask Rose Mary Woods when John would be coming home. Martha wanted to send the chauffeur to the airport to meet him. Rose Mary wouldn't take Martha's call and Martha couldn't understand it. When the Mitchells were in Washington, Martha thought she and Rose Mary were good friends. It was frightening, Martha said.

On John's flight back to New York, there were two CBS reporters, Daniel Schorr and Bernard Shaw. They questioned John Mitchell when the plane landed.

According to news reports of the CBS interview, John Mitchell said, "After conferring with the President" he expected White House aides would testify in the Senate's Watergate investigation. As for himself, "With all the hearsay evidence and all the rest of it, I just can't wait to get down before the Ervin Committee."

The next afternoon I received a call from a reporter friend saying the White House was denying that John Mitchell saw the President.

The next time we talked, I asked Martha to clarify this; she said John told her he definitely had seen the President; in fact, she had sent a message to President Nixon and John brought back the reply. Later she called to say she'd asked John "right out" if he'd seen Nixon and John said yes. The next day White House deputy press secretary Gerald Warren denied that Mitchell had seen the President, or had even talked with him by telephone.

Martha called Frances Lewine of Associated Press and said, "That's a god-blessed lie. You can say it's not so, that they're lying from the beginning to the end."

White House tapes, however, agree with Gerald Warren.

According to the tape of April 14, Richard Nixon, Bob Haldeman and John Ehrlichman met in the President's office. During the meeting they decided someone had to tell John Mitchell that he must take full blame for Watergate. The question was, who should talk to him. Ehrlichman explained to the President what had to be done.

EHRLICHMAN: The purpose of the mission is to go up and bring him to a focus on this; the jig is up. And the President strongly feels that the only way that this thing can end up being even a little net plus for the Administration and for the presidency and preserve some thread is for you to go in and voluntarily make a statement.

NIXON: A statement [*unintelligible*]

EHRLICHMAN: A statement that basically says—

HALDEMAN: He's got to go beyond that.
EHRLICHMAN: I am both morally and legally responsible.
NIXON: Yeah.

John Ehrlichman wanted the President to be the one to tell John Mitchell. He said Nixon should say, "My God, I've got a report here. And it's clear from this report that you are guilty as hell. Now, John, for [expletive deleted] sake go on in there and do what you should. And let's get this thing cleared up and get it off the country's back and move on."

The President maintained he shouldn't do it. The proper one, he said, was John Ehrlichman. The three went over the things Ehrlichman should tell Mitchell. At one point Ehrlichman said he'd tell Mitchell, "The thing is not going to go away, John, and by your sitting up there in New York pretending that it is, is just making it worse. And it's been getting steadily worse, by your sitting up there for the last couple of months. We're at the point now where we had no choice but to ask you to do this."

After more discussion it was decided to call John Mitchell immediately and ask him to come to Washington, saying the President wanted to see him. John Mitchell left New York with no idea that he was going all the way to Washington only to see John Ehrlichman, a man he disliked immensely.

The meeting in Ehrlichman's office was quite different from the one the Presidential assistant had fantasized about while in the President's office.

A tape Ehrlichman made of the conversation, without John Mitchell's knowledge, shows how much difficulty Ehrlichman had telling Mitchell what he was supposed to. It went, in part, like this:

EHRLICHMAN: Sorry to drag you down here this way, but things seem to be moving and I thought you'd better know what we know. Sit down.
MITCHELL: I'd like to know what you know.
EHRLICHMAN: Uh, late last night, uh, I gave the President the results of what I had been working on since about the 25th of March . . . Uh, he then asked that I talk to you and several other people about something that I discovered in this thing that, that troubled him very much, and that was that some people thought that their silence served his purpose at this point . . .

Now, obviously you're in a situation of jeopardy, and other people are, too. And, he does not—I mean this is just very hard uh, uh, for, for him, and that's the reason I am talking to you. And, and, uh, he just didn't want anybody to labor under the misapprehension that there was any overriding consideration in his interest of anybody remaining mute. That, that, uh—obviously, everybody's got to decide for himself if, if he's got a Fifth Amendment situation or, uh, put them on your approved situation and that's not what I'm talking about. I'm talking about, uh, the, uh, attitude that several have—John Dean for one, that he is better off not, not testifying than testifying because it was the, the President's interest.

The President now feels his interest institutionally, not, not individually necessarily, but the institution of the presidency is better served by having this thing aired, disposed of, and put, put behind us, so to speak. . . . Now, uh, I learned in the process of, uh, trying to reach people that—access routes—that Jeb Magruder has decided to make a clean breast of things and to take a guilty plea . . .

So that pretty well, uh, starts to work from the middle in all directions, and apparently he will be seeing the U.S. Attorney to carry this out either over this weekend, or immediately the first of the week. Uh, he, uh—on the four corners of my investigation, that will pretty well determine the ultimate outcome of things uh, if he does that and I—absolutely anyone's opinion [*unintelligible*], uh, in addition, it's coming unstuck in a number of other areas and uh, [*unintelligible*].

MITCHELL: Well, I'd like to know about it.

EHRLICHMAN: Well, the U.S. Attorney is focusing on the aftermath.

MITCHELL: Uh huh.

EHRILCHMAN: On the obstruction of justice aspect of this, and, uh, apparently has induced Hunt to testify through some arrangement or other. Now, that's not very reliable evidence. [*unintelligible*].

MITCHELL: From what I hear, that's probably true.

EHRLICHMAN: But, uh, that seems to be the breaks of this [*unintelligible*] . . . they expect that, uh, they will make a very wide-ranging case of the aftermath business.

MITCHELL: On what, uh, what basis?

EHRLICHMAN: Obstruction of justice.

MITCHELL: Huh.

EHRLICHMAN: Yeah, on conspiracy.

MITCHELL: In what way did they obstruct justice?

EHRLICHMAN: In inducing the defendants to withhold testimony, is their theory for corrupt [*unintelligible*].

MITCHELL: Is that factually true?

EHRLICHMAN: I don't, I, I can't say that it is . . .

MITCHELL: Uh huh.

EHRLICHMAN: Because he—uh, a, a lot of validation has been made with regard to John Dean . . .

MITCHELL: Well, certainly there wasn't any corrupt motive . . . Poor John is the guy that just got caught in the middle . . .

EHRLICHMAN: Sure, and that's what I said.

MITCHELL: Like, uh, like so many others that were first of all trying to keep the lid on this until after the election.

EHRLICHMAN: Yeah.

MITCHELL: And, uh, in addition to that, to keep the lid on all the other things that, uh, were going on over here, uh, that . . .

EHRLICHMAN: Well, the, uh . . .

MITCHELL: Would have been worse, I think than the Watergate business.

EHRLICHMAN: So, uh, uh, that's before them. Now, as far as what you do, obviously you're the, you're the captain of your own boat on this, but the President wanted you to have me tell you right now that he is extraordinarily troubled by the situation in which you find yourself, and, and therefore everybody finds themselves. That this, uh, in no way affects his feeling for you in any regard,

MITCHELL: What's his [*the President's*] first proposed action?

EHRLICHMAN: He hasn't any right to tell you what to do, uh—

MITCHELL: Oh, I'm not talking about me.

EHRLICHMAN: Yeah.

MITCHELL: No, no, no, no. What, what is Brother Dick doing about that?

EHRLICHMAN: Well, he, he doesn't have just a lot of options.

MITCHELL: Well, let me [*clears throat*] tell you where I stand. Uh, there is no way that I'm going to do anything except staying where I am because I'm too far out. Uh, the fact of the matter is that, uh, I got euchred into this thing, when I say, by not paying attention to what these bastards were doing, and uh, well you know how far back this goes—this, uh, whole genesis of this thing was over here—as you're perfectly well aware.

EHRLICHMAN: No, I didn't know that . . . Well, I certainly would not attempt to tell you what to do.

MITCHELL: No, I appreciate that.

EHRLICHMAN: The, the thing that was lurking in the, in the President's mind and that I could not disabuse him of was, is—"You think John thinks that he ought to hold back for me?" and I said, "Well, I haven't talked to John, I don't know what's in his mind."

MITCHELL: Hold back from the President?

EHRLICHMAN: Hold back—no, no, no, no. Hold back from coming forward on account of the President. In other words, if you were to think I shouldn't really—even say to yourself: "I shouldn't come forward on this because I would hurt the President," or something of that kind. He said: "Well, somebody's got to talk to him and say: 'Don't, don't hold back on account of the presidency.' "

MITCHELL: Uh huh.

EHRLICHMAN: And, and, that's really the burden of this conversation. I don't have any, I don't have any desire to have you take anything else away from here except that. And y—, and it's his, that's his message.

MITCHELL: It's not—I, I realize that. But with all of this, uh, uh, *(clears throat)* There's uh, certainly no possibility that I would ever turn around and say, "Yes, I was part and parcel of this."

EHRLICHMAN: Sure, sure. Okay. . . .

Before he left, John Mitchell casually let Ehrlichman know he was aware that Haldeman had approved making payments to the defendants from some of the White House funds.

That afternoon John Ehrlichman reported to the President on his failure to convince Mitchell he should come forward and confess: "He [Mitchell] is an innocent man in his heart, and in his mind, and he does not intend to move off that position."

Chapter Sixteen

"THERE WASN'T ANYTHING NORMAL ABOUT IT. THE HOME WAS FULL of tension—a contagious-type tension so strong you got wrapped up in it and reacted in ways you normally would not react. I mean, it made you another kind of person."

This is the way Alleta Saunders describes the atmosphere—and her reaction to it—in the Mitchell apartment during the week of April 16. Alleta had rushed to New York, from Mississippi, after a frantic call from Martha. The developments of the weekend had so filled Martha with fear and despair she knew she couldn't face another crisis alone.

After his visit to Washington, and the subsequent White House denial that he had seen the President, John telephoned Nixon, who wouldn't accept his call. Neither would anyone else in the White House. As Martha put it, "He is completely cut off. He can't get through to any of those bastards."

In one of the many phone calls she made to me early that week, she said, "Those little boys [Haldeman, Ehrlichman and their staffs] just hate John and they hate me . . . And with them in power and sitting in Washington they can do anything they want to to either of us." She added, "They would just love to put us both down."

We discussed a radio report, in another call that day, saying she would be subpoenaed to give a deposition, on May 2, in connection with the Democratic National Committee's $6.4 million suit against CREEP. She noted that she was "sorry they just want a deposition from me. I want to go to the Hill and testify publicly."

Martha also complained to me that she couldn't leave her apartment because the press was keeping an almost twenty-four-hour watch outside their building. She was annoyed, too, by the constant interruptions caused by the elevator men delivering notes, letters and telegrams from the media wanting statements from her. And although their unlisted telephone number had been changed again, the telephones were ringing incessantly. Finally, on Wednesday, Martha called and begged me to come to New York; she said the situation was more than she and Alleta could handle.

When I arrived I saw that Martha hadn't exaggerated about the media. Reporters and camermen were outside the building, on both sides of the street. Some were standing, others seated in cars. When they saw the District of Columbia license plates on our car, several dashed over to see who was getting out. Nobody recognized me.

Alleta was right about the tension in the apartment. The usually cheerful and easy-going Julia Carter broke down later and cried as she told me, "It just breaks my heart to see what is happening to these wonderful people." And Marty, who'd always been friendly, ran to her room and slammed the door when she saw me. Alleta explained, "It's because you're a member of the press; she hates all of you."

Although it was early afternoon, Martha was wearing a pale-blue, antebellum-type nightgown with matching peignoir. It was Martha's habit, during times of stress, not to get dressed; she would wear gowns and negligees, often changing them two or three times a day. She looked overwrought and exhausted—and frightened.

The Washington *Post* that morning quoted Jeb Magruder as saying John Mitchell and John Dean had approved the Watergate bugging operation and later arranged "to buy the silence of the seven convicted Watergate conspirators." Martha knew about the bugging operation from eavesdropping, but she still was devastated at seeing it in print.

In another *Post* story, her husband was accused of trying to persuade Democratic officials "to drop their lawsuit over the Watergate break-in of party headquarters." Martha said it was true, she'd heard John talking to a DNC lawyer; he also talked to Washington lawyer Edward Bennett Williams so often about the DNC suit, she said, that Williams and Mitchell became "buddy-buddy." Williams was the senior partner of the prestigious law firm, Williams, Connally, and Califano. Joseph Califano, later Secretary of Health, Education and Welfare in the Carter Administration, was the attorney for DNC.

In his book, John Dean also mentions Mitchell's involvement with the DNC suit against CREEP: " 'I'm going to call Dwayne Andreas for Maury [Stans],' Mitchell told me. 'And I'll tell him to pass the word to Mr. O'Brien that we might find a way to end the nuisance of his tax problem if he can find some way to end the nuisance of his lawsuit. I think he'll recognize this might be a very satisfactory solution to a tough problem for everyone . . .' " Dean explained that Andreas was a "Minneapolis businessman who had made large contributions to Hubert Humphrey's past campaigns and a $25,000 contribution to the 1972 Nixon campaign. The Nixon contribution had passed through the bank account of Watergate conspirator Bernard Barker."

MARTHA SAID IT WOULD BE A GREAT HELP TO HER IF I'D SCREEN THE PHONE calls and check all the notes, letters and telegrams the elevator men were slipping under the front door. I told her I would but that I also wanted to contact everyone in the media who'd sent messages and I wanted to go downstairs and give the press a statement from her. After I returned to Washington, I'd read in a local paper that I'd been *called* to New York "to keep an eye on Martha and her telephone, and button her lip."

Martha and Alleta composed a statement which said she was a concerned wife, one who trusted her husband ("there's nobody in the world that believes in her husband more than I do") and was confident the facts, when known, would prove him innocent. In answer to reporters' questions I filled in some details about the situation upstairs—Martha was up and about, not under a doctor's care, not on tranquilizers, was talking with friends and had a sorority sister as a houseguest.

One of the incoming calls was from John Mitchell; he seemed surprised to learn I was there. Earlier in the day, Zolton had driven him to Washington where Mitchell was to testify the next day before the grand jury. After the unpleasant experience the Saturday before (when newsman Daniel Schorr had taken the same plane with him from Washington to New York), Mitchell thought it safer to make the trips by automobile. Martha told me John thought Schorr was tipped off by the White House that John would be returning to New York on that particular flight. In his call, Mitchell said he would be staying at the Crystal City Marriott, across the Potomac from the capital, probably in the hope that the press wouldn't find him there. He was registered under Zolton's name. Another call was from Maurice Stans, who three weeks later would be indicted with John Mitchell and charged with conspiracy to defraud the United States and to obstruct justice in connection with a secret $250,000 campaign contribution from financier Robert Vesco. The indictment made Mitchell and Stans the first Cabinet members to be formally charged with criminal acts since the Teapot Dome scandal during the Harding Administration.

Martha talked to Maurice Stans for some time, and when he told her he'd called to tell John he was getting an attorney, she said, "You all should have listened to me, shouldn't you." He answered that he would listen from then on.

After she hung up, she explained that she'd told John and Stans as far back as August 1972 that the two were in trouble and should start preparing their defense. "They wouldn't listen," she said. "And, when I told Kathleen [Mrs. Stans] 'our husbands are in trouble,' she said, 'Oh, no they are not.' "

Martha talked about the countersuit Stans had filed against Larry O'Brien and the Democratic National Committee, saying she was present in the Mitchells' Watergate apartment when it was decided Stans would sue. "They didn't expect to win," she claimed. "The suit was brought because John and Stans thought it would break O'Brien financially. They didn't think the Democrats would put up the money to defend O'Brien." She also said John and the White House were so anxious to "get" O'Brien they started an Internal Revenue Service harassment against him.

(Later it was revealed that a CREEP lawyer had written a memo to the White House stating that the facts of Stans's case against Larry O'Brien "do not support a claim of actual malice" . . . and that John Dean wrote an answer to the memo saying, "The facts known to us do not support a claim of actual malice. However, the filing of the action would have obvious media advantages.")

Martha also expressed a desire to go before the Senate Watergate Committee when it convened the next month, and begged me to help her get there. I explained that she couldn't go without documented facts of the accusations she wanted to make against Richard Nixon and his Administration. She assured me she would be given the incriminating documents before her appearance. In the notes I jotted down that day I wrote that I had the distinct impression John Mitchell was "putting her up to this in order to scare the White House into sticking with him." I was sure that he had no intention of letting her go before the Committee but that he did want her to talk about it.

I also warned Martha that she shouldn't go up on the Hill if she were involved in any of the Watergate illegalities. She told me a friend had delivered money, $10,000 in cash, to her but that she didn't think it was illegal. As it turned out, it was. It was part of the unreported funds.

She then told me about money given to the Nixon campaign that resulted in ambassadorships for the donors. Although these people had to "buy" their diplomatic posts, Martha said they were good investments. She recalled that John had complained to her once that he was *losing* money serving the Administration, while a man he had helped get his Nixon ambassadorial appointment was *making* money serving abroad. The assets of the man's firm had jumped several hundred percent, she said.

Later the Senate Watergate Report said that ". . . over $1.8 million in Presidential campaign contributions can be attributed in whole, or in part, to persons holding ambassadorial appointments from the President." On February 25, 1974, Herbert Kalmbach, President Nixon's personal lawyer, pleaded guilty to "selling an ambassadorship." This concerned a $100,000 contribution by J. Fife Symington, then ambassador to Trinadad and Tobago, who was promised a European post in return for the contribution.

Other things Martha and I discussed that day included John Mitchell's reactions after going to Washington on the fourteenth, thinking he was going to see the President and then didn't: "You have no idea what it was like around here, the night Nixon cut John off. It was hell. John was completely floored. He didn't realize what was going on."

And we talked about Bebe Rebozo and how he was a principal political adviser to Nixon. Martha said when she had asked Richard Kleindienst to intervene to keep John from having to leave Justice, he had said, "The President and Rebozo want this." Our conversation was at a time when Bebe Rebozo still was being portrayed simply as a friend and companion to the President, someone who was appreciated by Nixon because he didn't have *political* expertise.

Another subject we discussed was the Democrats and how they had "sold out" to Nixon in the 1972 election. Martha named a prominent Democratic congressional leader who, she said, had asked his big contributors to support Nixon financially and that he and John had met to discuss it. "He was so against McGovern," she said, "he got money for Nixon." She also said Lyndon Johnson had been instrumental in getting John Connally to head the Democrats for Nixon Committee. And she repeated something she had told me earlier, that Connally had been promised he would be Vice-President.

I questioned how this could be—Nixon had a Vice-President, Spiro Agnew. Martha admitted she didn't know how Nixon was going to do it, but she'd heard John talking about it over the telephone. Several months later, when the Agnew scandal broke, Martha gloated, "What did I tell you? What did I tell you? This is the way Nixon is going to pay off to Connally and make him Vice-President!" And according to later reports, Connally *was* Nixon's first choice, but his advisers convinced him he never could get the nomination confirmed by the Senate; Nixon turned to Gerald Ford.

A friend from Rye came to see Martha that afternoon; she was visibly shaken from having to walk past the press. Other occupants of 1030 Fifth were feeling the same way, and their complaints were adding to Martha's distress. She wrote notes to some, apologizing for the inconvenience.

When Alleta, who had taken Marty to the theater, returned to the apartment she told me Martha had made several telephone calls the night before, some of them to the White House.

About six or seven in the morning, Martha called the White House again to ask the switchboard operator to put her through to Bebe Rebozo's girl friend's house. Martha had been trying, unsuccessfully, to reach Rebozo to have him "tell Nixon that he should be nicer to John." She thought the girl friend could tell her where to reach Rebozo.

When the operator wouldn't complete her call, Martha started detailing what she was going to do to Nixon. The operator switched her call to the Secret Service; Martha repeated to the SS agent the things she'd told the operator and added more.

Alleta, who'd been trying to get Martha to hang up, was shocked at this point to hear Martha tell the agent that her friend Mrs. Charles Saunders of Greenwood, Mississippi, was with her and that Mrs. Saunders was going to complain to her senators about Nixon. With that she hung up. Alleta grabbed the phone, called the White House and told the Secret Service, "Don't pay any attention to her.

"I told him [the agent] that she was drinking," Alleta continued, "and to please just bear with me and try to help me out. I said, 'She's on a tear.' And he just kept saying, 'Yes, ma'm. Yes, ma'm.' "

The next day, Friday, Julia left for Washington, taking Marty with her; Marty stayed with one of Martha's former secretaries. John Mitchell was testifying before the grand jury and there was a larger crowd of reporters and cameramen outside 1030 Fifth than there'd been the day before. John's secretary was at the apartment when I got there but left soon after. She appeared as distraught as Martha had been the day before.

But then, everyone—myself included—who was in the apartment for even a short period of time seemed to develop a seige mentality. Martha seemed a little less harried; at least she was dressed.

Again I answered the phones and returned calls to members of the press—among them several friends of mine who had left urgent messages with my answering service. I also went downstairs and gave the reporters a rundown of what Martha was doing.

One of the calls I returned that day was from Bonnie Angelo of *Time* magazine. She had a message for Martha from Senator Lowell Weicker, a Republican member of the Ervin Committee. "He says if Mrs. Mitchell is serious," Bonnie relayed, "he'd like to invite her on his own if the Committee won't."

Martha said she wanted to go before the Committee more than anything in the world. But she told me it would never happen, because there was *no way* it would be permitted by Senator Howard Baker, the senior Republican on the Committee and, Martha claimed, its White House "man." One of the things they had done, she said, was to convince Baker that Martha would not be a viable witness. All they had to do, she claimed, was to "feed him their old line that I'm an alcoholic." His wife was an alcoholic, Martha said, so it was easy to convince him that Martha —if the stories about her drinking were true—shouldn't testify publicly before the Committee.

At the time it wasn't generally known about Joy Dirksen Baker's drinking problem. Then in August 1976, when Senator Baker was being considered for the vice-presidential nomination, to run with President Gerald Ford, he volunteered information about his wife's long-time drinking problem. Later Joy Baker told Barbara Gamerekian, of the New York *Times,* that she had been hospitalized, as long as eight months at one time, and had had psychiatric treatment and contacts with Alcoholics Anonymous.

I also spoke to Shana Alexander, then with *Newsweek.* As Shana and I talked, Martha sat across the desk from me nodding or shaking her head, sometimes scribbling notes. For the next issue of *Newsweek,* Shana wrote a "Love Song to Martha Mitchell," in which she called Martha the heroine of Watergate.

Martha saved the column, to reread over and over again, each time shedding a few more tears. "She understands, she understands," Martha cried. She didn't even complain that Shana had mentioned "drink," which for Martha was an unmentionable word. "If you like to drink once in a while, well, so do I," Shana wrote. "Anyway, it's mostly the sober people who tell lies. Drinkers can hardly wait to tell you the truth, as every bartender knows."

In the same issue with Martha's "Love Song," there was a column about John Mitchell. It wasn't as complimentary. The title was "The Rise and Fall of Mr. Law and Order."

A story in the New York *Times* that Friday claimed that John Mitchell had told friends he knew about the proposals to bug the Democratic opposition "and that he had participated in three meetings at which these proposals were discussed. But he insists that he rejected the scheme on each occasion."

This reminded Martha that she'd listened over the intercom system when one of these meetings took place in Key Biscayne, Florida. She hadn't heard John approve the plan; neither had she heard him refuse. "There was no talk of 'yes' or 'no'," she said. "It was all 'what.' "

Martha learned from another *Times* story that John Mitchell had retained as counsel William G. Hundley, a Washington lawyer who was a "close personal friend and frequent golfing partner of Henry E. Petersen, Assistant Attorney General in charge of the Justice Department's Criminal Division and the man who heads the government's investigation and prosecution of the Watergate case."

Martha and I were discussing the book she wanted to write, one in which she planned to "expose Nixon and his dirty tricks," when the house phone rang. The doorman said two "detectives" were there and wanted to come up. I asked him to get their names. One of the men got on the telephone and said they were with the FBI. Martha, who had followed me to the phone in the service hall, heard me repeat "FBI" and went into a panic. I knew she was thinking about her call to the White House and her threats. So was I; the agent had asked if I were "Mrs. Saunders."

Finally one of the men told me they didn't want to see Mrs. Mitchell; they were there with a subpoena for Sandy Hobbs. At first they wouldn't believe she wasn't there; they *knew* she'd entered the building. I don't know if they ever believed me, but it became evident to them that we weren't going to let them into the apartment. They left after I promised that Sandy would call their office as soon as I could find her. The subpoena was from the U.S. District Court for the District of Columbia, requesting delivery, by Monday, of "any appointment book maintained by John N. Mitchell during the period June 1971 through November 1972." One of the signatures on the subpoena was that of Judge John J. Sirica.

Early that evening we went into the den to watch Walter Cronkite. When John Mitchell appeared on the screen, looking gaunt and shaken after two and a half hours before the grand jury, Martha dashed out of the room crying, "Oh, God! I can't stand it!"

SATURDAY, MARTHA WAS UP EARLY, OR PERHAPS SHE'D BEEN UP ALL NIGHT. Alleta said she was looking for an aspirin at five o'clock and ran into Martha. Soon after breakfast, Alleta left for Mississippi.

That day, John, who had returned from Washington, worked on legal papers, and Martha and I agreed that I shouldn't come over. But about five she called me in tears—tears of relief because "John Mitchell finally got through to one of those bastards!" He had talked at length to Bebe Rebozo, the first person close to Nixon he'd been able to reach since his disastrous visit to the White House exactly a week before.

John wanted to talk to me, Martha said, and asked if Bennie and I could come over. I told her we would stop by for about thirty minutes on our way to a dinner party. When we arrived Martha met us at the door and said John was waiting for me in the den. I walked down the long, green-carpeted hallway and found John Mitchell seated at his desk, in his black Cabinet chair, with a glass of Scotch in his hand. It was one of several he'd have before I would leave the room two hours later.

John Mitchell talked at length about wanting Martha to do a book and how he thought she really had a story to tell. He agreed that I should be the writer. But, he said, he wanted a friend of his, one of his clients, to handle all of the publishing arrangements. The friend, as I understood from what he said, also would have a say about the book's contents. And he, John Mitchell, would have final approval of the manuscript. Of course I knew—and I'm sure he was aware that I knew—he was letting me know there wouldn't be a book. There was no way Martha could tell the story she wanted to tell and have John Mitchell approve it.

Then, for no apparent reason, he told me he'd had a call that afternoon from Bebe Rebozo; he said he'd also talked to the President. There is no public record of a conversation between Richard Nixon and his former Attorney General on that date. Since John Mitchell brought up the subject of talking to the President, I asked him about his April 14 meeting at the White House, and he told me he *had* talked to the President.

We discussed the California incident. I asked if Martha really had been held down and sedated, and he said everything she'd told me was "essentially true." Why did Steve King and Lea Jablonsky—a young woman Martha considered her friend—let this happen? "These kids were scared to death . . . They thought they were protecting me," he answered.

After a pause he added, "Richard Nixon is lucky she [Martha] hasn't blown it all the way."

Unexpectedly, and to my amazement, he started talking about the Watergate break-in and its aftermath. This was on April 21, 1973, almost a month before the opening of the Senate Watergate Committee sessions; John Dean hadn't yet given his damaging evidence against the Watergate principals.

John Ehrlichman ran a whole espionage operation, John Mitchell told me. He chuckled and said Ehrlichman had even involved the then deputy director of the CIA in the illegal activities. That was General Robert E. Cushman, Jr., who by that time had left the CIA to become Commandant of the Marine Corps and a member of the Joint Chiefs of Staff; earlier he had served as Vice-President Nixon's military aide for four years. It came out in the Watergate hearings that Cushman had helped get false credentials for Howard Hunt and Gordon Liddy. "Cushman is really sweating," John Mitchell said that day in the apartment.

Mitchell talked for some time about the way Judge John Sirica had conducted the Watergate trials of the men who broke into the Democratic National Committee headquarters. It was obvious he was disgusted with Sirica. He said the Judge should be disbarred and indicated that once the Watergate mess was over, Sirica would be removed from the bench, though he didn't say how this would happen.

At one point in our conversation, I told John Mitchell that Martha thought their telephone was bugged and asked him if it might be. He answered, "It sure as hell better not be!"

He also talked angrily about Jeb Magruder, who secretly had gone before the prosecutors on April 14 and implicated John Dean and John Mitchell in the break-in and cover-up. "Jeb Magruder," John Mitchell declared, "should take a saliva test." Later that evening Martha told me the White House had someone who briefed them on everything that was said to the prosecutors or before the grand jury; she said John Mitchell always knew, within a few hours, about any testimony concerning him.

He discussed his part in the hush-money payoffs, although he didn't call it hush money. His story was that he had given permission for Fred LaRue to make a payment to the original Watergate defendants, but only because he thought it was for legal fees and because it was his understanding that was what had been done before.

His whole manner was that of someone telling a friend, in confidence, his thoughts and concerns about his innocent involvement in a serious situation. But John Mitchell and I were not friends. Obviously he wanted to use me as a conduit to get this information out, but I also had an uncanny feeling he was setting me up for something. I felt he was trying to use me to leak information, and then if I did he could offer it to Martha as proof that I couldn't be trusted with a confidence, that I wasn't her friend, which was what he'd been telling her for years. I did nothing.

(When John Dean's book *Blind Ambition* was published in 1976, I realized that Dean had had the same feeling of being "set up" when he met with John Mitchell, on April 10, only eleven days before my meeting.)

At this point in our conversation, John Mitchell said he'd like to say something about his friend John Dean, who had just had his secretary call the press to read a statement. "Some may hope or think that I will become the scapegoat in the Watergate case. Anyone who believes this does not know me, know the true facts nor understand our system of justice."

The statement he was going to make, John Mitchell said, was something I could write if I'd like to, provided I didn't attribute it to him. I told him I'd pass it on to a friend, which I did. The statement was never used; since it couldn't be attributed to Mitchell it had no news value. It was:

> John Dean is a most honest, dedicated and direct person, who had no personal involvement other than to protect people in the White House staff. And perhaps the greatest service he could provide the President is to come forward with all the indiscretions that he had become privy to during his stay in the White House. His integrity is unquestioned among all the people that know him and any revelations that Dean may make will be respected as credible by his many friends on Capitol Hill, [in the] Justice Department and in Washington. John Dean never initiated anything that was immoral or illegal. In a perhaps misguided concept in protecting the people around the President he has been caught up in questionable activities. Hopefully his statement of the past week is a clear indication that he is now going to help the President clear the White House staff of those that have besmirched the office of the Presidency to the end that President Nixon will have better and purer advisers in the future."

Although it wasn't publicly known, John Dean was talking to federal prosecutors at this time. John Mitchell knew. Perhaps he was trying to send a message to Dean to go easy on him.

Then John Mitchell talked about a "screwball" story, attributed to him, about support operations for Watergate. He wanted to make a statement, which again he didn't want attributed to him:

The press reports being leaked out of the [Watergate] grand jury inquiry stating that John Mitchell was the instigator of support for the defendants and counsel fees paid to their lawyers is absolutely contrary to the facts that have been testified to by the grand jury. Why the parties putting out the stories have been subverting the actual testimony must be a subject for further serious inquiry.

When I joined Martha and Bennie in the drawing room, Martha was beside herself with curiosity, but she knew that wasn't the time to ask why John had talked to me so long. Within a few minutes, Bennie and I left for our party.

LATER THAT NIGHT I WENT BACK TO THE MITCHELL APARTMENT. MARTHA had called around midnight and begged me to come over, saying she was alone and afraid. As it turned out, she wasn't alone. John Mitchell was there, she said: "He went to bed at nine o'clock with that goddamn radio in his ear."

I was amazed at Martha's appearance. Only a few hours earlier her clothes had been neat and tidy and her hair perfectly groomed. Now she was rumpled and disheveled; her hair was a stringy mess. Her face was bloated and flushed. Earlier Martha had been frightened and confused by the events surrounding her; now she was in a rage. As the evening went on she became loud, belligerent, vehement—her language was appalling.

Martha was "goddamn" mad at the Nixon Administration and what it was doing to her and John. She wasn't going to stand for it. She had kept quiet about dirty tricks so "King Richard" could be re-elected, and what thanks did the Mitchells get? The same kind of thanks she'd received for coming to Washington and working so hard for "Mr. President and his programs."

Now she was going to get 'em all, by telling everything. Some of what she threatened to tell had been reported by the press and denied by the White House; Martha furnished details. Others were new and startling. Though they seemed unbelievable at the time, most have since been proven true, by White House tapes or testimony.

Martha talked about the planning of Watergate, other campaign espionage, Internal Revenue harassment, wiretaps, Chile, the treatment of Nixon enemies, including the worst enemy of all, the press; favors bestowed on Nixon favorites—usually at taxpayers' expense; the way the Administration infiltrated the crowds, inciting the incidents of the 1971 May Day demonstrations that led to the mass arrests of thousands of people, including innocent bystanders; government "take over"—she insisted Nixon people were being put into key jobs throughout the government as a prelude to his taking control of the country.

She wasn't clear how this could be done, but she pointed out that just the month before *New York* magazine had written about a group calling itself Citizens for Nixon in '76, which had retained an advertising agency "to drum up grass-roots support for repeal of the Twenty-second Amendment so that Richard Nixon can run again for President four years from now."

(In February 1975, John Dean said that Nixon planned to keep power. He said the Nixon Foundation, set up in 1969 to build a presidential library, was "to be not merely a Nixon library but through the collection of contributions there was a plan afoot for Richard Nixon to perpetuate himself as a force in American politics." And the now defunct New York City newspaper, the *Trib,* reported in February 1978 that Jeb Magruder said Nixon "was so convinced that his kind of Administration was better for the country than anything the Democrats could offer" that he planned to establish "a perpetual presidency" by being able to pick GOP presidential candidates and destroy Democratic opponents. He would do this, Magruder reportedly said, by using the Federal Communications Commission, the Internal Revenue Service and such agencies to find "skeletons, however minor or ancient, in opposition political closets," and then leak the information to the press.)

Martha also said Nixon was set to revive the House Un-American Activities Committee, the one he'd used to destroy Alger Hiss.

It was incredible. I kept asking, "Martha, how do you *know* this?" She would say, "John told me," or that she'd heard John talking about it to someone else. She didn't mention looking in his briefcase after he'd gone to sleep at night or eavesdropping from the stair landing. I'd learn about that later from others.

She ripped into top White House aides who continued in their jobs while John was out, particularly Haldeman, Ehrlichman and Kissinger. There were others she named as having taken part in dirty tricks. And when she couldn't tie someone to a Watergate-type activity, she ranted away about his sex life. She named Administration men—at the White House and in the Cabinet—who "sleep with secretaries," others who were "queer," and some who were alcoholics. A wife or two came up in that category, too.

As astonished as I was at the information, I was shocked even more by the way Martha was presenting it. I had seen her upset and angry many times. But before she'd always appeared in control of her anger; now it seemed to control her. I just couldn't believe the Martha Mitchell I knew could be this ranting, raving woman.

But then I'd never seen Martha drunk on liquor while revved up on pills. At the time I didn't know about the drugs, but I suspected it was more than Scotch causing the shocking change in her personality.

From the time I met Martha, in early 1970, people continually asked me about her drinking. I always said she didn't drink as much as most people on the Washington political and social scene, which I believed.

Usually when we went out to lunch she ordered a champagne cocktail; if we ate lunch at her apartment or mine she had nothing stronger than a Coke. Before dinner Martha had a Scotch or two. I never saw her take an after-dinner drink. So one time when a press friend told me a seemingly wild story about Martha's actions after drinking martinis, I assured her the tale was untrue. Martha didn't drink gin, I stated positively.

But she did—often slipping off to drink it from a bottle kept on a closet shelf, while the person she was having predinner cocktails with in another room thought Martha was conservatively sipping Scotch.

MARTHA'S TIRADE, THAT NIGHT IN NEW YORK, CONTINUED UNTIL ALMOST five A.M., when all of a sudden she started speaking more slowly and her words became slurred. It was as if a battery were running down. She tried to get up to pour herself another drink but stumbled and fell back into the chair. When that happened, she looked surprised and immediately announced she was going to bed. She suggested that I do the same, in the guest room, because I shouldn't "be out on the New York streets at that hour."

Standing in the guest room doorway, I watched Martha weave down the hallway, bumping into one side of the wall and then the other. Within minutes, she was back, bringing me a nightgown, peignoir and matching slippers. She mumbled goodnight and went swaying down the hall again.

This is unbelievable, I remember thinking. Here she is so drunk she can't walk straight. She's had over a quart of Scotch that I know about, and no telling how much more. Yet she can remember to be a good hostess, to show concern for her guest's needs.

At nine o'clock I woke up with a jolt. John Mitchell—in pajamas and robe—was standing at the doorway, saying I had a telephone call. I dashed to the nearest phone, which was in the kitchen where John Mitchell was cooking his breakfast. The call was from Bennie; I assured him I was O.K. and would leave the apartment soon. Then, while John Mitchell ate breakfast I drank a pot of tea. The two of us sat at the ice-cream parlor table, in the kitchen, and talked for almost an hour. First he wanted to know what time I had come back to the apartment. And he laughed at his surprise "when the phone rang and a man asked if his wife were here."

We also talked about Martha's upcoming testimony in connection with the multimillion-dollar series of civil lawsuits brought by the Democratic National Committee against CREEP and its various officials. She shouldn't go through such an interrogation alone, I said. If he didn't know anyone who could go, I would come back to New York on May 3 to go with her. He said he'd let me know if it was necessary.

Martha had said Julia wasn't coming back for four or five days. I asked John Mitchell who was going to stay with Martha while he was testifying in New York on Tuesday and in Pensacola, Florida, the following day.

Martha was near the breaking point; I didn't think she should be alone. Although Bennie and I had planned to go home that day, I said we could remain in New York and I would stay with Martha during the day. I left the Mitchells, not expecting to come back that day, since John would be there. But she called that afternoon, saying she was "so sick" and would I please come over.

When I got there, Martha was feverish and in severe pain, her abdomen was markedly distended, and she'd been vomiting. I went into the den, where John Mitchell was sitting at his desk, and told him she needed a doctor. He made some excuse about not knowing any New York doctors.

"This is ridiculous," I said, "Martha's sick. She needs help. Someone has to call a doctor." John Mitchell sat silently for some time before he looked up and said, "She wouldn't have a doctor I called; she doesn't trust me anymore."

Of course it was true. But still, Martha couldn't be left writhing in pain, risking a perforated colon—which sometimes happens in severe attacks of diverticulitis—just because the two of them were in this impossible situation. I went back into the bedroom and begged Martha to tell me the name of someone she trusted who could recommend a doctor. How about the woman she'd told me to call if I didn't hear from her? Yes, she'd trust her, Martha said.

The doctor arrived in a surprisingly short time. He prescribed bed rest, wrote prescriptions, and gave Martha a shot for her pain.

That evening I stayed to sit with Martha while John Mitchell, for three and a half hours, met in the drawing room with three lawyers. He'd told Martha they were Maurice Stans's lawyers and that Stans was in "real trouble because two to three million dollars is missing from CREEP." It's doubtful the conversation that night was about CREEP missing funds, since this was only two days before John Mitchell testified before the Vesco grand jury, which later indicted him and Stans.

Martha was still in pain the next morning, but not enough to kill her sense of humor. At one point she was sitting up in bed, with a hot water bottle on her stomach, when she said, "Those jerks at the White House just hate my guts. And I wish they had my guts right now."

A story Martha loved to tell friends and reporters, after John left, was about the time John "cussed out the President." Martha didn't remember the exact night it happened, except that it was "after the White House cut him off, before he was indicted (on May 11), and [two friends] were here." It probably happened the evening following John Mitchell's testimony before the Vesco grand jury.

That night, Martha and the two friends were talking when John Mitchell came out of his den and dramatically announced, "Well, I just cussed out the President of the United States!" After that night, Martha said, both Bebe Rebozo and Robert Abplanalp were constantly in touch with John Mitchell. Martha called their persistent attention "stroking to keep him in line."

(Their later attempts to keep Martha in line weren't as successful. Martha said that Robert Abplanalp wanted to fly her and John in his plane to his private island in the Bahamas. She refused to go.)

Martha was feeling miserable the next morning. Again she was in severe pain and had been vomiting. She blamed it on "something I ate." Sometime that morning the telephone rang, and before I could answer it, Martha—who couldn't raise her head from the pillow without becoming nauseated—muttered, "Don't tell anyone I'm sick."

The caller was Helen Thomas. Martha rocked her head back and forth on the pillow, signaling that she couldn't talk. Helen and I chatted for several minutes, and when we hung up I was amazed to see that Martha was crying. "I can't have this, Winnie," she said. "I'm too sick to have the press calling me." She insisted I should have hung up when I heard who it was.

Her attitude was absurd, I said. Helen and I had been friends for years, and there wasn't any reason why we shouldn't talk. And besides, during my conversation with Helen I got the impression that Martha had asked her to call. If she hadn't, how did Helen know the new unlisted number? Martha denied she'd called Helen. As for the way Helen got the number, "People at the telephone company give it to the press."

Our argument ended when Martha got sick at her stomach.

The telephone soon rang again. It was a newspaper man, saying he was a friend of Helen Thomas's and that he was calling to check on Mrs. Mitchell. Martha became hysterical; she insisted that I call the telephone company to change the number. Within five minutes the Mitchells had a new telephone number, again unlisted.

Sandy Hobbs came by soon afterward. I gave her the new number and told her why it had been changed. She said it wouldn't keep the press from calling because "we suspect she [Martha] gives it out."

Later I phoned a newspaper friend and asked her to read the wire copy of Helen's story. In it she said, "Mrs. Mitchell attempted to reach a UPI reporter by telephone [last night] but failed . . ."

I knew Helen wouldn't say Martha had tried to reach her if she hadn't. But I also felt that Martha was telling the truth, as she knew it, when she told me she hadn't called. It was the first inkling I had that Martha sometimes suffered mental blackouts when drinking.

Chapter Seventeen

MARTHA WAS UP AND AROUND WHEN I LEFT TWO DAYS LATER, apparently completely recovered from her diverticulitis attack. In her calls that weekend she was ecstatic over Watergate developments. Jeb Magruder had resigned his job at the Department of Commerce, Patrick Gray announced he was leaving as acting director of the FBI, after Senator Weicker revealed Gray had burned politically sensitive files taken from Howard Hunt's White House safe, and the New York *Times* said John Dean had linked Richard Nixon to Watergate.

Then, on April 30 the White House announced the resignations of Bob Haldeman, John Ehrlichman, John Dean and Richard Kleindienst; Elliot Richardson was named to replace Kleindienst as Attorney General. Martha was gratified by the resignations, although she didn't think the housecleaning went high enough.

But the news that day that John Connally had left the Democratic party to become a Republican was "one of the funniest things I've ever heard; he's being used and doesn't know it."

Martha talked a lot about her upcoming pretrial testimony in the Democratic suit. And although she was getting more nervous by the minute, she could joke about it. When I told her I was a basket case, from working long hours to meet a deadline for a magazine article, Martha asked if I could find a second basket.

The morning Martha was going to testify a visibly irritated John Mitchell came out of their apartment building and snapped at a waiting throng of reporters, "Your *star* will be down in a few minutes."

Clutching a worn Bible she said was given to her when she graduated from kindergarten Sunday School, Martha left the apartment building accompanied by the bodyguard/chauffeur Zolton and attorney Plato Cacheris. As she pushed her way through a shoving crowd of reporters Martha at first refused to answer questions, saying, "I'm not going to stand here and give an interview on the sidewalk. When I want to give an interview, I telephone my friends."

The deposition took place in the West End Avenue law offices of attorney Henry Rothblatt, who was representing James McCord in a $15-million damage suit against CREEP. A bevy of lawyers representing the Democratic National Committee, CREEP, and various named defendants was there to question Martha. But before they began, the attorneys agreed that contents of the deposition would not be released until Martha had had "an opportunity to examine the transcript, reading it over carefully, to make sure that everything in the transcript" was correct and "to make whatever corrections the witness chooses to make." It further was stipulated that Martha would have twenty-four hours to read, make corrections and sign the transcript.

Later reporters would cite the "rambling, two-hour statement" she made that day as *proof* that Martha knew nothing about Watergate or Nixon Administration misdeeds. The media didn't take into account the fact that Martha was not permitted to answer questions about anything she would have learned in her husband-wife relationship.

And a close look at the transcript shows that Martha was skillful in her replies to questions she didn't want to answer precisely. The following exchange took place when one of the attorneys asked Martha if she had handled any CREEP money:

Q. Mrs. Mitchell, were you ever used as a courier to bring cash money from one of your trips back to the Committee Headquarters, the Finance Committee?

A. I think I'd be tempted to keep it, if I had it.

Q. The answer then is no, you never carried any funds?

A. As I've said before, gentlemen, they haven't paid me, and they can't ever pay me enough, for the work that I did for them.

Q. I'm not talking about payment. I'm asking if you ever were given some money in some city and asked to take this money back to the Finance Committee as you were going back to Washington.

A. Don't you know that I would never take money from anybody, under any circumstances, and carry it any place? I don't care who it is.

Q. I'm not insinuating anything. I'm just asking a question.

A. Well, I'm telling you that I would never, under any circumstances. If I did, I would go straight to the police, or straight to somebody, and yell very loud.

Q. Your answer then would be no to the question? You never carried any—

A. [*by Martha's attorney*]: The answer is no.

But the answer, according to Martha, was not "no." She couldn't have said that without committing perjury. Money—$10,000 in cash—had been delivered to Martha. She said she turned it over to John, who passed it on to the Finance Committee. And had the attorneys been able to ask her if she'd witnessed money being delivered to her husband, she would have had to answer "yes." Martha told a doctor, during her final illness, that "suitcases full of money" were delivered to the Mitchells' Watergate apartment. And during a visit to Key Biscayne, Martha told me, she saw Bebe Rebozo give John a large sum of money and she'd heard him say, "There's a lot more where this came from."

During her two-hour testimony, Martha hedged on another question or two, but for the most part she was frank and forthright in her replies. She even answered questions about John Mitchell until attorney Chacheris stopped that line of questioning.

Martha complained several times that the White House had leaked false stories that she was in an insane asylum. When asked who put out the stories, Martha identified White House social secretary Lucy Winchester and First Lady Pat Nixon as sources of the stories. She also said that leaks came from columnist Betty Beale, "who was prompted by the White House," and author Victor Lasky, who also got his information from the Executive Mansion. She said later that she learned this from a CREEP secretary.

She furnished details of the California incident, and for the first time she revealed why she had made her famous call from the Newporter Inn: "I decided that the best way to get my husband out of Washington after having talked to him was to make a public announcement."

Commenting on some of the people with whom she came in contact at CREEP, Martha said Robert Mardian was "pretty harmless." And Steve King, "even though I didn't like him personally, he seemed to be greatly admired. I guess, after all the hooligans that McCord had produced, King seemed like an angel." And Jeb Magruder was someone she had wanted "fired from the very beginning . . . I just didn't trust him." She admitted there was no basis for her distrust, "but I'm a pretty good judge of human nature."

Since Martha couldn't mention anything involving John, she really hadn't contributed much that was helpful to the case. But as attorneys said later, it was "amusing," "interesting," and "gave useful background."

An exuberant, chatty Martha left Henry's office to face a mob of two hundred reporters and spectators. She told the media if John knew about the Watergate bugging, "I didn't know it." She added, "He has always assured me that he has not been involved," and "I trust and pray to God [that he is not]."

Martha came home from her deposition feeling that she had "glided through the whole thing." There were messages at the apartment from several reporters asking her to call. The Washington *Post* and *Newsday* had sent their requests tucked into bouquets of flowers. Martha told me she was going to return some of the calls, but first, would I be home all evening? She wanted to call when the transcript arrived, so we could go over it line by line.

She called back several times to say the transcript hadn't arrived, although they'd promised it within an hour after she left the attorney's office. Getting more nervous by the minute, and bemoaning the fact that she had no one there to share her troubles, she sat alone and drank.

Martha momentarily forgot her problems when she heard the *CBS Evening News.* Commentator Eric Sevareid said that men of the Nixon Administration had been able "to blanket the airways with propaganda, to fix polls . . . and to win a landslide election. But they have forgotten . . . [that] just one person in possession of the truth and willing to talk can bring the whole show to a dead end. Men who could blow whole countries off the face of the earth at their own discretion were powerless if Martha Mitchell reached for the phone."

Reports on Martha's deposition, with verbatim quotes from her testimony, were coming in over the radio. Yet Martha hadn't received her copy. The agreement to let her read and correct it had been "a goddamn lie," she cried. Here was Martha "taken again." It was after midnight before Martha got a copy of the deposition.

Martha's deposition was taken on Thursday. My notes for Friday show that she telephoned so many times I lost count. With each call she was more pugnacious and strident—even more so than the night in April when I'd sat up all night with her at their apartment.

At two forty-five A.M. Saturday she again called. John had gone to bed at nine o'clock, saying he didn't know if he'd get up all day Saturday. Marty, who was asleep, had a head cold and an earache. Julia was in Washington "getting her teeth fixed." She complained that there wasn't anyone there to talk to.

At six-fifteen A.M. Martha was back on the phone. She wanted to implicate the President in Watergate and asked me to help her get the word out. Did she really know anything to prove the President's guilt? Yes. Could she furnish real evidence? She said she had it. Although I felt the evidence should be made public, as a friend I had to advise her not to do anything without talking it over with her husband. If she still loved him, as she said, and wanted the marriage to last, she shouldn't go off on her own on Watergate. We got into an argument which ended when she told me I was "nasty" and hung up.

THAT NIGHT MARTHA MADE A CALL FOR WHICH JOHN MITCHELL NEVER forgave her. She telephoned Helen Thomas to say, "Mr. President should resign immediately. I think he let the country down. It's going to take a hell of a lot to get him out . . . he's been compromised." She added that she thought he should step down "in order to give credibility to the Republican party and credibility to the United States.

"If my husband knew anything about the Watergate break-in, Mr. Nixon also knew about it," she said. Speaking of her husband, she said, "I don't think he is going to get out of it."

John Mitchell's reply to her suggestion that the President resign was in the form of a statement issued through CREEP:

> Martha's late-night telephone calls have been good fun and games in the past. However, this is a serious issue. I'm surprised and disappointed that United Press International would take advantage of a personal phone call made under the stress of the current situation and treat it as a sensational public statement.
>
> I think that under all the circumstances, Martha is entitled to more consideration and courtesy than that. Particularly from a reporter whom she had considered a personal friend. Any thought of the President resigning is ridiculous.

It was seven days before the public heard from Martha again.

When Martha didn't call me for two days, I checked at the apartment. John Mitchell answered and said she was visiting friends. "You should have taken my advice and had a woman friend stay with her," I told him. He said, "I know it now."

The woman I was to check with when I couldn't reach Martha also assured me that Martha was visiting in the country; Sandy Hobbs told the same story. But in the meantime there were rumors that Martha was in a medical institution. I thought my information was correct and passed it on. When John Mitchell was indicted in the Vesco case, however, on charges of perjury and obstruction of justice, and Martha didn't call, I suspected there was more to her absence from 1030 Fifth Avenue than a visit with friends. Also, Martha knew I was leaving that weekend for Warner Brother's fiftieth anniversary party at the Cannes Film Festival. She certainly wouldn't let me go without first getting a telephone number where she could call.

After I'd made a few more inquiries, I received a message from Martha. She was in Craig House, at Beacon Hill, New York, where she'd gone secretly to dry out in 1968 and again in July 1969, when her drinking was beyond her control. She'd been told about John's indictment and apparently was bearing up well. I had two more reports on her gradually improving condition before I left for France.

The issue of *Time* magazine on the stands Monday, May 14, reported that "only three days after Martha Mitchell delivered those brave, perhaps defiant words during a Watergate deposition hearing, her tongue was stilled. Unable to sleep, distraught and unhappy, she put herself under doctors' care and voluntarily entered a medical institution last week for treatment of a nervous breakdown."

The same day, both the New York *Daily News* and the New York *Times* carried stories with Martha's denial. A *News* reporter, staked outside the Mitchell apartment, found Martha "alive and well" when she arrived home around four-thirty P.M. the afternoon before, wearing a bright-orange pants suit, a loose white blouse and an orange coat, and carrying a bouquet of roses. "Do I look like I'm suffering from a breakdown?" Martha asked the reporter and a photographer.

The *Times* story was the result of a telephone call from Martha, made to the paper at John Mitchell's request and in answer to a letter to John from one of its editors, hand-delivered Sunday, May 13, to the Mitchell apartment, saying, "*Time* magazine, in an article coming out Monday, says Mrs. Mitchell has had a nervous breakdown and voluntarily has gone to a hospital. Is this true?"

A *Time* correspondent says the magazine learned about Martha's hospitalization from "a friend of John's." After Martha's denial, the magazine checked its source and was told the information was correct. He added, "John is not a bit unhappy about the way it came out."

"So you see," the correspondent explains, "John was doubly using us. He used us to show she [was at Craig House] and at the same time undermined our accuracy by making it look like the story was untrue. We were used twice."

When Martha came home from Craig House, or, as she put it, "after I'd been up to what's-a-ma-gig," she went into the den, sat down at the desk opposite John Mitchell and told him she was "sorry." She didn't ask any questions. If he was in trouble, she said, then she was in trouble too—because they were a team. Whatever he wanted her to do, Martha promised, she would do. She'd help him anyway she could. John Mitchell scoffed at her promises; he refused her apology. Martha said, "He cut me off, completely."

LIFE BECAME MORE AND MORE UNBEARABLE FOR MARTHA. JOHN WOULDN'T talk to her. She couldn't go out; the press was keeping a twenty-four-hour vigil outside the door. And lawyers kept running in and out of the apartment at all hours; she couldn't leave her own bedroom without being completely dressed.

Mudge Rose Guthrie and Alexander had taken John Mitchell's name off the door the day after he was indicted. "They couldn't wait to get rid of him," Martha said, although she was shocked when it happened.

Without a conviction, the firm had announced that John Mitchell was taking a leave of absence "in order to devote his time and attention to his personal affairs," and that "at his request his name has been withdrawn from the firm name." Everyone knew he wouldn't be back. Later it was reported the firm paid him $500,000 to leave.

Now his office was the den—the room where he and Martha had had drinks together and had eaten dinner from trays while watching the evening news; the room with ceiling-to-floor bookshelves filled with His and Her trophies and awards. Martha considered it "our" room; now it was "his."

Martha pleaded with the lawyers to tell her what was going on, but they wouldn't tell her any more than John would. Martha couldn't stand being shut out. Alone and rejected, she again turned to the bottle and pills. And as usual, the combination brought on violent temper outbursts, sometimes aimed at the lawyers. "When that happened," one of them recalls, "I always led the retreat."

Martha had been home from Craig House less than a week when, while eavesdropping on a telephone conversation, she heard John's friend at *Newsweek* telling him about a story in the magazine's upcoming issue. He said it would report that John Ehrlichman was heading a group planning to place the blame for the Watergate break-in and cover-up on John Mitchell and John Dean. The group started seeking the two as scapegoats after James McCord refused to continue with the cover-up. (James McCord told the Ervin Committee that he had been asked to keep silent about the break-in. He said he'd been promised executive clemency, financial support for his family and a job after prison in return for his silence.)

Newsweek also would report, according to Mitchell's source, that the plot was "to make sure he [Mitchell] was indicted" before he testified before the Ervin Committee.

Martha didn't wait for the end of the conversation before going downstairs to tell waiting newsmen and camera crews her husband was protecting the President. Martha apologized to the press, saying, "I've been mean to you all." She said she had to, "to get publicity in order to clear two guiltless people, my husband and myself—and you can place all the blame right on the White House.

"Where do you think all this originated?" she asked. "Do you think my husband's that stupid? And whom do you think he's been protecting? Whom? . . . Mr. President he has been protecting under no uncertain circumstances!"

She quoted John Mitchell as having told her, "If anything happened to Mr. President, the whole country would fall apart." Martha added, "And if you remember a few weeks ago I suggested that Mr. President resign. Well, it's a darn better idea that he resign than be impeached!"

The interview was aired on NBC–TV's *Nightly News* the same evening.

Martha said that when John heard the news, "He cussed me out about it. He said, 'You are hurting our situation.' "

John Mitchell got on the phone when I called Martha from the airport between planes on my way home from Cannes. Now that the den was his office, and since he never left the apartment unless he was testifying or such, it was impossible to talk to Martha without having him on the line. When she called, if he were awake, he picked up the telephone the minute he saw the light go on. Then, if Martha started saying something he didn't want discussed, he would punch the push buttons up and down, making such shrill beeping noises it was impossible to talk.

Another reporter, Wauhillau LaHay, says he did the same thing when Martha called her from their Watergate apartment a few weeks after the Watergate break-in: "I knew it was John Mitchell on the line, making the clicking noises, so I said, 'Listen, John, you are driving me up the wall with the damn clicking. Now you quit it,' and there wasn't any more clicking. He didn't say anything. But it was sort of funny."

It particularly outraged Martha that when John listened in on her conversations he either joined in or clicked the telephone. When *she* listened in on *his* talks she kept quiet and didn't disturb anyone.

Another thing that irritated her almost beyond endurance was that John criticized her for making calls to the press when he did the same thing. Martha claimed that John continually called reporters—most often at the New York *Times* and at *Newsweek*—to leak information.

ON MONDAY, MAY 21, JOHN MITCHELL ENTERED A PLEA OF NOT GUILTY TO charges of conspiracy, obstruction of justice and perjury in the Vesco case. According to press reports, he left the federal courtroom looking "pale and shaken." When asked how he felt, he replied, "I've been better." As he walked to his car he seemed shocked when someone in the waiting crowd yelled, "Hey, Mitchell, I hope they throw the key away!"

He still was shaking when he arrived at the apartment, where he tried to joke about his situation. But as usual when he was under stress, his "jokes" came out as sarcastic wisecracks, such as his telling Martha he hoped she had plenty of clothes so she could wear a different dress each day of the trial.

Martha cried, "I can't go through a trial," meaning she didn't feel she could stand the strain of seeing her husband in court, being tried as a criminal. But this and similar remarks were misinterpreted by some of John's friends, who leaked them to the press. One columnist wrote that one intimate predicted, "If John goes to prison, Martha will pack her bags and clear out."

At this point, Martha had no intention of clearing out. She still had the unrealistic idea that all of their troubles somehow would go away if John just would stop protecting Richard Nixon. But John was adamant about keeping the President's name out of Watergate. He wouldn't turn state's witness or plea bargain, as Martha begged him to do. "He thinks his only hope is clemency from Richard Nixon," she cried in frustration. "But he'll go to jail and that son-of-a-bitch, who planned the whole goddamn thing, will get off scot-free."

(Evidently John Mitchell had been offered clemency. According to the final report of the Judiciary Committee on the Impeachment of Richard Nixon: "On April 14, 1973, the President directed Haldeman and Ehrlichman to imply to Magruder, and also to Mitchell, who had been implicated by Magruder, the President's assurances of clemency . . . [Later Ehrlichman] reported to the President that he had spoken to Mitchell and that Mitchell 'appreciated the message of good feeling between you and him.' The President responded, 'He got that, huh?' The President added that there could be clemency at the proper time; but that they all knew that, for the moment, it was ridiculous to talk about it.")

Martha and John now were communicating only when one of them hurled insults or accusations at the other. Every time Martha publicly said anything against Richard Nixon, John Mitchell accused her of destroying him, her husband. She took this as proof that he'd been promised clemency if he would "stonewall it," as the President had told him to do during a White House meeting.

But as angry as she was with John, Martha in her own way still was trying to save him. She called Republican members of Congress, other important members of the party, and big contributors to Nixon's re-election, pleading with them to help John, and threatening them if they didn't promise that they would.

She was silenced only when stricken with another severe attack of diverticulitis. As soon as she could travel, Martha packed up and went to visit her Craig House psychiatrist, Wally Vogt, and his wife, at their house in Connecticut. She was afraid to go to Craig House for fear an employee would leak the news to the press.

The fact that Martha was breaking under the strain was evident June 19, a few days after she came home, when she had a running battle with the press stationed outside the building. The fight lasted six hours, and at one point Martha threw a doorman's cap at a woman reporter, hitting her in the face. Martha then struck the reporter two times on top of the head with her open hand.

The confrontation started around six P.M. when Judy Yablonky of Associated Press sent a note to the Mitchells' apartment, asking John Mitchell for "just a glimpse of you to let people know you are well and not a changed and broken man as per recent accounts." Judy also asked him when he planned to make a statement about the Watergate affair.

"Shortly before seven P.M.," according to the New York *Daily News*, "Mrs. Mitchell came out of the building. She was wearing her hair in its usual pompadour, but strands were falling in front of her face.

"Swaying and prancing up and down in anger, Mrs. Mitchell told the AP reporter: 'You have no right to be here, infringing on my privacy.' She appealed to a man passing by: 'Let me ask you, a private citizen, how do you get rid of people like this?' "

The *News* also reported: "A woman leaving the building to walk her two dogs stopped to sympathize with Mrs. Mitchell, then led her back inside."

The second encounter lasted almost an hour and started at around ten o'clock when Martha came down and again asked Judy Yablonky to leave. When she didn't Martha threw the doorman's hat at her. And according to the AP reporter, Martha "yelled an obscenity" and struck her on the head.

"I have never done anything wrong in my life, ever," Martha told the newswoman. "I wasn't even sent to the principal's office when I was in school."

She turned her attention to a male reporter standing across the street and called out, "You are part of the Communists—every one of you. If you dare come on this side of the street, I'll call Governor Rockefeller." She encouraged several passersby to "go beat them up. Go over there and beat those people up."

The tirade continued until Marty arrived home at ten-fifty P.M., in a chauffeur-driven station wagon. Taking Martha by the hand Marty pulled her back into the building.

THE NEXT MORNING, A GRIM-FACED MARTHA, FOLLOWED BY MARTY, THE chauffeur Zolton and Sandy Hobbs, left 1030 Fifth Avenue for Alleta and Charlie Saunders's house in Greenwood, Mississippi. Zolton drove the station wagon as far as Hershey, Pennsylvania, and Martha, Sandy and Marty drove on alone.

Martha was a perfect guest when she first arrived at the Saunders' antebellum-type mansion. Her hostess, who had gotten to know Martha quite well over the years, was impressed when Martha went eight days without "touching a drop, not even a glass of wine."

One of the things Alleta had learned about Martha was that she had a "marvelous" sense of humor and that she had the ability to laugh at herself: "I don't know how much she remembered of what she did [while drinking], and she may not have remembered. But she thoroughly enjoyed hearing exactly what she had done. She would say, 'I didn't!' And I'd say, 'You did!'

"And she didn't want you to treat [her life] as a tragedy. She wanted it to be a tragedy only when she wanted it to be." Even the California incident sometimes was comedy: "She could see the humor in it. One night she acted it out for me cold sober—taking all parts. It took her two and a half hours and it was one of the funniest things I've ever seen.

"She was a frustrated actress and she should have been one. If you see the old movie with Bette Davis, *All About Eve,* you see Martha Mitchell."

Martha talked seriously with Alleta, too, about her concern for the United States and about Watergate: "She felt she could save the country, singlehanded. I mean, she really thought it." Alleta and Ray West told Martha they thought the United States would exist with or without her, that she didn't have to try so hard. But Martha was thoroughly convinced that she could do more good for the United States, "and she was hellbent to do it."

It was an open secret in Greenwood that Charlie and Alleta's house guest was Martha Mitchell, but all the townspeople professed innocence about her presence when questioned by outsiders—mainly the Eastern establishment press. Even the local paper editorially ignored Martha's being there, which must have taken considerable restraint since papers all over the country were asking, "Where's Martha?" and speculating whether or not she would sit behind John Mitchell, as Maureen Dean sat behind John Dean, during his upcoming testimony before the Senate Watergate Committee.

As for Martha, she was happier than she'd been in months. She luxuriated in the lazy hours beside the pool, the unexpected—almost forgotten—safe feeling she had in the cozy and friendly atmosphere of her hosts' Southern hospitality, and in the "girl talks" with Alleta.

The idyllic situation ended on July 10, the day John Mitchell started his three-day testimony before the Senate Committee. Martha sat on the couch in front of the television set in Greenwood, and the more she listened to John Mitchell—outside the hearing room talking to reporters and inside at the witness table—the more distressed she became. She started drinking Bloody Marys; as far as is known, she didn't draw a sober breath during the rest of her Mississippi visit.

Among other things, John Mitchell testified that he hadn't talked to Richard Nixon about the Watergate incident, claiming he had kept secret the information about the break-in and cover-up because he "didn't want to scare Nixon." He added that he didn't think it was fair to Nixon to have these "White House horror stories come out during this political campaign."

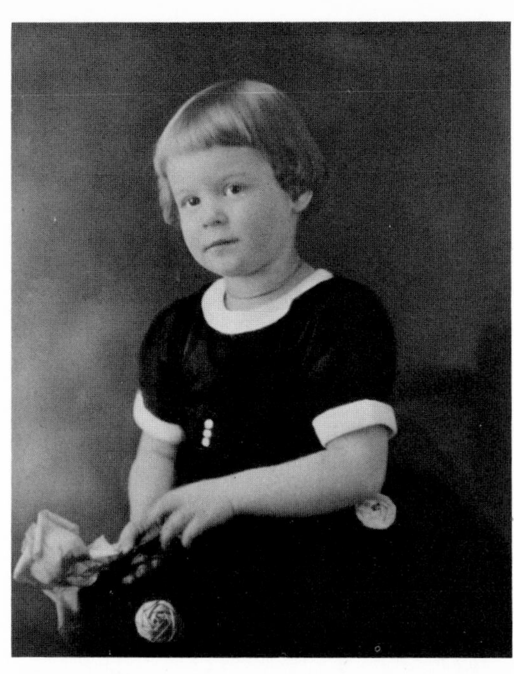

Martha Elizabeth Beall was less than five years old when her mother took her all the way from Pine Bluff, Arkansas, to Dallas, Texas, to have her picture taken at Neiman-Marcus. *Reprinted with permission from Saturday Evening Post Co. © 1971/ Courtesy of Muffett Studios*

Uncharacteristically for a woman of her day, Martha's mother Arie Ferguson Beall (left) was a "doer." She was active in several organizations and was a teacher of speech and drama for many years. Here, Miss Arie is seated with Lorine Hightower Toney, her roommate at Virginia College for Young Ladies. *Henry Marx/Pine Bluff*

The Pine Bluff, Arkansas, house where Martha was born is now a museum, containing some of the furnishings that were used there when Martha was a child.
Henry Marx/Pine Bluff

Former classmates of Martha's say that at eleven years old she already was becoming willful and headstrong, though she remained "sweet and affectionate."
Courtesy of Mrs. Sam Bridges

MARTHA E. BEALL

Glee Club '34, '35, '36, Band Maid '36,
Student Council '36, '37.

"I love its gentle warble,
I love its gentle flow,
I love to wind my tongue up,
And I love to let it go."

Editors of the 1937 Pine Bluff High School yearbook, the *Zebra*, recognized even then that Martha was a compulsive talker. *Henry Marx/Pine Bluff*

Martha met her first husband, Clyde Jennings, Jr., while working for the Army, in Washington, D.C., during World War II. *Bryn-Alan Studios/Jacksonville, Florida*

The night after Martha lost her vigorous campaign for a woman on the Supreme Court, she attended a National Federation of Republican Women banquet, where she was mobbed by hundreds of women eager to shake her hand and to get her autograph. *Washington Star/ Walter Oates*

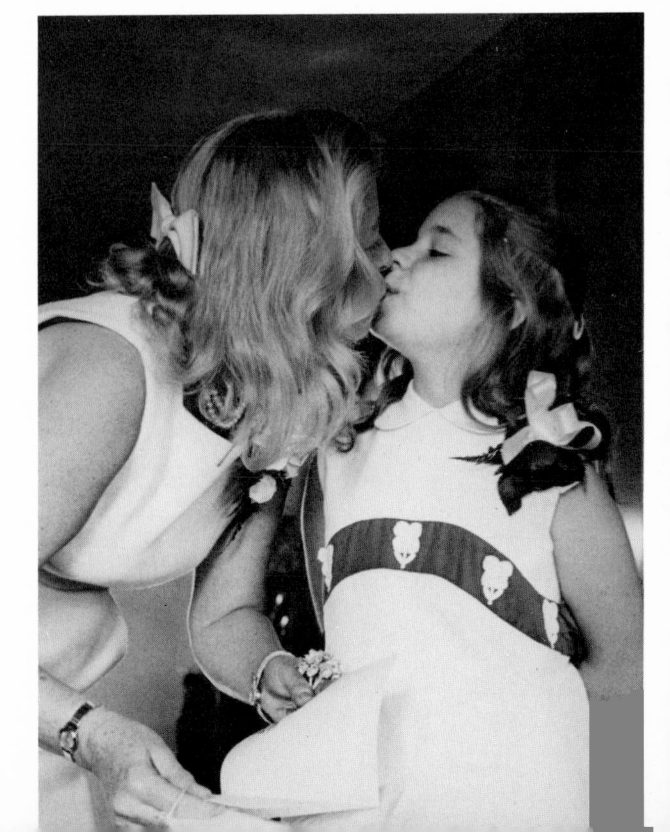

In May of 1970 there was no hint of their later estrangement when Martha affectionately thanked her daughter Martha Elizabeth (Marty) Mitchell, Jr., for her Mother's Day present. *Fred Ward/Black Star*

Martha was falsely accused of arranging to have this picture taken of her buying orange juice from Ann Haldeman, daughter of Nixon aide H. R. (Bob) Haldeman. *Washington Star/ John Bowden*

Martha, with her husband Attorney General John N. Mitchell, arrived at the White House for Tricia Nixon's wedding in the costume she'd later dub "my Queen's dress," after she wore it to meet the Queen of England at a Buckingham Palace garden party in 1971. *Matthew Lewis/Washington Post*

Although Pat Nixon, the perfect political wife, and the volatile Martha never managed to get along, they put on a show of çordiality at a Blair House luncheon in 1972. *World Wide Photos*

The British press was intrigued with Martha when she entertained its members at tea in her London Hilton Hotel suite. One reporter wrote that life in London would be "a lot less dull if we had Martha on the Westminster scene." *World Wide Photos*

Chief Justice Warren Burger was not Martha's favorite dinner partner; he wouldn't let her smoke at the table. *Fred Ward/Black Star*

Among Martha's admirers was a surprising number of young people, and she often accepted invitations to meet with them. Here she is talking to students attending a Frankie Welch (upper right) fashion seminar at the Sheraton Carlton Hotel. *Capitol Glogau/Courtesy of the Sheraton Carlton Hotel*

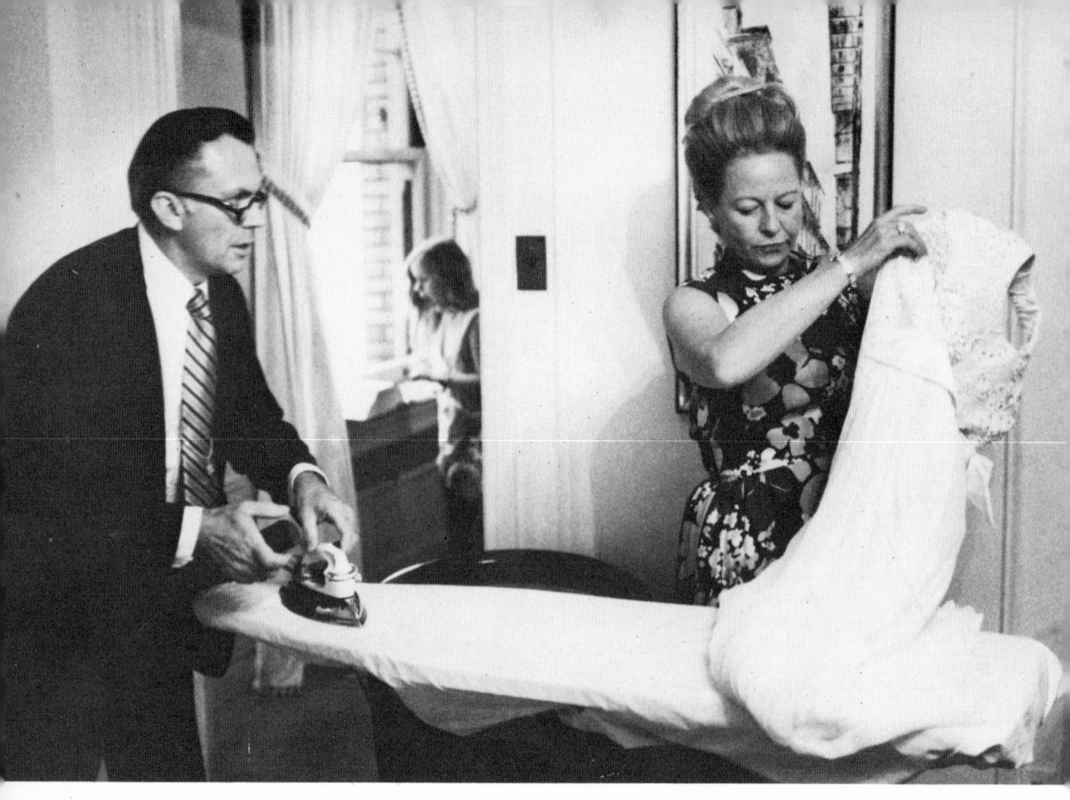

There was a public cry of outrage after *Life* magazine published this picture of an FBI agent helping Martha iron a dress. Marty is shown in the center background. *Harry Benson*

Martha met her son Clyde Jay Jennings (right) in San Francisco when he returned from Vietnam, where Martha always insisted he'd been sent only because he was her son. *Wide World Photos*

It was too much for Martha. She jumped off the couch and yelled (by some accounts she "hollered") at John Mitchell, "You're a goddamn liar! You're a goddamn liar! Tell the truth!"

When he talked to the press before his second day of testifying, John Mitchell said he had spoken "several times" to Martha the night before about his testimony. "She didn't think it good enough to have a repeat performance today." He added, "Martha said maybe I ought to stay home today. I told her I didn't have that simple a choice." Did Martha think the committee's questions were tough? "No," he replied, "she didn't think so. She had answers to all of them."

For days Martha swore at John's image on television. She even called former Senate Watergate Committee Minority Counsel Fred D. Thompson to tell him to advise Senator Howard Baker "to get John so mad tomorrow that he will blurt it all out, just blurt the truth out."

When John Mitchell left the witness table, Martha shouted at White House aides who followed him.

She telephoned John's lawyer, Bill Hundley, to "cuss him out," claiming he'd tricked her into going to Mississippi, when she wanted to be there when John testified.

She fought with Marty, as she usually did when drinking.

And she threatened suicide.

Sometimes when Martha drank to excess she became so distraught and depressed that she would announce, with great fanfare and drama, that she was going to kill herself. Of course her threats were bids for attention, but most of her friends recognized that her despair was real. Each of us responded in her own way.

One night in New York, Martha threatened to leap from her bedroom window. Afraid to move toward her for fear any motion on my part would cause her to jump, I feigned calmness, and quietly but firmly started talking. I told her she had a perfect right to take her own life, nobody could stop her, but I thought we should discuss methods more dignified than a leap out of an eleventh-floor window. In vivid detail, I described what her body, clad only in a shortie nightgown, would look like on the pavement below. Not only would it be crushed, I said, but most likely it would be in a vulgar position. (Martha was vain, and for all her flamboyance she was quite modest about her person; some of her friends even called her prudish.)

The more I talked, the more absurd everything I said sounded to me. But she listened, and finally, without saying a word, she walked away from the window. Looking at me intently, she crawled into her bed and said,

"You certainly have a lot of trouble with me, don't you, Winnie?" Her remark was so unexpected, I exploded with laughter.

We sat and talked, but not about suicide, for almost an hour. I heated a glass of milk for her—Martha always drank warm milk before going to bed, a holdover, she said, from childhood when her mother gave her a glass of milk before tucking her in for the night.

Martha's suicide threat at Alleta's was an entirely different type of dramatization. There was no screaming or hysterics that night.

"She stood up against the door," Alleta recalls. "She had on a shortie nightgown and her hair was twisted up on top of her head—and she pulled one foot up to the other knee, and put her opposite arm up high against the door frame, and said, "I have *just* taken a *full* bottle of *sleeping* pills."

Often when drinking, Martha accented every second or third word, sometimes even every word in her sentences—or as someone said, "She spoke in exclamation points."

Alleta recalls, "I said, 'Well, in that case you should sleep very well' . . . She repeated that she'd taken a *full* bottle, and I again said she'd sleep well.

" 'You just don't care,' Martha said. I told her I did, but that it would be inconvenient to have her dead on my hands. I asked her where she wanted to be buried and she answered, 'Arkansas, naturally.' I told her that was fine and suggested, 'Why don't you go on and get in the bed and go to sleep.' She said, 'Since you don't care, that is exactly what I intend to do.' "

Martha got in bed and went to sleep immediately. Alleta dashed into the bathroom, where she found an empty pill bottle. But she remembered there had been only two pills in it that morning. Then she checked a new bottle she knew Martha hadn't opened before. Only two were missing. Knowing that Martha had taken as many as five in one night while at the Westchester Country Club following California, Alleta says she reasoned "four won't hurt her and she'll have a good night's sleep." Which she did.

The next day, still complaining that "nobody cares," Martha continued her drinking.

During her stay in Mississippi, Martha had refused to be interviewed. But on her last day there she sat down in the garden with John Miller and chatted with him for UPI television.

In the exclusive interview Martha said, "Since I have been down South, I have found out the American people don't realize that these Senate hearings are not spontaneous like you and I are sitting here talking. These Senate hearings are as much rehearsed as any play on Broadway.

In other words, these men have crews that go in . . . and talk to whomever they are going to interview and it's rehearsed and rehearsed and rehearsed and then they put it on camera."

The American people, she said, "are sick and fed-up with Watergate. And they don't want to hear about it anymore . . . There are only . . . two cities that are keeping this thing going, plus the press, and that's Washington and New York."

She also said she was anxious to get back to "my husband because, whether I can do him any good, I can give him moral support if nothing else."

That night Martha left by train for Chicago, where she would transfer to another train for New York. Marty flew to New York, accompanied by Raul Saunders, Alleta and Charlie's son.

Since the *Panama Limited* doesn't come through Greenwood on its way from New Orleans to Chicago, Charlie Saunders took Martha to the station in Grenada, some thirty miles away.

Once at the depot, Martha didn't want to go inside, saying she was afraid someone would recognize her. Later she changed her mind, saying she'd go "incognito" into the little café, where there'd be ice for the Scotch she had with her.

As Charlie Saunders tells it: "Then this tough fellow came in, at least he looked tough. He had on shoes without any socks, and he'd been working all day; he was greasy and had on blue work clothes. He was sitting there at the counter when Martha decided he was Secret Service, checking on her. She wanted me to go ask him.

"I didn't want to disagree with her. She might fight me. And I didn't want to get in a fight with that fellow over there. Finally, Martha blurts out to him, 'You know who I am, don't you?' And he said, 'No, and I don't give a ——!' I thought I was going to have something on my hands."

Fortunately, just then the *Panama Limited* pulled into the station. "By that time all the railroad personnel had come out to view the getting on the train by Martha," Charlie continues. "The stationmaster was out there. I put Martha on the train, they took her bags, and they'd just pushed up the steel door—it comes up to your waist—and the train had started moving out when Martha came running to the door. As it pulled by she was hanging out, hollering and carrying on,. 'I told you those sons-of-bitches were going to do it; they gave me the smallest goddamn room on the train.'

"The station master came up and said, 'Mr. Saunders, is there anything I can do?' And I said, 'Yes, keep that train rolling.' "

Chapter Eighteen

MARTHA NOW ENTERED A PERIOD SHE'D LATER DESCRIBE AS THE time when "things were happening so fast, when the momentum was building up and things were getting hotter and hotter . . . God knows how anyone could live through it."

What she called "their nastiness" started the day she came back from Mississippi. Zolton wasn't sent to meet her at the station, although John knew her train time.

Once home, John was hardly civil to her. After some sort of confrontation, Martha locked herself in Marty's suite, which connected with the guest room and its bath. But before leaving her husband, she'd told him, while sobbing, "I don't want you. I want my John Mitchell back; you aren't John Mitchell."

According to Martha she never shared John Mitchell's bed again.

The night she moved into Marty's room, Martha called and talked in riddles about a story she wanted to put out. She was crying and saying, "I shouldn't talk about this," and "I'll be dead and in the East River." Without fully explaining what the big story was, she hung up.

She called back at two-fifteen, again worried about being "at the bottom of the river." The story she wanted told was that Richard Nixon was involved with the Mafia. (A few weeks later, she'd repeat her accusations publicly in a telephone call to UPI). She claimed, "The Mafia is in the whole damn operation; they got all of them involved."

A few days later, Martha called me from a pay phone on Madison Avenue to repeat the charges and to ask how she could protect herself. If she was seriously worried about being murdered, I suggested she make a tape and put on it everything she knew about Mafia involvement in government, how she came to have the information and where the proof was, if any. Evidently she took my advice and told someone; after her death John Mitchell asked one of her friends if he knew the whereabouts of "a tape Martha was supposed to have recorded about the Mafia."

Before we hung up I told her I was doing an article about Bebe Rebozo for *Ladies' Home Journal,* and I would like to talk to her about him the next day. She suggested I ask in the article, "If Bebe and the President are the best of friends, why hasn't Bebe been called before the [Senate Watergate] Committee?"

During this period—from the time she came back from Mississippi in July until John left her in September—Martha phoned me four to six times a day, with some calls lasting as long as an hour and a half. The only days she missed were those she spent with her psychiatrist and his wife —either at their house in Connecticut or at her Fifth Avenue apartment. Sometimes Martha called to tell more about the Mafia or White House horrors; other times she was lonesome and just wanted to talk, and in still others she asked for help or advice. Her main concern now was to find a lawyer. She'd been told by a friend, "You are going to have to start a new life for yourself, Martha. And you are going to have to do it all by yourself." Martha took this to mean that John was going to jail.

She was anxious to get their financial affairs in order. In particular she wanted (1) to get the apartment in her name only (John's lawyers told her it would cost $90,000 in taxes to transfer his half of the title to her; she didn't believe them); and (2) to do whatever was necessary to keep from being legally responsible for John's debts. "I don't want to pay his goddamn lawyers," was the way she put it.

"I want an unscrupulous lawyer, a real dog," she said. "Because it's dog eat dog now. I'm dealing with crooks and I need a bastard to handle them."

Martha wanted a lawyer who wasn't connected with Watergate, the Administration or John's law firm. Neither did she want a lawyer who was a friend of John or Nixon, nor one who could be "bought" by the Administration. That narrowed the field.

Others were enlisted in the search—among them television commentators, syndicated columnists, financiers, politicians and even a former U.S. Attorney General. Name after name was submitted to her, only to be rejected because "he's mixed up in it, too." Martha tried to get help from Chicago multimillionaire Clement Stone. "But," she claimed, "they turned him against me." Martha couldn't understand it: "I always liked Stone, even if Nixon didn't. Nixon wouldn't let him be an ambassador—he was crazy to be one—even after he gave all that money." (Over two million dollars, according to the Senate Watergate report.)

Tom Pappas, international financier and fund-raiser for CREEP in Greece, said he'd find a lawyer for Martha. But when he came to the apartment to talk about it, John Mitchell took him into the den and kept him there for a long time. Tom Pappas left without even telling Martha good-bye.

Finally, through a Washington attorney friend, I got the name of a respectable New York tax lawyer. At that point, Martha wanted only to get her financial affairs in order; there was no talk of legal separation or divorce.

After meeting with Martha on July 30 in his Park Avenue offices, the attorney went to the apartment to talk to John Mitchell. Martha called me in Key Biscayne, where I'd gone to do interviews for the Bebe Rebozo story. Shouting over the noise of the traffic on Madison Avenue—again she was at a pay phone—Martha told me the meeting had gone better than she'd ever dreamed. John, who had been treating her abominably, had been "absolutely great." She couldn't understand it, she said. Maybe it was because she had a lawyer, Martha reasoned.

Martha was surprised but pleased that John had liked her lawyer so much he'd asked him to write his will. At first the attorney said he couldn't, since Mrs. Mitchell had retained him, but John told him he didn't think Martha would mind, since the purpose of her business was only to straighten out some financial matters, such as getting the apartment in her name. Martha didn't object. After all, since John was acting so nice she was more than willing to meet him half way.

EUPHORIA OVER JOHN'S HELPFULNESS WAS SHORT-LIVED. HE WASN'T COoperating at all, she complained: "He keeps putting off and putting off what he should do." It seemed to Martha that John deliberately was sabotaging the transfer. (His delay tactics continued for almost three years. On the day Martha died, the apartment title was in joint tenancy. So instead of her half of the apartment going to her two children, as Martha had requested in her will, it went to John Mitchell.)

During one of her calls to me, when she was crying over the way John was treating her, there hadn't been any beep, beeping on the line. This was so unusual I asked if her husband were home. She said yes.

"Where is he?"

"Where the hell he always is, in the den. The only thing I can compare it with is when I was in Florida and knew the son of the 'big hood' from Chicago. I knew Sonny Capone, Al's son. Yes, ma'am. Well, this reminds me exactly of when I used to go over [to Capone's villa on an island near Miami] and Al Capone would be sitting in his huge library. Just sitting there. And it's the same thing I see with John Mitchell."

In mid-August Martha returned from a visit with her friends the Vogts. "I have had a nice vacation in the country," she reported. "In this lovely home near Danbury. You can get out in the woods and nobody bothers anybody; nobody locks their doors." She seemed relaxed and rested, a vast change from the day she left for the Vogts, claiming she "just had to get out," that she couldn't stand conditions in the apartment another minute.

Now she was talking about getting Marty ready for school, which started the next month. Martha was changing Marty to a private boarding school, the Convent of the Sacred Heart in Greenwich, Connecticut, in order to get her away from the press, which irritated Marty so much that one time she poured water out the window on reporters on the sidewalk eleven floors below.

As the time neared for John Mitchell's trial, tensions in the apartment became almost unbearable for Martha. John wasn't speaking to her. John's lawyers wouldn't tell her if, in their opinion, John would or would not go to jail, although one did speak to her long enough to mention the possibility of a divorce. And she and Marty, who for months had fought constantly, now weren't speaking at all.

Marty seemed to have felt that all the Mitchell problems were caused by Martha. At one point she told her mother, "It's all your fault that Daddy is in trouble. You're the one that talked."

But Marty didn't stop speaking to her mother until after two incidents, coming one on top of the other. The first involved a little friend Martha thought was a bad influence on Marty. According to Martha, Julia thought so, too. Martha forbade Marty to bring the child to the apartment.

The other incident was over a haircut. Marty got her father's permission to get her long, auburn hair cut, and Sandy Hobbs took her to the beauty parlor to have it done. No one told Martha. "I hit the ceiling when I saw Marty," Martha said. "My child's hair hadn't been cut since birth, it hung all the way down her back. The prettiest part of Marty was her hair . . . that on top of forbidding her to have that child in the house was the reason Marty stopped speaking to me."

I SAW MARTHA ONLY ONCE DURING THIS PERIOD, WHEN I WAS IN NEW YORK one day and went by the apartment. Martha looked and talked like someone heavily sedated; her eyes were glazed and her speech slow and slurred. In a call a few nights before, she'd talked about feeling groggy because she'd had so many pills. When I asked what kind she'd replied, "Normal pills."

"Normal pills!" I exclaimed.

"Oh, for God's sake, Winnie, who could go through what I have without pills? I've been persecuted more than anyone since Jesus Christ."

On August 22, during his first news conference in five months, Richard Nixon was questioned about not asking John Mitchell to tell him the details of Watergate. Nixon said that "throughout I would have expected Mr. Mitchell to tell me in the event that he was involved or that anybody else was. He did not tell me. I don't blame him for not telling me. He has his reasons for not telling me. I regret that he did not, because he is exactly right. Had he told me, I would have blown my stack . . ."

"John Mitchell has had it," Martha said after hearing Nixon's remarks. "But he won't admit it. Because John is too proud and he's had too much." She added, "My husband is trying to live and he thinks Richard Nixon is coming to his side."

Martha didn't share her husband's optimism about clemency. He was being used by Nixon, she claimed, and not only in Watergate. "Nixon stole John's law firm, just as he stole John Mitchell."

Still brooding over Nixon's remarks, Martha tried the next night to call the President. "All I wanted to do was give him a message," she reported. "But the White House said, 'Tell it to UPI.' " The following night she did.

Reaching Helen Thomas in San Clemente, where the President was vacationing, Martha told her Nixon had told "a damned lie" when he denied that John had told him about Watergate. She also told Helen about a campaign strategy book, outlining tactics, including espionage and dirty tricks, which she insisted Nixon had co-authored. Since she saw it with her own two eyes, Martha told Helen, the Watergate Committee should call her.

Another call Martha made that night was to Clare Crawford, to say the Watergate scandal had wrecked her life and that she was going to leave John "because he is going to jail." Martha lamented "what Watergate has done to our lives . . . we have been suffering." And although she said she and John loved each other very much, Martha declared she was "finished" with their relationship from the time she was "beaten up" in California.

Of course, Martha didn't want their relationship to be finished, and a few days later, when she realized what she had done, Martha called another reporter to say, "There has never been any such discussion with my husband. I'm staying to the bitter end . . . until John is convicted, disbarred or cleared."

While staying with Dr. and Mrs. Vogt, Martha had said several times she wanted them to come visit her. Now she set a date—the last week in August—for them to spend a few days at the apartment.

Later, friends of Mitchell's would leak the story that John "had a psychiatrist and his wife move in with them to give Martha constant care —and presumably supervision." But Dr. and Mrs. Vogt say this was not true. They claim Martha was a friend as well as a patient, and it was as friends that they stayed at her apartment. In denying that her husband was a psychiatrist in residence at the Mitchell apartment, Mrs. Vogt points out "there was no charge."

ON SEPTEMBER 2, 1973, MARTHA WAS FIFTY-FIVE YEARS OLD. NEITHER John nor Marty mentioned that it was her birthday; no one gave her a present. Three days later, on John's sixtieth birthday, Martha invited friends over to have dinner with him; she didn't go to the table.

No one knows what agonies John and Martha Mitchell put each other through their last few days together. But one friend describes the atmosphere in the apartment as "Tennessee Williams on Fifth Avenue, only worse."

Martha, whose greatest desire was to be accepted, loved and most of all needed, was bound to this man who had cut her out of his life, refused her help during his troubles, and spoke to her only to make taunting remarks.

And John, who according to his secretary Sandy Hobbs was "playing a role he'd never played before, the defendant, and who had to think of himself, not Martha," had a wife whose insecurity drove her to drink until she was a raving, swearing shrew.

Finally the pressures, the fears—of rejection by John and of having him go to jail, leaving her alone—plus the alcohol and drugs, drove Martha into a frenzy. Or as one observer put it, she went berserk. She ranted and raved and stormed around the apartment until a friend found it necessary to take Marty to her house. When Martha awakened and found Marty gone, she went to the nearest police precinct station to swear out a kidnapping arrest warrant against her friend. Once back in the apartment, Martha went on the attack against John. Now it was he who barricaded himself behind locked doors. This so infuriated Martha she hammered against the door, covered with a thick, beveled, glass mirror held in place by a wrought-iron filigreed frame, until she shattered the glass into little pieces.

Martha went into Marty's room and fell into a troubled sleep. John Mitchell left before she awakened; Martha never saw him again.

Chapter Nineteen

JOHN MITCHELL LEFT HOME ON THE MORNING OF SEPTEMBER 10, 1973, carrying only briefcases, his radio and minimal changes of clothing.

It had been planned for some time that John and his lawyers would stay at a hotel during his trial in order to be free to confer about the developments without disturbing Martha, or being disturbed by her.

According to what he told Julia, who in turn told Martha, since the Mitchells communicated only through a third party, John Mitchell would be away "two to thirty days," depending on the judge's ruling on a request for a trial postponement.

The change in Martha was amazing when she called that night; she was calm and didn't seem to be drinking. She was more like the Martha I'd talked with hundreds of times before Watergate. For the first time in months she was interested in events other than those directly related to her.

Martha had an insatiable curiosity; she seemed to want to know everything about everybody. She adored gossip, especially about members of the press and former Administration people. And I was fascinated with her tales of the quirks and foibles of high Nixon Administration officials.

There had been times when our hour-long conversations were filled with nothing but chit-chat.

John had moved to a hotel, she said, and she had gotten rid of all of his lawyers. It was a relief that her apartment no longer was "Grand Central Station, which drove me out of my mind." She complained, but not in a bitter way, about her attorney, who, she said, hadn't "done anything for me so far." No one was there with her except Julia, who "loves me and will never leave me." Zolton had gone with John. Marty was with friends and entered school the next day.

Her mail was "piling in," and just that day she'd received a telegram from Dean Martin's producer. "He asked me to call collect about something that was 'important, urgent and financially rewarding.' " She laughed and said of course she'd called him. They wanted her to be on their show, but she said she told him "maybe later."

A letter from Bill Moyers of Public Television also intrigued her. He'd said, "You have made many perceptive statements on American politics which have often been overlooked in the attempt to sensationalize your comments . . . our purpose is to give our national audience a greater understanding of you as a person . . ." Martha said she would call him, too.

At no time during our long conversation was Martha upset or swearing —her strongest language was one "darn." And she didn't even get disturbed when I told her I was going out that night to be on a late radio talk show, to publicize an article I'd written about Pat Nixon for *McCall's.* All Martha said was "good luck." Usually when I wrote about the First Lady her comments were stronger and she invariably asked, "Why would you write about *her?* She doesn't *do* anything."

And when I told her I'd be home shortly after midnight if she were lonesome and wanted to call, Martha surprised me by saying she'd be asleep by then.

The next day Martha still was calm, although she said the phone "rang all night and when I answered there was just breathing." Speaking of the press outside and the constant references to the trial on television and radio, Martha said, "People love sadness . . . I'm not kidding you; look how many go to funeral homes when they don't even know the family."

The only thing that really concerned her was the news that the trial was postponed. She wanted it "over with." She lamented that the attorneys would "come back here in full force" and again disrupt the household.

"Well," she suddenly said, "I'm going to watch the news; I want to know how long I'll be a prisoner."

At eleven o'clock that night, in the last of five calls, Martha no longer was calm. John hadn't come home after the trial was postponed, as both she and Julia had expected; they'd even prepared his dinner. It was several days before she learned he was at the Essex House under an assumed name.

"I got mad last night and threw John's clothes in the hall," Martha reported the next day. "And now Julia's gone." She hadn't left a note, but Martha knew it was a permanent move. Julia had taken all of her things.

Martha still couldn't find Zolton or Sandy. Neither her mail nor her newspapers had been delivered to the door. And she couldn't reach her lawyer; he was sitting at the bedside of his dying mother.

Martha said she did not understand what was going on. She was afraid. Could I come to New York? After rearranging a magazine assignment, I called back to say I'd be there the next morning. She'd tell the doorman a "Miss E. Condon" would be coming up, Martha said, explaining, "I don't want John Mitchell's spies to know you're coming."

It would be the first night Martha had spent alone since California. She was apprehensive about it, but with the extra bolts on all the doors she felt she'd be safe. Later we discovered that the door to a second stairway, off the laundry room, had a lock which could be opened with a credit card; we had a strong slip-bolt lock installed at once.

Sometime after midnight Martha called me, sobbing and crying and claiming there were Chinese people in the apartment.

"Chinese!"

"I woke up and there were two on my bed. Chinese. I don't know how they got in."

"Martha, you've had a nightmare. There aren't any Chinese in your apartment."

"I've waked up screaming for how many years now? I've waked up ever since California, but I've never dreamed of any Chinese sitting on the side of my bed!"

I tried to calm her: "You subconsciously were thinking of Kissinger's pro-China foreign policy." (For several days we'd been following the confirmation hearings of Henry Kissinger for Secretary of State.)

I said the wrong thing.

"Oh - - - -! I can't stand that. I can't tolerate it. Thinking about some goddamn born-German. My grandmother was German—half German. I know all about the goddamn Germans."

Remembering that William Rogers was leaving the State Department to make room for Kissinger, she cried, "Poor Rogers. He took it and took it while the State Department was being run from the White House. He was the President's friend for a long, long time. But he didn't buckle under. The President didn't like anybody who did not buckle under to him. The President had a hell of a hard time trying to get anybody in there in the first place. I was down in Florida and I went through all of it. Nobody wanted it."

"Why?"

"Oh, nuts. We are talking long distance and it is costing me money. Remember the name, E. Condon."

THE FIRST THING WE DID WHEN I ARRIVED WAS TO HAVE THE PHONE number changed. Martha wanted John Mitchell's name off the listing and asked that the bills be sent to her. "I don't want him knowing who I talk to," she said. But it was impossible to take his name off without his consent; neither could the phone be disconnected without his permission. So, the bills went to John Mitchell, and for months at a time they weren't paid. The phone company would threaten to cut off the service, and Martha's lawyers would negotiate with John Mitchell's lawyers until part of the bill was paid.

Martha had lost a lost of weight since I saw her three weeks earlier. Nine pounds and no wonder, she said, "I couldn't eat and I vomited each morning. I couldn't hold anything except iced-tea." But since the attorneys left, she claimed, "I've been eating everything in the refrigerator."

When I noticed the missing mirror from the bedroom door, Martha admitted she'd smashed it "to smithereens." But she claimed a faulty memory when asked about other events of the previous weekend.

"There apparently is something in people's minds," she philosophized, "that wants them to forget everything horrible, or things that are unpleasant." Following a traumatic experience, she continued, "It's as if every little thing, every little cell in my brain has to go through a certain reaction until Martha Mitchell gets over [the trauma]. I have done this all my life. And it takes a period of time for each cell in my brain to register; until then I just block things out."

Martha was so worried that I suggested we sit down and list all of her problems and then try to find solutions.

Mainly, she was afraid of five things:

1. They would kill her. Martha genuinely was afraid of being murdered. She thought the Administration was behind the attempt on Governor George Wallace's life. And only two days before we talked there was

a report out of Chile that deposed President Salvador Allende committed suicide during a violent military coup. Martha declared, "He was murdered by the U.S. We didn't want him. I know what the government was doing in Chile." So, she reasoned, an Administration that would kill a foreign politician and attempt to murder a local one wouldn't hesitate to kill her.

2. John would take possession of the apartment and not let her back in if she went out—even to buy groceries.
3. She'd never again receive her mail or her newspapers.
4. She wouldn't have enough money to live on.
5. She wouldn't have anyone to take care of her. "Someone has always taken care of me, Winnie," she said.

Number One wasn't a problem, I assured her. They missed their chance to kill her, if they'd ever wanted to. Now her untimely death would cause more trouble than it was worth to them. I halfway convinced her.

Number Two could be taken care of by my doing the shopping until her lawyer was available. Then he could do whatever was necessary to guarantee that John Mitchell couldn't come in without her consent.

"He's coming back in, Winnie, I'm sure of it," she insisted. "And he'll do it when I'm not here and then lock me out." There was evidence that she might be right about his coming back. He would need his clothes; John Mitchell had left with very little clothing. And although Martha said she had thrown his clothes into the hall, she tossed out only a few items. Most of his wardrobe still was there, hanging in two closets. Also, his files were in the den. And stacked in boxes all over the room were three-inch thick black foldover binders containing transcripts of every major radio and network broadcast since June 17, 1972, that mentioned John Mitchell or Watergate. Similar folders had Xerox copies of newspaper stories for the same period. Some of these clips and transcripts, which must have cost thousands of dollars, were paid for by CREEP. Others didn't have identification; Martha thought they came from the Justice Department, but she wasn't sure. John Mitchell also had been receiving the daily White House news summaries, whose distribution usually is limited to extremely high-ranking White House officials. These were sent first-class, special delivery; postage for each one ran around $1.20. The White House also sent such things as "Digest of Recent Comment Focus on Watergate, Reaction from Around the United States."

John Mitchell's logs from the time he entered government in 1969 were in the apartment, too, as were several United States code-annotated books from the Mudge Rose library, which he surely would need to prepare for his Vesco trial and for his appearances before one or the other of the grand juries he went before to testify.

Number Three seemed simple but it wasn't. Starting the day after he walked out, John Mitchell had his chauffeur/bodyguard stop by the Fifth Avenue apartment every morning to pick up the mail. Only after it had been opened, and presumably read, was her personal mail returned to her. Martha objected, but it did no good. Finally, she rented a Post-Office box and requested that all her mail be placed in it. This worked for about a week, but then all the mail addressed to John Mitchell and to "Mr. and Mrs. Mitchell," and some addressed to Martha alone, was sent to John's former law office on Broad Street (where Sandy Hobbs was given an office in which to handle Mitchell's business affairs). Only after it was opened and resealed was Martha's personal mail sent back and put in her P.O. box.

Martha was so distraught she called Jack Anderson and volunteered to work for him as a reporter in order to help him investigate the "dirty tricks" in the Post Office. Jack refused the offer.

Mail that managed to be delivered was a great comfort to Martha; often it was the only bright spot of her day. She called me in Washington regularly to report on the amount of mail and to read some of the more interesting letters. Often she'd cry over one, such as the note from a woman in Atlanta, a stranger, who wrote, "You're a wonderful person . . . you gave up your seat for me at a DAR meeting." Martha didn't remember the incident, but she found it touching that the woman had.

Rarely was there a critical letter after John left. People—most of them strangers, although there were several whose lives she had touched briefly in the past—wrote words of encouragement. Almost all urged her not to give up, saying she was doing the right thing.

Number Four was complicated. Martha said she knew nothing about the family finances. John always took care of them. She didn't know how much money they had, if it was in cash, stock or bonds, or if anything was in both their names—except for the apartment, which she knew was in joint tenancy. Neither did she know if she had an insurance policy that could be used for a loan.

A call to her bank revealed she had in her account a few hundred dollars—less than her usual balance, she said—and that nothing had been deposited for some time; in her purse she had around a hundred dollars. Later Martha would tell people John Mitchell had left her with only $975. I thought it even less.

Martha kept insisting she had to have money *now.* I told her, jokingly, "Martha, you aren't going to starve to death. If you never get a cent from John Mitchell you can live for months just by selling a piece of furniture now and then."

"Sell my possessions! You don't understand, Winnie, what possessions mean to people in the South. They cherished the few possessions they had left [after the Civil War], and they lived decently with them the best they could. I'll never give up my possessions; they and this apartment are all I have left."

Seriously, I told her, she was in an excellent financial position. I reminded her she'd been offered $50,000 for a magazine article. And her book should bring at least $500,000. (My estimate was low; a few weeks later one publisher was ready to pay one million dollars; Martha didn't think the time was right to sign a contract.)

Number Five, who would take care of her, was a more difficult problem to solve. Martha resisted all arguments that she didn't need anyone to take care of her, that she was perfectly capable of doing it herself. As she told me another time, she'd never felt she could "make it alone." And typical of Southern women of her generation, Martha honestly felt a woman needed a man to provide for her.

MOST OF THE REST OF OUR CONVERSATION THAT EVENING WAS A REHASH of things Martha had told me before. I was glad to hear that when told cold sober, the facts hadn't changed.

The next day was spent going over her mail—boxes of it weeks old and never opened—talking more about Watergate and trying to figure how to get her apartment in order. It was a mess. All work on the apartment was stopped when John Mitchell was indicted. There was a large window in Martha's bedroom that wouldn't stay up when opened; two rooms hadn't been painted; the butler's room and bath were piled high with paint cans and other debris. Also, there were no draperies at any of the windows in the drawing room, music room or dining room; unpacked boxes were in most rooms, including the master bedroom; and Martha's tall metal files from CREEP and several boxes of her campaign material were in the dining room.

Then, too, closets were jammed with the types of things families used to keep in the attic—Marty's outgrown clothes, from the time she was a baby; every birthday, Valentine, Mother's Day or Christmas card or note Martha had ever received from Jay, Marty or John (who until 1971 always signed his communications "Jack"); and box upon box of memorabilia from Martha's childhood. It seemed that she never had thrown anything away, that it was necessary for her to hold onto the past.

It was evident she couldn't live in such confusion. We decided to get the workmen back to finish their labor as soon as possible.

Martha cooked dinner that night, as she had the night before, and we were just starting to carry out trays to the den when my husband Bennie telephoned to say that *Newsweek* was running a story in their next issue saying John Mitchell had left Martha and that she needed medical help. The magazine wanted Martha's comments and answers.

"What will I do, what will I do?" Martha cried. She was sobbing and trembling so much I thought she would collapse. Suddenly she turned and ran back to her bedroom. When she came back she was calmer; she also had a drink in her hand, the first of many she'd consume before dawn.

"You're the only person in the world I can trust," she said. "You must tell me what to do."

"Look," I said, "if you don't trust anybody, why do you trust me?"

"Because," she answered, "John Mitchell hates you so."

I laughed and said, "Well, I guess that's as good a way as any to pick a friend."

Martha promised she'd take the advice I gave her, which was to do nothing. Then she poured herself another drink, refused her dinner and went to her room. All night long she either was on the phone or in the pantry getting ice for another drink.

We worked on the apartment, making list after list of things to be done, and we taped many of the Watergate-related things we'd been discussing for the past year. In all, it was a productive two days.

Then, while watching television Sunday night, Martha heard details of John's accusations about her in *Newsweek.* Again I told her not to respond in any way.

Martha wanted legal advice. We called her lawyer's associate and he told her the same thing: "Don't talk." By now the elevator men were pushing notes from the press under Martha's door. Some contained the wire copy of the *Newsweek* story.

Under the heading "A Sick Woman," the story read: "With every passing week, Martha Mitchell's outbursts about the Watergate scandal have grown more and more frantic . . . Martha's public tirades, a family intimate told *Newsweek,* have been more than matched by a series of unpredictable and sometimes violent outbursts at home. On one occasion, friends said, Martha pitched her husband's clothes out into the hall . . .

"Last week," the article continued, "the strain took its toll . . . John

Mitchell moved out of their Fifth Avenue apartment and into a New York hotel.

"His departure was plainly a last resort, according to friends. Mitchell feels his wife needs medical help, but cannot bring himself to take the necessary legal steps to try to have her committed. Over the last six weeks, he has twice attempted—unsuccessfully—to have her hospitalized."

My reaction to the story amazed Martha. I told her it couldn't have been better for her if she'd planted it herself.

"What do you mean?" she asked incredulously.

"In one article," I explained, "this man has said his wife is so 'sick' he twice thought of legally committing her to an institution. Yet he *walked out,* leaving her *alone*—this poor mentally ill woman whose condition is 'deteriorating.' What does this make him look like? A fiend? Or at best, a cold, insensitive, unloving husband?"

All the sympathy in the world would be with her, I said.

Martha looked at me like I was the one who should be committed and stomped off to her room. The night was a repeat of Friday's—Martha drinking to excess, pacing the floor, alternately sobbing and swearing and making phone calls. I didn't know who she called, but I learned about one the next morning when I heard on the radio what she'd said to Helen Thomas.

She confirmed that John had left, but she told Helen it was on the advice of his attorneys. "He walked out, yes," she was quoted as saying. "But I've been trying to get him out. If you've got a man twenty-four hours a day. I couldn't stand it. He was watching the football games."

I was upset—not that she'd called, but because of what she'd said. As I told Martha, it was O.K. for her to make a statement. I would have helped her draft one. But to say she wanted to get her husband out because he watched football! In the first place, it wasn't true. She wanted his lawyers out, I reminded her, not her husband.

All through my tirade, Martha kept repeating, "But he said *he* left *me.* He said *he* left *me.*" He had left her; I couldn't understand her trying to deny it. But I didn't know then, and wouldn't until after Martha's death, that her father had left her and that she'd suffered other rejections in her life. For Martha the most terrible thing in the world was being left or rejected.

As we talked that day, she must have been trying to convince herself that John had left only because she wanted him to go. Eventually she would reach the same type of illogical conclusion when Marty rejected her.

Martha had been talking about Marty the night she received the *Newsweek* questions about her marriage breaking up. She'd wondered how Marty was and where she'd spend the weekend, her first after starting school. Yet Martha wouldn't call the Convent of the Sacred Heart to find out.

"When she wants to talk to me, Marty will call," Martha insisted. I was just as determined that Martha make the first overture toward her daughter. "Then you call," Martha said. Several calls and two days later, I had Marty on the phone. When I identified myself, Marty immediately asked to speak to her mother. I handed the phone to Martha.

The first thing Marty said was, "They told me you didn't want to talk to me." Once Martha had convinced her that wasn't true, the two chatted away like any mother and daughter who'd been temporarily separated. There were no harsh words or recriminations. Martha genuinely was interested in hearing how Marty liked her school, her studies, the Sisters and her classmates. Marty seemed just as eager to share her first boarding-school experience with her mother. Finally, Martha said, "I love you and miss you, too." She hung up, turned with a stricken look and cried, "Marty said she loves me and she misses me." She broke into sobs.

A day or two later, Marty called from school and during the conversation Martha asked when she wanted to spend a weekend with her. Marty called later to say she couldn't come at all. "She said her father wouldn't let her," Martha told me in a call that day. "She said one parent always advises a child and John was advising her."

Finally, through the efforts of one of Martha's lawyers a date was set for Marty to spend a weekend with her mother. Martha was so excited about seeing Marty she spent hours planning every little detail of the visit—what they'd eat, what they'd do. She also was nervous about seeing her; memories of their last disastrous weeks together were still fresh in Martha's mind.

Zolton was to bring Marty to the apartment on Saturday; Friday afternoon Martha's lawyer called, saying John Mitchell was insisting that Martha get out of the apartment for several hours so he could come get his files and clothes. He had requested this before, he knew Martha's answer; she wanted him to make a list of what he needed and she would put them in the hall. She absolutely refused to let him in the apartment for fear he wouldn't leave and she would be locked out. But now, the day before Marty's visit, he was back demanding she let him in. Martha was awake all night, worrying about John and his request.

On Saturday morning, Martha went across the street to the garage where the Mitchells kept their car and waited for Zolton. She insisted on going with him to pick up Marty. She never explained why she did this, but since she thought Marty had spent Friday night with her father, Martha probably hoped to see John. She'd been trying to reach him by phone throughout the night.

But Zolton didn't drive to the Essex House. He went to Sandy Hobbs's apartment building. Sandy came out with Marty, saw Martha and asked, "What are you doing here?" The two had a verbal battle on the sidewalk, with Sandy accusing Martha of deliberately instigating a confrontation and Martha vowing she would never let Marty go to Sandy's apartment again.

Once at her apartment, Martha dashed to the phone to instruct her attorney to get a court restraining order preventing John Mitchell from allowing Marty to go to Sandy's apartment. Marty went to her room, which she hadn't seen for more than a month. Unfortunately, one of the first things she saw was her mail, which inadvertently had been opened along with Martha's letters.

Martha admitted to me that she and Marty had had a "terrible fight" over the opened mail. But they'd made up, Martha said, and now Marty didn't want to leave to go back to school. "She wants to stay with me," Martha told me on the phone Sunday, the day Marty was scheduled to leave.

But according to Sue Morrison, John Mitchell's former secretary and a close friend of Jill Mitchell Reed, his daughter from his former marriage, Marty was in the apartment less than an hour. After fighting with her mother, Marty left and took a taxi to the Essex House, where she spent the weekend with her father. She refused ever to visit Martha again.

Evidently Sue's version of the weekend is correct. Marty wasn't there when Junie Dankworth arrived that Saturday afternoon after an urgent call from Martha. It was the first time Martha had talked to Junie since July 4, 1972, when the two spoke briefly after Martha's return from California.

During Junie's five days in New York, Martha never once told her that Marty had been there and walked out. Just as she never told me.

Chapter Twenty

MARTHA'S FIRST CONTACT WITH ANYONE CONNECTED WITH John Mitchell was eight days after he left, when her lawyer met with his lawyer. Following the meeting, Martha's attorney came to the apartment, bringing two hundred dollars in household money and a startling announcement. He said he also had talked to her psychiatrist, Dr. Vogt, and the two had decided she should go to Craig House "to get away from the press." He, the attorney, had made arrangements for her to leave the next day. Zolton would take her to Beacon, New York.

No, he assured her, John Mitchell had nothing to do with this plan. It was his opinion she should go, and her doctor concurred.

The attorney was in the apartment for over an hour, during which time I was in the breakfast room finishing a magazine article I'd been working on when Martha asked me to come to New York. Martha kept running in and out, on the pretense of going to the kitchen for Cokes, giving me a running commentary on what he was saying.

Martha asked her attorney if John would pay the assessment on the apartment; he'd work that out later, he said. Later we'd learn that John Mitchell had refused to discuss any financial arrangements unless Martha went to a psychiatric institution, and unless I went home.

She agreed to go to Craig House but remained concerned about what would happen to the apartment while she was away. She didn't want to leave it unattended. The attorney assured her that wasn't a problem; he would come the next morning with a locksmith who would change the locks on all the doors the minute Martha was out. The lawyer would keep the only set of keys.

Martha didn't want that. Instead, she came in and asked me if I'd stay there while she was away. I had no legal right to do that, I explained. John Mitchell would throw me out. Still, Martha wanted me to ask the attorney.

No, indeed, he said. He also insisted I had to be out of the apartment before eleven o'clock. If Martha wasn't going until noon, I asked, why couldn't I stay until I saw her on her way. Because, he repeated, I *had* to be out before eleven o'clock. No reason was given.

He hardly was out the door before Martha came to tell me, "I'm not going." She certainly was not going to accommodate *them* by committing herself, claiming, "If they ever get me in there they'll never let me out.

"John Mitchell has snowed this attorney," Martha added. She wasn't so sure, either, but what he was "using" her psychiatrist in some way. Now she'd have to get another attorney, Martha said. And although Dr. Vogt was her friend and she trusted him implicitly, she said she wouldn't see him again because she didn't want "any doctor who knows John Mitchell."

I was glad Martha went to her room and closed the door; I needed to be alone to have time to think about this latest development and what, if any, my role should be in it. As I saw it, one of two things was happening. Both were frightening.

1. Martha was perfectly sane and John was trying to railroad her into an institution in order to keep her from spilling the beans about Watergate and the dirty tricks.
2. She was the "sick woman" John Mitchell claimed and truly needed psychiatric help. In that case, why did her husband leave her alone?

MARTHA WAS UP ALL NIGHT. ABOUT DAWN SHE TOLD ME SHE WASN'T going to see the lawyer when he came back; I could tell him her decision. "They aren't going to put me away," she announced before going to her room and to bed. I was left to face the attorney alone.

When I told him Martha had changed her mind and was asleep and couldn't be disturbed, he shouted and ranted and was so antagonistic toward me I finally asked why he would act in such a manner. Because, he said, I had ruined his plans by talking Martha out of going. And besides, I had eavesdropped on his conversation with Martha the day before. None of this was true.

When he saw there was no way to get Martha to go to Craig House, he cancelled the locksmith and Zolton. Then he told me I had to be out of the apartment before noon. I protested, saying she couldn't be left alone. He said he'd send his secretary over. I asked why he'd want me, a friend, to leave her with strangers. He repeated that I *absolutely* could not stay in the apartment. That decision was up to Martha, I told him. He left in a huff.

Martha didn't eat her dinner that night—a usual sign that she was upset and drinking. I had my dinner with Bennie, who had come to New York after Martha asked me to call him, saying, "This isn't anything for two women to handle." We went to bed early; I was exhausted from my encounter with the attorney and from being up the night before.

I awakened with a start. Martha was banging on the door, crying, "Help me, Winnie! Help me!" I dashed into the hall just in time to see her entering her bedroom. When I got there, Martha—in a pale-blue billowy nightgown and her blond hair streaming down her back—was standing in the middle of the floor, looking toward the door. Once she saw me Martha rushed to the window, screaming that she was going to throw herself onto the sidewalk below.

At that very moment, Bennie called, "Where is the orange juice?" He is a diabetic, on insulin. I knew the shock of being awakened abruptly by Martha's screams for help was putting him into an insulin reaction.

Martha also heard his call and stopped her rush toward the window. "Don't you move, Martha," I commanded her. "Bennie is going into insulin shock. You just wait; I'll be back."

As fast as I could, I squeezed oranges and mixed the juice with sugar. Bennie finished two large glasses of the mixture before he could tell me to go to her, that he was all right.

Martha was sitting on her bed when I came in, but the minute she saw me she again ran to the window. Grabbing the two handles she raised the lower pane—and it slowly came back down. The defective pulleys, which hadn't been repaired when John Mitchell stopped the workmen, were too weak to keep the window raised.

Martha looked back at me with a puzzled look on her face, turned and raised the window again. The moment she turned it loose, the window again slowly made its descent.

The night had been too much for me; I started laughing, hysterically. Martha looked at me as if I'd lost my mind. I tried to speak to her but couldn't stop laughing. Finally she walked back, got into her bed and said, "Winnie, you'd better go get some sleep."

I didn't. I spent the night taking Maalox, for indigestion, and walking back and forth from our room, down the hall past Marty's suite to Martha's bedroom—first checking on Bennie and then on Martha. Both slept well.

The next morning, as usual, someone had taken the mail—the elevator man said it was Zolton. Her newspapers were also missing. I felt this was petty harassment, staged to upset Martha. There were other things, too. Bennie discovered that the peekhole in Martha's kitchen door had been painted over with sticky green paint. It would have been impossible to identify someone knocking on the door without opening it. We never told Martha, it would have added to her fears. Another harassment was the unsolicited merchandise and accompanying bills. Someone subscribed to things for Martha: she received boxes of cooking utensils, beauty products, dictionaries (a premium for joining the Book-of-the-Month Club), magazines—including *Playgirl,* which shocked Martha's puritanical sensibilities.

And Martha's imagination wasn't running wild when she said something was wrong with her telephones. There often was a clicking or popping sound on the line, and sometimes at the end of a call, when the receiver was placed back on the cradle, the line didn't disconnect for several seconds. If the phone was picked up during this time, a grinding noise would be heard. She repeatedly reported it. Once when I was there, I insisted that someone come check the phones. The repair man said nothing was wrong. Then I dialed a number, hung up and handed him the phone. He was embarrassed to hear a grinding noise instead of a clear line. Later he reported there had been trouble "with a cable." I was given the same excuse almost two months later when I discovered my home telephone didn't disconnect after Martha called me.

MARTHA CONTINUED TO BE TERRIFIED THAT JOHN MITCHELL WAS going to find some way to have her committed. Hadn't he said, in *Newsweek,* that he'd "twice attempted—unsuccessfully—to have her hospitalized." (Evidently he had considered committing Martha, but one of his attorneys discouraged it, saying Martha's public support was such "you can't commit her; you'll be killing Joan of Arc.")

If she were that afraid of being sent to an institution, I told her, then she should have her own psychiatrist, one who would go to court, if necessary, to testify as to her sanity. Martha agreed and asked me to find one.

Before I could do anything about it, though, Martha decided she'd prove her own sanity. Without telling me, she called Clare Crawford and told her she wanted to go on television.

I was amazed. Only two days before, saying she wanted to "save everything for my book," she had turned down $50,000 from a magazine for the story of her last few weeks with John and what her life was like now that he'd left. Yet, she was going on NBC–TV, without pay, to tell the same story.

How could she do it, especially when she needed the money? Because, she said, a magazine story wouldn't come out for at least two months. She wanted to tell it *now.* Time after time, when Martha was drinking, I'd see in her this need to do something or have something *now.*

Martha and I fought over her doing the NBC–TV interview with Clare. I thought it was foolish for her to give away the information, and also, she was so distraught I doubted she could make a credible appearance.

The NBC interview took place in Martha's drawing room. Martha spoke softly and looked like the sad, abandoned wife she was. She went on television, she said, because "of those nasty horrible stories that these lawyers have put out against me and [because] my mail has now begun to say they're sorry I'm in the hospital, to please take care of myself—so I decided it was time for me to tell the American public that I am sitting in my apartment, I'm perfectly capable of doing anything I want to do, and there's absolutely nothing wrong with me except I'm mentally tortured from the torture I'm getting put though."

Obviously she also had gone on TV to send a message to John to come home. At no time did she criticize him for leaving, and when Clare asked if she wanted her husband back, Martha answered, "Of course. Of course."

She put the blame for any troubles they might had had on his lawyers who "for some unknown reason like to come [to the apartment] late in the afternoon or they come at night and stay and they stay here until sometimes twelve o'clock at night or one o'clock [in the morning]."

Sure, she said, she threw his clothes in the foyer because after some provocation she "got mad and like any woman does, it's just like typical of a woman if you get mad you do something. [But] what are you going to do? He's not here. You can't hit him on the head. So I've got to do something so I took his clothes—not his clothes, a few ties and a few shirts—and threw them out here in the foyer."

Yes, of course she knew a lot, but "I mean I would never in the world say anything that would hurt my husband's trial or be a detriment against my husband . . . I just have not that kind of heart; I don't want to hurt anybody."

She admitted that she "blew up" one night, but "when you're under pressure and under strain you say things and do things that you wouldn't do ordinarily. It's just a state that you get in that you can't explain and you'd have to go through something like this before you'd know what it's like."

Why did she think her husband hadn't contacted her, Clare asked.

"I guess he's mad at me for throwing his clothes out, for one thing," Martha said, adding, "not really out because they . . . took them to him. And then, I think that he just thinks that I'm just overly wrought and that I should have some kind of care but I'm not."

Had she ever been hospitalized for nervousness? "I've never been committed to anything . . . except the good of my country," Martha answered.

Martha also took the opportunity to talk about the "fake" Martha. For some time the press had been reporting calls from a woman who said she was Martha Mitchell, and unsuspecting reporters often printed statements made by this woman, only to have them denied by Martha the next day. The conclusion was reached that the woman was a "fake." Martha expressed the view that "they" had hired this woman to discredit her. "Let me mention to you, Clare," she said, "these telephone calls that I get credit for, they've got somebody that mimics me . . ."

There may have been someone imitating Martha, but a lot of the so-called fake calls were made by Martha herself. They probably were made during some of her frequent "blackouts." I remember one night, trying unsuccessfully to get Martha off the telephone while she was swearing at one of Marty's school teachers. Later, when her lawyer told Martha she had antagonized the school's Sisters by yelling at one of them, Martha called me in tears. "You know I wouldn't be disrespectful to a Sister," she cried. "I have the greatest respect for them." She went on and on about her deep religious feelings and how it was impossible for her to have done such a thing. I'm sure she believed it.

Another time she was devastated that the "fake" Martha had been calling her gynecologist and using threatening and abusive language. Martha had made the calls. She reasoned that since she had been the one who wanted a baby and that John had not, she should have custody of Marty; she felt her doctor should come forward and verify those facts. Martha didn't remember the calls to her doctor, but there were many times when

I was at the apartment when I'd heard her, during one of her rages, telephone the hospital where her gynecologist was associated.

I never knew until a day or two later if Martha had been in a blackout. But once when I was describing Martha's dramatic personality changes to a psychiatrist whose speciality is alcoholism, he said I could have been witnessing the very moments when she went into an alcohol-induced mental blackout.

As I told it to him, her personality would sometimes change even as I watched. It was frightening to see. The first time I saw it happen, Martha and I were sitting and talking before dinner. She'd had only two drinks, as far as I knew, but she'd made several trips to her room, where I soon learned she kept a generous supply of both pills and liquor. She was telling me something about her relationship with John Mitchell when within seconds the expression on her face and in her eyes changed from hurt and sadness to bitterness and fury. Even the tone of her voice was not the same. She became an entirely different person, in actions and in appearance. It was like watching Dr. Jekyll become Mr. Hyde.

While impressing her supporters, Martha's NBC television appearance didn't help her with John Mitchell. Her attorney still couldn't get an agreement from him about her support money, and Martha still was being pressured to enter herself in Craig House.

Martha was desperate; she again asked me to find a psychiatrist, one who'd keep John Mitchell from "putting me away."

Through Dr. Richard A. Steinbach, professor and chairman of the Department of Psychiatry at Georgetown University Hospital, who I had met while researching an article, I got the name of a doctor he thought would be "right" for Martha.

He recommended Hungarian-born Dr. Sandor Lorand, a distinguished pioneer of the psychoanalytic movement, Professor Emeritus of Psychiatry at the State University of New York Downstate Medical Center, and author of numerous professional books and articles. He often was called upon to give expert testimony in New York courts.

Dr. Lorand, about eighty years old then, was the same height and build as her father, Martha said. "The Good Doctor," as Martha always called him (although not to his face), was an authoritative figure, one demanding respect. Yet he was kind and gentle. Martha adored him.

Immediately after Dr. Lorand talked to John Mitchell, telling him that in his opinion Martha should stay at the apartment, the pressure ended for her to commit herself to an institution.

Dr. Lorand first saw Martha at her apartment four weeks after John left. He was with her for what seemed hours to me; his opinion was that Martha should not be in an institution. According to what Martha told me, Dr. Lorand thought the fears she had, as a result of the traumatic California experience, could be aggravated if she were confined to a hospital.

The Good Doctor saw Martha periodically until the night before she left New York for Virginia, where within a few weeks she entered a hospital and learned she had a malignant blood-cell disease, multiple myeloma.

Martha wasn't very good about going regularly to the doctor's office, but she was quick to call him to come to the apartment when things became so bad she felt she couldn't handle them. She also called the doctor from out of town whenever she needed support, and Martha seldom went on a television program without talking to him a few hours before air time. She was afraid to go on these shows, but Dr. Lorand told her she could do them.

I do not know Dr. Lorand's diagnosis of Martha, but I recall his fury when a magazine article, published after her death, quoted Dr. Klaus Mayer as saying Martha was "manic." She definitely was not manic, Dr. Lorand stated. Dr. Mayer says the same thing. "This is how quotes get [distorted]," he says, adding that Martha "was a lively person, she was an up and down person. She was everything but cool. She was active and jumpy and very sad. That is what I said—but not in the psychotic sense, in the personality sense. She was mecurial. But manic? No!"

The last time Dr. Lorand saw Martha she was at her apartment. Emotionally it had been a trying time, and Martha had taken to her bed. Dr. Lorand sat and talked with her. Then as he started to leave, Martha asked, "Would you just put your arms around me?"

The doctor kindly answered, "Sure. I like you." He put his arms around her and she hugged him, real tight, saying, "Oh, it's nice to have someone's arms around me."

MARTHA HADN'T BEEN HAPPY WITH HER ATTORNEY (RETAINED IN THE first place only to get the apartment in her name) from the time he'd tried to get her to go to Craig House. And she was more upset with him after he and his associate told her the Ervin Committee wanted her to testify but they got her "out of it." Martha was eager to go before the Committee. Now, she said, she was going to find someone who would arrange for her to testify.

Since I still thought she might get herself in trouble if she testified,

I again quizzed her about her possible criminal involvement. Had she done anything other than receive the $10,000 contribution? Nothing, she assured me. Was she *sure?*

The only thing she did, Martha answered, was to get rid of his Nixon Foundation files when John asked her to destroy them. (The Richard M. Nixon Foundation was created in 1969 to finance and build a library for Richard Nixon's presidential papers. John Mitchell was one of the foundation's seven-member executive group.) According to Martha, John Mitchell asked her to destroy these files sometime after they moved to the Fifth Avenue apartment. But she claimed she had handed the files to someone else to dispose of them.

The same day Martha decided she was dismissing her attorney she received a letter from him saying he was removing himself as her legal adviser. He gave as his reason the fact that he had been hired by both the Mitchells to arrange property transfers and that he wasn't a matrimonial lawyer and didn't want to be one.

Martha was elated; she immediately retained attorney Mary (Deede) Goodhue. Within a short time Deede saw John Mitchell and got a commitment from him for a temporary financial settlement. He would pay the apartment assessment and all of Martha's other bills. She could keep and use her credit cards and charge accounts. And every Friday he would deposit $350 into Martha's account at the Chase Manhattan Bank, to cover her cash expenses and the salary of one live-in domestic. He also promised that acknowledgment of the deposits would be sent promptly by the bank to Martha. When Martha needed transportation, she was to order a limousine and send the bill to her husband.

Deede also arranged for John Mitchell to inform Dr. Lorand of how Marty could be reached for emergency purposes when she was not at school. John Mitchell also agreed that efforts would be made to have Marty spend every other weekend with Martha and to have her keep in touch with Martha by telephone at regular intervals, "both when she is at school and at least once on the weekends she spends with her father." Marty's first weekend with her mother was the one that turned out to be the last, although through no fault of Deede's.

As it turned out, John Mitchell did not pay Martha's bills—even the lawyer and doctor fees he had promised to assume. But Martha wouldn't know that until later. So now with a new psychiatrist and a new lawyer, Martha felt a rare sense of security. She called old friends and went out with some of them. She and Pat Mosbacher lunched together and afterward went shopping along Madison Avenue. Martha and I went to the

American Fashion Designers' showings at the Plaza Hotel, where she had her first encounter with a large press group since her separation.

And one afternoon Martha said, "Let's go out to dinner tonight." I was surprised, since two women dining *à deux* at a restaurant wasn't Martha's idea of fun. She said she wanted to go to Trader Vic's, claiming she was hungry for their Chinese food.

Martha seemed preoccupied all through the dinner, which she didn't eat. She absent-mindedly answered my questions and didn't contribute to the conversation. Martha just kept her eyes on the entrance, after first carefully scanning the room, and watched everyone being seated. Later I learned she'd been told that John had had dinner at Trader Vic's a night or two before we were there.

MARTHA'S FEELING OF WELL-BEING ENDED ABRUPTLY ONE EVENING when she found a copy of John's divorce settlement with his first wife. Every day Martha had spent hours in the den, going through the files containing the Mitchells' financial records, looking for information for her lawyer. It was in those records that she came across a full file folder on John's financial dealings with his former wife, now Elizabeth Katherine Suyker.

Martha couldn't believe—and neither could the various friends and her many lawyers who saw the legal papers—that her husband had agreed to pay his first wife 35 percent of his gross annual income and that the payments would continue even if she remarried. "He kept telling me that he was through with her, completely," Martha cried. "He said he had done everything that he was supposed to do for her."

John Mitchell also agreed to each year submit his income-tax returns and other financial data to his first wife, in order for her to know what her payments should be.

In the files, too, Martha found that John Mitchell hadn't kept up his payments to Mrs. Suyker; neither had he transferred certain insurance policies irrevocably designating her as beneficiary, which also had been agreed to in the separation agreement.

As a result, Mrs. Suyker had taken him to court, in 1972, to collect the back payments. He had settled his claim with her about the time he took out a $150,000 loan. The loan papers, which Martha found in the Mitchells' financial files, were signed by both John and Martha Mitchell. But Martha had no recollection of signing such a document; in fact, she maintained the signature was forged and even told this to the bank making the loan. "I really upset them," Martha reported after her call.

Also, John Mitchell in 1972 had renegotiated a new divorce settlement with Mrs. Suyker, one in which he paid her a lump sum and agreed to pay her $25,000 annually. And he transferred the insurance policies.

In searching their financial files she also found a stack of unpaid bills, including storage fees on their furniture from Rye, which had been put in a warehouse when they went to Washington in 1969. Moreover, they were in arrears on their income tax and Martha cried when she saw that John hadn't paid her dues to American Federation of Television and Radio Artists. She was proud of being a member of AFTRA, which she had had to join when she appeared on *Laugh In.*

Martha was so devastated over losing her AFTRA membership that I called to arrange for her to be reinstated. While talking to a representative I learned that membership included a health-insurance plan plus a life-insurance policy. Neither of us knew at the time how important the insurance would be to Martha later. It paid her hospital bill during her stay at Northern Virginia Doctors Hospital, where her malignant blood condition first was diagnosed. And it paid a large portion of her hospital bill at Memorial Sloan-Kettering Cancer Center during her final days.

Soon Martha found in the files things of interest other than financial and divorce information. On legal-size yellow paper there were pages and pages of notes, in John Mitchell's hand, evidently written when he was preparing testimony for his appearance before the Senate Watergate Committee. Martha spent hours trying to decipher their meaning.

Some of these notes were among the papers Martha gave to the Washington *Post* when the prosecutor's office ignored her calls. A picture of one was printed in the *Post,* in June 1974, with an accompanying story by Carl Bernstein and Bob Woodward. John Mitchell had written: "When I left Committee (7/1) the only documents that were destroyed were personal communications on campaign from R.N. and HRH. All other campaign documents were left in office taken over by MacGregor with exception of material on state committees which was forwarded to state coordinators."

According to Woodward and Bernstein, the notes represented "the first indication that communications from either the President or Haldeman might have been destroyed following the Watergate arrests . . . Although the Senate Watergate hearings produced extensive testimony about the destruction of documents related to the Watergate break-in and Nixon campaign contributions," the article continued, "no testimony was developed suggesting that any material from the President or Haldeman was destroyed at any time."

Mitchell's notes said he destroyed campaign correspondence with "R.N. and HRH," but Martha found several letters and memos from Richard Nixon and Bob Haldeman in the den files—just as she discovered correspondence to and from John Mitchell and John Ehrlichman, J. Edgar Hoover, and others in government, Congress and industry. The notes held a spellbinding fascination for Martha. She spent endless days and nights in the den reading, her mood changing dramatically, depending on the contents of a particular file. Often she'd find a letter or a memorandum that proved she had been correct about a particular statement—often one that had been denied by the White House. Then she'd rush in to me—or telephone if I were home—to gloat: "You ask for proof! Well, here it is. And you didn't believe me!"

In that category was an EYES ONLY memorandum from the President, dated June 6, 1972—eleven days before the Watergate break-in. Martha saw it as proof of her claim that Richard Nixon ran his own campaign. Richard Nixon wrote:

> One of the factors that brought Goldwater down to such a shattering defeat in 1964 was the success of the media in tying him to ultra-right-wing supporters like H. L. Hunt, the John Birch Society, etc. While we will not have the media cooperation in a similar effort directed against McGovern, at least we can try to develop a tactic to the extent that it will sail. For example, the fact that Abby Hoffman, Jerry Rubin, Angela Davis, among others, support McGovern should be widely publicized and used at every point. Here an ad or a piece of literature from a veterans's group might be in order. This must be carefully done but nailing him to his left-wing supporters and forcing him either to repudiate them or to accept their support is essential. In fact, one effective way to operate here is to have a prominent Democrat or Independent, or a veterans' leader or a labor leader, demand by letter or otherwise that McGovern repudiate the support of Abby Hoffman and Jerry Rubin and any others who are well known of this type that you can find. Keep calling on him to repudiate them daily until you finally break through the media blackout into the clear. I consider this a top priority objective.

Also in the files was a joint will prepared by John's lawyers that Martha had refused to sign. "It would give John's kids the right to come in and take my furniture that belonged to my family," Martha claimed. "There would be nothing for Jay."

It worried her to think that her "family heirlooms" would go to anyone but Marty and Jay. One time when she was in Washington, Martha asked her lawyer to send her the correct wording for her to use in preparing a will, in her own handwriting, in which she could leave everything to Jay and Marty. While Junie and I watched, Martha wrote her will. It was left in Junie's possession.

After Martha died, Junie sent a copy of the will to Martha's attorney, now William Herman. As it turned out, the will was not valid in New York, since handwritten wills are valid only under certain conditions, which were not applicable in Martha's case. But the will was valid in Virginia, where it was written, because Martha had assets in the state. She had money in the Burke and Herbert Bank, in Alexandria, where I had opened a savings account for her when shè wanted money outside of New York City "so John can't find out I have it." Nevertheless, the will was never filed for probate, and under New York law Martha, legally the wife of John Mitchell although they had been separated for more than two and a half years, had died intestate.

Chapter Twenty-One

AT SOME POINT MARTHA DECIDED SHE WANTED TO USE THE FILE cabinets in the den for her own records. John Mitchell's papers, she said, could go on the shelves in one of his closets. She was going through the files when she came across four or five folders of classified documents. They must contain important information, Martha reasoned. She asked me what I thought. I didn't know, but Bennie was there that night and I said he'd know, since he's a retired Naval officer who'd had top security clearance.

Bennie was in Marty's sitting room, watching a sports event on television, when I walked in and said, "Martha wants to know if these are important." Still with his eyes on the television, he reached for the files. Suddenly he threw the folders to the floor, unopened, and shouted, "Goddammit, don't ever hand me anything like this again!" The files were so top secret, he didn't want his fingerprints on them.

I didn't know what to do. If Martha knew they were *that* secret, some night when she was mad at John she'd get on the phone and read them to a reporter, and probably get herself into a lot of trouble. On the other hand, I couldn't destroy them. Finally, I walked back to the den, said, "They're nothing," and tossed them on the pile of files to go on the closet shelves.

But I worried about them all night.

It was foolish to waste good shelf space on the files, I told Martha the next morning. Why not put them in cardboard boxes. She thought it a good suggestion. I packed the boxes, carefully putting the classified documents on the bottom of one, and sealed them with heavy, wide tape. Bennie stacked them in a back closet where they stayed for several weeks—until Martha got so mad at John Mitchell she tugged the heavy boxes out, opened them and scattered their contents all over the den floor.

Another time, when she thought John was being unnecessarily difficult, Martha's anger reached a point where she couldn't bear the sight of his portrait on the dining-room wall.

The oil painting, by artist Gloria Schumann, was in a frame so heavy it took two men to hang it. But Martha, alone, removed it from the wall. Then with turpentine and such kitchen supplies as SOS pads, Ajax, Clorox, mayonnaise and Heinz catsup, Martha erased John Mitchell's face from the canvas.

The damaged portrait stood in the butler's room for weeks, until one day, when Philip and Mary Robertson were visiting, Martha asked Philip to dispose of it. After cutting the canvas from the frame and putting it in a large shopping bag, Philip walked into the drawing room where Martha, Mary and Junie Dankworth were sitting and asked, "Anyone want to say good-bye to John?"

"Good-bye, John," said the three women in unison.

Carrying the damaged canvas under his arm, Philip walked down Fifth Avenue to the fashionable Stanhope Hotel, across the street from the Metropolitan Museum, where he placed John Mitchell's distorted portrait in a public trash receptacle.

STILL, MARTHA WAS OBSESSED WITH THE DESIRE TO TALK TO JOHN Mitchell. She sincerely felt all their differences would be solved if only he'd see her. Many of her outrageous acts were reactions to the unbearable frustration she felt over the way he completely ignored her. She called the Essex House almost daily demanding to speak to him. Once Martha even went there to try to find her husband; she created such a furor in the lobby that the hotel security men had to ease her out.

A few weeks earlier I saw Martha coming down the hall, wearing a coat, starting out on another attempt to see John. When I learned where she was headed, I reminded her that she didn't know which room John Mitchell was in or how he was registered; she said she'd go from floor to floor, knocking on every door.

"Looking like that?" I asked. Her slacks and shirt were rumpled and on her bare feet she wore sandals. Her hair was stringing down her back and she wasn't wearing makeup. "You'll look great on the front page of the *News* tomorrow, dressed that way."

She stopped, gave me an angry look, turned and went back to her room.

Bennie asked, "What happened?" I told him Martha was determined to go to the Essex House to find John Mitchell, but I'd tried psychology on her and it had worked.

I'd underestimated Martha.

About thirty minutes later there was a knock on the bedroom door. Martha was in the hall, wearing an attractive dress, a mink coat and high-heeled shoes. Her hair was tucked under a hairpiece and her face expertly made up. "How do I look?" she asked.

"Fantastic," I answered truthfully.

She threw me a triumphant look and stalked out of the apartment.

It couldn't have been more than twenty minutes before Martha rushed in, raced down the hall, calling over her shoulder, "If anyone comes here, even policemen, don't let them in!" She dashed into her room and slammed the door.

Yanking the door open, I went in after her. "What do you mean 'policemen'? What have you done?"

She refused to tell me until I threatened to march the police—or anyone else who might come to the door—right back to her bedroom. Only then did she confess that she'd gone across the street to the garage and had a fight with the attendant when he wouldn't let her take the Mitchell car. She'd rushed back to the apartment when he called the police.

SOON AFTER SHE DISCOVERED THE FILES ON JOHN MITCHELL'S DIVORCE, Martha started complaining that she couldn't reach her lawyer Deede Goodhue. "Some man always answers the phone and says she isn't available," Martha said. Of course, Martha was calling at all hours of the night, and Deede's husband took over answering the telephone to save his wife from having to listen to Martha's endless complaints.

"I need another lawyer," Martha said one day. "This situation is impossible." She had learned that Deede was away for the weekend; Martha thought her problems so urgent they couldn't wait until Monday.

Even when her problems weren't urgent, Martha demanded constant availability of her lawyers, although she often didn't let them know where she was for weeks on end. Sometimes Martha's lawyer would be calling all over the country, trying to find his client when there were important documents to sign, or even once when she was scheduled to appear in court.

The attorney Martha retained following Deede, the third in a series, learned early on that his client was hard to find. Martha had seen him once in his Madison Avenue office, then had arranged for him to come to the apartment to look at the files.

While the attorney and an assistant were in the den, checking various papers and documents, Martha took off for Pine Bluff to spend Thanksgiving with Ray West, Jr. She didn't tell her attorney she was leaving. Nor did she inform her maid of one week.

Mary Casey, a young friend of Junie Dankworth's who was staying at Martha's until her own apartment was available, was left in charge, but with instructions to call me if there were problems. After the attorney left, Mary telephoned to say he'd walked out with four large boxes of materials from the files, but that he "really was upset" when he wanted to speak to Martha about something and learned she not only wasn't in the apartment but she wasn't even in town.

FROM THE TIME MARTHA WROTE THE ONE ENTRY IN HER DIARY, "DEAR Heart," she had said she was writing a book. "I am a sponge," she said. "I have been soaking up material and it's fabulous." And anytime she didn't want to answer a particular question she'd say, "That goes in my book." But she didn't keep notes, record tapes or dictate her thoughts to anyone. Then, sometime in December 1972, Martha asked me to write the book. "You've written so much about me already," she said, "you might as well do this." I said I would. But a few days later she said John Mitchell insisted the book couldn't be published until Nixon was out of the White House.

After John left in September, Martha said she was ready to do the book. She still didn't keep notes or record or dictate her thoughts, saying she had to be questioned in order to have her memory "triggered."

I put a yellow legal pad and pen on her nightstand, just in case her memory was triggered without questioning. She used it once to jot down possible titles for the book; she thought my working title, *Martha, Martha,* too frivolous. She preferred either *The Proud Shall Fall* or *This Is the Way It Was.*

Our first interviews were reviews of things Martha had been telling me since Watergate. They went so well the first few days, I optimistically thought we'd finish within a month to six weeks. Then I planned to talk with people connected with various phases of her life—this would take me to six states, including California, Florida and Arkansas. Of course, I'd interviewed Martha in depth many times for magazine and newspaper articles, and I already had a rather complete background on her—some of this material had been published, some hadn't. And there were my notes from our hours and hours of gossip over the past four years. It looked so easy, I thought I'd be writing by the first of the year.

One of the reasons the interviews were going well was because Martha was easy to question—when she wasn't drinking. She wasn't uptight about her image, as most people are when being interviewed. She had an uncanny memory for detail and a dramatic way of presenting it. And she had a great sense of humor—even when the humor was against her.

Sometimes, though, I found her pixyish humor startling. For instance, the day Julie Eisenhower's story appeared revealing that Richard Nixon often played the piano late at night in the White House, alone and in the dark, I said to Martha, "The first night you sit down at your Hammond organ and play in the dark, I'm going home."

Several days later, at two o'clock in the morning, I awoke to the thunderous sounds of "Nearer My God to Thee," played by Martha, and loud enough to cause the whole apartment to vibrate.

Martha laid down only two restrictions for the book's contents. She didn't want any mention of her drinking. "I don't drink as much as half the people in Washington," she claimed, adding, "and for God's sakes, I never drive when I've had a drink."

Neither did she want any "cuss words" in the book.

"But, Martha," I protested. "That's the way you talk; your conversation is sprinkled with swear words."

"I don't care. I don't want any goddamn cuss words in the book."

She was adamant. No cuss words and no mention of drinking.

When Martha was upset or drinking she wouldn't sit still long enough to answer questions. Neither would she stay off the phone. So when the *Newsweek* story about John's leaving came out, followed by the trouble with her first attorney, our interviews stopped. It was almost two weeks before we again did any significant work.

Interruptions such as these continued throughout our association as author and collaborator. There were other problems, too. One was that Martha was angry with me often. During one period in 1974, she was so "mad" she didn't speak to me for two months. She sent messages. Her attorney would call to say, "Mrs. Mitchell would like to know if you are working on the book." Or Junie might phone to report, "Martha wants to know when 'Winnie is going to finish that goddamn book!' "

SOMETIMES WHEN I WENT TO NEW YORK, PLANNING TO WORK WITH Martha she would be sick with a diverticulitis attack and couldn't work. Occasionally, Martha became so depressed after such an attack that she took to her bed and spent days in her darkened room.

I was sitting beside her bed, during one of her low periods, when she had a violent coughing spell. Martha had a morning cough, which I thought was caused by smoking. Part of it may have been aggravation, but Martha also had a fungal infection in her lungs, which she perversely ignored.

But this particular morning, I talked to her about her "smoker's cough." She was killing herself, I said. And if cigarettes didn't get her, I continued, her drinking would. Instead of being upset with me, as she usually was when drink was mentioned, Martha said, "But what you don't seem to realize, Winnie, is that I'm trying to kill myself."

"Why?" I asked.

"I don't want to live; I have nothing to live for."

"How long have you felt this way."

"A long time. A long, long time."

"Then what stops you from committing suicide, when you threaten to do it?"

"My religion. I don't have the choice. God will take me when He's ready." She repeated, "I don't have the choice."

Martha's doctors say she wanted to live; I don't believe it. Neither does Marta Sweeney, a friend who took Martha into her home the last summer before she died. One day when Marta was mourning the recent and tragic death of her son, Martha said, "Don't mourn for him, Marta. He is fortunate. I wish I could go to sleep and never wake up. All I want is to be in Pine Bluff in a grave alongside my mother."

Another time, when Martha had taken to her bed, I thought she might feel better if we listed the things she wanted, what she hoped to accomplish, the way we'd listed her fears when John left.

Our conversation went something like this:

"Martha, what do you want?"

"I don't want anything. I really don't want anything."

"What are your hopes?"

"I don't hope; I really don't hope."

"If you don't want anything and you have no hopes, you must be ready to give up."

"No, I don't think I am ready to give up. I've never been able to give up."

"Then you must be waiting for something."

"No, I don't think so. It is a very peculiar situation, because I am a nonentity, a person who has all of a sudden become a person who has no meaning. What do you want when you become a person like this?"

"How can you say you're a nonentity when so many people know you and write you such supportive letters?"

"You are a nonentity as far as you yourself are concerned, not as far as the public is concerned."

"Do you really feel you are nothing?"

"I feel I am nothing."

"How do you go on if you feel this way? What keeps you going?"

"My pride, my Southern pride—the fact that I shouldn't have come to the North. It was the war, the Second World War that brought all of this onto me; I never would have been in a predicament like I am if I hadn't been cast into the Second World War and left the South."

I remember thinking that Scott Fitzgerald had said the same thing about his wife Zelda. "She might have been happy with a kind, simple man in a Southern garden," Scott told his daughter Scottie. "She didn't have the strength for the big stage—sometimes she pretended, and pretended beautifully, but she didn't have it . . ."

MARTHA DIDN'T WANT AN AGENT FOR THE BOOK, CLAIMING THERE WASN'T any sense in letting an agent get 10 percent of it when "he wouldn't do any work." Neither would she sign a working contract between us, although her current lawyer thought she should have one and submitted a proposed contract to her. Martha insisted, "We won't cheat each other, Winnie."

We started talking to publishers. Martha wanted these meetings, she said, because it was important that she and the editor of the book were "simpatico." Martha quickly ruled out two women editors, although one was prepared to offer a better contract than anyone else. Martha thought a woman wasn't capable of "handling" her book, just as she thought Deede Goodhue was handicapped by being a woman when dealing with John Mitchell or his lawyer.

The way Martha and I went about selling the book was unique in publishing circles. We didn't show anyone an outline. Martha absolutely refused to let anybody see one, claiming it would be leaked to the press. I didn't argue the point. Since I didn't have a written letter of agreement with Martha, I was content not to have my outline floating around. And had Martha seen it, she might have read it over the phone some night.

So we *talked* to editors about the book, but never in a structured form.

Thomas Congdon, then a senior editor at Doubleday and Company, insisted he had to have something in writing to present to the editorial board. I understood his problem. One day, Tom and I sat down, and I told him the basic outline—where the book started, how it developed and many of the anecdotes it would contain. He wrote his own outline. Later he'd tell a columnist that it read like a "Gothic novel." He compared Martha to a Victoria Holt heroine "beset by sinister forces, some of which she could perceive, some of which she could not perceive."

Martha had been right about not giving out an outline; Tom's was leaked to the press—to the late Joyce Illig, a book columnist—not by Tom, but by someone unknown.

After a lot of pressure and pleading, Joyce didn't print the outline. But Martha heard about its contents and didn't speak to me for several days. I had mentioned her drinking while talking to Tom; he wrote about it in his outline.

Before Martha and I reached an agreement with any of the publishers interested in the book, she told me she couldn't sign a contract until her financial arrangements with John Mitchell were settled. A week or so later, Martha said she'd changed her mind; she wanted a contract *now.* Martha did this several times, and invariably her decisions to have the book published were made when she was upset with John Mitchell.

From the first, Bennie said Martha never would sign a contract. He felt she couldn't write the book she wanted to write and ever expect her husband to come back. "She still wants John Mitchell," Bennie would say. "So she isn't burning any bridges behind her."

I didn't agree. But following Martha's death, one of her attorneys said the same thing. She not only wouldn't sell the book, he said, but she wouldn't let any of her attorneys start divorce proceedings. Her financial problems could have been solved, satisfactorily, in the divorce courts, he claimed. Martha could have had the apartment and substantial alimony: "But she still loved John Mitchell. She wanted him back."

Although Martha wasn't ready to sign a contract, she still wanted me to work on the book, saying it then would be ready when she'd sign, which would be after working out a financial settlement with John Mitchell. In that case, I said, I'd have to continue writing magazine articles and only work on her book between other commitments, and then only on a first draft, which I'd update when she signed a contract.

Martha said she understood. But when I was writing about someone else, she constantly interrupted me. Once, when I was on deadline, and she knew it, Martha called me eighteen times in one evening.

SINCE SHE WOULDN'T SIGN A BOOK CONTRACT, MARTHA, TOO, NEEDED another source of income. John Mitchell only sporadically deposited her household money in the bank; the bills were not being paid either. Martha constantly worried about her furniture in storage. Eventually she had to pay the overdue storage charges to keep the company from putting her possessions up for auction. She wrote her last check to the storage company from her hospital bed a few weeks before she died.

Yet with all her financial problems, Martha refused to accept any of the dozens of offers she had from magazines and newspapers, claiming her "secrets" were reserved for her book.

The cluttered condition of the apartment also distressed Martha more each day. The workmen she'd called back to finish their projects had walked out after John Mitchell notified the contractor that he wouldn't be responsible for their pay.

The problems of both the money and the clutter could be solved easily, I told Martha. If I finished the *Ladies' Home Journal* article about her redecorating the apartment—the story John Mitchell had been vetoing for months—I was sure the *Journal* would send a crew to put the apartment in order, otherwise they couldn't take the pictures needed to illustrate the article.

To get her some fast money, I said, I could write a magazine story telling what she thought of Washington society. I had a thick folder of remarks Martha had made to me on the subject, gathered during our many interviews and conversations but never printed. If I wrote that story for Martha, in the first person, she could stop worrying about money for a little while.

Martha thought both articles would be "great." Then, in reference to the *Journal* story, she asked if sometimes magazines didn't give a contribution to the favorite charity of the person being written about. I said yes, that had been done; what charity did she have in mind? "Martha Mitchell," she answered.

Martha received her "charity" money from the *Journal* and a check from *McCall's* for the article, "My Life in Nixon's Washington." Martha didn't deposit the checks in her regular account since "John Mitchell will know about them." The Chase Manhattan Bank, where Martha had her checking account, continued to send her bank statements to John Mitchell, even though Martha had repeatedly asked that they be sent to her. So Martha opened another checking account one block away at the Security National Bank. At the same time she rented a safety-deposit box, in which she put many of the papers from the files in the den; these included anything with Richard Nixon's signature, which she said she planned to sell to an autograph collector.

Chapter Twenty-Two

As much as Martha loved her apartment and the security it gave her, she couldn't stay there for any length of time without having to get away. Shortly after John left, Martha visited Junie Dankworth in Arlington, Virginia, just across the Potomac from Washington. Although Martha was there six days, she didn't call the press or make an effort to see any friend except me. She seemed content just to relax and talk with Junie and her family.

Then, in November, Martha flew to Arkansas to spend Thanksgiving with her cousin Ray West. And no sooner was she back in New York than she started worrying about Christmas. She claimed she couldn't survive it alone. Marty was still refusing to see her mother, and at the time the relationship between Martha and Jay wasn't good either. This had come about when Jay wouldn't agree with Martha on Watergate. He didn't accept her "facts," neither did he believe in Nixon's guilt. Jay felt everything Nixon did might have been within the powers of the presidency. And in turn, if it was within the President's powers to order the break-in (if, indeed, he did order it), then it was within his powers to direct the men who carried out the orders. Such views were maddening to Martha.

When Jay visited at the Fifth Avenue apartment, shortly before John

Mitchell left, there were times when Martha felt he sided with John against her. It was several days after her husband walked out before Martha would even telephone her son, at the University of Mississippi where he was studying law.

WHAT WAS I DOING FOR CHRISTMAS? MARTHA ASKED. BENNIE AND I WERE taking M'Liz and Charles Beardsley, our daughter and son-in-law, and their two children, Sean, 11, and Colin, 8 months, to Williamsburg for an eighteenth-century Christmas. Martha said she'd go along.

I explained that it was impossible. We were driving down in their station wagon, and there wasn't room for another person. Then Martha wanted to know what my friend Clare Crawford was doing for Christmas. About a week before, after hearing about our Christmas plans, Clare also had made reservations for herself and her two children at Williamsburg. Martha said she'd go with Clare and immediately phoned to inform her.

Clare wasn't happy. It would be the first Christmas since she and her first husband had separated; at best it would be difficult for her children, Victor, 8, and Charlene, 6. Clare thought they might resent having a stranger share their holiday. But as Clare later said, what could she do? Martha went with her to Williamsburg.

As soon as they reached the inn, Martha took to her bed and kept room service busy delivering individual orders of Scotch; because of Virginia laws the inn couldn't sell liquor by the bottle. But Martha didn't get loud or belligerent, as I fully expected her to do. She was quiet and sad; she looked like a lonely child, propped up in bed in her ruffled nightgown with her hair hanging loose. The rest of us took turns sitting with her from the time she awakened in the morning until late at night.

In her conversations with me, Martha wasn't critical of anyone. She didn't blame Richard Nixon for her unhappy situation, as she had before and would later. She just talked of Christmases past, including the last one with John Mitchell, and how happy they had been. She could recall every Christmas present John Mitchell had given her. Often, she said, he let her know what her present was going to be by enclosing, with an affectionate note, a picture of a mink coat, silver tea service or something else he thought she would like, which she could then go and pick out herself.

According to Martha, this Christmas of 1973 was the only miserable one in her life.

Martha left her room only two times—once for our "family" Christmas dinner, and again the next day when she insisted on going to a toy store with the three older children, "so they can pick out their own Christmas presents from me."

Back in Arlington with Junie, with Christmas over, Martha's mood changed. She happily went to holiday parties at Philip and Mary Robertson's and with the Dankworths or Bennie and me. She went out to lunch —one day with me to the Sans Souci, where she was greeted warmly by other Washington celebrities, such as Art Buchwald, Jack Valenti, Pat Nixon's press secretary Helen Smith, and former Senator Eugene McCarthy, who called her "Martha, doll." All of this was reported by the press. But when she and Junie lunched at the Jockey Club it went unnoticed that two women with close Nixon ties were their companions. They were Nancy Lamberding—then with the State Department's Office of Protocol and later social secretary in the Ford White House—and Nancy Chotiner, wife of long-time Nixon political crony Murray Chotiner. Soon after, when Murray Chotiner, who was killed a few months later in a freak automobile accident, called to wish Martha and the Dankworths a Happy New Year, Martha was asleep. "Tell Martha that's the way to start the New Year," Chotiner prophetically advised. "If she stays asleep she won't know how horrible 1974 is."

Martha also went to the Laurel Race Course with Bennie and me and sat at a corner table in the President's Lounge quietly handicapping the horses. She said she'd learned about horse racing by going to the track at Hot Springs, Arkansas, "from the time I was a child." Evidently Martha learned well: she won every race. Following one, she went to the winner's circle to present a trophy to the jockey who rode her horse to victory. Other guests in the President's Lounge were charmed with Martha; one said she thought Martha had been maligned by the press. "She is not outspoken and gregarious," the woman insisted. "Mrs. Mitchell is quiet, still and reticent."

The day after New Year's, Martha flew to Florida to visit her Miami University sorority sister Alma Jane McCauley and her husband. She planned to stay three weeks, but she came back early because they tried to limit her drinking and disconnected the phone at bedtime—all for her own good. Martha complained that her old friends had turned into "health-food faddists." Alma Jane laughs at this description, saying they served steaks, salads and lots of vegetables.

BY MID-JANUARY MARTHA SEEMED TO HAVE PULLED HERSELF TOGETHER. She was working around the apartment and getting her wardrobe in order. She even gave her first seated dinner in the dining room, where the portraits of John and Martha flanked the carved Carrara marble mantel. There were only four of us at the long table—Martha, *Ladies' Home Journal* articles editor Mary Fiore (now managing editor of *Good Housekeeping* magazine), Bennie and me. Martha planned and cooked the excellent meal.

Also at this time our interviews were coming along nicely. And Martha had started thinking about her future. We went over and over her various offers and talked with some of the people who'd made them.

David Frost wanted to interview her in London; Tom Snyder of the *Tomorrow* show wanted to do the same in Los Angeles. Martha wanted to do both, if I'd go with her. I said I would. We started working on the arrangements.

WTTG-TV's *Panorama* show, in Washington, asked Martha to be a guest. She didn't want to be interrogated by the capital press but said she'd "turn the tables and interview them." *Panorama* asked her to co-host the show for a week.

And, again, she said she was ready to sign a book contract. We worked out the details of a contract with Ellis Amburn of Delacorte, and the proposed contract, which Martha said she liked, had just been approved by her lawyer (at this point, Martin R. Gold) when she surprised all of us by saying she wanted an agent. She had resisted having one for months. Why now? Because, Martha said, a friend had told her she should have one and recommended lawyer/agent Paul Gitlin, whose clients included Harold Robbins, Gay Talese and the late Cornelius Ryan.

By mid-February I was through with my interviews with Martha and had set dates for seeing her friends and relatives in other states. I sent Paul a letter, saying that I could start writing the minute he had a contract. (Ellis Amburn had withdrawn his bid.) But Paul never had a chance to negotiate a contract to present to us—not after Martha went on the *Today* show.

Martha's disastrous appearance on the *Today* show followed a series of events that started when Martha read an item in the New York *Post* that said John Mitchell had taken Marty out of her school. Martha's attorney called the school and was told the item wasn't true. Marty was there. In fact, the school spokesman said, Marty was having two teeth pulled the following day.

Evidently there had been previous discussions about the teeth, and according to Martha, her dentist had advised against the extractions. She was terribly upset. Before the night was over, Martha was in hysterics and drinking heavily, and her doctor was trying to reach John Mitchell to discuss Marty's teeth.

At some point that night, Martha called the New York *Post* to complain about an earlier article, in which a friend of John's had said Martha had been "of little solace to him when he needed her the most."

"I can't even find him, talk to him, see him," Martha complained to the *Post.* "I've done everything in my power to get to this man . . ."

The next day Martha was even more distressed. Hoping to get her mind off Marty's teeth and braces, I started talking about various requests for interviews that had come in to me for her. Among them was a message from Clare Crawford who wanted to interview her for *People* magazine.

She reminded me angrily that she had told Clare, several days before, that she would not give her an interview for *People.* Since I knew it, why would I "put this on" her now? Our conversation ended in a shouting match.

Martha called Clare, intending to tell her not to send her any more messages. Instead, she talked to Clare for almost two hours, telling her the whole story about life in the apartment before and after John left. She also invited Clare to come up that night to stay with her. And the next morning photographer Alfred Eisenstaedt came to the apartment to take pictures of Martha to illustrate the *People* article.

Ladies' Home Journal, which had been promised exclusive picture rights to Martha's apartment for its March issue, heard about the pictures for *People* before the day was out. Mary Fiore called me and sent Martha a hand-delivered note. The calls back and forth on this went on for days, with nothing being solved. Then Martha saw an advance copy of *People.*

NOTHING THAT HAD HAPPENED IN THE PAST TEN DAYS HAD ANGERED Martha as much as the *People* cover. The picture of Martha showed her with bags under her eyes, her lipstick smeared and her face swollen. Martha claimed the photographer deliberately "doctored the picture to make me look bad." Inside the magazine the pictures were no better.

As she read the article, Martha's fury switched from the photographer to Clare. Martha was quoted as saying, "I haven't had a drink since God knows when. . . . I have used drink to overcome some problems, but now that I've gotten medication—a minor tranquilizer—I don't drink."

Martha claimed the quote was "a goddamn lie."

She said the same about a quote she made about John Mitchell: "He was drinking and taking tranquilizers. There were nights our daughter Marty and I and the maid had to drag him to bed.

"I'd never say such a thing about my husband," Martha cried. I reminded her she had said the same thing to both Junie and me several times. Now she was angry with me, claiming it was my fault that she'd given the *People* interview. If I hadn't delivered Clare's message, she said, she wouldn't have known about it.

When I reminded her I'd always delivered her messages, Martha said, "Next time someone calls you tell them I run my own business and if they want to communicate with me they can write me at 1030 Fifth Avenue. Tell them you are just my biographer—or whatever the hell they call you."

She called back to say she had talked to Barbara Walters and that she was going on "national television to go down the *People* article, point by point, and show everyone where Clare lied."

When Paul Gitlin heard about it, he called Martha to advise her "not to go on the air and say for free what's going to be in the book." And Dr. Lorand told her to think about it first.

Before the day was out, Paul Gitlin talked two or three times to Barbara Walters, who was unhappy with him for telling Martha to stay off the show. By now *Today* was promoting Martha's upcoming appearance. Two publishers Paul had been negotiating with for the book called to say they would be watching Martha on TV.

Finally Paul agreed that Martha could go on the show but insisted that the questions be limited to "feminine stuff, no Watergate, and nothing from the book."

Martha was up all night worrying about the show; by now she didn't want to do it but was afraid of what Barbara Walters "might say about me if I don't." She went on. It was a fiasco.

Martha obviously was in no condition to appear before a live television audience. And the questions weren't the "feminine stuff" she'd been told to expect. Martha rambled in her answers and did her best to stonewall it.

But Barbara repeatedly asked her what she knew about the Administration activities, until at one point Martha answered, "Barbara, you can't say that I know anything . . . I am now so confused about what I have read and what I have heard and what I have seen that I could not be a good witness, not in the slightest."

"Do you think the President should be impeached?" Barbara asked.

"I have no idea whether the President should be impeached! I couldn't answer that," Martha replied.

Barbara also asked Martha, "When people say Martha Mitchell is an alcoholic, Martha Mitchell drinks too much, is that so?"

"In my explanation, no . . . I am not . . . I assure you I am not," she said. Martha added that falsely being called insane and alcoholic was "the normal thing the White House puts out about people they want to discard."

Newsday reported that Martha "sounded completely incoherent. She was so bad, insiders at NBC were saying that it had not been kind of Barbara to put a woman in that condition on a national show."

A few hours after the show, Paul Gitlin gamely told Judith Martin of the Washington *Post,* "She behaved like a lady—I don't know what more you're supposed to do on the *Today* show."

The two publishers Gitlin had been negotiating with watched the show, and as far as I know never again seriously considered offering a contract for the book. And within a few weeks, Paul no longer was Martha's agent.

"I'M IN WORSE SHAPE THAN I WAS SIX MONTHS AGO," MARTHA LAMENTED shortly after her *Today* appearance. She didn't have a lawyer. No one was bidding on the book. She couldn't find out anything about Marty—where she spent her weekends, how she survived the dental surgery. One night Martha reported her "missing" and sent police out looking for her.

Also, she was so sick she had a nurse in attendance. Martha was in pain with diverticulitis and an infected tooth. Probably the first signs that Martha had a major physical problem were her recurrent toothaches. As early as 1973 a New York dentist told Martha he saw signs indicating she should have a complete physical. Again in mid-1974 another New York dentist told her essentially the same thing. He refused to work on her teeth unless she saw a medical doctor. Martha did not take the dentists' advice; when her dental pain became too severe she medicated herself, with codeine.

But in March 1974, Martha was less worried about her teeth than her other difficulties, which included the unpaid bills—representing thousands of dollars and now arriving with threatening notes.

I went to New York for five days to help get her affairs in order.

Although Martha had said she would appear on *Panorama* and Tom Snyder's *Tomorrow,* she had been reluctant to set dates for either. There also were other requests she'd been temporizing on. Now we arranged for her to co-host *Panorama* the week of April first. On the sixteenth we would fly to California, where she'd tape the *Tomorrow* show. And in May we'd go to Alabama to interview Cornelia Wallace for *McCall's* magazine. I thought that would keep her busy while also providing the money she so badly needed.

And even though she wouldn't be paid for it, Martha said she'd be one of the celebrities at a Counter-Gridiron carnival the night after her *Panorama* week ended. It was being staged by many of her Washington press friends to raise money for the Reporters' Committee for Freedom of the Press, while serving as a protest against the annual white-tie dinner given by the Gridiron Club, then an all-male fifty-member journalism society.

The *Panorama* staff and its viewers were enchanted with Martha. She was as uninhibited in her questions as she'd always been in her answers. And she thoroughly enjoyed herself. When asked to give the weather report, Martha read, "Fifty-two degrees at National Airport, relative humidity sixty-one percent, the wind south at eight miles per hour, the barometer twenty-eight point nine." Then, laughing uproariously, she asked, "What does that mean? Does that mean it's not going to rain? It doesn't mean a thing to me . . ."

Martha worried about doing a good job. Before saying she'd go on the show she'd made me promise I'd help her. Now she did her homework. Every night we talked for one or two hours about the next day's guests, forming questions and gleaning enough material from a new book (which she never received more than eighteen hours before airtime) for Martha to discuss it intelligently with the author, even though she hadn't read it. She was a quick study, and I watched every day's show to hear her repeat word for word the questions and statements I'd coached her on the night before.

As far as I know, Martha didn't drink that week. She went to bed early and was up each morning in plenty of time for a leisurely breakfast. As the show's host Maury Povich said, she was "Great, just great."

Dozens of people called the station wanting her for an interview, a speech or an appearance on another television program. Charles Ashman, who later co-authored the book, *Martha: The Mouth That Roared,* asked her to do a television show the next week in Toronto, Canada. She said she would if I'd go with her. We made arrangements to fly to Toronto on Monday.

Martha also was a tremendous success at the Counter-Gridiron, so much so that ultraliberal members of the press were surprised to find themselves confiding that they *liked* her. Former Attorney General Elliot Richardson sold autographed copies of his famous doodles, Watergate prosecutor Jill Wine Volner and CBS's Dan Rather ran a booth selling nonsexist chocolate kisses, former Senator Eugene McCarthy ran the ring toss, and White House lawyer Leonard Garment played the clarinet in a dance combo.

But the superstar was Martha. Patiently sitting in her phone booth, she cheerfully called anybody anyplace in the world for five dollars plus the long-distance charges. People lined up twelve deep to place their calls and to listen via an intercom to the two-way conversation. Some unfamiliar with Martha's pixie sense of humor were amazed at what their calls brought forth. CBS correspondent Fred Graham, who paid for a call to the Arkansas *Gazette,* had to dash to a pay phone to set things straight after hearing Martha tell a *Gazette* editor that she would be running against Senator J. William Fulbright in the fall election. Sometimes the shocks came from those Martha called. Congressman John Brademas's elderly Greek mother, reached at her home in Indiana, told Martha, "I want you to know some of us think Tricky Dicky is the worst ever." Martha told her she had "a lot of company."

Martha loved it. She could have gone on all night, and probably would have if there hadn't been a closing time. Martha was wound up, like an entertainer coming off stage—which she was, and had been, all week. Around eleven o'clock we took her to Agostino's, a popular Washington restaurant, where she met Hal Gould, Helen Thomas and her husband Douglas Cornell for a late supper.

From Agostino's Martha and her party went on to the Junkanoo, a Caribbean nightclub, where she danced with friends and strangers until three-thirty in the morning.

Still she wasn't ready to quit. Hal and a friend went back with her to her Wardman Tower suite, where they talked until after dawn. Even then, as her guests said good-bye, Martha claimed, "I could keep going; I feel like I've got my second wind."

MARTHA AWAKENED THE NEXT AFTERNOON FEELING "DOWN IN THE dumps," probably because she was suffering a letdown after her week on stage and her night on the town. As the day went on she became more depressed and she started drinking heavily. Sometime during the night she called Junie to come stay with her, claiming she was afraid to stay alone. Martha was up all night.

Between the two of us, Junie and I got Martha packed and to the airport for the flight to Canada. Martha didn't eat lunch on the plane; she drank. And from the number of times she rummaged around in her cosmetic case, I suspected she was taking Valium, Librium or a similar pill. I had learned about the drug supply in her cosmetic case one night when Martha had gone into hysterics and threatened to kill herself. I called Dr. Lorand, who asked what sedative medicines she had on hand. When I told him Martha said she didn't have such drugs, he said, "She has something. Look for it." I made a fruitless search of the medicine cabinet; then I saw the cosmetic case on the bathroom floor and discovered that it contained several vials of capsules and tablets—Valium, Librium, codeine, Seconal, among others. There wasn't any makeup in the case.

On the first night in Canada, Martha was belligerent and noisy and as far as I know she didn't go to sleep at all. But when Charles Ashman and the show's producer Norman Baer came to see her around noon, Martha was a charming Southern belle. She also did well that night on the show *Anything Goes.*

I talked at length with Martha after we got back to the suite. We couldn't travel together again, I said, or we would wind up bitter enemies. I suggested that when she taped the *Tomorrow* show, and later went to England for the David Frost interview, she should have her companion Maggie Hogan go with her. (Maggie had been hired by Martha after two maids had proven unsatisfactory; she came through a nurses' bureau recommended by Dr. Lorand. Maggie was the first of several companions the bureau sent to Martha.)

Martha protested, saying people would think she was "crazy for sure" if she traveled with a nurse. I reminded her that no one, except Dr. Lorand and I, knew that Maggie wasn't a typical maid. She hadn't even told Junie. Finally Martha said she'd take Maggie. For the next six months it was a perfect arrangement. Maggie took care of her beautifully. It wasn't easy, and sometimes Maggie had to call Junie or me for support, but she was a better traveling companion for Martha than I was.

Pamela Burke, of the *Tomorrow* staff, remembers that Martha was a huge success on the show: "Basically she was a great actress. Offstage, off camera, she was in this total dither . . . then she got on, and she was just as calm and comfortable and well mannered, you'd never know the agony she went through backstage. She was an actress."

Martha loved Tom Snyder and Pam Burke; she added them to her ever-growing list of media phone-pals, to be called in time of crisis or sometimes just to chat.

Often Pam tried, unsuccessfully, to get Martha back on the show. Then there came a time when Martha demanded to be on and Pam was hard put to keep her off. Martha heard that Jeb and Gail Magruder were being interviewed by Tom Snyder; she thought she should be on the show, too, to challenge him about things he'd said about her in his book. Or as Martha put it: ". . . to meet Jeb Magruder face-to-face and let people know he is a goddamn liar."

Before leaving for California, Martha had arranged to meet with attorney Melvin Belli in Los Angeles. She was firmly convinced that all New York lawyers were friendly to John Mitchell; and if not friendly "John can get to them." Also, she wanted a name "big enough not to be afraid of the Administration." And, she claimed, her other lawyers hadn't been mean enough; she thought the flamboyant Belli would be.

After talking to Belli in Los Angeles, Martha was ecstatic that he was "going to take care of my problems. And he's doing it for nothing." I questioned that. But she insisted it was true. Actually, what their letter of agreement said was that Belli and his law firm would receive "fees and costs expended by way of court award from [her] husband."

The letter also stated that Belli and the firm agreed "to be available to you at all times to counsel you and to represent you with respect to all other matters which may arise, separate and distinct from those matters hereinabove set forth and shall receive for their services in this regard fees which will be agreed upon as such matters arise."

Martha, who loved intrigue, almost had too much of it in her first few days as Belli's client. After taping the *Tomorrow* show she had gone from Los Angeles to Phoenix to visit a long-time friend, and one of Belli's investigators went there to accompany Martha to New York. She was afraid to fly alone.

In New York, Martha was taken to the Plaza Hotel, which is on Fifth Avenue, only fifteen blocks from her apartment. One of her attorneys says this was done because Martha didn't want to go home for fear there would be press outside the building.

Meanwhile, Martha's companion Maggie, who had come back to New York when Martha stopped at Phoenix, was at the apartment—by now frantic because Martha hadn't arrived when expected.

About midnight Martha called me with an incredible tale about Belli's associate taking her to the Plaza Hotel, where Mel Belli and several other lawyers had dinner in her suite and discussed her future. She said she sneaked out after the men left. Martha had been in such a hurry to get away she'd left her luggage.

All during the telling of the story Martha kept saying, "I don't know why they took me there!" Most likely Martha was having one of her alcohol-induced mental blackouts—on the flight to New York, according to a witness, she had eleven martinis.

A FEW DAYS LATER MARTHA SAW A PICTURE IN THE NEW YORK *Daily News* of her husband in an animated conversation with his secretary. According to the *News,* John Mitchell had been dining with "his pretty secretary, Sandy Hobbs, who was [seen] kissing him enthusiastically at a party celebrating his court victory last weekend." (Both John Mitchell and Maurice Stans had been found innocent by the Vesco trial jury.) It was too much for Martha. She went to bed with a severe attack of gastritis. Junie Dankworth left for New York to be with her.

Martha learned, a day or two later, that Belli had been suspended from practicing law for thirty days because he'd appeared in a liquor advertisement. He couldn't see her or talk with her; she could communicate only with his associates, principally New York attorney Richard Creditor. Martha just went to pieces. Again she threatened to kill herself.

"You may have the perfect goddamn ending for your story," Martha called to tell me before running to the window, raising it and threatening to jump out. Junie Dankworth talked her back. This went on for hours. Suddenly Martha took the phone from Junie—who had called me for help—and said, "Winnie, we've been through hell together and we'll go on!" She paused and added, "Isn't it strange you've also been through this with [a friend of mine who was suicidal]?" Martha said she'd help my friend straighten out her life and even offered to raise her child. Martha hung up to call the friend and offer her services.

In the meantime, Melvin Belli was interviewed by Maxine Cheshire. Belli told the columnist that "a process server is looking for" John Mitchell "at this very moment." Martha would ask for $2,500 a week maintenance, Belli added. He also said Martha would seek custody of Marty, and he revealed that he had wired John Mitchell asking for a meeting but there was no answer. The next step would be to learn what Mitchell's assets were.

"Because Mrs. Mitchell thinks her husband may have a Swiss bank account," Belli said, he planned to take a deposition regarding that allegation.

Martha was upset to see in the *Post* parts of her confidential conversation with her attorney. But when Belli called and told her the information was released "to get a reaction from Mitchell," Martha decided it would "scare the hell" out of John Mitchell.

It didn't.

Again he refused to discuss financial support of any kind unless certain conditions were reached. Among other things, he wanted to sell the apartment, pay off the $150,000 loan (the one Martha claimed contained her forged signature) and then discuss a payment to Martha. He also insisted that she sign a joint federal income-tax form for 1973. Martha had filed a separate 1973 tax form for income she had received in December for two magazine articles. Now John Mitchell wanted her to sign an amended joint return—a blank one. She would not be allowed to see how much income he reported; neither would she have any way of knowing if it was an accurate accounting of his income. Martha refused and sought advice from a childhood friend, Donald Alexander, Commissioner of Internal Revenue. Alexander or someone in his office told her not to sign a return if she didn't know its contents, since she could be held liable for any inaccuracies in the return. Yet John Mitchell's lawyers were still insisting as late as 1975 that she file an amended return.

Finally, in July, Martha's lawyers started proceedings for a separation suit in Manhattan Supreme Court. Marvin Segal, whose law firm represented John Mitchell, told newsmen: "This is a kind of friendly proceeding. There is no rancor between them, no ill feelings on either side . . ." Nothing could have been further from the truth.

A day or two after the suit was filed, a Mitchell friend leaked to Maxine Cheshire that Martha's phone bills "sometimes were into five figures," and claimed that Mitchell had "been providing for her adequately . . ." But when her attorney Richard Creditor took the case to court in October, he said John Mitchell was $2,000 behind in a $350-a-week payment he had agreed to pay. A month later Martha was awarded $1,000 a week; she had asked for $3,000.

A thousand dollars a week sounds like a lot. In Martha's case it wasn't. By the time she paid her income tax and maintenance her lawyers figured she would have less than $70 a week. The previous temporary settlement Deede Goodhue had reached—of $350 a week with John Mitchell paying the bills—was a better one for Martha. The trouble with it was that John didn't always pay the $350, or the bills. At the time the $1,000-a-week settlement was reached, the unpaid bills included groceries, medicines, telephone (eight months past due), limousine rental and storage on furniture and furs.

Martha was frantic to get the apartment in her name. She said it was the only "solid" thing she had; she thought she could rent it for enough money to live on. John had proved he couldn't be depended on to pay her temporary alimony, so what could she expect once he went to jail and his only set income, according to what her lawyers could find out, was his government pension?

At the time of the settlement, John Mitchell's gross income was listed as about $5,281 a week. But in the November 11 issue of *New York* magazine, Dan Dorfman wrote that John Mitchell had three checking accounts in one bank totaling around $140,000. One account, he said, had maintained a monthly balance since February of $100,000; "and from then right on through September, ten large deposits were made in this account totaling $220,000." Dorfman admitted he didn't know where the money came from. He also noted that Martha's checking account in the same bank, as of October 8, was $1,299 overdrawn.

Richard Creditor called me soon after Martha had retained the Belli firm to say Mel Belli wanted to see me. Since I'd be in New York the next week, we arranged to meet at five-thirty P.M. the following Monday, in the Oyster Bar of the Plaza Hotel. I asked Bennie to go with me. When we arrived Mel Belli and his young son were eating an early dinner before going on to a sporting event. Richard Creditor and two other men were at the table with Belli.

That morning Martha had warned me not to talk to Belli about the book. She said she'd asked him to help with her numerous business offers, but that she didn't want to pay him for helping sell something she thought everyone was eager to buy. Later I'd learn that she hadn't informed Belli of her decision.

Bennie and I sat down at the table with Belli and his associates, and ordered drinks. As soon as the waiter left, Belli asked, "What can I do for you?"

"Nothing," I answered.

He looked surprised. Didn't I need help on the book, he wanted to know? No, I said, it was in good shape. How about help in finding a publisher? That was no problem, I answered.

From that point on, the conversation went nowhere and as soon as he'd finished his dinner, Belli and his son left.

I wasn't surprised a few days later when Martha told me that Mel Belli wanted her to get another writer.

Chapter Twenty-Three

IN MID-MAY MARTHA AND I FLEW TO MONTGOMERY, ALABAMA, FOR *McCall's* magazine, to do a Cornelia Wallace interview (scheduled before I told Martha we couldn't travel together). As usual, Martha was nervous about flying. She was especially frightened when we changed to a small plane in Atlanta. The trip to Montgomery was rough, and between martinis Martha sent messages to the pilot to "stop hitting those air pockets." Martha often sent instructions to airline pilots. One of her college friends, the wife of the senior pilot of an international airline, says Martha sometimes told the pilots of her husband's airline that she'd "tell Jim Smith [not his real name] if you don't fly this plane more carefully." One sent word back to her that "this is the way Jim told me to fly the plane. It's the way he would do it." Martha was content.

Surprisingly, Martha was friendly with me during the whole trip, perhaps because she and Junie had been fighting, so bitterly that Martha had moved from the Dankworths' house to a hotel. Today I was her "only friend in the world." Junie was the one who'd "sold out to Mitchell."

Cornelia and Martha had met before, one afternoon at Key Biscayne in January 1973, in the house owned by Bebe Rebozo, where the Mitchells were spending the holidays. Later, John and Martha went to the Key Biscayne Hotel for a dinner celebrating the Wallaces' second wedding anniversary.

By the time the evening was over, Cornelia and Martha were like "lifelong friends." They both agreed it wasn't just their Southern heritage that "made things click" between them; it was also the empathy they both felt for another political dirty-tricks victim.

The day Martha and I went to the Governor's Mansion to interview Cornelia, the two talked almost exclusively about dirty tricks. The first time she knew there was "hanky-panky going on in the Nixon Administration," Martha told Cornelia, was when she heard they were sending money to Alabama to defeat Wallace in the 1970 gubernatorial primaries. (According to Senate Watergate testimony, $400,000 was given to his opponent.) "I was so mad, I laid John Mitchell low," Martha said. "I told him it was a poor game they were playing if money was the only thing that talked. I said I thought they should get their candidates elected in the proper form, in a gentlemanly way."

Martha felt the same way, she added, about their paying money to the Wallace campaign official who "sold out to Nixon." Cornelia asked who that was; Martha gave a name.

Cornelia looked shocked. She turned to me and ordered, "Turn off that tape!" Martha gave her the details of how she had listened to many conversations John had had about the Wallace defector with various people at the White House and Justice. Cornelia said they always had suspected someone but hadn't known who it was.

We had to stop the morning interview when George Wallace, in a wheelchair, came into the room. He and Martha, who called him "sweetie," were talking when I heard him say to her, "Let me tell you something. When you've got your health—and you've got yours, you may think you don't have it good and you may be a little nervous at times—but when you've got your health, and you can walk and you can cross that leg and raise that toe . . ." His voice trailed off before he added, "You take my place and I'll take yours, then I can walk out of here . . . being in good health is being a multimillionaire."

Later I asked Cornelia if she or the Governor were bitter about the attempt on his life, in May 1972, when Arthur Bremer shot the Governor, leaving him paralyzed from the waist down. The bullet not only shattered Wallace's spine but his hopes for the Democratic presidential nomination. Cornelia said neither she nor her husband was bitter.

"I'm bitter," Martha said, "about what happened to me in California."

THE WALLACES GAVE A DINNER PARTY FOR MARTHA THAT NIGHT AND invited about thirty guests, including a girlhood friend from Pine Bluff and Charlie and Alleta Saunders, who flew in from Mississippi. Since George Wallace, a teetotaler, didn't allow alcohol to be served at the Mansion, toasts were made with nonalcoholic Catawba wine, served in tall-stemmed crystal goblets. More than one guest was unhappy with a whole dinner party without drinks, Martha among them. But she was quite charming to the Governor. Martha took the attitude that the two had much in common, since both had been victims of conspiracies.

George Wallace, like most Southerners, is a great *raconteur*, as were two or three of his male guests. As the evening wore on, the men told one funny story after another, more or less monopolizing the evening. "Poor Martha," said one guest. "She doesn't have a chance."

But Martha didn't want to entertain. She wanted a drink, as did several others, including Cornelia's mother, Ruby Folsom Ellis Austin. The sister of former Alabama Governor James ("Kissin' Jim") Folsom, Big Ruby—as she is known throughout the state—is a friendly, flamboyant, fascinating woman who doesn't deny that she likes partying and drinking.

Following the dinner, which ended about eleven o'clock, Big Ruby took Martha and me to a party at Will and Ruth Waller's house; he was the Governor's doctor and Ruth was from Pine Bluff. I left the party about one A.M.; Martha, who was having a good time with old friends, got in around four. She wasn't happy at having to get up five hours later to go to the Governor's Mansion, where New York photographer Otto Storch was waiting to take pictures of her with Cornelia.

Again, Cornelia asked us to have lunch with her and the Governor, but Big Ruby said we were eating with her at a downtown café. Cornelia took me aside to say she didn't want her mother and Martha going to that particular place, since it was primarily a cocktail lounge. She called Mr. G's, a restaurant on the outskirts of town, and made reservations. A state trooper, Clark McCord, took us there in a state limousine.

The four of us walked into Mr. G's and immediately were whisked into a private room—one large enough for a banquet. It was what Mrs. Wallace had requested, the waiter said.

Soon Big Ruby, a dramatic storyteller, was revealing intimate details of the time Cornelia talked her into entering a Florida clinic specializing in the treatment of people with drinking problems. I was so fascinated with her tale, I asked, "Do you mind if I tape this?"

"Hell, no!" said Big Ruby.

Big Ruby ordered a bourbon, Martha a martini. Then they ordered another, and another, for a total of five each before we left; neither one ate lunch. All this time, Martha and Big Ruby were sharing their life histories. No newcomer to politics, Big Ruby was First Lady of the Governor's Mansion when her brother was in office; she could match Martha's tales of political dirty tricks and often topped them. She sympathized with what had been done to Martha's credibility, shared her anger at her treatment in California and wept with Martha when told how Marty had been brainwashed against her mother.

Neither one wanted to leave when I insisted we had to get back to the hotel. By now it was four o'clock and Martha and I were being picked up at four-thirty to go to two parties. We were going with my friend Scottie Fitzgerald Smith, who had moved to Montgomery to research a book about her mother Zelda's family.

Martha rode to the second party with Mary Katherine Blount, whose husband Winton ("Red") Blount was Nixon's Postmaster General. It was obvious Martha was upset about something when she entered Mrs. Thigpin Hill's drawing room as if she were a ship in full sail and plunked herself down in the middle of the sofa. I learned from Mary Kay that on the way over in the car she had tried, as a friend, to talk to Martha about her drinking, and at one point had told her she had to "straighten up." Of course, Martha was incensed.

But instead of venting her anger at Mary Kay, Martha soon was arguing Alabama politics with a native Alabaman. By this time, Martha had a drink of Scotch in the hand with which she kept motioning. The Scotch kept almost slipping over the edge of the glass; the entire attention of the group of about twelve people was riveted on the drink.

Mrs. Hill's house, probably the most beautiful in Montgomery, is furnished with precious antiques. I was worried that Martha would ruin one of them with her Scotch and was wondering what I could do to prevent it, when Martha called across the room, "Scottie, why don't you like me?"

"I like you," Scottie answered.

"No, you don't," Martha said. "Winnie keeps telling me you hate me." With that I dropped a hot hors d'oeuvre on the arm of the antique chair in which I was sitting.

I protested that I hadn't told Martha that Scottie hated her. "Oh, yes, you did. Yes, you did. Yes, you did," said Martha who often repeated words or phrases for emphasis when she was drinking. Of course, I hadn't. But once in 1970 or '71, when Martha had said she'd like to know Scottie better since she thought they "could be good friends," I'd laughed and told Martha it probably would be impossible since she and liberal Democrat Scottie were poles apart politically.

Now Martha was telling Scottie I had kept them from being friends in Washington, but that they should be now since they "had so much in common."

Hoping to get Martha's attention away from Scottie, one guest suggested to a dignified Montgomery matron, "Why don't you sit by Mrs. Mitchell and get to know her better?"

"I don't want to know her better," said the matron. "I just want to watch."

Mary Kay and I knew we had to get Martha away from the party. A decision was made to have the Blounts' son and daughter-in-law take Martha back to the hotel. Surprisingly, she went without a fuss, although she made a snide remark to Mary Kay and me about our wanting "to get rid" of her.

Scottie and I had planned to have dinner together, but I thought I should be with Martha. The door between our rooms was open when I came in and I saw Martha sitting in bed, crying. When she saw me, she sobbed, "I thought you'd deserted me, too!"

She calmed down after I assured her I hadn't and we sat and talked for about thirty minutes. Her anger was replaced with unhappiness and self-pity, because she, Martha Mitchell, had to run "around the country working for magazines when John Mitchell should be taking care of me."

Then she said she was "tired, so very tired," and wanted to go to sleep. Later, I was watching television when I heard Martha talking on the telephone. She seemed to be talking to someone in the press. Her conversation was still going on an hour and a half later when I dropped off to sleep.

At four-twenty A.M. I heard a loud noise, which sounded like a door slamming. I thought it was across the hall, but it probably was Martha. Several days later I'd learn from two newspaper articles that she had gone out after I fell asleep.

Claude Duncan of the Alabama *Journal* and Peggy Roberson of the Birmingham (Alabama) *News* (who was in Montgomery on her way home from a vacation) both wrote about a meeting they had with Martha that night in the hotel's cocktail lounge.

According to the *News* article, Martha came downstairs at their invitation after warning them not to write a thing about it until after her plane left, since she had "slipped off" to join them while her biographer was asleep upstairs.

Miss Roberson noted that "Martha is fearful, though apparently hungry for company. She ducked, and sometimes put both hands over her face and shuddered when new customers came into the lounge.

" 'Who is he?' she demanded, when a man in a raincoat came through the door. 'Is he FBI?' "

Speaking of politics, Martha told Peggy Roberson that "the country made a mistake back in 1968. Voters should have elected George Wallace. In 1976, 'I expect to vote for George Wallace and work for him every way I can. I think he would make a perfectly wonderful president, even in a wheelchair.' "

At the airport the next day Martha had two double martinis. She had another two on the flight to Atlanta, where on her way off the plane she stopped to thank the pilot and co-pilot for a smooth trip; then she stood at the door and shook hands with all the passengers as they left the plane. Martha was the last off.

By now Martha was becoming more public in her drinking. It was almost as if she had given up trying to hide the problem from everyone except family and close friends.

That afternoon on the flight to New York she walked up and down the aisle, telling the first-class passengers "they" were going to kill her the way "they" killed Mrs. Hunt in a plane crash, but she didn't mind except for "taking all the people with me." The only way the stewardess could keep her in her seat was to serve her another martini; Martha had five on the flight. At one point a young man, obviously irritated by the commotion, asked, "Martha, do you know what you are doing?"

"No," Martha answered sarcastically, "what am I doing?"

"You are talking yourself right into a strait jacket."

Even that didn't keep her quiet.

In New York Martha needed help to get off the plane. Then, when she heard me tell the airline representative we'd be going into town by taxi, Martha exploded, saying Martha Mitchell only rode in limousines. There were no limousines available; she wouldn't leave the airport. We were taken to one of the airline offices to wait for one.

Knowing that anything I said might touch her off, I sat without saying a word. My silence seemed to upset her as much as anything I could have said. She ordered me to leave, to go back to Washington. As much as I wanted to go, I knew Martha shouldn't go home alone.

I told her I'd go home with her and leave the next morning. No, she said. It had to be *now.* I gave the representative her address and called

Maggie at the apartment to explain the situation and to give her the name and phone number of the airline representative. Then I flew to Washington, where I notified Junie that she was "on duty." I had been dismissed. Martha called Junie at one A.M. to see if she knew "why Winnie left me at the airport."

I heard from Martha six times before dinner the next day. She called to get her lawyer's phone number (she'd lost it) and to talk about John Mitchell. Now one of his conditions for discussing a separation settlement was that she give him all his clothes and papers.

Later that night her mood had changed completely. She had been drinking, and she was in a rage when she called to inform me a newspaper friend had told her I wasn't working on the book and that I was just "taking" her. I asked how I was doing it. Martha admitted she didn't know, but her friend had said I was. She was in such a temper I told her I wouldn't discuss it that night, to call tomorrow. She hung up but five minutes later phoned back to say she didn't want her name on the Wallace article. It was a month later before I spoke with her again.

The next day her lawyer Richard Creditor called to talk about the article and the book. The article, I explained, could be written one of two ways—with her by-line, as Martha's story about interviewing Cornelia, or without her by-line, as my observation of the interview taking place. But we had to know which way to go.

As for the book, it was progressing slowly, because without a contract and advance money I had to do my regular magazine writing for income. Richard Creditor understood and seemed sympathetic to my problem.

AS SO OFTEN HAPPENED WHEN MARTHA CAME HOME FROM A TRIP, SHE GOT the blues. A small item in *Women's Wear Daily* also added to her distress. John Mitchell, according to *WWD,* had dined with a male companion at the Miyako, a Japanese restaurant, where he "spent more time with his eye on two young women than he did on his chopsticks." He also made a "slight pass" at them on his way out, *WWD* reported.

Martha again took to her bed, eating nothing and drinking only iced tea, Cokes and buttermilk. Dr. Lorand helped her over her blues, and within a few days she again was on the telephone. She called to accept invitations from two talk shows to co-host their programs—one in June and one in August. And she said yes to a request from Marji Kunz, of Knight News Service, for a day of beauty at Kenneth's, one of New York's better-known beauty salons. "There's nothing that does more for my spirits when I'm down than a trip to the beauty parlor," she said.

Soon after her day at Kenneth's Martha called the Washington *Post* and asked them to come pick up some of the politically embarrassing papers she'd found in the den. She thought their publication might bring about the early resignation of Richard Nixon. Martha, like a lot of people, including some congressional leaders, had thought he would resign. But in mid-May Richard Nixon issued a statement in which he vowed not to quit "under any circumstances." His refusal to quit threw Martha into a rage.

In an interview lasting fourteen hours, over a period of three days, Martha told Donnie Radcliffe of the *Post* the highlights of about 50 percent of the material I'd gathered for the book. Donnie's article, along with pictures of Martha and the apartment by *Post* photographer Harry Naltchayan, was published on the eve of the second anniversary of the Watergate break-in.

In the meantime Richard Creditor had written *McCall's* to say Martha now wanted her by-line on the Wallace story and that the article should be submitted to her for approval. Of course, neither the magazine nor I dared submit it to Martha; she might read it to a press friend. It was agreed that I would telephone Martha to say I was coming to New York to read the article to her; if she hung up on me, *McCall's* assistant managing editor, Barbara Blakemore, would take it to the apartment and go over it with Martha.

When I called, Martha talked with me just as if nothing had happened. She was chatty and cheerful as she told me about the talk shows she would co-host. One was *The Pat Collins Show,* on New York's WCBS–TV, which she was doing the next week; since I was coming up Saturday, she asked me to stay over to go with her to the studio. She'd loved the day of beauty at Kenneth's, she said, although she had been embarrassed when she "ran into Happy [Mrs. Nelson] Rockefeller—of all people—in the shampoo room." And she said Jay was coming to visit and bringing his fiancée.

It would be Martha's first meeting with her future daughter-in-law, Janis Crawford, of Tylertown, Mississippi. Later Martha reported that she adored her; Janis says, "She was so good to me. Just from the very first she seemed to adopt me, not as a daughter-in-law but as a daughter—a real daughter. I think the fact that we were both Southerners brought us close."

Martha performed commendably as co-host on *The Pat Collins Show.* Television critic Marvin Kitman, of *Newsday,* wrote, "Martha Mitchell as a talk-show host may be the one good thing to come out of the Nixon Administration."

She held her own with such guests as David Halberstam, Joe McGinnis, Carol Channing, Gloria Steinem, Carl Bernstein and Bob Woodward. When Pat Collins asked if Martha was one of the sources for their book *All the President's Men,* Woodward and Bernstein refused to say. But Martha giggled and asked, "Haven't you heard? I'm Deep Throat." And Martha teased a ruffled Bob Woodward into admitting that he had voted for Richard Nixon in 1968.

Martha was happy the whole week. But the last day of the show, Martha told me, crying and distraught, that the program, which she'd been telling me all week might not be renewed, had been.

"But, Martha," I asked, "isn't that what you wanted?"

"It's renewed for *her,*" Martha answered. "What about me?"

It was the first I knew that Martha had thought she would be asked to co-host the show on a permanent basis if the ratings went up and it was renewed. She cried that she had "made" a Washington newswoman, she had "made" a woman in television, "and now I've made Pat Collins! When am I going to do something for myself?"

As disappointed as she was over the outcome of *The Pat Collins Show,* Martha didn't fall apart, perhaps because Jay was there. Jay saw Marty and John Mitchell at their Essex House suite, and Martha was so eager for news of Marty that she interrogated him about everything her daughter had said or done. Jay told her Marty and John Mitchell had moved to a smaller suite, one with a bedroom alcove instead of a separate bedroom, which at night was separated from the sitting room by a curtain. Marty and John Mitchell did a lot of their own cooking, he added. And in answer to Martha's questioning, he admitted that Marty had gained weight.

A few days later, unfortunately, John Mitchell again did something to upset Martha. It isn't known what it was, but it didn't matter. Anything John Mitchell did against Martha—refuse to see her, not pay her bills, make a snide remark about her that wound up in print—hurt Martha deeply. And these things often triggered in Martha the most erratic behavior.

This time she lashed back at John Mitchell by telling a member of the press that her husband was keeping Marty in dinky little rooms, where she didn't even have a bedroom of her own, and that he'd let her get "so fat she must weigh two hundred pounds." Martha's revelation alienated Marty and Jay.

The day after Jay left, I went to New York to interview Martha for a *Ladies' Home Journal* article. Many times Martha had said that Richard

Nixon broke up her marriage; the *Journal* wanted her to expand on her remarks. The interviews went along beautifully the first day and the morning of the second. Then her attorney called to say that John Mitchell had submitted some sort of a paper, in their separate maintenance discussions, claiming that Martha had spent over $30,000 since he walked out nine months earlier.

The interview stopped. Martha was too distressed to go on; she spent the afternoon on the phone—sometimes calling her lawyers to rail at them, other times telephoning friends to complain about "that liar John Mitchell."

At seven-thirty, Martha came marching down the hall, dressed to go out. She informed me she was going to a hospital, where a doctor could give her a shot for the "unbearable pain" in her hand, the one she'd injured in California. "It's just killing me, just killing me," she claimed.

Martha didn't look to me like a person in severe pain. She looked nervous and aggravated—in fact, almost frantic. Although Martha protested, I insisted that Maggie go with her.

They went to New York Hospital, where the emergency room was crowded with people. Martha went from patient to patient, holding out her hand to show them what "Richard Nixon did to me."

A doctor examined her hand, x-rayed it and told her there wasn't anything wrong except the beginning of arthritis. Martha exploded; she told him he didn't know anything about injuries. After the doctor prescribed home treatment and gave her a shot for her pain, Martha left the hospital without paying. She told the nurse to "send the bill to Richard Nixon."

Two days later Martha signed the necessary papers for her attorneys to file suit against John Mitchell for separate maintenance.

Still, there were days when Martha functioned well enough to travel and appear on television shows. In July she went to Detroit to appear on Dennis Wholey's *A.M. Detroit,* where she said Richard Nixon was a very private person who had an inferiority complex and was "not sure of himself." From Detroit, Martha went to Washington to again co-host *Panorama* with Maury Povich. The staff couldn't believe how much Martha had changed. Where she had been content before to do her own hair and to ride back and forth to the studio with one of the staff, she now demanded a hairdresser and a limousine. As one *Panorama* regular puts it: "She wanted all the color-me-Barbara Walters."

When Martha and Maggie arrived home from Washington, the telephones were out of order and the apartment showed signs of having been entered. Martha called from the street corner to report the latest instance of what she thought was "their" harassment. (Several months later Martha came home from a trip to find someone had broken into the secret safe in her closet, where she kept some of the revealing documents from the den files. The building superintendent Alfons Suss, who reported it to the police, says the safe door was completely off the hinges.)

Martha blamed John Mitchell. She called the Internal Revenue Service in Washington and urged them to check her husband's income-tax returns.

The House Judiciary Hearings on Impeachment were being televised that week, which reminded her that she'd "been a fool, a goddamn fool," for falling for the Administration's line: "I can't tell you how mad it makes me that those jerks were smarter than I was." The week wasn't totally without joy, though. The Supreme Court announced its decision on the Nixon tapes; he had to give them up.

I FINISHED THE *Ladies' Home Journal* ARTICLE, "HOW RICHARD NIXON Broke Up My Marriage," and went to New York to read it to Martha. She was in a happy mood. We went to lunch one day and to dinner two nights with friends. The *Journal* story delighted her; she said she'd love to watch "King Richard's face when he sees it."

Ladies' Home Journal liked it, too, or so we thought.

While I was packing to go back to Washington, Martha told me I'd have to take home with me "all the stuff you want to read," claiming if I didn't take the material, she'd throw it out. I had put aside in the den, to read later, several of the black folders containing the television transcripts and some of the *Congressional Record* clippings. I protested that I couldn't take them home, saying I didn't have room for them in my apartment, nor did I have a way to get them home.

Martha gave me a large battered suitcase, which I filled with the papers. Just before I closed the case, she threw in some of the letters and memos she'd considered important, saying, "You keep these since you're so worried I'll give them to the papers." This was in reference to a conversation we'd had the night before when she'd asked the whereabouts of a particular paper and I'd told her it was in the file with the papers she'd given the Washington *Post*; at the same time I'd suggested she put important documents where she couldn't get to them every time she had the urge to talk.

I no sooner arrived home than I received a call from a *Journal* editor, saying the magazine's lawyers wouldn't let them use the story. They claimed it was "too hot to handle." I got the feeling they were afraid an impeachment trial could be going on at the time the story would be published.

Of course, they would pay for the article; they also would retain the rights, as stated in the contract, until late December, which was about three months away. And Martha and I were expected to abide by the clause in the contract, stating we would not discuss the article or its contents.

Martha was upset when I told her about the *Journal*'s decision. But she calmed down when I explained that we could resell the article in December.

The next morning I was shocked when Martha told me she had called her lawyer Richard Creditor and told him to "make them [the *Journal*] print that story." But when Creditor called me, after he'd talked with the *Journal,* he said Martha wanted a new contract which would give us the money but wouldn't restrict her talking—conditions I felt the magazine certainly wouldn't meet.

Negotiations over the new contract went on for five weeks, during which time Richard Nixon resigned as President. Finally it was agreed that the *Journal* would publish the article in its December issue. But at some point during the writing and rewriting of contracts, the *Journal* bought all rights in perpetuity to the material; they did not revert to Martha and me.

Also, the *Journal* wanted the article changed from "How Richard Nixon Broke Up My Marriage" to "How Politics Wrecked My Marriage." Martha wasn't happy about the emphasis the article would now take. She wanted everyone to know how she and Richard Nixon constantly engaged in a power play "for possession of John Mitchell." For the longest time John Mitchell tried to play both sides. "Finally when he had to choose between us, he stuck with the President. Looking back on it, I don't know why I was surprised. I should have suspected the direction he'd take that spring night in 1973, when he came home from a trip to Washington and told me, 'I've made a deal; I won't have to go to jail.' Sticking with the President was his only chance for survival. By this time his fate was totally and completely tied in with Richard Nixon's."

What puzzled Martha was how John Mitchell, a man she considered to be "so smart, so honest, so brilliant," could have gotten himself into such a position.

"It's more confusing to me," she added, "that John Mitchell would get himself into such a mess for this particular man, Richard Nixon. Less than ten years ago he despised him. He . . . talked to me and to our friends about Nixon's questionable political tactics in his early election campaigns."

Looking back, she said, she should have been suspicious of Richard Nixon the night she and John gave the dinner party for the Nixons, at the time the two law firms were considering a merger: "One of the first things I learned while growing up in the South was 'never trust a man who won't look you in the eye.' Nixon didn't once all evening, or at any other time."

She talked about Richard Nixon taking her husband on trips—always without her. "I didn't even exist," Martha claimed, "nor in my opinion did any woman, as far as Richard Nixon was concerned. He wanted men around him." She said that as far as she could see, the only time Richard Nixon wanted women near was when he thought it would help his public image.

When talking about Richard Nixon's desire to have everyone at his beck and call, Martha said, "It was worse for his good friend Bebe Rebozo than it was for us. He had to come all the way from Florida when the President called. I remember once when Bebe had planned a dinner for his mother, whom he adored, and his sisters and their families. He had to cancel the party on a few hours notice, pack a bag and head for the airport. The President handled everyone like that; it was as if he were a king sitting there giving out orders to all his little men."

But what concerned Martha the most, she said, was when she realized Richard Nixon was destroying John Mitchell's honesty and his sense of right and wrong: "Many times John and I would talk something over and I knew his thinking on the subject before he went to the White House to discuss it with the President. When he came home, John would have done a flip, he was now quoting Nixon's interpretation of the subject.

"I talked to him, constantly," she continued, "about how he had to stand on his two feet, how I wasn't sure the President was right in many of his decisions. I pointed out that Bob Haldeman and John Ehrlichman were influencing the President, and I asked him, 'Are you sure you agree with those two characters?' It bothered me that John Mitchell was becoming a Yes Man, a carbon stamp for the President's utterances. Any woman loses respect for a man who lets this happen to him."

John Mitchell probably made his choice between the President and Martha, she said, in June 1972, the week following the Watergate break-in: "He undoubtedly played an important role in having me detained and forcibly sedated at the hotel, against my will. Protecting the President had become more important to John Mitchell than protecting his own wife.

"I don't know what is in store for him, for our daughter or for me, but as I try to get my affairs in order, I continue to reflect on the past; I forage for the answer. How could a weak, insecure man—a conglomerate of nothing—manipulate and overpower a strong, confident person like John Mitchell?

"Perhaps that's the answer—through his own overconfidence, John Mitchell brought this all on himself. While I honestly believe John didn't realize what Nixon was doing to him until it was too late, I also know that he has always been the most gullible man in the world . . .

"Also, it wasn't in John Mitchell's character ever to admit he was wrong. So when he found himself in this Nixon-made mess, he continued to hold his head high. Why not? Until now his pride had seen him through. But Richard Nixon's White House was more than one man's pride could handle."

Chapter Twenty-Four

WHILE ALL THE BICKERING AND BARTERING WAS GOING ON OVER THE *Ladies' Home Journal* contract, Martha was keeping herself busy—taping the Mike Douglas show, taking a trip to Washington, attending her son's wedding in Mississippi and visiting relatives in Pine Bluff, Arkansas.

Martha was such a hit on the Mike Douglas show that she was asked back three times, appearing the last time only a few weeks before she entered the hospital. The Philadelphia *Bulletin* reported that as a co-host she was "dynamite . . . she was whimsical, angry, charming, outrageous, cunning and humorous. In other words, completely unpredictable."

Martha was ecstatic the day Richard Nixon announced he would resign the Presidency. She had heard about the upcoming announcement just before taping her last Mike Douglas show. She listened to the resignation speech over radio while riding in a limousine between Philadelphia and New York.

She called me around midnight to talk, for over an hour, about the resignation and what it would mean to the country and to her. She felt it "exonerated" her, and she called her hometown paper, the Pine Bluff *Commercial,* to say just that. "I was the first woman in the whole United States that asked for him to resign, a year ago in April, remember,"

Martha told the *Commercial.* "And that's when they called me crazy or drunk."

When asked what she thought about the question of immunity from further prosecution for Nixon, Martha said, "I think that everybody who has been involved in a criminal offense should be prosecuted. I don't care who it is, there's nobody in America that is beyond prosecution. And if we set an example like this, it will continue."

The next day Martha had her usual post-trip blues. She was lonesome and again dissatisfied with her attorneys; Mel Belli had called her from California to say her separation case against John Mitchell, scheduled for a court hearing the following week, had been postponed. "I'm being screwed from all angles and I'm sick of it," she cried.

"I've called Jay to come up and I'm going to give him everything I have," she declared. "Then I'm going to jump out of the goddamn window. This is the end of Martha Mitchell!" She hung up, then stormed through the apartment, a pair of scissors in hand, cutting the telephone wires.

Martha was on a rampage all night; later I'd learn this was when she mutilated John Mitchell's portrait, the one dumped in a garbage can. It was after dawn before she fell into a restless sleep, only to awaken within a few hours.

Maggie was frantic when she called me, claiming Martha woke up "still mad at everybody." I gave Maggie Dr. Lorand's number and told her to call him.

For some unexplained reason the telephone in Maggie's room was still working. When I called to see if Maggie had reached the doctor, Martha heard the phone ringing and came in to see who was on the line. She took the phone and repeated her threat of the night before.

"So enjoy yourself, Winnie," she added. "I won't be around for you to worry about anymore after tomorrow." She suggested that I call photographers to take pictures as she jumped. It was two months before she called again.

Leaving John Mitchell's faceless portrait on the dining-room floor, where the chemicals she'd used to erase his features seeped through and ruined a portion of the beautiful herringbone-patterned parquet floor, Martha took off for Washington a few days after we talked, taking Maggie with her.

Martha went to Stouffer's National Center Hotel, near National Airport, where she stayed until time to go to Mississippi for Jay's wedding. She didn't leave her room, except to keep a dental appointment, for the next two weeks. She stayed in bed and on the phone. One of her calls was to Lloyd Shearer of *Parade.* She told him, "You are talking to a jackass. Did you ever see a woman jackass? Well, I am one, because I truly believed what the Nixon Administration told me . . . Gullible? Honey, you don't know how gullible I've been . . .

"Am I drinking much? I'm not drinking at all. I'm trying to get my personal life put together . . . What I want is what all of us want, a little tranquility, a little peace of mind."

Her only visitors the first week were the Dankworths—Junie, Ted and Piper. Then one evening she saw Marta Sweeney, the mother of one of Jay's best friends, and her daughter Sudee. Somehow, Jay learned that his mother was at the hotel and came to her door; Martha wouldn't let him in.

She was angry with her son because he'd asked his father, Clyde Jennings, to his wedding. Jay wanted both of his parents to see him get married; Martha refused to go if Clyde was there. Finally, Clyde told Jay he wouldn't come since his presence might create a "scene."

Even when she heard that her first husband, now remarried, wouldn't be there, Martha didn't tell Jay she was going. He knew she was on her way only when he boarded the plane to fly to Mississippi and saw Martha and Maggie seated in the first-class section with Mary and Philip Robertson.

Martha had been difficult about the wedding for another reason. She didn't want Jay to get married. When he first told her his plans in June, Martha asked Marta Sweeney to "please, please do something so Jay doesn't get married.

"I need him; he can't get married," Martha said, adding, "Jay is my son—he owes me this."

Jay was adamant; the wedding took place as planned. And as Alleta Saunders tells it, "Martha did everything she was supposed to do. Once she had decided to go, she couldn't have been nicer. She was lovely and did not cause anybody any trouble."

TYLERTOWN, MISSISSIPPI, IS A TOWN WITH 1,700 RESIDENTS; ALL WERE invited to the wedding by the traditional method of publishing the wedding invitation in the local newspaper, the Tylertown *Times.* Most of them must have accepted. Following the ceremony, guests lined up four and five abreast for five blocks, to get into the reception at the home of the bride's parents, Dr. and Mrs. Benjamin L. Crawford, Jr.

Paul Pittmann, writing in the Greenwood, Mississippi, *Common-*

wealth, noted that Martha was "fairly opinionated. She thinks, for instance, that former President Richard Nixon is a 'dirty son of a bitch.' To her credit, she doesn't mince words."

Since tiny Tylertown was short on hotel rooms, Martha and Maggie and the Robertsons stayed some twenty-five miles away at the Holiday Inn in McComb, Mississippi, in three connecting rooms.

Martha refused all interviews, except for one with a long-time friend, Alice Fulbright of the Memphis *Commercial Appeal.* Martha told Alice, "I'm still being tormented like hell," and admitted that "John and I never will patch things up."

Although Martha was doing all the right things, she was moody and unhappy when she was alone with Maggie or the Robertsons. Philip and Mary remember that they almost had to force her to go to a wedding eve cocktail party given for Jay and Janis by four of Martha's old friends—Alleta and Charlie Saunders, Ray West, and Mrs. William Hicks. Philip and Mary remember that "Martha balked all the way from our room to the party—until the minute we walked in the door. Then it was a complete change of personality. She was on stage and she was in her glory."

The wedding was scheduled for four P.M.; by three-fifty everyone had arrived—except the mother of the groom. Her limousine had a flat tire. It was driven into a service station and, with Martha and Mary and Maggie still in it, onto the lift to have the tire changed.

Since Martha didn't want to crush their clothes during a twenty-five-mile drive, Philip rented a room at a small motel in Tylertown where they could change. When the car pulled up in front of their cottage, they saw a large sign on the door, WELCOME MARTHA—TYLERTOWN.

A police escort took the limousine through the little town to the church, where about 3,000 people were standing outside, waiting to see Martha Mitchell. "They saw her get out of the car," Philip remembers. "And they all started stampeding toward us. And with that two policemen picked Martha up—one had her under each arm—and two more took Mary. All I remember is that I was running along behind Martha, with a policeman beside me, and I saw Martha with her feet still moving, like she was walking, although they were six inches off the ground."

Following the ceremony, Martha refused to let the cameramen take her picture until after Philip took her aside and reminded her they had been standing outside, in a ninety-four-degree heat, for hours. Only then did she walk toward the cameras, smiling and answering reporters' questions on the way to the car.

"Watergate is the greatest thing in the world for this country," she said. "We're gonna get all the politicians true blue again. They're not going to be dishonest." And she announced she had postponed the publication of her book "until all this Waterjunk—gate—junk gets out and then I can contradict it."

Just as Martha created controversy by being late to the wedding, she caused a furor when she went back to the motel to change her shoes after the wedding. People saw the car pull away and thought she wasn't going to the reception. Many people left. But once she got to the Crawfords' house, Martha stood in the receiving line—shaking hands, hugging and kissing—for over two hours.

Martha went back to Arkansas with Ray West after the wedding. They were in Hot Springs when President Gerald Ford pardoned Richard Nixon. According to an Associated Press story, "Mrs. Martha Mitchell, declaring her bitterness about President Ford's pardon of former President Richard Milhous Nixon, said yesterday that she believed the whole thing had been prearranged before Nixon left office. 'I knew Nixon had something up his sleeve when he left the White House.' "

In a separate interview with KATV of Little Rock, Martha was vehement about the pardon, declaring, "Nixon's just as guilty and responsible as anybody else . . . I don't feel sorry for him . . ."

When Martha spoke of Nixon's responsibility and guilt, she was stating what John Eisenhower, son of the late President Eisenhower, later said. Eisenhower told the Philadelphia *Bulletin* in 1975 that Nixon "admitted his own complicity" in his resignation statement and in his later acceptance of President Ford's pardon. Eisenhower added that he didn't "subscribe to all those clichés . . . about his innocence and persecution."

His remark probably was no more than Nixon expected; Martha once told me that Nixon "just hated John Eisenhower."

A FEW WEEKS AFTER JAY'S WEDDING, MARTHA FLEW TO ENGLAND FOR THE David Frost show, arriving after an all-night flight from New York and came off the plane "in fine fettle," says Ian Johnson, producer of *The David Frost Interviews.* "She was bright and breezy and full of fun."

The London *Daily Mail* put it another way: "She chatted her way off the airline and all the way through customs. And the former Southern belle . . . hadn't dried up when she arrived to meet the press."

Peter Rosier, the public relations director of BBC, says that "the main point we made to Martha was, 'You get five minutes and that's it, because we want a television program left after you've spoken to the press.' So we started the press off and we finished about six or seven minutes later. But because she spoke so quickly, because she was on the ball and she had calculated exactly what she was going to say, she said in six or seven minutes what it would take most people to say in two or three hours."

The *Daily Mail* wrote: "BBC men who paid Martha's fare over here and who had been fidgety throughout the interview, brought it to a hasty conclusion . . . They were suffering from the rather wild fear that she might run out of things to say before appearing on tonight's Frost show."

Ian Johnson and Peter Rosier took Martha and her paid companion Maggie in a chauffeur-driven Daimler to the Savoy Hotel, where a suite with a Thames River view was waiting. Then, without mentioning it to any of the Frost people, Martha let Maggie leave for Ireland to visit her family.

The BBC staff had registered Martha at the Savoy in secrecy and under the name of David Frost's secretary, Libby Reeves Purvis.

"But Fleet Street soon got word she was at the Savoy," Ian Johnson says. "So they were hammering on her door for a story, in an unscrupulous way. The hotel wasn't able to send them off . . . Martha got excited." She threatened to go home unless she had a constant companion. Later Martha said that David Frost was upset with her and reminded her "that was the reason they'd paid Maggie's way to England."

At some point Martha telephoned Maggie in Ireland and told her they were going home. Maggie rushed back to England and the airport, where she got on the flight she'd been told to take, only to discover Martha wasn't on board. Martha had changed her mind about leaving after the BBC enlisted two of their researchers to take turns looking after her.

The David Frost show was taped in the Mayfair Hotel's small theater. "David did his normal introduction," Peter Rosier says. "But what clearly was wrong was that Martha was feeling buoyant to the point that the program was basically a three-way conversation . . . the audience was just as much a star of the show as David Frost and Martha, on that particular occasion."

"It was a supreme piece of one-upmanship," Ian Johnson recalls. "But I think David handled it very well."

On the program, Martha discussed Watergate, California, the Nixon pardon and her marriage. She said she would almost be willing to bet her life that Nixon planned Watergate and that she thought her husband, then waiting trial for his part in Watergate, knew about it in advance.

She talked about the pardon "deal" Richard Nixon must have made with Jerry Ford before resigning. When David Frost seemed skeptical,

Martha said, "Well, I don't know how much the English people know about politics in America, nor do I know how much the English people know about Richard Nixon. But we must take into consideration that this man never did anything that could harm himself." So, she reasoned, Nixon would not have walked out of "the top job in the country" without having something to rely on if he was "going to be criminally prosecuted."

Earlier she had mentioned that she had been living a "nightmare." David Frost asked, "Do you feel you're coming out of it now?"

"I must say this, David," Martha answered. "The night that Nixon resigned was the first time I really felt the whole thing. I could have been living through a novel or a James Bond . . . but the night he resigned I actually realized what had happened and that was the beginning of—I had to stand up and realize I had two feet to stand on and that was it."

As was her custom when she appeared on a show, Martha took time to speak with everyone working on the program—the hairdresser, cameramen, secretaries and others. "A guest on the Frost show who takes an interest in the production team always makes a much better impression than someone who walks coldly in and out," Ian Johnson says, adding, "I don't think they will ever forget her."

Neither will Ian Johnson or Peter Rosier. Ian, who from the time of the Frost interview called Martha every time he was in New York, "just to keep in touch," says, "I really liked her. As you well know, she was a woman you couldn't not like."

Peter feels the drawback to Martha was that she presented her claims in an unfortunate way, making everybody switch off "because of the way she said it." Had a more suave person said the same sort of thing in a more logical fashion, Peter thinks she would have been believed.

"Martha was a victim of all sorts of things," he continues. "But she was her own worst enemy, because she made you believe she was a *nutter*, when in fact all the rest of them were . . . If you ask me what I think of Martha, today, I think she was an extremely unfortunate lady who in fact was talking some sort of sense . . . She probably was the most underestimated person within the whole of the Watergate tale . . . All the applause went to the Washington *Post*. But she was talking [about dirty tricks] long before the *Post*. And I think if the Washington *Post* had listened to Martha Mitchell they would have been there a lot quicker."

The show was taped on Friday, and David Frost had invited Martha to spend the weekend with him and his mother at his country house north of London. Martha had accepted, but for some reason she never explained, Martha left after only three nights in London.

She refused to go through the routine security check at Heathrow Airport, and she "made a scene" about being checked by a woman security officer. A British Airways official said Martha was "shouting and refused to be touched by one of the security girls. In the end, when we told her she would not be able to fly if she were not searched, she calmed down and we used an electronic device to search her."

They found a can of hair spray in her hand luggage and routinely confiscated it, since it was thought an aerosol can could be used as a weapon during a hijacking. Martha was outraged. As she boarded the plane she was heard to ask someone, "Do you know who I am? I should have flown Pan Am. I know the President."

Women's Wear Daily reported that Martha spent the "six-hour flight upstairs, drinking champagne on the rocks and insisted that her lunch be served there against regulations. When she arrived in New York she was escorted past U.S. Customs, waving her passport, saying, 'Put me in jail.' "

Martha reached her apartment in a fighting mood. Unfortunately, the only person around was Maggie, who after arriving and finding an empty apartment had been frantically calling Martha's friends to see where she was. Martha got into a heated argument with Maggie and fired her on the spot, insisting that she leave that night. The nurses' agency sent over another companion, a South American woman named Ana Storm.

The next few days were rough ones for Martha. She had the inevitable post-trip letdown; also, diverticulitis, bad news from her attorneys (attempts to negotiate a settlement had "not been fruitful"), and the daily news reports were increasingly upsetting.

THE WATERGATE COVER-UP TRIAL FINALLY WAS GOING TO START. JOHN Mitchell was charged with six counts: conspiracy, obstruction of justice, two counts of lying to the grand jury, one count of perjury before the special Senate Watergate Committee, one count of lying to FBI agents. He was facing a possible thirty-year prison term and a $42,000 fine.

A Washington *Post* story, the day before the trial, mentioned that John Mitchell's social life was perking up and told how he and Marty had spent the summer together on Long Island, fishing and swimming. It upset Martha to read that her husband was having a good time when she was so miserable, as did "his sudden interest in Marty." But what really offended her was a remark about her suit against John Mitchell: "Custody [of Marty] is not shaping up as a big issue in the suit . . ." Martha wanted it to be a big issue and she was frustrated that it wasn't. But after a lot of arguments with friends and attorneys, Martha finally had been convinced she would be destroyed if she took the custody battle to court and Marty testified against her mother.

One week after John Mitchell went on trial in Washington, Martha went with her attorney to Manhattan's State Supreme Court to seek $3,000 a week support from her estranged husband. Her attorneys asked for $35,000 counsel fees. Later, John Mitchell's lawyer challenged the counsel-fee charges, representing 318 hours and 40 minutes spent on Martha's business, saying, "They have . . . stated, 'This office has had to literally run the plaintiff's life . . .' It would appear that either these are not counsel fees, or that the lawyers are asking for compensation as den mothers."

As soon as she got home from court, Martha phoned me, for the first time in two months. No mention was made of her long silence. She was disturbed that John Mitchell had filed papers in court "full of damn lies about how much money I spend and what the apartment could rent for." In answer to the motion submitted by Martha's attorneys, Marvin Segal, who represented John Mitchell, introduced a letter from a New York real estate firm, saying it could rent the Mitchell apartment to "a member of royalty who would wish to lease the apartment furnished for three months, commencing October 10, 1974, at a rental of $15,000 (fifteen thousand dollars) per month."

At one point Martha's lawyers stated in court that "the alleged agency involved has denied such an offer." But whether it was true or not didn't matter; Martha was sure in her own mind that Mitchell would find a way to keep her out forever once she moved out of the apartment for any reason. She was determined to stay.

As the evening went on, Martha became so distraught from her day in court that Junie went to New York to be with her. Martha stayed in bed the whole time Junie was there, getting up only to take baths and put on clean nightgowns.

Then Philip and Mary Robertson went up to stay with Martha so Junie could go home. Martha threatened to jump out the window the second night the Robertsons were there. Philip took her suicide threat seriously and dealt with it directly; he nailed down all the windows with spike-sized nails. It was an effective suicide deterrent, but later Martha, her maids and friends almost suffocated on warm days.

Philip remembers that he and Mary were sound asleep the next night when around three o'clock "Martha opened the bedroom door at the same time she turned on the light and yelled, 'You've *got* to do *something*!'

"Mary jumped up and hit the canopy with her head; it scared her to death. Martha kept crying that she couldn't stay in that room by herself and we had to come in and talk to her."

They went in and sat on Martha's bed for about an hour, all the time trying to convince Martha she should go to sleep. Finally she said she would if Mary would lie down beside her. But Mary wouldn't stay alone with Martha. Philip crawled in on the other side of his wife; to his surprise the three slept well the rest of the night.

Martha perked up the next day and felt so well they went out for a night on the town. There was a piano player at the restaurant where they had dinner, and just as Martha and the Robertsons stood up to go, the piano player finished playing and everybody applauded. Martha thought they were applauding her; she took bows and walked around to all the tables, saying hello and greeting the other customers. Philip remembers that it "really was very sad."

Shortly after that was when the judge rendered his decision in the Mitchells' separate maintenance case, awarding Martha temporary alimony of $1,000 a week. Since John Mitchell's income was $5,281 a week, Martha's lawyers immediately submitted a motion for reargument.

Martha was dejected over the decision, but she didn't go to pieces over it, perhaps because her friend Bonnie Swearingen, wife of John Swearingen, chairman of the board of the Standard Oil Company (Indiana), was in town from Chicago and the two went out daily—for lunch at "21", to dinner with friends and one night to Madison Square Garden to hear Frank Sinatra, where Martha was mobbed by people wanting her autograph. Martha loved it.

She also was happy that Bonnie had put her in touch with someone—she wouldn't tell his name—who, Martha hoped, would handle her affairs. She said he had booked her on three television shows in Chicago, plus a promotion there for Flair Merchandising, Inc., and had arranged for her to do one of the CBS Bicentennial television spots sponsored by Shell Oil. Martha laughed when she read the material chosen for her, saying it was quite appropriate:

> Two hundred years ago today, the nagging wife in a rhymed satire was getting a good laugh. Her husband had been a delegate to Congress and she was sure he and his friends bungled the whole business.
>
> She *berated* him!
>
> "Would of instead of delegates . . . they'd sent delegates' wives,
> Heavens, we couldn't [have] bungled it so for our lives . . .
> Instead of imploring their justice and pity,

> You treat Parliament like a pack of banditti,
> When I think how these things must infallibly end,
> I'm *distracted* with fear. *My hair stands on end*!
> Oh! my country! remember that a woman unknown
> Cried aloud—like Cassandra, in oracular tone,
> *'Repent!* or you are *forever, forever,* undone!' "

Before she took off for Chicago, Martha again warned me not to speak to Mel Belli or Richard Creditor under "any circumstances." She was furious with both of them.

Martha claimed they still wanted her to sign a joint income-tax return, saying it would save John Mitchell $30,000 if she did. When Martha asked what she would get out of it, she said they told her John Mitchell would then sign over an insurance policy to her. Martha asked, "Who will pay the premium if he goes to jail?"

As Martha understood it, John Mitchell would not pay her any more money until she signed the return, and that every day she didn't sign would be against her. "I got so damn mad I hung up," Martha said. Also, Mel Belli was trying to get her to give up the apartment. "Mitchell and company," she reasoned with ire, had her attorneys working for him.

"It's unbelievable, this man [Mitchell] is still sitting on the throne of Justice, ruling the world."

MARTHA STARTED HER DAY IN CHICAGO ON A SEVEN A.M. SHOW. HOSTESS Sadi Freeman asked Martha if she had a drinking problem; Martha left the studio in tears.

Later that day Liz Carpenter saw Martha in a Chicago restaurant: "She obviously was on kind of a high; she was revved up. Martha was carrying on and she was overly loud . . . It was sad, because you realized that here is a woman who needs love, who needs help. And she has been cut off from a lot of things that she cares about."

Liz had the feeling that Martha was on an emotional binge: "She had been on television all day and I think Martha, who had a lot of exhibitionism and ham in her—she loved the spotlight—was still playing to it in an exaggerated form."

Martha's conduct so disturbed Liz that she telephoned me when she got back to Washington, saying, "Something has to be done about Martha. Someone has to help her."

The problem, as Martha's son Jay pointed out after her death, was that you can't help someone who doesn't want to be helped. A lot of people tried, though, including one of her lawyers. He recognized her problem as being a dependency on alcohol and drugs, which he at first thought he could help her overcome. And he did see her through some bad periods. But finally he said he reluctantly had reached the conclusion that "she'll have to hit bottom before she comes back."

"I'VE GOT MYSELF BACK TOGETHER," MARTHA CHEERFULLY REPORTED THE day she returned from Florida, where she'd gone with Bonnie Swearingen after her Chicago appearances. The two women flew to Miami in a private plane, Martha reported, and she'd done a promotion for a discotheque: "Honey, let me tell you something. When five hundred kids stand up and cheer you get yourself back together in a hurry."

The news from her lawyers wasn't good, though. She said they again were trying to get her to sign the income-tax form. They also wanted her to give John Mitchell his clothes and papers. She called them back and said she'd given her husband's clothes to the doorman. She hadn't. As for the income-tax return, she again called her friend at Internal Revenue and was told not to sign it.

Martha talked so often to Internal Revenue over a period of several months that at one point someone got confused and sent her a check. Martha wanted to keep it since "the Nixon Administration caused me so much trouble."

AGAIN MARTHA WAS DISSATISFIED WITH HER LAWYERS. SHE WANTED another firm to represent her. One of her complaints was that her attorneys couldn't even get Mitchell to pay her phone bill. It was eight months overdue; the telephone company was threatening to discontinue the service. Martha called an official to tell him, "I have given millions of dollars of publicity to the telephone company," and that it should give her free service for life. The phone wasn't disconnected.

The same day Martha was complaining about her lawyers Mel Belli and Richard Creditor, she was incensed at the way the trial was going in Judge Sirica's court. She called Junie three times after midnight to say she was taking the four-fifteen A.M. Amtrak to Washington "to go to the court and confront Mitchell face to face." Junie didn't believe she was serious.

But about nine o'clock, Martha's maid called Junie, saying Martha was not in the apartment and all the lights were on, indicating she'd left while it was still dark.

Junie and I were in a panic. We knew if Martha showed up at Judge Sirica's court and created a scene, he would put her in jail. Evidently the

Judge had thought she might try to get into the trial; Judge Sirica told John Mitchell's lawyer, William Hundley, that he would hold him personally responsible if Martha put in an appearance, saying, "I will not have her in my court."

Shortly after noon, Martha called Junie. Her first question was, "What time is it?" Her second, "What day is it?" She again was at Stouffer's National Center Hotel, across the Potomac River from Washington. Junie went right over; a few hours later I relieved her.

Martha was at the hotel for six days, insisting every morning that she was going to the trial. Junie and I never left her alone during the hours court was in session. We kept stalling her, each day saying the next would be a better one to go to court. We found things to keep her busy, or perhaps it was the other way around. I know that both Junie and I always had something to do for Martha. One day Martha had Junie write a letter for her to Mel Belli, saying she no longer wanted him to represent her. I was delegated to talk to her old friend Henry Rothblatt, who had seen her through the trying times of 1968. Martha considered Henry her friend; she trusted him. In fact, she would have retained him first, if he hadn't been "messed up in Watergate," as the original attorney for the Cubans in the break-in. Later when Henry couldn't get the apartment in her name, and her temporary alimony increased, Martha became unhappy with him, too.

When I talked to Henry Rothblatt, from Stouffer's, he agreed to take Martha as a client; we arranged for her to see him later that week in New York.

We finally got Martha to go home by setting up an appointment for her to have her picture taken for *New York* magazine. Junie drove Martha to Union Station, and just as they were passing District Court, where the Watergate trial was in session in courtroom No. 2, Martha asked, "Which building is the one where they're having the trial?" Junie answered that she had "no idea."

MARTHA'S PICTURE IN *New York* MAGAZINE WAS SUPPOSED TO APPEAR IN the Christmas shopping guide, to illustrate the ultimate over-fifty-dollar gift—a $1,500 photograph by portraitist Francesco Scavullo. She was to receive the original photograph, a check in the amount of her income tax on the $1,500 gift and the publication rights to the photograph after the issue of *New York* was off the stands. Only a cutline explaining the gift idea was to appear with the photograph.

But as it turned out, Martha was such fascinating copy *New York* didn't use the picture as a gift suggestion. The magazine put it on the cover, and inside ran two articles about her—one by Priscilla Tucker and Joan Kron telling how the photograph was produced, and the second an interview with Dan Dorfman. Martha never received the photograph, although she did receive a check for the taxes on it.

In the photograph, Martha looked like a glamorous movie star. She was lying on the floor, with her chin resting on her hands, wearing Tourmaline mink, pearl and diamond earrings, three diamond rings, a long strand of pearls she said was a gift from the Emperor of Japan, and one of her blond "falls."

Martha breathlessly reported that it had taken eight hours to produce the photograph. Hairdresser Maury Hopson had given her a "fantastic but natural-looking" hair-do. Makeup specialist Way Bandy had "designed" her face, she said, with contouring pencils (brown along the chin and jawline, white on the ledge at the top of the cheekbone, according to *New York*).

Yet when the magazine appeared on the stands and a friend called Martha to ask who did her makeup, saying, "You were so gorgeous," Martha snipped, "I did my own makeup; he only helped with my eyes." She added, "That's the way I look all the time."

Chapter Twenty-Five

JUST AS SHE HAD THE YEAR BEFORE, MARTHA STARTED PLANNING early for the holidays. She quickly accepted Mary and Philip Robertson's invitation to be with them in Washington for Christmas and New Year's. And she invited Jay and his bride, Janis, and Ray West to spend Thanksgiving with her at the apartment.

Martha was excited about the Thanksgiving dinner, the first she would have cooked in several years. She spent days working on the menu. Then, two days before Thanksgiving, when Martha tried to find out where Marty was spending the holidays, no one would tell her. She brooded over it and became so upset she drank to calm her nerves.

The more she drank, the more outraged she became, until finally she called the police and had them go search the house of one of John Mitchell's business friends, looking for Marty. It isn't known why Martha thought Marty would be there; the couple hadn't seen her for months.

Her rage still not spent, Martha called the office of John Mitchell's attorneys to tell them she knew her husband was lying on the stand and that she had written Judge Sirica to tell him. As far as anyone knows, she didn't.

Twenty-four hours later, a sober Martha was in the kitchen, cheerfully cooking Thanksgiving dinner for Ray, Jay and Janis and two of Jay's friends. Janis says it was an absolutely marvelous meal.

The day after the dinner, Martha flew to St. Croix, Virgin Islands, to help promote a celebrity golf tournament. Someone from the tournament promotion staff met Martha at the airport, took her to the Buccaneer Hotel and left her. She was terrified at finding herself alone, at night, on a strange island and refused to stay unless a security guard was posted outside her door.

She created such a commotion the tournament officials had to move her someplace else. She was taken to the Gentle Winds resort, where she stayed with the manager Keith King and his wife Lee in their two-bedroom house.

From St. Croix she flew to Miami to be a guest on a Mike Douglas show. Three days later she arrived home, obviously on a high. When Martha called me she was effusive and boastful as she chatted about moving to Miami, where she'd always had such "wonderful times." And she insisted she wanted to sign a book contract, immediately, because the time was ripe. She was still euphoric when she said good-bye.

Martha was on the telephone until three A.M. and then was up and out by eight-thirty; she told her companion Ana that she was going to the Convent of the Sacred Heart "to get Marty out of school."

For over a year—ever since Marty's visit to the apartment—Martha had one attorney after another trying to get Marty back. No amount of pleading or threatened legal pressure could get Marty to see her mother. Finally Martha's psychiatrist, Dr. Lorand, talked to John Mitchell and was able to convince him that Martha and Marty should meet "face to face." Arrangements were made by Martha to go to the school, since Marty refused to come to the apartment.

The night before she was to see Marty, for the first time in more than a year, Martha became so nervous she took a drink to calm herself. Then she was up all night, drinking and making phone calls. During one call, a well-meaning friend, who had no knowledge at all about the true relationship between mother and daughter, advised her to "bring that child home with you; she should be with her mother."

The idea appealed to Martha. But she felt she couldn't face the unpleasant task alone. She invited a CBS-TV reporter to accompany her to the school, explaining that she wanted someone to go with her "to see that I try my best to do what I'm supposed to do as a mother."

When Martha, who had continued drinking in the limousine on the way to the convent, arrived at the school with a TV reporter and camera crew, the three nuns and school business manager who met her at the door refused to let anyone in except Martha.

The meeting with Marty was a disaster. As one of the people involved says, "It was a situation antagonistic to Marty. There was no chance of success. If she had gone quietly (and alone) the confrontation might have been all right."

Martha's version of the meeting, told to various friends and the press, has Marty blaming Martha for John's troubles, calling her mother a "drunk and an alcoholic," and saying, "I never want to see you again."

Losing her temper, Martha slapped Marty and told her, "I never want to see you again either!" Sacred Heart Sisters, present during the argument, had to pull the two apart.

Explaining her actions to CBS–TV reporter Trish Reilly, Martha said all the Mitchells had tempers and claimed that in the past John Mitchell had beaten her up, presumably in a fit of temper. She also said she and Marty were so afraid of him there had been times when they'd barricaded themselves behind locked doors.

Martha was devastated that her plans to "make up" with Marty had gone wrong. She kept asking, "What can I do now?" It was the same question she would put to her psychiatrist over and over again when he came and sat with her for almost three hours before she calmed down.

Of course, there was nothing she could do then, except wait and hope that in time Marty would change her mind and want to see her mother again.

Never after those first hysterical outbursts did Martha indicate in any way that she thought she should do something to win her daughter back. "Marty will come back," Martha would say. "She knows who took care of her and gave her love when John Mitchell was too busy to pay any attention. Marty knows what I did for her, how close we were and how I took her every place with me."

TO ADD TO MARTHA'S TROUBLES, THE DAY SHE CAME HOME FROM MARTY'S school there was a notice from American Express saying her card no longer could be used. Also in the mail were more bills, with threatening notes. And Martha said she couldn't pay Ana her salary, now two weeks past due.

I reminded Martha that she had checks, from promotions and television appearances, that she was holding for deposit until she came to Washington. She could cash one of them. Martha was indignant: "You know I can't use that money, Winnie. It is for my funeral!"

Martha worried a lot about her burial. For one thing, she didn't want John Mitchell "to have a goddamn thing to do with it."

She talked to Ray West, telling him what she wanted. She talked so many times about it that Ray finally said, "Martha, why do you keep telling me all this?" She answered, "Because you're my family and you'll have to do it."

Martha was just as worried about the disposition of her property as she was over her burial plans. She could go into a panic just thinking about "John Mitchell and his goddamn kids getting the things my mother and grandmother left me." One night when she'd been threatening suicide she suddenly said she wouldn't do it since she had to "stay alive to keep John Mitchell and his children from having my things."

With the help of Dr. Lorand, Martha got through the next days of depression, and on December 20 she left for Washington to spend the holidays with Philip and Mary Robertson.

Philip and Mary soon discovered they had a most unusual guest. Martha slept until four or five most afternoons and stayed up all night. She wanted them to stay up with her and talk, but Philip was working and had to get up early. Because time meant absolutely nothing to Martha when she was drinking, she did such things as dash into their bedroom at two A.M., when they were asleep, to complain that she couldn't reach a telephone number she was calling. When Philip suggested it might be too late to be calling someone, Martha answered, "It's on the West Coast, so it really doesn't matter."

Christmas Eve, Martha and the Robertsons went to a friend's house, and after dinner Martha said she wanted to go to church. They went to the eleven o'clock Christmas Eve services at the Metropolitan Methodist Church.

As Philip tells it: "The services started with the minister, Dr. William Holmes, talking about people at this Christmastime who were without their families, mothers who were without their children . . . And it really hit right home with Martha."

She became so upset, saying "I have got to get out of here," that Philip took her home. When they got there, Martha said she was going upstairs to take an overdose of sleeping pills and commit suicide.

In trying to calm her, Philip suggested she might want to talk to the minister who had preached the services. Martha said she would, and Philip arranged for Dr. Holmes to come over. When he saw the lights of the clergyman's car, Philip went to the door to meet him and to tell him the problem. When the minister walked into the room where Martha was, she beamed and stood up and said, in her best Southern-belle manner, "Well, how are you? Why, you look just like Billy Graham." Then she sat there and was so charming that Philip feared Dr. Holmes would think he was out of his mind.

All arguments in the Watergate cover-up trial ended at three-fifty P.M. on December 27, and Judge Sirica sent the jury out for a weekend of rest. Three days later the Judge gave his instructions to the jury, and it started deliberations. Martha was overcome with anxiety.

New Year's Eve she refused to go to a party with Junie and her friends, after saying she would go. She told Philip she didn't want to be out partying while the jury was out, because she didn't think it looked right.

After deliberating fifteen hours and five minutes, over three days, the Watergate cover-up jury reached its decision at four twenty-five P.M., New Year's Day. Twenty-five minutes later the verdict was read to the defendants.

John Mitchell, H. R. (Bob) Haldeman, John Ehrlichman and Robert Mardian were found guilty on all counts. The fifth defendant, CREEP lawyer Kenneth Parkinson, was found not guilty.

As soon as I heard the verdict on the radio, I called the Robertsons. Philip said they hadn't heard the news. I asked if he wanted me to come over to tell Martha; he said he'd do it but would call me if Martha wanted me to come and be with her.

Philip walked back into the room. He didn't know quite how to tell Martha. Finally, he said as kindly as possible that the verdict was in and John was guilty on all counts.

Martha started to cry. She said, "You certainly don't know how to break news very gently." Then, Philip says, "She got absolutely where she could not talk. She couldn't speak at all. Her mouth quivered. She shook all over. It scared me, really. And she was in this condition for about ten minutes."

Then Martha asked for a drink. When he returned with some wine, Martha told him, "I don't want to speak to anybody from the press; just tell them I have no comment."

With that, the telephone rang. It was the Los Angeles *Examiner.* Philip told the reporter that "Mrs. Mitchell doesn't want to talk at the present time." As he hung up he heard "a heavy *swish* and then a sort of a crunch." He jumped up and looked out the window. The tallest tree in the garden, a pine some eighty feet tall, had been knocked over by a freak wind. It came down on the telephone pole right in back of the house. Philip lifted up the telephone; it was dead.

He told Martha and Mary about the tree. They didn't believe it. The day was clear, there hadn't been a storm. They looked out the window and Martha started laughing. "I think this is one of the funniest things," she said between gales of laughter. "It is an Act of God. This is the way He has cut me off from the world. Now I won't have to do anything about the calls."

Martha seemed to rejuvenate herself and she was fine for about two hours, but then she picked up the telephone and found it still without a dial tone. She kept going back and picking up the phone, as if she really wanted to talk to people, but there was no way she could.

Martha especially wanted to talk to Judge Sirica. Since she couldn't phone him she said she'd go see him if only she knew where he lived. Philip laughed, and Martha insisted on knowing why. He told her that one could see Judge Sirica's house from their upstairs windows. Martha wanted to go over immediately, and she got mad at Philip when he wouldn't tell her which house belonged to the Judge.

"Then the eleven o'clock news came on and they showed reporters outside Sirica's house," Philip says. "She said she knew the press was trying to get in touch with her too and couldn't. The news program also had an interview with Parkinson, who got off, and Martha was outraged at that."

As the evening wore on, "Things got a little out of hand," Mary says. "She [Martha] became hysterical. We didn't know what to do."

Philip went to an outside telephone and called me.

When I got there, Martha was sobbing and wringing her hands. She was alternately angry (at Richard Nixon for getting John Mitchell into this mess) and overcome with sorrow that her husband, the father of her child, was going to jail. "And he is going to jail, Winnie," she cried. "People have told me this, but I didn't believe it."

A few days later, when she was back in New York, Martha told me that when the verdict came through it was like an awakening for her. For two and a half years she had been drifting through a fog: "Every morning I used to wake myself up and I would shake my head and say, 'You're wrong, Martha, this isn't happening to you. You are dreaming it, Martha.' "

On the other hand, she felt "free, since I no longer had to carry the burden of feeling that I had been wrong. It was a feeling within myself that I had to meet with God and know that I did right when I went against my husband in many, many things, in order to help my country."

But Martha realized this "was the end of the line and I had to face it. I was by myself. I had to depend on myself. Either I would survive or I wouldn't survive. It depended on me." She added, "I will survive."

Although Martha claimed she would survive, some of us now feared she might not. She was on liquor and Librium, plus sleeping pills. It was a rare day when she wasn't under the influence of one or all of them. And her moods changed constantly, depending, probably, on events, the amount of drugs she took and their interaction on each other.

She was high. She was low. She was maudlin. And sometimes she just seemed to take leave of her senses. January 4 was a typical day. She called me seven times, between nine forty-five A.M. (an early hour for Martha) and fifty minutes after midnight. First she was depressed. She said she'd been awake most of the night, worrying about the unpaid bills, her lack of money and "who will take care of me."

In another call she was exuberant. Martha had talked to Rex Reed ("he *loves* me"); he had told her all of her money problems would be over if she hired his agent, Sanford (Sandy) Leigh. Martha took Reed's advice. Now she was full of optimism. She said Sandy Leigh would handle everything.

"Who the hell have you been talking to?" were her first words in her after-midnight call. She was furious that I'd been on the line with someone else when she wanted to chat about her future career. The frustration of having to wait to talk to me had put her into an absolute frenzy, as I realized the minute I heard her voice.

When Martha had her dramatic shifts in moods—always, as far as I could tell, caused by alcohol or drugs or a combination of both—her close friends could recognize them just by the tone of her voice. It was soft and childlike when she was sad and in a "poor little me" mood; tearful and maudlin when you were her only friend in the world and she needed help; loud and harsh during times of outrage.

There was a special tone which signified her "Grande Dame" mood. Then she spoke slowly, in a condescending tone, pausing between each punctuated word, which was spoken in a broad Southern accent. At those times I always felt Martha was playing a role. As Jay Jennings says of his mother: "She should have been an actress. She was able to pick and choose her façade, according to what she wanted to portray. She was able to play her part convincingly."

JUST AS THE FOURTH WAS A TYPICAL DAY, JANUARY WAS A TYPICAL month. Martha was emotionally up or down; there were few in-betweens. In response to a desperate plea, during a low period, Junie went to New

York and stayed several days. Then I dashed up after a call in which Martha sounded so drugged I was afraid she accidentally might kill herself. Another night she was so distraught it took visits from both Dr. Lorand and Henry Rothblatt to pull her through.

Ana was becoming increasingly distressed over Martha's behavior, and Junie and I feared she'd quit, which she did in late February. In addition to being afraid of Martha when she was in one of her alcohol/drug-induced rages, Ana was reluctant to take the responsibility for Martha's welfare or the apartment's contents.

For one thing, there was the overnight guest who wanted to go into the locked den "to do some work" after Martha had gone to bed. When Ana refused to open the door, the woman kept insisting she had to get in. Ana stood firm, but she was unhappy at having to tell Martha's house guest what she could and could not do. And Ana had noticed that items mysteriously disappeared every time a particular visitor came to see Martha. One day, Ana told Junie she'd seen this person walking out with something. For a while Martha too suspected this "friend." But evidently she changed her mind, because later she resumed the friendship.

Surprisingly, Martha did accomplish some things during January. She went to Canada to appear on a television show. She and Junie met at Martha's apartment with a representative of the American Program Bureau and arranged for Martha to speak, on February 14 in Youngstown, Ohio, at an annual Junior League meeting. She met with John Mitchell's probation officer. Also, Martha had several promising meetings with Sandy Leigh.

Martha was being deluged with every kind of offer. Some of them, Sandy thought, were "ludicrous," others seemed out to exploit her. He wanted to plan for Martha a long-range career in broadcasting, on the lecture circuit or in writing. In any of these he thought she could have a "perfectly wonderful, dignified career . . . She was an American heroine, of a kind, and to demean that by throwing her into commercials or into dinner theaters or silly things like that would have killed all the qualities about her that people most admired."

Sandy Leigh had meetings with several lecture bureaus that were interested. They were offering $2,500 and $3,000, and he thought he might be able to get more. But every time he approached Martha with an offer, she refused. "I never figured this out," he continues. "I said, 'You know, Martha, you keep telling me you've got money problems, and yet you are turning down an easy twenty-five hundred to three thousand dollars a week for a half-hour prepared little speech over a rubbery chicken à la king.' I said, 'I really don't understand.' " Martha would only say, "We'll get to that later," or "I don't think I want to do that right now."

Although she wouldn't do the lecture circuits or sign a contract for a book, Martha, who all her life had wanted to be on the stage, was anxious to accept a dinner theater offer to play a leading role in *Arsenic and Old Lace.*

"She thought she could do anything," Sandy says. "But even if she could remember the lines, it was a part she was totally wrong for; even if she were an actress.

"And if she had a drinking problem," he continues, "she would have been in lawsuits up to her ears for nondelivery. Also, she wanted the limousines and the this and the that. I said, 'You are never going to get that kind of treatment in a dinner theater.' "

Finally the offer of a radio interview show met the approval of Sandy Leigh, while also appealing to Martha. Sandy negotiated it for over a month, but he says she was making demands which were unrealistic: "Also, I think the parties that were interested in her decided she wasn't up to it. And at the same time I realized I was wasting an awful lot of my time on what I considered a project that was never going anyplace."

Among all her frustrations that January, the biggest was that John Mitchell was not sending her the full amount of support ordered by the court. An example of how he met the payments is the way he paid Martha on January 22, 1975. On that date, with John owing her $12,000 for twelve weeks, Steve Peskin, a partner of Henry Rothblatt's, came to Martha's to deliver six checks. One, dated December 16th, was for $2,156.24, which Mitchell's attorney said represented a $6,000 payment to Martha, since he claimed John Mitchell had paid the apartment maintenance until December 16. Yet no one had told Martha he had made the payments; she had been worrying about being evicted. Another check, dated December 23, was for $1,000. Then there were two dated December 27—one for $488.92, the other for $511.08; and two more dated January 16, for $544.53 and $455.47. There was no explanation as to why the checks were backdated. The total of the checks was $9,000.

This method of payment infuriated Martha; she "knew" John was doing it deliberately to harass her and to "drive me out of my mind."

NEW YORK WAS IN THE MIDST OF A SEVEN-INCH SNOWSTORM THE DAY Martha and Junie left for Ohio, where Martha was scheduled to make a speech before the Youngstown Junior League's annual Town Hall, on Valentine Day 1975.

Their trip was to be as stormy as the weather.

Martha had been irritated with Junie ever since she read that John Dean was receiving $4,000 a lecture while she was getting only $2,500, although both had the American Program Bureau as their booking agent. At Martha's request, Junie had made the arrangements with the Bureau, and Martha thought she should have negotiated a fee comparable to John Dean's.

The same day Martha learned that John Dean's lecture fee was larger than hers she also received a copy of the speech she was supposed to make. It was about Valentine's Day, a subject Martha herself had picked, since she would be delivering it on February 14. Martha had spent hours doing her "homework." She had produced several pages of notes on the history of the day, and insisted on having them incorporated in the text. But when she saw the completed speech, she hated it and said she'd never make it.

Martha also was annoyed because the speech hadn't been prepared in large type, as she'd requested. She couldn't see it without her glasses, and she had no intention of wearing them in front of two thousand people. There wasn't time to have a new speech written or to copy the existing one in large type.

Since Martha wouldn't fly in bad weather, she and Junie went by train. This meant leaving a day early in order to take a train to Pittsburgh, where they were met and taken by limousine to Youngstown, Junie spent the whole twelve-hour train ride copying the speech in large block letters on cue cards.

The committee for the Junior League Town Hall took Martha and Junie to dinner the night before the event, which was to start with Martha's speech, include an Anne Klein fashion show and end with a luncheon with Martha as the guest of honor. Someone seated next to Junie at dinner casually asked the subject of Martha's speech. When Junie said, "Valentine's Day," the woman responded, "No! We don't want anything like that."

The women went back to the hotel with Martha and Junie, and rewrote the speech with Junie's help. Then they copied it in block letters, with crayons, on large cards. During the whole time Martha was her charming best. But the minute they left, she turned on Junie. She didn't like the speech. She didn't like anything about being in Youngstown. And she especially didn't like the hotel—it didn't sell liquor.

Sometime in the wee hours of the morning, Martha and Junie wound up in a screaming match; Junie went to her room and slammed the door.

The sound of people talking in the sitting room awakened Junie. She got up and opened the door a little to see who it was: "There was Martha, all dressed, looking bright-eyed and like a million dollars—that's the first time I suspected she took pep pills—just leaving with the Junior League women. Martha heard the door open, turned and looked at me and said, 'Oh, Junie, I'm afraid you won't be dressed in time.' With that, they left."

Junie made it to the Symphony Center, where the Town Hall was taking place, just as Martha dramatically threw away her speech and called for questions. But Junie stayed in the dressing room downstairs, too angry with Martha to listen.

Relations between the two didn't improve on the way home. And once in New York, Martha and Junie got into such a violent argument that Junie repacked her bags and left for the Plaza Hotel to spend the night. As she was leaving, Martha, who had been standing in the hall screaming obscenities at her, suddenly turned, lost her balance and fell against a small table standing outside her bedroom door. When she hit the table, a cranberry glass lamp which had belonged to her grandmother crashed to the floor and broke into a dozen pieces.

Junie started back to help Martha, but Ana, afraid of another tirade, waved her back, saying she'd take care of everything.

Martha broke two ribs when she hit the table, although the fall didn't seem severe enough to have caused such damage. It's possible she was already suffering from multiple myeloma, the blood condition which brought her to the hospital seven months later. In multiple myeloma, the bones become porous and brittle and break easily. She would suffer several other mysterious breaks before going to the hospital.

Finally Ana quit, saying she was afraid to stay in the apartment with Martha, who immediately called the agency and got another companion. The next day, John Mitchell was sentenced to two and a half to eight years for his part in the Watergate cover-up. When Martha and I talked, she was the calmest she'd been for some time. Her only comment about the sentencing was, "Mitchell will appeal and appeal until his friend [Supreme Court Chief Justice] Burger gets him off."

(In April 1977, when the cover-up case was before the Supreme Court for appeal, someone at the Court leaked to National Public Radio correspondent Nina Totenberg that the Justices had voted to deny the appeal, five to three, with Justice William Rehnquist having disqualified himself. Chief Justice Burger, the report said, was delaying an announcement because he hoped to convince two other Justices to switch their votes in favor of reviewing the case. According to Nina Totenberg, the three Justices who voted to hear the case were Warren Burger, Harry Blackmun and Lewis Powell, Jr., all Nixon appointees. Following the furor over the leaked revelations, the Court took no action for a month, after which it voted not to hear the appeal. John Mitchell went to prison on May 22, 1977.)

As John Mitchell was leaving District Court he said of his sentencing, "It could have been a hell of a lot worse. They could have sentenced me to spend the rest of my life with Martha Mitchell."

On the same day that Judge Sirica was sentencing the Watergate cover-up defendants, a Manhattan Supreme Court judge refused to grant a quick trial in Martha's separation suit. Now she would have to wait at least six months before going back to court to ask for an increase in her separate maintenance.

Her husband's insensitive remark, plus the delay in her separation suit, was more than Martha could bear. She took to her bed for two days, getting up only when her anger overcame her melancholy. Now she was upset with her lawyer Henry Rothblatt for losing their plea for a quick trial. Martha claimed he was "playing footsies with John Mitchell." A week later she hired a new attorney, William Herman.

Martha also was disturbed with Sandy Leigh and said she wasn't going to pay him 10 percent of her earnings. "I can get offers on my own, without an agent," she declared. Within a few days Martha and Sandy agreed they should sever their client/agent relationship.

EARLIER IN THE YEAR MARTHA HAD ASKED ME TO GO TO MEMPHIS WITH her in March, when she was to speak at a seminar. I refused. We'd almost become permanently alienated following the Alabama trip, I told her. And of course it had been a disaster when we went together to Canada.

But Martha kept after me to go. Norfleet Turner, a college friend of Ray West's and head of the Data Communication Corporation, had asked her to speak, Martha said. She would be paid around $3,000.

As an inducement to get me to go with her, she added that she was going from Memphis to Pine Bluff, and if I went along I could meet and interview her friends, which I would have to do at some point before finishing the book. Against my better judgment, I said I'd go.

At Martha's request, Norfleet Turner called me to discuss her schedule for the three-day seminar. Her first night should be free, I told him, without revealing that following a flight Martha probably wouldn't be in condition for any of the festivities. He wanted her to hold a press conference the morning after. That was fine, I said, if it wasn't too early. We settled on eleven o'clock.

Instead of a speech at the luncheon, as he and Martha had agreed, I suggested a question-and-answer period, with local reporters and commentators asking the questions. He thought that a good idea. The only other event he wanted her to attend was the final night dinner where opera singer Marguerite Piazza would entertain.

Then, without telling me, Martha talked with Norfleet several times and approved a new schedule, which would start the night we arrived. She was to make an appearance at a seminar cocktail party, give an exclusive interview to Anna Byrd Davis of the Memphis *Press-Scimitar* and then go to a dinner at the Hunt and Polo Club. The next two days were to be just as busy.

In the meantime, Martha booked herself on a television show in Boston three days before we were to leave for Memphis. Once in Boston Martha learned that Bill Safire had been a guest that morning on WCVB-TV, the station Martha would be on later in the day. Apparently Safire had talked quite a bit about the Mitchells, and none of it had been favorable to Martha. Safire said that Martha was a woman who desperately craved attention and publicity, adding, "She has to be a celebrity." He said he remembered that for "many years when she needed John Mitchell he stood by her like a rock and then when he needed her she ran out." Martha's current outspokenness, Safire claimed, was "a personal thing to hurt her husband."

Martha still was in a rage when she got back to New York the next day. Because she'd been "insulted" in Boston, she said she wasn't going to Memphis. Then she said she would, but by train, which was impossible since she would arrive after the luncheon. Finally she said she'd fly. But at one A.M. of the day we were to leave—Martha from New York, I from Washington—Martha was still storming around her apartment. She hadn't packed. I didn't know if she would make it to the airport.

Chapter Twenty-Six

MARTHA WAS ON THE PLANE WHEN I GOT ON AT WASHINGTON. She had boarded it in New York, with the help of a friend of Norfleet Turner's, a woman who had picked Martha up at her apartment and then flown with her to Washington. The woman seemed relieved to vacate the seat next to Martha and let me occupy it.

Once we were at the Hilton Inn in Memphis, Martha ordered a bottle of Scotch and headed toward her room, announcing over her shoulder that she was going to bed. I told her that if she reneged on her agreement to go to the interview and the dinner following, it would be terribly embarrassing for her cousin Ray West, who had introduced her to Norfleet and who was in Memphis to be with Martha.

She was extremely fond of Ray; I knew she always tried to be on her good behavior when he was with her. Reluctantly, Martha dressed and went to the interview, where she told Anna Byrd Davis that she would drop a bombshell while in Memphis that "is going to be the biggest statement that Martha Mitchell has ever given." When asked about the bombshell by reporters the next day, Martha didn't seem to remember having promised any and lamely said her bombshells would be in her book.

Martha was quite emotional at the Hunt and Polo Club dinner and cried often as she talked with long-time friends from Arkansas. She also took an instant dislike to Marguerite Piazza, who was beautiful and charming and received a lot of attention from the other guests. Martha didn't like to share the spotlight.

When we returned to the hotel, Martha stayed up most of the night, finishing the bottle of Scotch. As expected, she was in a foul mood the next morning. Halfway through her bacon and eggs (not cooked to her liking), Martha wanted to know when the hairstylist would arrive. On learning that no one had been engaged, she said she wouldn't go before television cameras at a press conference until someone did her hair. It was too late to get a hairdresser. Martha could do her own hair as well as, if not better than, a professional stylist; I told her so and added, "So you either can do your own or have your picture taken with it looking like that."

I knew that was a mistake the minute I said it. Martha gave me a peculiar look and disappeared into her room. After the cameras were set up and the reporters were in place, Martha, wearing a pants suit, which I'd never before seen her do in public, slowly walked in. Her limp and uncurled hair was tied back with a tacky little ribbon. Halfway through the press conference, she untied the ribbon and let her hair hang loose. It looked terrible.

Martha started her press conference dimpling and laughing, but she quickly lost her happy look. The first question dealt with John Mitchell's remark following his sentencing, when he said it could have been a "hell of a lot worse," had they sentenced him to spend the rest of his life with Martha.

"You don't have to quote that to me," Martha said, "I know it. But I won't answer. I've never said a word about John Mitchell and I won't."

Martha told the reporters she was retiring to private life as soon as she completed her Memphis visit and a scheduled television appearance in Washington. "I'm tired," Martha said, "tired of the constant, daily harassment from the 'powers that be,' tired of the whole mess. I'm signing off. This is the end. No more. I don't need it."

Martha's question and answer session following the next day's luncheon didn't go well. Since she'd been out until after three A.M., she was tired, and her rambling answers showed it. Some questions she didn't answer at all, which was unusual for her. Those she referred to me. I was seated beside her but behind the lectern and out of camera range, which made it a bit awkward.

When asked about her book, she said it would contain several bombshells, since "I have some papers that haven't been released. And they can't kill me to get them—they're all on tape."

Of Henry Kissinger she said, "I don't think he's sexy." Asked why she called Helen Thomas so often, Martha said she liked the press and she liked Helen and "besides, she's Lebanese. The Lebanese in Washington liked me."

The then President Ford was weak, because he hadn't "made any outstanding judgments on our problems." She added, "I don't have any crystal ball but I think this country is going into a depression like nothing ever heard of."

When asked what she thought of Gerald Ford's pardon of Nixon, she replied, "We have a double standard of justice in this country. I have a friend who has a child down in Mississippi. The child was arrested not because he possessed marijuana but [because] he happened to be in a car with a friend who had marijuana and the child got ten years in prison . . . On the other hand, We have someone [Nixon] who almost completely tore up our country [and he received a pardon]."

She said she thought Mitchell, Haldeman and Ehrlichman would also receive pardons, since "John Mitchell said to me, months before the indictment, 'We've figured out a way we don't have to go to jail.' " While talking about a possible pardon in an interview earlier in the month, Martha had said, "I know deals were made. I know part of it, but I prefer not to tell you how I know. But I knew before Mitchell walked out of our apartment . . ."

Under protest Martha went that night to the dinner where Marguerite Piazza entertained, but she arrived an hour late. She sat through dinner without eating. A woman at her table remembers that "she pouted like a small child all the time Marguerite was singing."

One hour before Ray West was to pick us up the next morning to take us to Pine Bluff, Martha announced she wasn't going, although her visit had been planned for weeks. Various friends were entertaining for her, and one couple had asked fifty or sixty people for dinner that very night.

She said she wasn't going because "Martha Mitchell doesn't ride three in the front seat." (Ray had told her the luggage would fill the trunk and back seat.)

What did she plan to do? I asked. She'd stay in Memphis, Martha said, and then get on the same plane I'd be on when I came back through Memphis, from Arkansas, two days later.

Ray couldn't do any more with her than I had. She stayed in Memphis; Ray and I went to Pine Bluff. And as far as I know, Martha didn't leave her room for the next two days. She seemed reasonably content to spend her time in bed and on the phone.

When I picked her up in Memphis, our plans were for me to return to New York with her, get her settled and then come back to Washington the next day. But Martha decided we'd get off the plane in Washington, since she'd have to be there in five days anyway to do two *Panorama* shows.

Martha seemed to be in a stupor during most of the flight to Washington, which made it even more surprising when after more than an hour's silence she suddenly turned to me and said something to the effect: "Winnie, I know you don't think so, but I know what a good friend you've been to me. You've saved me so many times. I appreciate it more than you'll ever know."

At the Wellington Hotel in Washington, Martha had room service send up a bottle of Dewar's and signed the $36 chit, saying *Panorama* would pay for it. For three days Martha didn't leave her suite. Jay and his wife Janis came over one night for dinner, which they brought in from a Chinese restaurant. Martha and Jay disagreed over something and they fought before he left. I went over to spend a day with her, but we, too, got into an argument and I went home early.

That night, Hal Gould took Martha to a St. Patrick's Day dinner dance at socialite Rose Marie Bogley's nearby Maryland estate; Martha hired a limousine to take them there.

Martha had had several drinks before they left her hotel, and as the evening went on she continued to drink. After dinner Martha and Hal went into the living room to dance, and Hal remembers that when "Howard Devron and his little band struck up 'Martha, Martha' she went into a little act, with her own little dance by herself. She was oblivious to anyone else in the room."

Back at the hotel, the limousine driver came up to Martha's suite to receive his pay. She wrote him a check and Hal remembers thinking, "Isn't it funny that she would spend $118 to make an impression when it wasn't necessary."

Hal was amazed that Martha could handle the transaction as she did: "But, as you know, Martha never quite lost control. She'd get out of her hair [a hair piece] and her shoes, but she could still manage to *carry* her shoes and her hair."

Martha shed a few tears that night when talking to Hal about John Mitchell. And she confessed that she'd always love him. But on the whole, it seemed to have been a pleasant evening for her.

THE NEXT FIVE DAYS WERE HAPPY ONES FOR MARTHA. SHE WENT OUT WITH friends—to Sans Souci, the Jockey Club—successfully co-hosted two *Panorama* shows and temporarily made up with Jay.

But her euphoria was to be short-lived. On Friday afternoon, May 21, Maxine Cheshire told Martha that for some time John Mitchell had been going with Mary Gore Dean, an attractive and rich Georgetowner. Mary Dean was the widow of Gordon Dean, first chairman of the Atomic Energy Commission and the sister of Louise Gore, the wealthy Republican who introduced Spiro Agnew to Richard Nixon.

It never had occurred to Martha that John Mitchell ever would find someone else; she always thought he still loved her. She was heartbroken. She sobbed, uncontrollably. I offered to go sit with her, but she said Jay would be there in a few minutes.

The next day Martha was in a disgruntled mood, and her disposition hadn't improved that night when she again went to a Counter-Gridiron carnival to make phone calls all over the country for five dollars each, plus the cost of the call. Martha smiled at the people paying for the calls and joked with those she telephoned. But the people working in her booth soon realized it wasn't the same as the year before, when Martha cheerfully went about doing her part to raise money for the Journalists for Professional Equality.

Now she was complaining and demanding and often rude. When the telephone lines temporarily went out of order, she called to the crowd lined up to place calls, "The CIA cut me off!" But inside the booth she threatened to leave.

While on a rest-break from working with Martha, I visited the book booth where I saw copies of William Safire's then-new book, *Before the Fall.* Thinking it might cheer Martha to receive a present, and knowing she wanted to read Safire's version of the Nixon White House, I bought her a copy. But when I took it to Martha, she looked at the 704-page, two-and-a-quarter-pound tome and querulously asked, "What do you expect me to do with that? I can't carry it all the way to New York."

I was angry with her and would have told her so if I hadn't noticed that other workers in the booth had paused to see what would happen next. So I smiled, leaned close to Martha's ear and hissed, "You take this book graciously, Martha, or I'll hit you over the head with it." Martha looked startled; I'd never before spoken to her like that. She grabbed the book out of my hand, and after a pause she said in her broadest Southern drawl, "Why, thank you, Winnie!"

But on her way out, Martha walked up to where I was talking with friends and said she was going to have a late dinner with Hal Gould and would I *please* take the book home with me. *"Touché,"* I thought. Then I laughed and said I'd be glad to. Martha grinned the way she would when she'd bested someone. She said, "Bye!" and left. It was the only time I'd seen her happy all evening. It also was the last time I'd ever see Martha.

AFTER THE COUNTER-GRIDIRON CARNIVAL, HAL GOULD TOOK MARTHA OUT for a late supper, as he had the year before. In the car on the way back to the hotel, Martha started crying. She said she knew that she and John would never get together again. There was a note of finality about the way she said it. Her husband had found somebody people said looked like her, somebody with money, somebody with position.

When they reached the hotel, Martha asked Hal if he would come up and "just sit with me for a few minutes." She sobbed softly for a while and then said, "Well, I guess I might just as well go to bed. There's nothing else for me to do." Then she walked Hal to the door and stood there, with her shoes off and her hair fallen apart and the tears streaming down her face. She said, "Darlin', Martha's going to get herself together, you'll see."

Although he didn't believe it, Hal told her he thought she would. He spoke of the benefits of prayer and suggested that she ask for God's help. "Oh, I do, darlin'," Martha replied. "I'm close to Him."

Martha awakened around noon more depressed than she'd been when Hal left. Later in the afternoon she was supposed to go as Helen Thomas's guest to a repeat performance of the Gridiron show—a series of satirical political skits. She had looked forward to it, but now she didn't want to see people; she only wanted to go to bed and "never wake up."

At my urging she got dressed and went, but she left within a few minutes because someone "insulted" her. She said that before the show she had been talking to some people at the cocktail party when a woman standing nearby said, "There is that bitch, Martha Mitchell."

Martha dashed out of the room and came back to the hotel alone. I offered to come over, but she said no, she just wanted to have dinner in her suite and go to bed. Later, Martha called to tell me she was going to kill herself; there was no reason left to live. Although I'd never really thought that Martha would commit suicide, unless by accident, I knew she now was so desperate she might stage anything in an effort to get John Mitchell's attention away from Mary Gore Dean. After saying, "I'm going to do it, Winnie," Martha hung up. I called back and we talked some more. This kept up for some time—Martha hanging up to kill herself, my calling back to talk.

Then the line was busy and finally a woman whose voice I didn't recognize answered the phone. She said Martha was out to dinner. Of course I knew this wasn't true and I told her so. Finally she said she also had been a guest of Helen Thomas's at the Gridiron repeat, that Martha had taken her "drinks too fast" and had had to come home. The woman was worried about Martha and had come by to check on her. When I asked her name she said she was "Diane . . . just Diane."

About midnight Hal Gould called to say he'd just called Martha's suite and a "strange woman answered the phone and said Martha was out to dinner." He wanted to know what was going on. I didn't know, but I suggested we each get a good night's sleep; tomorrow would probably be a rough day.

It was.

ABOUT NOON MARTHA CALLED, AS I KNEW SHE WOULD, BASED ON PAST performances. When I snappishly asked why she hadn't talked to me when I called the night before, she said she didn't know what I was talking about. In answer to my questions, she steadfastly maintained that she had been in her suite all evening, that a relative of Helen's, a Diane Beury, and her husband had come over to check on her and had stayed with her all night. She swore she didn't know that either Hal or I had called.

She was huffy about my questioning her and I was still rankling over the night before, not to mention my trip alone to Arkansas. Our good-byes were curt, although I believed neither her pique nor mine would last for any length of time.

Not long afterward I heard from Betty Beale. She wanted to know why the book wasn't finished. I told her the book would be finished when Martha wanted it finished. Martha was back on the phone within thirty minutes. In her Grande Dame voice she said, "I have been told that you said the book would be finished when I wanted it finished."

"That's right," I replied, still miffed. She wanted to know why I'd say such a thing and I answered (1) it was true, and (2) I was tired of covering up for her. She hung up, but not before letting me know what kind of friend she thought I was for "talking about me behind my back with Betty Beale."

Later that day Martha informed me that she had found someone else to write the book. This had happened before and I'd always say we'd discuss it the next day. Of course, she'd forget, and it wouldn't be mentioned again until the next time she was angry with me about something I'd said or done. But this day I said, "Fine. Just let me know where to send all those papers you had me drag all the way to Washington."

She screamed, "I always knew you were on the other side."

I wasn't surprised when I didn't hear from Martha for the next two days. But she didn't call Junie either, which was unusual. She'd never stayed mad at both of us at the same time.

Three days after we'd talked, Martha returned to New York and I received a letter from Washington attorney F. Joseph (Jiggs) Donohue, saying he had been consulted by Martha and that she had asked for the return of all items "which she supplied you over the past two years." I called and told him the same thing I'd told her other attorneys when they'd contacted me; when I received permission from Martha, in writing, I'd be glad to discuss her affairs with him.

Ten days later I hadn't heard from either Martha or her attorney. When I called Junie to say good-bye—I was leaving for the Netherlands for the press opening of the Marriott Amsterdam—she said I probably wouldn't hear from the lawyer. She felt Martha didn't want the papers delivered to him, but that someone was "pushing" her on it.

But that night, when Martha learned I had gone to Amsterdam without telling her, she became so infuriated at me that she sat down and wrote a letter to Jiggs Donohue, giving him "permission to get *all* material" from me, and to tell him, "Diane . . . says you will take good care of me . . ."

ABOUT THIS TIME, MARTHA AGAIN SEEMED TO PERK UP. SHE STARTED GOING out to parties—usually escorted by a procession of bright young men in publishing or advertising—and her conversations with Washington friends were filled with information about offers she was receiving to do promotions and to appear on television. One night she went to a publishing party where she discussed her book with several editors. As soon as she got home, she called Junie to say the consensus was that the book should be published immediately; Martha wanted Junie to find out when I would finish it!

In late April, Martha went to Nashville to tape a Mike Douglas show at the Grand Ole Opry; when she arrived back at her apartment she found the coverplate off her bedroom phone and the wires exposed, and her closet safe broken into. It is not known what, if anything, was missing from the broken safe.

Martha was upset for several days over the break-in, but pulled herself together to go to Washington to be on a WWDC-Radio *Empathy* program. Fred Fiske, host of *Empathy,* says they had planned to give Martha a good deal of air time, but they had to cut her short because she was so "nervous."

IN THE LAST FOUR MONTHS BEFORE SHE'D ENTER THE HOSPITAL, MARTHA went out more than she had the whole time since John left. She told her friends she was having a "great time." But people who saw her during this period say she was very lonely.

The building superintendent, Alfons Suss, recalls: "She would ask me to come up and fix a window or check the heat, anything to get someone there to talk with her. At first I didn't understand . . . But she was a nice woman, just lonesome." He also remembers that Martha used to come sit with his late first wife, an invalid, when he had to go out.

In late May, Martha's lawyer told me she wanted the papers pertaining to the book, immediately. Since I was leaving on an out-of-town assignment, we made arrangements for them to be picked up the following month.

In the meantime Martha called the two editors she'd liked most when we were talking to publishers—Ellis Amburn of Delacorte, and Tom Congdon of Doubleday—to tell them she was ready to have the book published. Ellis was no longer interested in the book; he had the feeling she never would do it. But he liked Martha. When she wasn't drinking, he says, "she was adorable." He became her escort to many Manhattan parties.

On June 4, Tom Congdon went to the apartment to see Martha about the book. Then he arranged for Martha to have lunch with him and author Max Gunther, on June 9, at the Stanhope Hotel. Later Max Gunther talked with Martha about the book several times, even when she was in Memorial Sloan-Kettering Cancer Center a few months before her death.

"But, she never told anything; she never revealed anything, ever," Tom Congdon says. "And it made me nervous, because we didn't know if she really could reveal anything, whether she had lost her power to reveal, or if she had become so suspicious she couldn't talk to anyone, perhaps."

On the third anniversary of Watergate the media reported it along with interviews with some of the Watergate figures. Martha was on the phone all night fussing at reporters. Or as Martha Angle, of the Washington *Star,* reported, she called, "lambasting the press for 'glorifying' the perpetrators of the nation's worst political scandal in history." Martha also told the *Star,* "These men have become celebrities because they had committed crimes, sins against our country. To me it's just asinine for the press to be giving them all this publicity."

ON JUNE 23, I TURNED OVER ALL OF MARTHA'S PAPERS AND OTHER materials to Diane Beury, whom attorney Jiggs Donohue had named as his representative to receive them. Martha came to Washington a few days later to look over the papers. She stayed with her friend Marta Sweeny in Virginia, planning to be there three days. She wound up staying three and a half weeks. In early July, when Marta lost an assistant at her shop, a boutique called The Pink House, Martha immediately pitched in to help. She answered the telephone, waited on customers and talked to the press. Sales boomed with her working as a saleswoman: when customers asked for her autograph, Martha suggested they buy something and she'd sign the sales slip.

For Martha, the three and a half weeks she spent in Virginia with Marta were the best of the year. With few exceptions she was relaxed and happy to be away from her problems. Since she hadn't told her attorney where she was going, he couldn't tell her about her latest legal problems with John Mitchell. Also, she wasn't reminded of her unpaid bills each day; now the dunning letters from her creditors were left unopened in the entrance hall, where the elevator men put her mail each morning.

After dinner, when Martha and Marta were alone, they'd sit up and talk for hours. Martha would settle down in a large living room chair, tailor-fashion, in her bare feet, and say she really felt at home there. The two would laugh at fate and how it worked out that they were very dear friends. Marta says, "I knew and dated her first husband, Clyde Jennings; he was a divorced, charming Southern gentleman from a good old Virginia family. It was funny that Martha and I would end up friends."

Martha helped Marta during a time when she was "at the depths of grief" over the tragic death of her son. "I would come home from the shop a little late in the evening and she would say, 'You were out at the cemetery, weren't you?' And I'd say, 'Yes, I stopped by.' Then Martha told me how her grandmother never went to the cemetery after the funeral; she just went to church. Martha said, 'There is where you'll find Robbie, not at the cemetery.' "

And when Marta's cousin died and she went to church at eleven o'clock—the time his funeral was being held in a distant city—Martha wouldn't let her go alone. The two sat in the little empty church, and Martha held Marta's hand.

But it was Marta who comforted Martha on July 3, when Martha heard on television that John Mitchell had been disbarred in New York: "She ran to the bedroom and when I walked in she was looking out the back window. She turned around and there were tears running down her cheeks. She said, 'Oh, why did John do it? Why did John do it? He worked so hard to get where he was in life.' "

When Martha came back to New York, she again started drinking heavily, with the predictable results. Her moods changed rapidly, from exhilaration—when talking about partying with New York friends and the offers she said she had for a movie, television shows and commercials—to despair, when she talked about her $1,000 electric bill, along with others, and what was going to happen to her and Marty when John Mitchell went to jail.

Chapter Twenty-Seven

ON THE TWENTY-EIGHTH OF JULY, MARTHA WAS INFORMED BY HER attorney, William Herman, that he had received a Notice of Motion from John Mitchell's lawyers, saying they were going to court on August 5 if they did not receive all of Mitchell's clothes, personal property and papers by the next morning. Martha couldn't understand it. She cried, "Why would he want these things? He's going to jail!"

Nevertheless, she worked all night getting his possessions together and putting them in the foyer, sobbing as she labored that she was severing all connections with Mitchell and that "after nineteen years it is all ended." Zolton picked up what Martha had put out and gave a receipt to the building superintendent.

New York County Supreme Court records show that the chauffeur came for the things after Martha called John Mitchell's law firm and put a message on the answering service which stated: "Your clothes are in the foyer. You will never get your papers." The court record also states that the clothes were "heaped" in the foyer and that family photographs were "torn and damaged to boot." A Mitchell friend says Martha had taken scissors and cut to bits photographs, documents and various certificates. But as she'd vowed on the answering service phone, she did not put out any of his records, correspondence or other items relating to his periods of private practice and public service. Since she did not include these things, Mitchell's lawyers proceeded with the motion to the court.

The motion requested delivery of papers "in the apartment." Saying she didn't have the papers, Martha showed William Herman filing cabinets which were virtually empty, with only a few of Martha's papers and unpaid bills in them. She didn't mention that months before she had cleaned out the files, putting all the other papers into boxes. As for the clippings, releases and transcripts her husband was seeking, Martha told Bill Herman they were hers.

John Mitchell's lawyers demanded an affidavit from Martha, saying she did not have the papers requested. She told Bill Herman, "I'm not going to make an affidavit; I'm telling you I have nothing and he's getting nothing from me."

Martha went off on a trip, and her lawyer put in an affidavit saying she was out of town, but she had told him there was nothing of her husband's in the apartment. The judge decided the motion in Martha's favor. But while the motion was still pending, the other side put in an additional affidavit, substituting "anything in her possession, whatever it may be" for "in the apartment."

William Hundley, one of John Mitchell's attorneys, called me to ask if I had any of the papers they were seeking. Mitchell was trying to write a book, Hundley said, and urgently needed the material to refresh his memory. I told him about the suitcase full of clippings, transcripts and letters that I had turned over to Diane Beury.

A few weeks later William Hundley called back to question me further about the contents of the suitcase, which he said had been delivered to Helen Thomas's apartment after Diane Beury had picked it up at my apartment.

By the time the Mitchell lawyers amended their motion, Bill Herman couldn't find Martha. She deliberately hadn't told him where she was going. Bill Herman had to tell the court that, incredible as it seemed, he couldn't find his client.

SOON AFTER SHE PUT JOHN MITCHELL'S CLOTHES IN THE FOYER—ONE account has it that she sprinkled them generously with salt and cleanser —Martha telephoned Ellis Amburn to ask if she could join him and his guests for a weekend on Fire Island. She was sad. She was lonesome. She didn't want to spend the weekend alone. Ellis said he'd be glad to have her.

Martha arrived at Fire Island in one of her bitter and belligerent moods. She complained about her transportation to the Island, let her host know she wasn't pleased at having to share a bedroom with another woman guest, and generally was so nasty Ellis finally told her he thought she'd be more comfortable in her own apartment and suggested she go home. Martha refused to leave. The situation became so explosive that Ellis left his own cottage to spend the night with friends, leaving his guests —among them Pat Loud, the mother in the public-television documentary series, "An American Family," and her son Lance.

The next day, Lance Loud escorted Martha to the ferry, which the two were dashing to catch, when she slipped and fell to her right knee. Later Martha would tell a dramatic story about falling up the gangplank after being "pushed" as she was getting on the boat; still later she'd say she was pushed and fell between the ferry and the dock and had to be pulled out. According to witnesses Martha slipped, but Lance caught her before she fell completely to the ground.

Once back in the apartment, Martha, too lonesome to stay in New York, called Marta Sweeney to ask if she could come to Virginia the next day instead of two weeks later. Martha also had arranged for the two to tape a Mike Douglas show the following day in Philadelphia.

The taping went well, but Martha surprised her television host when in answer to his question, "Martha, if you had to do it all over again would you do anything different?" she answered, "Yes, Mike, I would be quiet as a mouse."

The first time Martha visited Marta, in June and July, it was a tranquil period. But the second time she started drinking right away. She stayed up all night drinking Scotch, and she slept until noon or later each day. And when she was up, she was on the phone constantly.

Also, Martha was having problems with her teeth. A consultation with a dentist and a periodontist determined that Martha had a medical problem and it was recommended that she see a Washington hemotologist. She didn't.

One evening during her visit, Martha went out on a "blind date" with a retired Navy captain, a Naval Academy classmate of Ted Dankworth's, who had been a White House social aide during the Kennedy, Johnson and Nixon administrations. The Dankworths took Martha and the captain to a popular restaurant, where Martha surprised her hosts by being uncharacteristically reserved. From the restaurant, the four went on to a Washington nightspot where they danced for hours.

Martha reported to Marta, who had waited up for her, that she'd had a wonderful time and that she had held the captain's hand and "danced close so that anyone who looked would blabber." Martha admitted she was putting on a show for such people as a Mitchell attorney and a Washington *Post* reporter who'd been in the crowded restaurant.

But holding the captain's hand and dancing close, Martha admitted, "wasn't hard, because I loved it, he was so handsome and charming."

Plans were made that evening for Martha and Junie to visit him soon in Virginia Beach. Martha and the captain discussed the trip the next day by phone, but Martha never went. Ten days after their date Martha wasn't feeling well, and soon after she entered the hospital.

Even before their evening out, Martha had complained about being "terribly tired," which she said she couldn't understand. Her friends, knowing that she was "staying up all hours of the night," weren't disturbed by her lack of energy.

Also, Martha was consuming large amounts of Scotch, and it was a rare few hours when she wasn't ranting and raving about something. Undoubtedly, she already was in physical pain from the disease which later would be diagnosed as a bone-marrow malfunction. And the mental anguish caused by her problems with John Mitchell was almost unbearable.

Anything anyone did or said seemed to set her off. She screamed abuse at Jay and reminded him he was "just like your father," which to Martha was the ultimate insult. She complained to Nick Thimmesch about an article he wrote in which he quoted John Mitchell as saying it had been a good year "because I got rid of you-know-who."

The week of August 25 Martha calmed down enough to go to Marta's Pink House to help get out invitations for a party Marta was giving at the shop. Martha became faint, and Marta had to have someone take her back to the house.

Then on Saturday, August 30, when Marta had a dinner party for some out-of-town relatives, Martha was too sick to get out of bed. She asked Marta to bring everyone back to her room, saying, "I want to meet them." She complained, "I don't feel sick, but I don't feel well. I feel nauseated, but I can eat. So what's wrong with me?"

The next day she mentioned that her back and shoulder were hurting. And while bending over to get something out of the refrigerator, she cried out, "Oh! That pain!" Marta dashed in but Martha brushed her aside, saying she was all right.

On Monday, September 1, Martha was in tears. She said her pain was so severe she couldn't stand it. Marta called her doctor, Thomas O'Brien.

When he walked into the bedroom, Martha—ever the Southern belle—smiled, turned to Marta and said, "Well, you said he was a wonderful doctor, but you didn't tell me how *handsome* he was!"

Dr. O'Brien examined Martha and told her she must come to his office the next day for x-rays. There was a problem, he said, which might be a pinched nerve. In any event, more tests were necessary. He wrote a prescription for a medicine to relieve the pain.

When Martha saw it, she said, "That's only Tylenol; I'm not taking that. Give me my purse." Marta was amazed to see Martha remove a large bottle of codeine tablets. For the rest of the day and throughout the night, Martha drank Scotch and took codeine.

On Tuesday, Martha's fifty-seventh birthday, she refused to go to the doctor's office for x-rays, claiming she didn't need them, that nothing was wrong with her. Of course, the Scotch and codeine had deadened the pain; she probably thought she was over whatever had been bothering her. Finally, she was persuaded to go, but not until the next day.

In the meantime, Marta had planned a little birthday party for Martha, but she wouldn't come out of her bedroom. When Junie called to wish her a happy birthday, Martha cried, "Why don't people leave me alone!" Jay, who still was upset because of the phone calls, brought flowers to Marta's shop and asked her to take them to Martha. His mother didn't call to thank him, but she carried the flowers around the house with her for the next few days.

Saturday morning Martha seemed to be feeling well, and for the first time in days she wasn't angry with anyone or about anything; her attitude was more of bewilderment at the predicament she was in.

A letter from her lawyer Bill Herman had arrived for her in Junie's morning mail. Martha asked that it be read to her over the phone. It said that Martha had to be in court, in New York, the following Monday. Junie had someone take the letter to Martha, and for the rest of the afternoon Martha called Junie repeatedly. With each call she seemed more upset and increasingly outraged at John Mitchell.

Martha also was making other calls. She telephoned Dr. O'Brien to say she was so sick she had to enter the hospital at once. She called Marta and "ordered" her to come home immediately to take her. "She was drunk, very drunk," Marta says. She contacted Dr. O'Brien who said there was no rush, she could take Martha to the hospital after the shop's closing time.

When Marta got home, Martha was in the kitchen frying a steak and making toast. She refused to leave until after she ate. Ed Doran, a next-door neighbor, and Marta waited almost thirty minutes while Martha drank Scotch and ate steak and toast with catsup on it. Martha didn't mention being in pain or feeling ill.

Marta felt that Martha wanted to go to the hospital so she wouldn't have to go to court. Since Martha hadn't complained of pain at any time during the day, and since her decision to go to the hospital came so fast after Bill Herman's letter, it's possible that Martha *did* use the hospital as an excuse.

BY ALL ACCOUNTS, MARTHA WAS "ABSOLUTELY IMPOSSIBLE" THE NIGHT she entered Northern Virginia Doctors Hospital. She swore at the nurses, the aides and Ed Doran, who had gone to the hospital with them. She also called Marta "every name in the book."

One thing that outraged Martha was when the nurse told her she couldn't smoke in bed. Martha screamed, "They're not going to tell me to cold-turkey cigarettes. I've been smoking for thirty goddamn years and I'm not going to stop."

When the nurses asked if Martha had any money or jewelry, Marta said she would check. She was counting the money when Martha yelled, "Goddamn, here I am wracked with pain and you stand there counting my goddamn money."

Just then Dr. O'Brien walked in. Immediately Martha was all smiles. She cooed, "Oh, Doc. I am *so* glad you're here." Marta left; she was so angry with Martha that she didn't enter her hospital room again for over a week, although she came every night, bringing flowers and sitting in the waiting room while her mother and daughter visited with Martha.

During one visit, Marta's daughter Sudee explained that her mother wasn't coming in because Martha had been "so nasty to her." Martha said she didn't remember that.

"Then I went in to see her and I was shocked," Marta says. "She looked like she was at death's door. I had taken her in drunk, not sick; I didn't know what was wrong."

Martha didn't have on makeup and her hair wasn't combed. Food and water were spilled over her dinner tray, and when she wanted a drink of water two nurses had to help her up to drink it.

When Junie visited, she was disturbed to find Martha, "like a zombie," falling off to sleep while talking, although no sedation had been prescribed. Later nurses searched her belongings and discovered a supply of various drugs.

It was three weeks before the doctors could complete their tests and make a firm diagnosis, partly because of Martha's self-medication but mainly because Martha kept refusing to take the scheduled tests. Finally Dr. O'Brien appealed to Jay to intercede with his mother to get her to take them.

Although she was weak and "not feeling well," Martha was optimistic enough about her condition, on September 20, to say that she would go to Philadelphia on the twenty-ninth to accept the Charisma Award from the Golden Slipper Club, a philanthropic organization. She planned to go to New York first to get the proper clothes.

But on the twenty-seventh Martha again was in a drugged state. At one point she fell asleep and dropped her lighted cigarette on the blanket. The nurses were concerned because she wouldn't eat; all she would take were Cokes, ice tea and coffee.

Since she felt "terrible and hurt all over," Martha couldn't go to Philadelphia. One of her complaints was that her leg hurt so badly she needed help to walk. Another was that her cough was becoming much worse.

Enough tests were completed by September 29 for the doctors to make a diagnosis. On that day Martha was told that she had a serious blood condition and that her chest "was not good." (The x-rays probably showed her old fungal infection, which Martha hadn't mentioned to her doctors.) Martha did not tell Junie or Marta about the diagnosis.

In fact, the next day when she was complaining that she felt "sick," Martha claimed the doctors still didn't know what was wrong with her. She also worried about having no money, although Junie knew she had a considerable amount in American Express checks in her purse. Martha was also concerned about where she would go when she left the hospital; Junie told her she could come to her house.

Dr. O'Brien received the results of more tests on October 1; he was pleased to find that Martha's blood condition was not as bad as he first thought. It's doubtful that Martha understood, though. People she talked to that day say she was so confused she sometimes didn't even know who they were.

THE FIRST PUBLIC WORD OF MARTHA'S HOSPITALIZATION CAME ON OCTOber 4, when a news story quoted Ray West as saying Martha had been hospitalized for "back injuries she received after she slipped getting off a boat." The same article quoted Maxine Cheshire as saying a "family spokesman" confirmed that Martha was in the hospital and that "her trouble has nothing whatsoever to do with the consumption of alcohol.

It also has nothing to do with nerves. It is a physical ailment . . . We are hoping people will not try to track her down."

Martha asked Helen Thomas to come to the hospital the next day—October 5—to hear Dr. O'Brien explain the nature of her illness and then to write the story.

Both Helen and Fran Lewine of Associated Press, who had talked to Jay, had stories on the wire that night saying Martha had a blood-cell disorder and was receiving chemotherapy treatment. Neither story mentioned multiple myeloma.

A later Associated Press story quoted Dr. O'Brien as having told Martha that her prognosis was favorable. He said, "I anticipate the immediate future favorable . . . but that could be changed. Maybe in a year from now, two years, we don't know. I've known people who have gone along five, six, seven years and are still doing fine."

Another news story quoted one of her doctors as saying her blood condition was manageable but in a fairly advanced stage. She had received chemotherapy, which the doctors referred to as "aggressive treatment." It had brought her calcium level back to normal, the doctor said, adding "this is a blood disease that is going to require long-term treatment every four to six weeks."

(Martha's blood condition, multiple myeloma, is incurable but in some cases it can be arrested. A doctor who later treated Martha, Klaus Mayer, chief of hemotology at the New York Hospital of Special Surgery and a member of the staff at Memorial Sloan-Kettering Cancer Center, describes multiple myeloma as a disease in which there is an increased number of plasma cells in the bone marrow. "What happens in this disease," he says, "is that these cells get out of control; they don't function properly because the patient isn't able to make normal antibodies and can't fight infection properly. Also, the disease keeps the patient from making red blood cells properly. The third thing that happens is that because these cells do multiply in an uncontrolled manner they erode the surrounding bone, making holes; the bone looks like Swiss cheese. As a result the bone becomes very brittle." This eventually would cause Martha to have some fifteen fractures. Dr. Mayer adds, "Multiple myeloma is *not* cancer.")

THE MORNING AFTER THE UPI AND AP STORIES APPEARED, MARTHA HEARD a commentator say, erroneously, on the *Today* show that she had cancer. She later said it shocked her to tears. Yet she was calm a few minutes after the show went off the air when she called Junie to ask if she'd heard the news. It was Junie who was so upset she couldn't talk.

Martha was bright and cheerful on October 7. Her visitors were surprised to find her looking "great." Again she wore makeup and her hair was combed and held back with a ribbon.

Dr. O'Brien arrived to see Martha while Marta was there. Marta told him how wonderful it was to see Martha looking so much better. The doctor, too, was delighted with Martha's response to her first chemotherapy treatment, which Marta felt was "just like a miracle."

Martha again was bright and seemed happy on Thursday, the ninth; Marta asked when she could leave the hospital. Martha said she didn't know. When Marta left she told Martha she'd see her tomorrow and Martha said, "Fine."

And yet, as Marta walked into Martha's hospital room Friday night, a nurse said, "Oh, you just missed her. She left twenty minutes ago." Martha had checked out without telling either Marta or Junie that she was going or where she had gone.

Jay had picked up his mother on Friday, October 10, and secretly taken her to an apartment building at 2501 Calvert Street, in northwest Washington. "It was the building where Helen Thomas lives," he says. "Diane Beury moved in with Mom, into this two-bedroom apartment. Diane had rented furniture for it and her husband sometimes stayed there with them." (The Beurys lived in nearby Lanham, Maryland.)

The move was made, according to Janis Jennings, because Martha wanted out of the hospital: "It seemed a blessing at the time that Diane would take care of Mom."

Jay didn't tell anyone where his mother was, because "that's the way Mom wanted it." For the next two or three weeks, Jay and Janis went to see Martha three or four times a week. Diane was always there, occasionally her husband, and once or twice, Janis recalls, Helen Thomas was there, too.

Then one day Jay got a telephone call from Diane, saying his mother didn't want to see him anymore. "The telephone number was changed," Janis says. "And it was impossible to get in unless they were expecting you." Jay went to General Delivery to pick up the mail, only to be told Martha no longer had a postal box; there was a forwarding address, which the Post Office refused to give him.

When Martha didn't show up for her chemotherapy treatment, the doctor called Jay, who sent an urgent message to Martha through a friend of Diane's. There was no reply. He sent another. Only then did he get a telephone call, during which his mother spoke to him and said she was receiving care. But if Martha was seen by a doctor during this period, he didn't get in touch with her Virginia doctor, Thomas O'Brien, to ask for her records.

The phone call was the last Jay heard of his mother for almost two weeks. It was November 18 when Diane Beury called him at two A.M. and said she had to have John Mitchell's telephone number in a hurry, that Martha was dying. Jay asked where his mother was so he could go to her. He wasn't told. Jay learned by radio that his mother had been entered, in critical condition, in a New York hospital under the name Diane Mitchell.

Martha had been brought to her New York apartment on the night of November 16; it was the first time she'd been there since early August. A doorman, Tim O'Neal, recalls the ambulance pulling up in front of the building and Martha being lifted out. "The poor thing," he says, "she was on a stretcher; she was the same as dead."

Dr. Klaus Mayer was called by Diane Beury on November 17 to come see Martha. "I remember that the apartment was an awful mess," Dr. Mayer says, "with a lot of suitcases all over [indicating a recent arrival]." As far as he knows Martha had not had any treatment from the time she had chemotherapy at Northern Virginia Doctors Hospital, six or seven weeks before. Jay thinks Martha refused treatment during this period because she "didn't want to own up to anything unpleasant; she always felt she could escape by not acknowledging whatever it was that was unpleasant."

Dr. Mayer says that when he saw Martha "she was sick, very sick; she had a very high calcium—I drew blood on the spot." He says Martha was taken by ambulance the next morning to Memorial Sloan-Kettering Cancer Center.

Later Martha would claim she didn't remember any of the circumstances surrounding her entering the hospital. "I discussed it with her many times," Dr. Mayer says. "She couldn't remember where she had been, how she got to her apartment or how she got to the hospital." Dr. Mayer later told a family member that Martha was so sick she wouldn't have lived another week had she not received "aggressive treatment" immediately.

Diane Buery rode in the ambulance to the hospital with Martha and furnished the information for her entry. "Then," Dr. Mayer says, "we never saw Diane Buery again."

Within hours after Martha entered the hospital the press reported that she was critically ill with multiple myeloma, which some writers called cancer, although her doctors said it was not.

After hearing the news of his mother's hospitalization on radio, Jay called Memorial Hospital but couldn't learn a thing; the hospital didn't know Martha had a son and evidently didn't believe Jay when he said she did. Jay was beside himself with worry. He spent the next few days trying to find out about his mother's condition. He also wanted to know what had happened to her during the past two or three weeks. She had been weak when he last saw her, but he had thought the myeloma was arrested, at least for the time being.

Ray West was the first person Martha wanted to see. One week after she entered Memorial, Ray received a call from Martha. Her voice was almost unintelligible as she asked him to come to New York, saying, "I need you." He told her he'd be there as soon as possible.

Then Ray called back to talk to the nurse. He had house guests coming from Dallas for Thanksgiving, and he wanted to know if he could wait another week before coming to the hospital. She told him, "Mr. West, my advice to you is to come as quickly as you can." He was on the plane the next day.

When Ray walked into the hospital about ten o'clock Thanksgiving morning, the doctors and nurses were "just elated." Until then they'd had no family connection. Dr. Mayer was trying to get a history of her disease, but he didn't have any information except her records from the Northern Virginia Doctors Hospital that had been sent to him.

Ray was shocked at Martha's appearance. She had lost a lot of weight. Her skin was quite yellow and her abdomen grossly distended. And she couldn't move out of the bed at all except in a wheelchair.

Martha's doctors didn't know whether she was going to live or not. When Dr. Mayer talked to Ray about her chemotherapy treatment, he said what they had given her in Virginia was "peanuts" compared to what they were giving her in Sloan-Kettering.

Ray immediately called Jay and told him to come up. He also thought it urgent that Marty see her mother; he wanted to go get her. But Martha said, "No, they'll only take her away from me again."

DURING THIS PERIOD MARTHA SAW TWO PEOPLE WHO WEREN'T FAMILY. One was J. W. Canty, a young man Ray had introduced to her the year before, who had walked into her hospital room, unannounced, five days after she was entered.

And she saw Kris Forsberg (her former secretary at CREEP). John Mitchell had sent her over to find out about Martha; the doctor wouldn't tell him anything because Martha had told him not to. Later Martha said,

"I knew Mitchell sent her; he wanted to see how near death I was. He wants everything in the apartment for his kids."

Ray called John Mitchell, too, to tell him Martha's condition.

Dr. Mayer's office was flooded with calls from friends of Martha's who wanted to visit her. Martha refused to see any of them. Jay thinks it was because Martha—unlike some people who cling to others when seriously ill—had withdrawn.

The doctor had good news for the family in mid-December. Martha had responded beautifully to chemotherapy. There was talk of sending her home, if someone could be found to take care of her. Martha still needed a wheelchair to get around; she had a fractured right leg that wouldn't heal, and she refused to have it operated on.

Also in mid-December, although she didn't know it, a decision was handed down on the motion John Mitchell's lawyers had filed, requesting the return of his documents and papers. Justice Guy Gilbert Ribaudo wrote the decision, in which he mentions "the publicity attending Martha Mitchell in the various media regarding her illness." He added, "It appears that Mrs. Mitchell is quite ill and the court was chagrined to think that it had entertained any doubts when her attorneys consistently and insistently informed the court that the whereabouts of Martha Mitchell were unknown to them." Because of her illness, the Judge wrote, "the court must conclude . . . that an affidavit from her will not be forthcoming for a long time. Accordingly, the court will consider all the papers that have been submitted."

The court record also stated that the affidavit from John Mitchell requesting the documents and papers said that Martha still had "various pieces of jewelry . . . autographed pictures to him from several former Presidents of the United States . . . various gifts bearing the Presidential Seal such as golf clubs and other items."These were in addition to "six unopened cartons, and two to four file cabinets of personal materials . . . twelve binders of newspaper clippings and documents which were compiled by members of the Department of Justice for his use . . . personal financial records including bank statements, records and other bank material . . . voluminous papers relating to the hearings before the U.S. Senate Committee on Watergate and the trial in the Southern District of New York: United States v. Vesco and others . . ." Mitchell's lawyers didn't explain how papers relating to the Vesco trial could possibly be in Martha's possession. The trial was held several months after John Mitchell walked out.

Other items sought by Mitchell were "eight drawers of his speech materials while in the Justice Department, testimony before various congressional committees, private papers within the Justice Department, and extensive correspondence accumulated during his years of private practice and government service."

The Judge ruled that the matter of the papers couldn't be decided by affidavit alone, that "a hearing is necessary to determine the whereabouts of the particular items sought, and this would perforce entail a confrontation between the parties."

"There is a possibility," the Judge continued, "that some new information relating to the 'Watergate' scandal may be uncovered that could possibly have far-reaching effects when the history of the Nixon Administration is written into our national history."

He ruled that a hearing be conducted "on or about May 1976, a specific date to be set by the referee in view of the plantiff's present illness and unavailability."

The Judge's decision ended with an extraordinary paragraph: "In conclusion, the personal compassion of the court is that it sincerely wishes Martha Mitchell a very speedy and healthy recovery in the near future and since this is the season of the year of 'Peace on Earth' and 'Goodwill,' I wish the plaintiff a Happy and Healthy Christmas and a blessed New Year."

AT CHRISTMAS TIME, EFFORTS AGAIN WERE MADE TO GET MARTHA AND Marty together. Both mother and daughter said no. Martha thought Marty had rejected her, but she felt that someday Marty would "understand" and come back. Martha wanted Marty to make the decision herself.

John Mitchell also refused to see his wife. One of his attorneys said it was his impression that Dr. Klaus Mayer had told John a confrontation between the two would be too disturbing for Martha. Dr. Mayer denies this. He wanted Martha to see John: "I thought it would be good for her to be able to talk to him." And Martha wanted "to just sit and talk to John." If John told her, personally, that they couldn't make a go of it, she would "take it," she would accept it.

Jay spent Christmas Day with his mother. He thought she was "better" but worried that she still was weak and in pain.

Piper Dankworth visited Martha on New Year's Day: "They let me stay only ten or fifteen minutes . . . She kept saying she wanted to go home, but she was pleased with all the get-well cards she'd received. The nurses had put them up with tape and they almost completely covered the four walls."

On January 20 Martha was moved to the nearby New York Hospital for Special Surgery to have her right hip socket replaced with a plastic ball; Ray West finally had convinced her the operation was necessary. The operation was not entirely successful, though; Martha could walk only with the aid of a walker.

Something else happened, however, that was miraculous. Martha had a striking change of personality within days after her surgery. She became one of the "most reasonable" patients Dr. Mayer had; until then she had been one of the most difficult. Martha told Dr. Mayer, "You know, I must have been cuckoo before."

Dr. Mayer admits he has no medical explanation for her tremendous personality change. He ponders the questions: Was it the alcohol? Was it the drugs? Was it something given to her in California? Martha always thought she had been given a long-lasting mind-altering drug during the California fiasco. "I haven't the foggiest idea what LSD does over a long period of time—or other drugs like this," Dr. Mayer says. "If you read the [Jack] Anderson story and how they tried to make her sound crazy—well, it certainly was in the interest of a lot of people to make her sound crazy. And the fact that she did drink was taken advantage of, completely; they made her out to be a complete drunk even when she told the truth."

Martha also thought something she had been given caused her multiple myeloma. Dr. Mayer says, "The press asked me over and over again whether I thought anything could have been given to her to give her the disease. If so, medically I have no knowledge or reason to believe this can be done." He pauses, then adds, "But who knows? In ten years we might find something."

During her difficult period, Martha would fire her nurses—none lasted more than two or three days. Now the nurses "loved her." The floor nurse, Vilma Crescinoni, and the day nurse, Valerie Jones, think Martha was a problem the first few days after her transfer because she was not feeling well and was frightened.

Following her hip surgery, there were times Martha would cry with pain and times when she was upset. She also went through the cycle seen in other patients with terminal illnesses—she had periods of denial and fear, then anger and "why-me?" and eventually acceptance. But through it all, the nurses found her a likable patient.

Although there were few people from the outside who Martha would see, she loved visiting back and forth with other patients and their relatives. Some of the people who visited other patients kept Martha supplied with cakes and cookies and brownies.

One woman who came to Special Surgery to see her boyfriend was so concerned about Martha she wanted to pay all the expenses to fly Martha to Mexico for the illegal laetrile treatments.

"She was a delight," Dr. Mayer says. "She was so positive, so full of life and interested in other people besides herself." He recalls Martha's kindness to one patient and her husband: "The man, a black man, had to go back home in the South and his wife was pretty sick. Martha made it her business to visit the wife every day."

Martha, too, was delighted with the patients, her doctors and the hospital staff. She told a friend, "I am so happy. This is my home." As one of her doctors says, "She hated to be alone. She had to have the security of people around her, taking care of her. The hospital met that need."

Chapter Twenty-Eight

MARTHA WENT HOME ON MARCH 6 IN AN AMBULANCE WITH ONE of the two practical nurses she had engaged to care for her. She hadn't wanted to leave the hospital—with its security, its care and her new friends—for the loneliness of the empty apartment.

Her homecoming was even more depressing than she'd imagined.

The apartment, which she'd left almost four months earlier, was dirty and in disarray. Soot covered the windowsills. Unpacked suitcases cluttered the entrance hall; others were open with the contents spilling out in the master bedroom and the drawing room, where the pale-blue silk sofa—a memory of happier days—was draped with dresses in cleaners' bags.

There was no electricity; it had been turned off for nonpayment. And a few days later the telephone company called to say it was disconnecting the telephone. The nurse finally made arrangements to have both services continued.

The whole apartment looked as if it had been left in a hurry. Beds were unmade, the kitchen sink and drainboards were piled high with pots and pans containing decayed food. And the meat, vegetables and dairy products left in the refrigerator had spoiled when the electricity was off.

Repeated cleanings over several days failed to eliminate the foul odor.

Martha decided she would sleep not in her own king-size bed but on a little sofa bed in Marty's sitting room that was closer to the kitchen, where the nurses would be spending a lot of time.

She kept falling out of the bed, however, while trying to get up without the nurse's help. Salvadore d'Angelo, a doorman, and another building employee, Rocco Michelle, had to put Martha back to bed at least five times, usually in the evening. Perhaps she fell because, as some thought, she had a lot of spunk and she wanted to do for herself—but there was another reason, too, as a relief nurse discovered a week after Martha came home.

The nurse surprised Martha, standing in her walker in the master bedroom, as she was taking something from beneath a chair cushion. Martha jumped when she saw the nurse and dropped a vial of Seconal capsules. Later, more pills and capsules were found under other cushions and tucked between the pages of magazines. There probably were more in her makeup kit and a large white straw purse, which she insisted on keeping next to her bed at all times.

Martha was upset with the nurse for discovering her secret, and she dismissed her immediately. The next day Martha called Junie, for the first time in five months. "Things are so terrible," Martha cried. "I need you more than I ever did." Junie went up the next morning.

Martha cried when she saw her friend; she wouldn't let Junie out of her sight. She kept holding her hand; even when she dozed off, Martha wouldn't let go. Junie would try to slip her hand out when Martha dropped off to sleep, but she'd wake up and say, "Come back; I want you right here."

Junie was surprised to see large plastic garbage bags full of unopened mail. In addition to the letters and telegrams, there were dozens of gift boxes stacked in front of the fireplace in the master bedroom. Most of them contained beautiful nightgowns or bedjackets; some never had been out of their boxes.

Martha didn't watch television or read the papers. She didn't seem to want to know what was happening. Neither did she want to take her chemotherapy treatments. She begged Junie to have her taken off the treatment program, which was two weeks of medication and then two weeks without. Martha even called Ted Dankworth and pleaded with him to find her a doctor who wouldn't make her have chemotherapy.

One day when Junie was there, Martha was in such severe pain the nurse had to call the doctor. It bothered Martha that "John Mitchell can ride around in a chauffeur-driven car and I can't even afford to have someone here who can give me a shot."

Once, while looking for a little table to put beside Martha's bed, Junie started to walk into the den. She opened the door and turned on the lights: "It looked as though somebody had opened the window and a tornado had gone through the place. I couldn't even see the carpet; it was completely covered with papers (letters, scrapbooks, documents). Other papers were piled high on the television, the couch, the chairs and all over the desk." Martha had scattered them the summer before when in a blind rage, brought on by her husband's legal moves to get the papers.

Junie was looking for something else for Martha when she discovered all of Martha's sterling-silver flatware was gone. It never was found after Martha's death. It's unthinkable she would have parted with it, since much of the silver came from her grandmother and Martha, who had a great sense of family and family possessions, always intended for Jay and Marty to have it.

When it was time for Junie to go home, Martha refused to let her leave. Junie had to slip out while Martha was asleep.

The next day Martha had an appointment with her doctor; she refused to go. As she had told Junie, she did not want to have the chemotherapy. Her new nurse pleaded with her not to miss her treatment. Finally, five days later, on March 22, the nurse took Martha to the doctor. He administered her treatment and told her she looked "great."

When Martha and the nurse got home, Martha couldn't find her keys. She accused the nurse of taking them. Once in the apartment, Martha went all through the house, in her walker, checking for various items. When something was missing, she accused the nurse of having taken it. By the time the night nurse arrived, it had been agreed that another day nurse should be there the next morning.

That night Martha again fell out of bed while reaching for a bottle of pills hidden underneath it. "She had sent me back to her bedroom for something," Katherine Foster, the night nurse, recalls. "But I ran back when I heard a noise. She told me, 'I've broken something.' "

Several Seconals were scattered across the floor. The nurse called an ambulance and Martha was taken back to the New York Hospital for Special Surgery; she had shattered her shoulder, broken an arm in several places and cracked some ribs.

By now Martha's myeloma was generalized throughout her body. All of her bones were affected—the skull, ribs, spine, pelvis—making them so brittle that the slightest shock would cause them to break.

Philip and Mary Robertson saw Martha in the hospital the night after she entered. They found her looking "quite well, considering what she'd been through." Her hair was pulled back with a pink ribbon, she had on makeup and her nails looked freshly manicured. She seemed content to be back in the hospital.

And although it was out of character for Martha to talk of unpleasant things, she discussed her most recent injuries, which a month later required surgery because the bones would not heal. Even more surprising, Martha told the Robertsons she had given up smoking cigarettes, a habit dating back to her youth. In recent years she had consumed up to four packs a day, maybe even more during times of sleepless nights.

She wasn't even distraught that the storage company had again sent a notice that it was going to sell her things if she did not pay more on the bill. Martha asked Philip to get her purse out of the closet. In it was a check for the storage bill, filled out by three different people: one had put the date on, one had written out "Morgan Manhattan" and someone else had filled in the amount.

Martha signed it flat on her back, holding the check above her. Her signature wasn't legible, but Philip sent it to the company, and since he never heard from them he presumes the check was cashed.

Before they left, Martha asked the Robertsons *please* not to tell anyone—not even Jay—that she was in the hospital again. Then, evidently changing her mind, she said, "Call Winnie and tell her I'm going to call."

THREE NIGHTS LATER MARTHA CALLED PHILIP, UPSET: THE DOCTOR HAD told her she had only three months to live. She asked Philip to come to New York to sell her furniture, jewelry and other belongings she had previously vowed to hold onto to the last. She was penniless, Martha told Philip. Her private nurse had quit because she hadn't been paid, the doctor had not received his money, and there was an outstanding $80,000 hospital bill.

"I want to die in comfort," Martha told Philip, while pleading with him to sell her possessions.

Philip immediately called Martha's doctor, who could speak freely with him since Martha had given him permission. First, the doctor said, he had not told her she had only three months to live. (As it turned out, another doctor—one of the surgeons—had told her this.) The doctor acknowledged his bill had not been paid, although he'd been treating Martha since November. And it was true there were some outstanding hospital bills. There seemed to be some argument—or as one hospital spokesman put it, "foot dragging"—between AFTRA, with whom Martha had a policy, and John Mitchell's company as to which one was responsible.

(After Martha's death, one of the people to whom she owed a medical bill asked me if I could call AFTRA to find out the status of her policy, since I had the policy number. When I called, the AFTRA representative told me to contact Mrs. Mitchell's sister. The representative seemed shocked when I said Martha never had a sister. Someone representing herself as Martha's sister had presented some bills, which AFTRA paid.)

As much as Philip wanted to help Martha with her financial problems, he knew he couldn't start selling the Mitchells' community property. He called Ray West in Pine Bluff, but Ray felt he didn't have the authority either.

Martha was without funds because John Mitchell had ignored the court's order to pay a thousand dollars a week and was seven months in arrears. But Martha was unaware for some time that John had stopped her separate maintenance payments; she thought the checks were in the unopened mail at her apartment.

Martha's attorney, Bill Herman, assumed the payments had been discontinued when he stopped receiving photocopies of the checks, but he had been unable to reach Martha or to find out where she was. He started writing letters. For seven months he wrote—about the hearings concerning John's papers; about the various lawsuits by her unpaid former attorneys, and by Dr. Lorand against John Mitchell, in which she was named; and about the separate maintenance payments that had been stopped. There was no answer. Finally, in early April—almost eight months since he'd seen his client—Bill received a call from Clifford Kunz, Martha's University of Arkansas chum, asking him to come to the Hospital for Special Surgery to see Martha.

Cliff Kunz hadn't seen Martha for some thirty years when, in 1974, he met Ray West at a New York party. On hearing that Ray was from Pine Bluff, Cliff said he'd once known a girl who was from Pine Bluff; her name was Martha Beall. Ray laughed incredulously and said, "She's my cousin. I'm visiting her now." Ray immediately called Martha and put Cliff on the line. After that they talked often, and Cliff, like many others, was the recipient of late-night calls from Martha.

When she entered Memorial, Cliff visited her a few times in late November and December, and then soon after New Year's he started seeing her every day, because "she had nobody she could depend on."

Cliff Kunz saw that Martha took her medicine, although she didn't want it, and he wiped away her tears when she cried with pain. But when he thought she cried from self-pity he told her to stop or he'd leave: "I said I couldn't stand to see a woman cry. Then she'd stop."

Since Martha loved candy sour balls, Cliff saw that she always had a supply. And she also had a special fondness for Peppermint Park's vanilla ice cream; almost every day he'd bring her a pack.

She always wanted Cliff Kunz with her when her dinner tray arrived; he spent hours by her bedside feeding her. He laughs and says, "Martha liked to be a waited on. But she also liked to think that there was a man who was doing these things for her. That was part of her makeup. Men always had done things for her; she was a true Southern belle and there is no other way to explain it."

CLIFF KUNZ DENIES THAT HE DID ANYTHING FOR MARTHA THAT OTHER friends of hers wouldn't have done had Martha let them. He says he did it "out of friendship and true love for Martha. Because I adored her; there is no question about that."

Although they never dated "as such" when they were at the university, Martha and Cliff Kunz were the best of friends. In describing their relationship he says, "Every girl has one boy she can talk to and say what she wants to say. I was that boy for Martha. There wasn't anything we didn't talk about."

And that's the way it was when they renewed their friendship in New York. He believes she told him things she wouldn't tell others: "And I just listened and showed enough interest that she wouldn't think I was bored.

"Martha was typical of so many Southern women," he continues. "I have known a lot of them in my day . . . And if you think that Tennessee Williams's women are not typical, then you just don't know Southern women. Because they are typical."

Cliff Kunz insists that people should not feel guilty because they weren't able to do anything for Martha at the last: "She wouldn't let them; she wouldn't allow it. She didn't want to see anybody."

Why would Martha, a woman who couldn't stand being alone, cut herself off from people she surely knew were her friends? There were several reasons.

Martha genuinely didn't want anyone talking to her about her illness. "She knew she was going to die," Cliff Kunz says. "There is no question about that. But you could not tell her anything unpleasant, she would not listen to it at all." He adds that always before she had been able to "bulldoze her way through or sweet-talk her way out of things."

Also, according to one of her nurses, Martha didn't want many people to see the way she looked. Martha could cover the surgery scars on her body and the needle marks on her arms with long-sleeved, frilly nightgowns. But her face showed the suffering she'd endured. Her hair was thin from the chemotherapy treatments. And her teeth, which she'd loved to flash in her wide, dimpled smile, now were without caps; all had fallen off due to the nature of her illness.

Another reason she didn't see some people may have been the one she gave when Junie asked why Martha hadn't called her friend Alma Jane McCauley. "Because I feel so guilty," Martha said. Although Alma Jane had been a loyal, supportive friend over many years, Martha hadn't been in touch with her for months.

And, Cliff Kunz says, Martha refused to see or talk to some people because she "was very bitter" about most of them. She thought they had taken advantage of her, that some had been nice to her just so they could use her name.

When Bill Herman went to see Martha, he says, "She was in pretty bad shape. But she was able to talk to me. I stayed about five minutes but she indicated to me quite clearly that she wanted me to go ahead. She wanted me to represent her."

A few days later Bill Herman went into court with a motion to enter judgment against Mitchell for being in arrears on the separate maintenance payments. Waving a sheaf of bills and medical reports from two hospitals, he told a New York Supreme Court Justice that his client was "desperately ill, without funds and without friends."

He said, "She owes nearly $10,000 on her cooperative apartment and large bills to Consolidated Edison, which has threatened to turn off her electricity." He also said there were ambulance, wheelchair and grocery bills, and charged that John Mitchell owed Martha $36,000 in back temporary alimony. When Mitchell's attorney claimed he had no money and was "rooming on borrowed funds," Bill pointed out that he maintained a private chauffeur and recently had received $50,000 on an expected $150,000 book advance. Bill Herman also said that John Mitchell wanted to sell the Fifth Avenue apartment and put Martha in a nursing home. The judge granted the motion and the judgment was entered.

ON MAY 14, ALMOST TWO MONTHS AFTER SHE'D GONE BACK TO THE HOSPItal with her broken shoulder, Martha went home—again with two practical nurses to care for her. One was Katherine Foster, who had continued as Martha's night nurse during her hospital stay.

Cliff Kunz was overjoyed when he found in Martha's unopened mail four or five checks that John Mitchell had sent her in August and September. It bothered him for her to be concerned with financial problems when she was "so sick and helpless." But his joy over the checks was brief; Mitchell had stopped payment on the checks after Martha entered the Virginia hospital.

Furthermore, the Counseling Employment Agency, which supplied Martha's nurses, had been notified by John Mitchell's lawyer, Marvin B. Segal: "This will serve specifically to inform you that Mr. Mitchell will not be personally responsible for any of the bills incurred with regard to the aforementioned assistance [two practical nurses] for Mrs. Mitchell . . ." The letter ended: "You are therefore hereby further notified that for all expenses in connection with the aforementioned services, your firm and the individuals employed can look solely to Mrs. Martha Mitchell."

Every time Martha got back in bed, after walking to the bathroom, she would be in terrible pain. She had to lie in one position; she couldn't even turn over on her side without activating the pain. Finally she said, "As long as I stay this way I don't hurt so much, so I'm not going to move."

This was a dramatic change from only a few weeks before. Then it had looked as if her myeloma had been arrested. Dr. Mayer had been encouraged. But now she was in agony. Tears would stream down her face and Bill Herman would "stand there like a fool with my handkerchief dabbing her tears." There were times when she was in such misery that a doctor had to be called to come give her a shot.

For a while Martha wouldn't see anybody except Cliff Kunz, her doctor and her lawyer. Neither did she want to talk on the telephone; she was too weak and in too much pain. But in the last week of her life, Martha consented to talk with one old friend and to see another.

Cornelia Kittle, who first met Martha when she was married to Clyde Jennings, says she did everything to get in touch with Martha but had been unsuccessful. This time when she called a nurse answered the phone and Martha got on the line. "She told me how much pain she was in and I begged her to let me bring her down here to Virginia with us. We have a big house, I wanted her to come. She said it would be 'wonderful.' "

Alma Jane McCauley, her sorority sister from the University of Miami, also reached Martha that last week, after months of trying. She asked if she could come to see her and Martha cried, "Oh, would you?"

ON WEDNESDAY, FIVE DAYS BEFORE MARTHA DIED, ALMA JANE SPENT TWO and a half hours with her: "She was so sad. She put her arms around me and she cried and cried. She knew she was going. I could tell . . . I held her in my arms and I talked to her."

Martha was having severe pain in her shoulders when Alma Jane was there. It was part of her disease, she explained; the pain would be centralized in one area one day and in another area the next. Hot water bottles seemed to ease her more than a heating pad, so the nurse kept bringing bottles and putting them in place.

By then, Martha was completely without money, although she didn't mention it to her friend. John Mitchell hadn't paid her any of the $36,000 the judge had ruled he owed her. Martha knew she had the account in Alexandria, Virginia, but she didn't have the bank book and she couldn't remember the name of the bank.

She told Cliff Kunz to get "Winnie on the phone," that I'd know how to get the money. Since she couldn't remember my phone number, he called information. Unfortunately, he spelled my last name wrong. For the next four days, he frantically called the answering service of someone named "McClendon," leaving urgent messages.

Ever since Bill Herman had said publicly that Martha was without friends or funds, she'd been receiving forty to fifty letters a day from people all over the country, telling her they were on her side, they missed her in the headlines and that she did have friends. Some of the people enclosed small checks.

On Thursday Cliff called Bill to tell him he had checks totaling $158 and that Martha, who was in terrible pain right then, desperately needed the money. He asked Bill Herman if he would bring $158 in cash, saying he would have Martha endorse the checks to him.

Early Friday, Bill drove into town. He stopped on the way to the apartment to go to Martha's bank on Madison Avenue and Eighty-fourth Street to arrange to get into her safety-deposit box later in the day, so that he could sell some of her jewelry to pay the nurses' salaries, by now around a thousand dollars overdue.

As soon as Bill gave him the money, Cliff Kunz sent the nurse out to buy food. The grocery store, where Martha always shopped, had stopped her credit, as had the pharmacy where she got her drugs. Everything had to be paid for in cash.

Martha endorsed the checks—three for $25 each; seven $10s; two $5s;

and one for $3. It was the last time she wrote her bold, flamboyant signature.

All of the financial manipulating so distressed Martha that at one point she cried, "What's going to become of me? What's going to happen to me?"

The key to her safety-deposit box was missing. She thought it might be in her locked cedar closet, but that key couldn't be found either. Cliff tried to get a locksmith to come open it. Finally it was too late to get in the bank; Bill said he would go on Tuesday, Monday being a holiday. Then he wrote out a personal check, to the Counseling Employment Agency for $203, which was their fee for supplying the nurses.

(By Tuesday it was too late; Bill Herman did not get the jewelry to sell. So the nurses were not paid the monies due them or for the additional days they worked before accompanying Martha back to the hospital—$847.50 for Linda Francis and $480 for Katherine Foster.)

Jay called his mother Friday night and found her in "great spirits." She talked seriously about what she was going to do when she was feeling better and was up and around. She had received numerous offers from various people to do interviews, stories and so on, and she was considering which ones she ought to do.

On Saturday morning, however, Martha was clearly depressed when Cliff Kunz arrived. She hadn't been able to reach her doctor for several days. At one point she asked, "What are they doing, just parking me over here to die?"

Cliff called Dr. Mayer and reached him right away; the doctor had been in Boston. Martha wouldn't let Cliff talk to him on the phone in her bedroom; she didn't want to hear a discussion of her ailments.

From the music room, Cliff told the doctor Martha had been throwing up and that she had some "awful big blood blisters and big welts full of blood" on her arms. They were increasing, he said, and "were building up."

The doctor found that disturbing and said he would come see Martha around nine the next morning. When Martha was told the doctor was coming by, she was overjoyed; she "just perked right up."

Cliff sat by Martha's bed for several hours, and they chatted about many things, including the bridge hand in the *Times* that day. When he asked if there was anything he could do for her, she answered, "You know what I'd like to have? Some good watermelon." He went to the delicatessen and bought a wedge of watermelon, which the nurse cut into little cubes. Cliff fed it to her.

About noon that day, Ray West called. The nurse Linda Francis says,

"We were so glad when she said she'd talk with him. He had called several times before but she was in pain and she wouldn't talk."

Ray's conversation with Martha lasted almost an hour: "Martha said the 'cells have been arrested and I am not any more dangerous than you are.' I didn't understand and I asked her to repeat it. Again she said, 'I am no more dangerous than you are.' In other words, I am going to be all right."

Knowing the seriousness of her disease, Ray couldn't understand her optimism. He felt she was trying to bolster him. As soon as they said their good-byes, Ray telephoned Dr. Mayer at his home to ask if he should fly to New York. The doctor said, no, since "this can go on indefinitely."

Saturday was the best day Martha had had since coming home from the hospital. She told everybody that she had no pain and that she was feeling happy. "And she really was happy," Linda Francis says. "I was kind of taken aback with that happiness."

But shortly before midnight Martha again started vomiting. She was in severe pain, and every time the night nurse Katherine Foster started to leave the room for something, Martha cried, "Don't move." Katherine Foster felt that Martha was afraid.

Between seven and seven-thirty Sunday morning, May 30, one of the nurses called Cliff to say Martha had started vomiting large amounts of blood and was in agony. The nurse didn't think they could wait until nine o'clock for Dr. Mayer; Cliff told her to telephone him at once.

When the doctor came, Martha asked him to help her, to please help her. Dr. Mayer said he was trying and that she must go back to the hospital. At first he thought they could get her downstairs in a wheelchair and take her to the hospital in his station wagon. But both Martha and the nurse protested, saying Martha was too sick. Later Dr. Mayer said, "She knew even better than I how sick she was at this point." He called an ambulance and then notified Bill Herman, who called Cliff Kunz.

Martha became unconscious a few minutes after the doctor left and before the ambulance arrived. She was comatose when she arrived at Memorial, where she was taken to the cardiac intensive-care unit. Dr. Mayer notified John Mitchell of his wife's deteriorating condition. According to a Mitchell friend, Marty was at the apartment with her father when the doctor called. Neither of them went to the hospital.

The doctor also tried to notify Jay and left messages with his answering service. Jay didn't receive them because he was in Philadelphia spending the weekend with his father and stepmother at the National Philatelic

Convention. Sunday night Jay went to bed not knowing his mother was near death in Memorial Sloan-Kettering Cancer Center.

The nurse Linda Francis joined Katherine Foster, who had gone to the hospital in the ambulance with Martha, and the two tried to go in to see Martha. But the doctors and nurses told them to go home. Linda Francis resents that the newspapers said Martha died alone, without friends, since both of the nurses would have been there had they not been sent away. "I really was interested in that patient," Linda says. "She needed love and we gave her real love."

Both Bill Herman and Cliff Kunz went to the hospital; they too tried to see Martha, but the nurse wouldn't let them in. The two sat in a hospital lounge, watching a ball game on television while waiting for periodic reports from nurses and doctors. About three o'clock a resident doctor told them her condition was stable, that nothing was going to happen in a hurry; he suggested they leave.

Dr. Mayer had gone home. When they talked to him on the phone, he repeated what the resident said: there was no reason to stay around, there wouldn't be a change in her condition for quite a while.

Cliff Kunz also resents reports that Martha died alone, without friends: "Bill Herman and I would have been there all night if the doctors hadn't told us there wouldn't be any change in her condition."

Shortly before midnight Martha developed pneumonia. Her body wasn't in a condition to fight it. By now the myeloma, a rare and vicious disease, had spread not only to all of her bones but into the adrenals, kidneys and lymph nodes. She was bleeding from stomach ulcers and hemorrhaging around the adrenals and heart.

Martha died at 4:25 A.M.

Epilogue

SHORTLY AFTER NOON ON JUNE 3, A BEAUTIFUL SUNNY DAY, MARTHA Mitchell was buried in her native Arkansas in the shade of massive oaks at the foot of her mother's grave. It wasn't exactly what she had wanted; her desire was to be buried *next to* her mother. But then, none of her final wishes were carried out strictly as she had hoped. Some of them were ignored completely, including those she'd incorporated in her last will and testament.

One of the main things Martha didn't want was for John Mitchell to have anything to do with her funeral arrangements. She thought she'd taken care of this by giving her cousin, "by marriage," Ray West, Jr., explicit instructions about her burial.

But since John Mitchell still was her husband at the time of her death, he was the one Dr. Mayer notified first. John Mitchell didn't go to the hospital; Dr. Mayer went to his East Side apartment to see what his wishes were.

Martha's son, Jay Jennings, was asleep in a Philadelphia hotel room when his mother died. Clyde Jennings had gone down to breakfast early and heard a waitress ask another customer, "Say, did you hear Martha Mitchell died?" He went upstairs to tell Jay what had happened.

Jay immediately called John Mitchell to say he was in Philadelphia and could be in New York within an hour and a half. He was assured by his stepfather that the trip was not necessary.

Another call John Mitchell received was from Ray West, Jr., who told him that Martha wanted to be buried in the Ferguson family plot, in the Bellwood Cemetery, just outside of Pine Bluff.

"John was glad I called," Ray remembers. "He said they hadn't known what she wanted."

With John Mitchell's consent, Ray West began planning Martha's funeral, according to her instructions. I talked several times to Ray the day Martha died, and the next, giving him messages from various people who would be there.

Philip and Mary Robertson, Piper Dankworth, and Bennie and I were flying to Arkansas together. Ray arranged for a special section in the church to be reserved for us and for others who were coming in from out of town.

Martha's husband and daughter did not accompany her body to Arkansas. No member of the family met the plane.

When we arrived in Pine Bluff we learned that John Mitchell had taken over the funeral arrangements from Ray. As a result no seats would be reserved, except for those set aside for Mitchell, Marty, Jay and the three Wests. Later, Mitchell added Alleta and Charlie Saunders to this list. I asked Ray about seats for dignitaries, such as the Governor of Alabama's wife; he repeated that John Mitchell didn't want any seats reserved.

Mitchell also had said that neither he nor Marty would go to the funeral home, and he requested that there be no visitation at the Ralph Robinson & Son mortuary, where Martha's body would be until time for the services at the First Presbyterian Church.

Associated Press later reported: "Hundreds of residents of this Arkansas River community were kept outside locked doors at Mitchell's orders."

Firm rules also had been set by John Mitchell for the handling of the press. Reporters were to be kept away from him, and photographers placed so far from the secluded side door of the church (where Mitchell and Marty would enter) that there would be no chance of getting a picture. Later, when Dr. Desiderio Demeco, a professor at the University of Arkansas, took a picture of the casket inside the church, his film was confiscated.

And all the media, which included network television camera crews, would be stationed thirty feet from the gravesite at the cemetery.

Predictably, tempers ran high. One reporter asked a mortuary spokesman why they would lay down such strict rules for Mitchell, saying, "This man is a convicted felon."

"His fifteen-year-old daughter isn't" was the reply.

When told that reporters could sit only in one of the last rows of the sanctuary, Myra MacPherson of the Washington *Post* complained, "We won't be able to see a thing." She was told, "You are a very perceptive young lady."

The night before the funeral, I was with a group of Martha's friends gathered at the home of Pine Bluff agricultural executive George Dunklin and his wife "Lib," when Philip Robertson came up to me and said he'd arranged for us—the Robertsons, Piper Dankworth, Bennie and me—to go to the funeral home to pay our last respects to Martha. Kay Woestendieck, who had come in from Arizona, heard us discussing our plans and said she wanted to go, too. We six and George Dunklin slipped out of the house and went to the Robinson mortuary.

Although Martha had many friends who would have been glad to sit with her, she was alone in a little flower-filled parlor. She lay in an open casket, a metal one, in a shade called "pink pearl." She wore a long-sleeved, high-necked dress of delicate pink organdy embroidered all over with small rosebuds, some the color of the polish on her nails. Her blond hair was upswept in the pompadour hair style she loved. Her expression bore no signs of the suffering she had undergone during the past four years—from Watergate, desertion by her husband, rejection by her younger child, and finally her vicious blood-marrow disease.

As I stood by her casket, I was reminded of something Martha once said in an interview with Myra MacPherson: "When I was growing up, come Sunday I couldn't wait to wear my go-to-church clothes. Today, when I wear something fancy and pretty it still gives me a lift."

I also thought that she'd be "mad as hell" if she knew that John Mitchell was keeping the citizens of her beloved Pine Bluff from coming to the funeral home. As she once said, such things as the traditional burial rites "are so important in the South, Winnie."

John Mitchell spent his whole time in Pine Bluff trying to avoid the press and as many of Martha's friends as possible, but Jay Jennings genuinely seemed to appreciate that so many of us were there. He thanked everyone for coming so far, at a dinner Ray West, Sr., gave the night before the funeral for those from out of town.

Surprisingly, the evening was not morose; one friend after another related anecdotes about Martha with affectionate humor. As Martha would have said, it was her kind of party. Jay put it another way: "This is what she would have wanted, all of her close friends together, laughing while they remember her."

The next morning when we arrived at the church, around nine-thirty for a ten-thirty service, the sanctuary already was half filled. And standing on the curb, across the street with the crews of six television cameras and twenty-five or more reporters, were small groups of townspeople and tourists.

Shortly after Martha's closed casket, draped with pink carnations, was brought into the church, John Mitchell walked in through a side door with Jay and Marty. Neither Mitchell nor Marty appeared to look either at the casket or at the two ministers who conducted the services, Dr. W. L. McColgan, pastor emeritus, and the Reverend Richard A. Dodds, the current pastor. Mitchell and Marty stared straight ahead or gazed at the church windows. One woman noted: "He's trying to ignore her in death as he did in life." Jay, with tears in his eyes, seemed to be struggling to keep his composure.

During the ninety-minute service, the Reverend Dodds spoke of Martha's zest for life, the breadth of her sympathies and the strength of her convictions. He compared her pilgrimage through life to that of Abraham in his search for the Holy City. Martha lived in some "great cities—Washington, D.C., New York City," he said, "and she discovered that the great cities have their limitations . . . their imperfections. She understood this and she had a way of sharing her thoughts and beliefs in these matters."

As Martha's casket was taken out of the church, Marty started to follow it up the aisle. But John Mitchell grabbed her arm and pulled her back. They left by the same side door through which they'd entered.

Mitchell, Jay and Marty rode together in a limousine in the funeral procession to the Bellwood Cemetery, where some of the graves pre-date the Civil War. Neither John nor Marty spoke to Jay during the ride to or from the cemetery. They talked together about things unrelated to Martha.

Immediately following the five-minute graveside service, John Mitchell left without speaking to any of the people who had come to his estranged wife's funeral, although some—including Cornelia Wallace and a group of Martha's Chi Omega sorority sisters—were standing directly behind him.

Prominent among the floral displays, which included a piece from President and Mrs. Ford, was a large green and white spray with white chrysanthemums spelling out in block letters the message: MARTHA WAS RIGHT. The funeral home and the florist refused to say who had sent it.

Some people were offended at the "Martha Was Right" floral piece; in fact, on spotting it the six pallbearers quickly stationed themselves in front of it to keep it from the family's view. But others thought the anonymous sender had made the right gesture.

Many of Martha's obituaries mentioned how she had been "right" and had told the truth, only to be ignored. Mark Goodman, writing in *New Times* magazine, said, "With a telephone receiver in one hand and a glass of whiskey in the other, she first sounded the alarm . . . We did not listen to Martha Mitchell, and we paid for it."

Explaining why Martha wasn't believed, Eugene Patterson, of the St. Petersburg (Florida) *Times,* said, "Because she told the truth indiscreetly . . . she was written off as a kook in Washington." He also wrote, "She married the the wrong man, connected with the wrong political crowd, and tried to find her place in the wrong town at the wrong time."

FOLLOWING THE FUNERAL, JOHN MITCHELL AND MARTY WENT TO SAN Clemente, where they visited with the Richard Nixons for almost two weeks. A Mitchell friend says the former President and former Attorney General "interviewed each other for their books."

Once back in New York, John Mitchell went to 1030 Fifth Avenue for the first time in over two and a half years. He did not ask Jay to accompany him; with John Mitchell, however, were Marty and his eldest daughter Jill Reed, who later became temporary executrix of Martha's estate. According to what John Mitchell told a friend, neither Marty nor Jill wanted any of Martha's clothes, with the exception of the two dresses Marty took, plus a fur-trimmed coat she liked.

Martha's complete wardrobe—evening gowns, dresses, coats, suits, shoes, lingerie—was stuffed into large plastic garbage bags and carried from the building by Zolton. One observer said at one point that thirty-five of the large bags were removed. It is not know where the clothes were taken; Vanya Abbott, a Pine Bluff native who, with her husband Bob, bought the Ferguson house and turned it into a Martha Mitchell museum, was told the clothes had been given to the American Cancer Society. But when she called the Society in an effort to get some of Martha's things for the museum, she was told they had not received them.

Fortunately, someone went through the pockets of the garments before putting them into the garbage bags. In one negligee they found her pearls—the ones Martha said were a gift from the Japanese government. Many other pieces of Martha's jewelry, including her diamond rings, were never found.

The furnishings in the apartment, many which came to her through her family, were disposed of in various ways. Some of them showed up for sale on New York's Third Avenue. Included in this group was a little French desk Martha especially treasured and a cobalt-blue, porcelain antique chandelier which had hung in the music room.

Many things were left in the apartment for the new owners, Moses (Moey) Segal, a Florida lawyer/investor, and his wife Leonore, to use until their own furnishings arrived.

One day a few months after Martha died, I stopped by the apartment and was allowed to go through it with the Segals. When the apartment was sold, left behind were such things as the large, blue satin, down-filled sofa (later spotted on the trash heap in an alley alongside 1030 Fifth Avenue); a fruitwood chair and crystal chandelier, which Martha said had belonged to her grandmother; the dining-room furniture and two little love seats she cherished.

Several of Martha's pictures were on the hallway wall, and at the end was a large mirror that had belonged to Miss Arie. In the butler's pantry were many of her dishes and pieces of bric-a-brac; the bedroom contained two of the Ferguson family's Victorian chairs, the king-size, red velvet bed and other pieces of furniture she'd bought for the Mitchells' first apartment on Gramercy Park. On shelves in the den were many of her books and some of her papers, including a graduation diploma from junior high school. The Segals told me they were disposing of everything belonging to Martha just as soon as their own things arrived. And they did.

As I went through the apartment, seeing these objects I knew Martha loved, I again heard her say, "You don't understand, Winnie, what possessions mean to people in the South. They cherished the few possessions they had left [after the Civil War] and they lived decently with them the best they could."

Martha had cherished her possessions and she desperately wanted them to belong to Jay and Marty after her death. But as this is written, Jay Jennings still has not received anything from his mother's estate.

Since her death, Martha has become something of a folk heroine. Every day people—strangers and friends—visit her grave, some bringing flowers. One unidentified person placed a pipe into the ground above her grave and put an American flag in it. Some of these people then join others in a visit to Martha's childhood home, which contains some of the furniture from the time Martha lived there.

Two things happened in September 1977 which intensified interest in Martha. (1) Her hometown paper, the Pine Bluff *Commercial*, announced that it was starting a Martha Mitchell fund drive in the hope of raising enough money to erect a suitable memorial to the town's famous daughter—probably a fountain in the new civic center. And (2) Richard Nixon went on television and told David Frost, "If it hadn't been for Martha, there'd have been no Watergate."

People were outraged at Nixon's accusation. The *Commercial* was flooded with letters and contributions from men and women defending Martha and condemning Richard Nixon.

They wrote, "Thank God she told the truth, which is more than we can say about those involved in the scandal" . . . "She was a kind of dippy saint, a dizzy yet right-on-the-target woman to whom freedom and honesty meant more than protocol and 'appropriate' behavior" . . . "I could not believe that even Richard Nixon would have the effrontery to make the statement [about Martha causing Watergate]" . . . and "If it weren't for her, this [corruption in government] would still be going on and only get worse."

Some people, though, saw Richard Nixon's attack on Martha as a "fitting tribute," since by so doing he had honored her beyond all expectations.

Two more honors came to Martha in early 1978. Her girlhood home was placed on the National Register of Historic Places; and U.S. Highway 65 Expressway, which runs past the Bellwood Cemetery, was renamed the Martha Mitchell Expressway.

And Martha would have loved knowing that her name lives on, in close association with the address "Mr. President" Nixon was forced to vacate. When an invitation arrived at the Carter White House for the Special Assistant to the President for Special Projects—a young woman named Martha Mitchell—it was returned, marked "Deceased."

Index

ABOUT THE AUTHOR

WINZOLA MCLENDON is a journalist with over twenty-five years of reporting experience. A White House correspondent, she has covered the East Wing of the White House through five Administrations. Her articles on the Washington political and social scene, and other subjects, have appeared in many publications, including *Good Housekeeping, Ladies' Home Journal, Look, McCall's, Town & Country* and *The Washingtonian.* She is co-author with Scottie Fitzgerald Smith of *Don't Quote Me: Washington Newswomen and The Power Society.*

Mrs. McLendon first met Martha Mitchell while interviewing her for a magazine article in early 1970. The meeting was the beginning of a long association in which Mrs. McLendon was accepted by Martha Mitchell in the dual role of intimate friend and working member of the press. The wife of a retired Navy captain, Mrs. McLendon lives in Washington, D.C.